THE FIELDS OF GROUP PSYCHOTHERAPY

The Fields
of
Group
Psychotherapy

Edited by

S. R. Slavson

INTERNATIONAL UNIVERSITIES PRESS, INC.

New York   New York

Manufactured in the United States of America

CONTENTS

v

LIST OF AUTHORS

BARUCH, DOROTHY W., Ph.D.: Consulting Psychologist, specializing in childhood and family problems, including psychosomatic aspects of allergy (with Hyman Miller, M.D.); Author of *One Little Boy* (with medical collaboration by Hyman Miller, M.D.), *How to Live with Your Teen-ager, New Ways in Discipline,* etc.

BRODY, MORRIS W., M.D.: Practicing psychoanalyst; lecturer at the Philadelphia Psychoanalytic Society; Associate Professor of Psychiatry at Temple University Medical School, Philadelphia, Pa.

BRUNNER-ORNE, MARTHA, M.D.: Medical Director, Westwood Lodge, Westwood, Mass.; Chief Psychiatrist and Director of the Re-education Clinic for Alcoholics, New England Hospital, Boston, Mass.; formerly: Department of Medicine, Vienna University Hospital; Research Fellow, Mayo Clinic, Rochester, Minn.; Psychiatrist, Ring Sanatorium and Hospital, Arlington, Mass., and Consultant in Mental Hygiene, Wellesley College.

DURKIN, HELEN E., Ph.D.: Instructor and supervisor in the Adult Therapy Department of the Postgraduate Institute for Psychotherapy, and Chairman of Committee on Research in Group Psychotherapy; formerly: Psychotherapist at Brooklyn Juvenile Clinic and New Rochelle Child Guidance Clinic.

FREEMAN, HENRY, M.S.: Supervisor in Casework and Group Therapy, Community Service Society of New York; formerly: Caseworker, Family Service Association, Cleveland, Ohio, and at Norwich State Hospital, Norwich, Conn.; Caseworker in Charge of District Office, Family Service Society, Hartford, Conn.

GLATT, MAX M., M.D., D.P.M.: Assistant Psychiatrist, Warlingham Park Hospital, Croydon General Hospital, and Mayday Hospital, Surrey, England.

HADDEN, SAMUEL B., M.D.: Assistant Professor, Department of Psychiatry, School of Medicine, University of Pennsylvania; Chief of the Neuropsychiatric Department of the Presbyterian Hospital, Philadelphia;

Psychiatric Consultant to the Philadelphia General, Bryn Mawr, Misericordia and Fitzgerald-Mercy Hospitals.

HARRISON, SAUL I., M.D.: Instructor in Psychiatry, Temple University School of Medicine and Hospital, Philadelphia, Pa.; Assistant Attending Psychiatrist, St. Christopher's Hospital for Children, Philadelphia, Pa., and Consulting Psychiatrist, Child Study Institute, Bryn Mawr College, Bryn Mawr, Pa.

HULSE, WILFRED C., M.D.: Associate Attending Psychiatrist, The Mount Sinai Hospital, New York; Consultant Psychiatrist, Foster Care Division, Department of Welfare, City of New York; Chief Supervising Psychiatrist, Jewish Community Services of Long Island at Hillside Hospital, New York; Research Associate, New York Medical College.

KALLEJIAN, VERNE, Ph.D.: Director of Education, American Hospital Association, Chicago, Ill.; Formerly on the staff of the Institute of Industrial Relations and Human Relations Research Group, University of California, Los Angeles; member of the staff and Policy Committee of the Western Training Laboratory in Group Development; conducted human relations training programs for educational, business, community and national organizations.

KLEMES, MARVIN A., M.D.: Consultant, The Institute of Industrial Relations, University of California, Los Angeles; consultant to industrial organizations and to Human Resources Associates, Los Angeles, Calif; formerly member of the Policy Committee of the Western Training Laboratory in Group Development.

KOTKOV, BENJAMIN, Ph.D.: Formerly chief psychologist: New England Medical Center, Numbered Army General Hospitals (during World War II), Boston Mental Hygiene Clinic of the Veterans Administration, and the Mental Hygiene Clinics of Delaware. Consultant to the U. S. Public Health Service in group psychotherapy, directed the training of group psychotherapists.

LEVINE, LENA, M.D.: Associate Medical Director of the Margaret Sanger Research Bureau, New York City; Psychiatric Consultant of Mothers' Health Center, Kings County; Consultant on Marriage Counseling of the Planned Parenthood Federation of America; Chief Gynecologist of the Gynecological Hygiene Clinic of Jewish Hospital, Brooklyn, N. Y.; Lecturer on Contraception, Premarital and Marriage Counseling, Family Living. Author of *Women Needn't Worry—The Menopause* (with Beka Doherty).

LINDEN, MAURICE E., M.D.: Director of the Division of Mental Health of the Department of Public Health, City of Philadelphia; Associate in Psychiatry at the School of Medicine and Member of the staff of the Functional Clinic, University Hospital, University of Pennsylvania; Research Associate at the Institute for Research in Human Relations, Philadelphia; formerly Program Director of the Gerontologic Study Center at Norristown (Penn.) State Hospital.

MACLENNAN, BERYCE W., B.Sc. (London): Director of Group Therapy, Youth Consultation Service, New York; formerly Research Psychologist, Special Unit for Research in Rheumatic Diseases of Children, Taplow, England; Caseworker and Group Therapist, Community Service Society, New York; Consultant on Delinquency, Association for Psychological Treatment of Offenders.

MILLER, HYMAN, M.D.: Associate Clinical Professor of Medicine at the University of California at Los Angeles Medical School; former Senior Consultant, United States Veterans Administration, Wadsworth Hospital.

ORNE, MARTIN T., M.A., M.D.: Chief Clinical Psychologist, Westwood Lodge. Formerly: Re-education Clinic of the New England Hospital.

REES, T. P., O.B.E., M.D., M.R.C.P., D.P.M.: Consultant Psychiatrist and Medical Superintendent of Warlingham Park Hospital; Visiting Psychiatrist, Mayday Hospital, Croydon and Croydon General Hospitals; Medical Director, Croydon Child Guidance Clinic.

ROSENTHAL, LESLIE, M.S.W.: Associate in Group Therapy, Jewish Board of Guardians, New York City; Consultant, Henry Street Settlement Guidance Unit, New York City.

SCHEIDLINGER, SAUL, Ph.D.: Consultant in Group Therapy, Division of Family Services, Community Service Society; Lecturer, Graduate School of Education, City College of New York, and the New York School of Social Work. Formerly: Assistant to the Director of Group Therapy, Jewish Board of Guardians; Consultant Psychologist, Walden School; Instructor, Graduate School of Education, New York University; Author of *Psychoanalysis and Group Behavior*.

SCHULMAN, IRVING, Ph.D.: Chief Clinical Psychologist and Director of Group Psychotherapy, Child Study Center, Institute of the Pennsylvania Hospital, Philadelphia, Pa.; formerly: Psychologist, Guidance Institute, Reading, Pa.

SLAVSON, S. R.: Consultant in Group Therapy; Jewish Board of Guardians; Youth Consultation Service; the Hudson Guild Psychiatric Service, and Actvity Group Therapy Center, New York; Editor, *International Journal of Group Psychotherapy;* formerly: Consultant in Group Therapy, Bridgeport (Conn.) Mental Hygiene Society, Newark (N. J.) Child Guidance Clinic, Community Service Society of New York, and Council of Child Development Center, New York; on the faculties of the School of Education, New York University, Springfield College, and Yeshiva University; Author of *Creative Group Education; Character Education in a Democracy; Science in the New Education; An Introduction to Group Therapy; Recreation and the Total Personality; Analytic Group Psychotherapy; Child Psychotherapy,* and *Re-educating the Delinquent;* Editor of *The Practice of Group Therapy.*

STEIN, AARON, M.D.: Assistant Attending Psychiatrist in charge of Adult Group Psychotherapy, The Mount Sinai Hospital, New York; Adjunct Attending Psychiatrist, Hillside Hospital, Glen Oaks, N. Y.

THORPE, JAMES J., M.D.: Director, Fairfax County Child Guidance Clinic, Falls Church, Va. Formerly: Psychiatrist, National Training School for Boys, Washington, D. C.; Psychiatrist, U. S. Public Health Service Out-Patient Department, Washington, D. C.; Psychiatrist, U. S. Public Health Hospital for Drug Addicts, Lexington, Ky.

PREFACE

The present volume can be considered an extension of THE PRACTICE OF GROUP THERAPY published in 1947, which reflected the state of this newly evolving branch of psychiatry and psychotherapy up to 1945. In the ten years that followed great strides have been made toward clarifying the picture that existed then. The PRACTICE was the first effort toward specificity in the application of group therapy. In that volume the various contributors for the first time pointed up the undesirability of the blanket use of terminology and indiscriminate application of group treatment, a step that was in a real sense a pioneering effort which subsequent developments proved to have been sound.

The growth of group psychotherapy has had few parallels in the development of the healing arts. The ready acceptance it has received is testimony to its inherent value and its even greater promise for the future. As some of the proponents of group psychotherapy will replace extravagant claims and overconfidence by scientific objectivity, its service will be even further enhanced.

A most striking phenomenon in the spread of group psychotherapy is the absence of active opposition to it throughout its brief history. Normally, all social innovations pass through four stages before they become integrated or assimilated by the body *sociale*. The first step is that of being ignored, which is the phase of passive resistance; the second is attack or active resistance. These are followed in turn by ridicule, which is a resolution of the discomfort engendered by the conflict between dawning recognition of truth and the resistance toward accepting it; and finally, by quiet acceptance of it. At the present (1955) and for some years past, psychiatry itself is and has been in the third stage, judging by the quips one perennially encounters on the radio, in the theater, in cartoons, in newspapers, in books, and in ordinary conversations. This is the stage antecedent to full acceptance and integration into the culture.

Group psychotherapy was spared these birth pains. It was met with singular receptivity not only from professionally trained persons and patients, but from the general community as well. Group psychotherapy uniformly evoked favorable response and unresistive acceptance from the intelligent man on the street, from newspapers, popular magazines and other media of communication, giving testimony to its acceptability. It has been my conviction for many years that while the intelligence of masses cannot be trusted, their intuitive and instinctive responses are unfailing. Aggregates weaken the ego and rational understanding, but sharpen instincts, a process that is readily understandable if viewed from the aspect of biologic and social survival.

The term "group" has always held a special fascination for man, partly because his survival in nature was conditioned by association and group life, and partly because group living presented the individual with special and arduous difficulties. Thus, all appeals to group action and group association command *ipso facto* attention. The keen response to *groupism* had been greatly intensified in recent decades, especially since the two World Wars.

The hospitable support of group therapy may be explained by reasons other than instinct. The few most articulate proponents of this method have for two decades now pointed out the limitations of group therapy with the same emphasis as they did its values and advantages. The focus of their attention was the patient and not a blanket method. This attitude resulted in more or less discriminative application and vigilant choice of patients who can benefit from treatment in groups. Later this discrimination was extended from generalized concepts to the evolvement of *different types* of therapy groups most suitable for *different kinds* of patients. It is felt that this objectivity and adherence to methodology and scientific modesty certainly prevented the opposition in those professional quarters from which it was most likely to come.

However, one must not be lulled into a state of self-deception and assume that group psychotherapy is universally accepted by all schools of psychiatry and psychotherapy, or by all practitioners. There exists an aloofness on the part of some because the idea of group psychotherapy does not fully accord with their specific systems of thought, perhaps even dogma. But interestingly enough, only demurral couched in a weak voice is heard, not active or vociferous opposition. There is also, on the other hand, a healthy skepticism—an attitude of watchful waiting until this new clinical fledgling will grow its wings and demonstrate its potency. This is an entirely justifiable and scientifically sound attitude that has always served to safeguard instrumental science and the tools of social living. It is hoped that the present volume will serve as an added instrument to enhance conviction and as an impetus to an extended understanding of group psychotherapy, and the acceptance of it.

The contents of the PRACTICE OF GROUP THERAPY was focused upon the discriminative use of this method of treatment in relation to specific clinical or diagnostic entities, and its suggestions do not seem to have been tarnished by test and the passing of time. In fact, an increasing number of practitioners have found them to be valid, as the literature unmistakenly testifies. In that volume positive and negative indications for selection, the process and results in cases of primary behavior disorders, psychoneuroses, psychoses, psychopathy, stuttering and allergies received special attention. The various treatment methods with children and adults were also described. This more or less limited variety in the content reflected the state of development and practice at that time; only in a few areas was group psychotherapy employed then. Many further applications have been made of it since, and the present volume is an effort to concretize these. Here we cut across clinical categories and attempt to show how group psychotherapy is applicable to special treatment tasks that the practitioner constantly encounters in his day-to-day work. At first glance the two approaches may seem contradictory, but the reader will find in the first chapter evidences of the fact that they unmistakably harmonize.

The chapters in this volume that deal with practice have been written in accordance with a definite plan. Repetitions have been avoided and, as in the case of the PRACTICE, it is a unitary and integrated book rather than a "collection" of discrete papers.

In am deeply grateful for the forebearance of the different authors who have cheerfully participated in this cooperative-coordinate writing venture. My thanks go to the International Universities Press, Inc., and especially to Professor A. Kagan, its president, for his warm understanding and his help in the development of group psychotherapy and to Miss Lottie M. Maury of his staff for painstaking and intelligent editorial assistance.

This book, as was the PRACTICE, is the result of the cooperation of the members of the American Group Psychotherapy Association, Inc., and reflects the pioneering work of that Association.

S.R.S.

New York
September, 1955

THE FIELDS OF GROUP PSYCHOTHERAPY

Chapter I

SYMPTOM VERSUS SYNDROME IN
GROUP PSYCHOTHERAPY

●

The readers of this volume will perhaps recall that I have consistently recommended grouping of patients in analytic group psychotherapy with adults—unlike that in activity groups for children—on the basis of similarity of pathology or syndrome. Such similarity enhances identification among the members of a group, evokes empathy as well as more insightful interpretations and better understanding of each other's problems and those of one's own.

Similarity of the *nuclear problem* accelerates the therapeutic process not only for the group but for the individual patients as well, since a communication by one applies to others and therefore evokes responses and memories in all. The absence of such a unitary basis causes considerable divergencies and sidetracking in the interviews, but when this requirement is met, treatment is greatly accelerated. An added advantage is that the group responds and acts *as though* it were a single patient, and interpretations are applicable to all. Thus, the group becomes in effect one patient, which makes possible treatment *through* the group as differentiated from treatment of patients *in* a group.

The basic difference between these lies in the fact that the interaction and responses of patients to each other, their interpretations, advice, efforts at help, empathy and support create a setting favorable to therapy through the group. That is, the group as such is the therapeutic agent as well as the therapist. Therapy in a group, to which one must resort occasionally under any conditions, becomes predominant when the dissimilarity or divergencies of the problems of the patients are so great that they cannot participate together and the therapist has to turn to an

3

individual and work through with him problems that concern him only. In these circumstances, the other patients become spectators, or observers, rather than active participants. They are more or less detached, with little direct emotional contact with what is occurring at the moment and in many instances are unable to follow, or only dimly so, what goes on between the therapist and the participating patient.

This does not mean that all the spectators remain unaffected emotionally by the peroration between the therapist and the participating member. There may be some others who are preoccupied with the same problem or suffer from a situation similar to that under consideration at a given time. In that sense, they are receiving therapy through the group. However, the closer one can establish syndrome similarity for all the participants in a therapy group, the better. The procedure is then more efficient and the therapy more effective.

I have said in my paper on "Criteria for the Selection and Rejection of Patients for Various Types of Group Psychotherapy" (1955) that there are always common areas that apply to all patients coming for treatment. One of these are feelings toward parents and/or siblings. There is always universality when this problem is brought forth. Though the actual hostilities and reactions may be somewhat different, basic negative feelings are reflected by all patients. Still another universal area is the distortions and disturbances in the matter of sex. Difficulties in the area of sex are the nucleus of the psychoneuroses, but they are also present in nearly all emotional disturbances and social maladjustments.

However, despite these similarities, the specific preoccupations of patients can be at great variance and, because of it, there is a lack of confluence and unity that prevents common understanding and emotional activity. Occasionally an adult patient complains to the group therapist in an individual session that his problems are so different from those being considered in the group that he does not quite understand what goes on; nor does it have much significance for him. This, of course, is most often a manifestation of resistance, but it cannot be regarded as such in all cases. As the patient elaborates on his problems, it becomes clear that in actuality his claim is correct. Usually parallel individual and group treatment are recommended where the common or universalized problems are worked on in the group and specific or individualized difficulties are considered in individual sessions, a fact that would not be necessary were it possible in practice to establish absolute similarity of syndrome or pathology. Perhaps an illustration of this is a borderline schizophrenic. When placed in a group of psychoneurotics he walked up to the therapist after a group session and said: "Doctor, why do these people talk so negatively about their parents? Were their parents really so bad? My parents were very good to me, and I don't understand why these people have such strong feelings about theirs."

In groups, the compulsive, narcissistic and egotistical persons who monopolize the discussions set off disturbances and resentments in the others. Such group tensions may become valuable grist in the therapeutic mill; however, if the need to dominate others and to be the focus of attention is a characterological difficulty instead of a neurotic defense on the part of one member, the psychoneurotic members will not be able to deal with the situation. This type of tension, and even the discussion of the mechanism of the offending patient, may become unproductive for the group. Perhaps the following contrast would illustrate this point.

A psychoneurotic patient whose problems stem from the oedipal situation discusses his difficulty in the group in the course of which he continually brings forth his hostility toward either one or both parents. His productions consist predominantly of complaints against the latter and narrations of how badly they had treated him. As he proceeds to reveal his hitherto withheld feelings, he narrates memories of situations that had been traumatic and were the cause of his sexual disturbances. Another member of the group is equally anxious, but his anxiety stems from strong homicidal thoughts and death wishes the patient had had as a child toward a sibling. The mother had preferred that sibling either because of physical appearance, special talents, or difference in sex. While the oedipal element is present in both of these situations, the actual reactions (syndrome) have a different content; and when either one of these two patients talks about his problems in the group, the other would make little contact and have little or no emotional empathy with the recital.

Further, a third patient's anxiety arose from early sexual play or actual incestuous intercourse with a sibling. He would not only be unable to become emotionally involved in the recitation of either one of the other two, but would be greatly frustrated. There are patients in a group whose anxieties originated in the prephallic and preverbal stages, because their survival was threatened through neglect or harsh treatment in their earliest years. They had been allowed to go hungry for long periods of time. Such biologically anxious patients would not be able to participate fully or adequately in group interviews. In one group, a married woman who had very strong, unresolved oedipal conflicts and remained strongly attached to her father, had repeatedly attacked her stepmother because the latter had blocked her father's affections for her; or so she thought. This was not understood by most of the other members in the group whose relationships with their fathers had not been quite as intense. Therefore, they wondered why this woman was so preoccupied with the reactions of her father and her stepmother. They were unable to empathize with or understand her.

Symptoms, as differentiated from the pathological syndrome, are not a valid criteria for grouping patients. For if we take any physical symptom as an example, we would find that it may be caused by a variety of neurotic conditions. It may be a resolution of a neurotic conflict; it may serve as a defense; it may be a form of hypochondriasis; a compulsive-obsessive manifestation, or a means for achieving secondary gains. In sound psychotherapy we address ourselves not to the symptom but to the causative intrapsychic states. The cathartic process aims at reaching these genetic causatives, and they must be considered as basic in the grouping of patients. Thus, the nature of the pathology and the core or nucleus of the problem should be the unifying element of the patients.

While this ideal grouping is the objective, it must be recognized that in actual practice it is very seldom possible to achieve. There seldom exists a sufficient pool from which one can select patients who fall within any rigidly defined category. It would also be difficult to determine in advance the nature of problems with such exactitude as to make the group perfect. However, the principle has to be kept in mind and as far as possible carried out.

In addition to the recognizable common problem areas in all patients already noted, there may be others in which two, three or four may be able actively to participate either directly or as spectators. Such subgroupings shift in accordance with the theme that may be occupying the group at a given time. Thus, silence is not always resistance. At times the theme of a group discussion is so remote from the problems of some of the patients that it does not touch off their feelings or associations.

The present volume may at first impress one as contradicting the principle of grouping by syndrome similarity. However, a further examination of the *areas* chosen for discussion here will reveal the fact that we are not dealing with strict *clinical entities*. Rather, certain areas of maladjustment manifestations have been selected for consideration. Alcoholics, drug addicts, allergies, the aged, unmarried mothers, and the others described here—all, in their specific responses, have a great many psychic difficulties in common. Alcoholics are a good example of this. Alcoholics are universally persons with weak ego development; they are orally dependent, and are frightened and at times overwhelmed by life's demands. They have feminine identifications with homosexual trends and are strongly masochistic. Alcoholics nearly always come from families where the mothers were strong and the fathers weak personalities.

Despite these common elements in all alcoholics, in my experience, even they have to be divided into two categories: those with character disorders, namely, persons with weak egos and strong dependencies, and those who are psychoneurotic. We found that when these two groups had been separated, considerable change in the tone of the therapeutic process and results occurred. When alcoholics with character disorders were in the same groups with the psychoneurotics, they were all greatly disturbed, and therapy was retarded and at times even bogged down. There has been a noticeable improvement in the group treatment when they have been separated. This was confirmed by two other group therapists who followed the plan. The syndrome similarity enhanced the identifications and empathy. This fused the groups into more unitary reactions, increased insight, and accelerated improvement. The content of the interviews in the two types of groups was strikingly different, and the patients were able to proceed more easily and more effectively.

Another example of the commonness of syndrome in the areas described in this volume are the aged. Dr. Linden's pioneering contributions in this new field are well known, and his studies of the psyche of the aged indicate that there is an ever-present alteration going on in their ego and libido structures that brings them into one category. This will also be seen in the case of unmarried mothers where there are definite "constant factors" present in the psychic structure of girls who have children out of wedlock, even though there are considerably "different variable factors" and "precipitating factors" present as well. However, the variables too occur with striking frequency and the determining traumata are impressively common.

In the case of those who commit delinquent acts, rigid distinction has to be made between the neurotic, the psychopathic, the organic and the psychotic states. Here, as well, group psychotherapy can be employed properly only when these clinical considerations are taken into account. Such considerations are necessary in all other areas.

In the chapter on mental hospitals, for example, the use of therapy groups for different types of patients and situations is recommended: the psychoneurotic receive analytic group treatment; they participate in general group discussions, while *activities* in a group and in a hospital community setting are provided for the deteriorated psychotics. The authors of the other chapters that deal with specific areas have similarly in no way negated the basic and, in our opinion, the most important single element, namely, the grouping of patients according to pathology and syndrome. Thus, this book as a whole does not in any essential way counter this foundational grouping criterion.

Psychotherapy in its ultimate form is a process in which intrapsychic balance is established in the functioning of the id, ego, and superego, so that maximum efficiency and equilibrium result in the individual's adjustment within himself and to his environment. This usually entails modifications in the instinctual urges, the strengthening of the ego and the correcting of the either overdemanding or too permissive superego. Each has to be brought to a level of appropriate functioning before inner balance can be established and effective adjustment ensue. When pleasure (id) urges are fixed at an infantile level and the pleasure drives are over-intense and unsublimated or not refined, the id overwhelms the ego controls so that they cannot function adequately.

Similarly, when the superego is overstrict or overlax, the individual's capacity is inadequate to select and judge in accordance with group or social mores. Under such conditions, the ego is not able to function appropriately, that is, either to carry out the demands of the superego or to repress the id urges. Under ideal therapeutic conditions, correction of these dynamic elements requires regression on the part of the patient to those earlier states in his background where particularly strong trauma occurred and fixations took place. This type of intensive psychotherapy cannot be made available to all that need mental treatment. Less intensive therapies have, therefore, been evolved, which, though deriving from dynamic psychiatry and psychoanalysis and using the same tools, aim at less profound intrapsychic changes.

Some of the chapters in this volume demonstrate how improvement in instrumental functioning can be achieved without radically altering the intrapsychic structure of individuals in basic respects, beyond reducing tensions and making behavior and motivations available to the ego for evaluation and control. In some instances and in the cases of some types of patients, the aim was to give them tools with which they could resolve problems within themselves and to guide their acts in relation to the outside world. This was made possible with some through controls that come from understanding, in others through internalized powers resulting from identification with the therapist and fellow members.

The ego debilities that result from the feeling of being unique and isolated are overcome through group relationships. Instead of relying solely upon himself in bearing the stresses of life, the individual shares his burdens with others who support and guide him. His capacity for relationship, trust and faith in people is thus increased through fellow group members whose basic intent is one of helpfulness and support rather than hostility and destructiveness. With this added strength, the individual can deal with reality with more satisfying results, which in turn again strengthen his ego powers and favorably alter his self- and social images.

However, it must always be kept in mind that severe personality distortions can be corrected only by individual psychotherapy and most often by a thoroughgoing psychoanalysis. For an individual who had been exposed to severe sexual trauma, to extremely intense anxiety for prolonged periods, or to paralyzing ties to important persons, requires the latter type of therapy which involves libidinal transference, therapeutic regression and emerging insight. Sometimes individual treatment may be a preparatory stage for group therapy, or the latter can be introduced at certain points as parallel treatment.

In the less disturbed situations, however, the group can sufficiently affect the feelings and functioning of an individual to normalize his life. In some instances even sexual fixations are loosened and their intensity reduced through the relationships in the group. However, the greatest significance of all psychotherapy, which is equally true of group psychotherapy, lies in the fact that much of the unconscious and particularly preconscious interfering feelings and attitudes are made available to the examination and control of the ego. Innumerable episodes show that groups are of greatest value in this regard. The interchange, the guidance, support and help, universalization and the reduction of guilt and anxiety that result from it, decrease and eliminate the defensive rigidities of the ego that dim the light of self-examination and understanding, and, therefore, its appropriate functioning.

I have suggested in *Child Psychotherapy* (1952) that we can assume a fixed maximum quantum of ego energies for a given individual derived from his constitutional potentials and psychologic conditioning. This reservoir of energies is drawn upon for the various needs in the establishment of inner and outer equilibrium and for the effort that living demands. Thus ego energies are employed intrapsychically in holding down hostility, dealing with anxiety, resolving or eliminating conflict and guilt feelings, and in overcoming feelings of shame, inadequacy and self-deprecation. The more the ego energy potentials are consumed for establishing disturbed intrapsychic equilibrium, the less energy is available for appropriate dealing with reality, for personality expansion and for growth.

I expressed this relation in the formula

$$EE = RE + IE + GE + OE$$

where EE represents the total available ego energies; RE, energies consumed in repressing feelings and impulses; IE, the energies used in integrating the various forces for action; GE, energies for growth and personality expansion; and OE, the quantum of forces needed for dealing with outer pressures and demands. In this formula RE represents all the energies needed for dealing with conflicts, hostilities, guilts, defective self-image and other corrosive and noxious elements.

It is clear from the formula that the greater RE requirements are, the less are ego energies available for the other more efficient and desirable functions. As the wasteful ego energy draining is eliminated or reduced through corrective experiences and psychotherapy, the more energy becomes available for growth, expansion of the self, and reality control.

Even analytic group psychotherapy deals largely, though not entirely, with reorientation and change in the ego structure and functioning of patients through increased feeling of security, favorable changes in self-image, self-perception and self-evaluation, through a more adequate reality testing which members of groups help evolve in one another. Of equal importance is the fact that the group discussions break down the barriers existing between impulse and ego in all patients. Unlike ordinary groups, therapy groups reinforce and buttress ego functioning as against impulse pre-eminence. Patients in treatment are invariably in the throes of impulsivity and irrationality. The group serves as a reflecting mirror that commands the individual's attention to his own behavior and responses. Their unsuitability for social living and human adaptation becomes apparent. The group discussions throw the light of reason and understanding upon the individual's functioning and his feelings, thus detaching the ego involvement in them and liberating it for its assigned functions in the psychic economy.

When the essential structure of the individual is not organically or constitutionally deficient, when a conscious or unconscious desire to establish an inner and outer homeostasis and to adjust to the world more adequately is present, he gives up most of his impulsivity for the more effective behavior that results from ego controls and rational judgments. It is this bridging between the preconscious (and in some instances the unconscious) and the ego which is the greatest service that group psychotherapy offers.

This process is demonstrated in most of the categories that form the chapters in this volume. We see it demonstrated in the group treatment with delinquents, psychotics, alcoholics, unmarried mothers, the aged, and many of the others. But note must be taken that while ego reinforcement occurs also in patients suffering from psychoneurotic symptoms, the sexual and nonsexual libido organizaton and fixations in these patients have to be unraveled. Their symptoms are erogenized and so cathected as to require transference and insight therapy that in the more serious cases, at least, can be supplied on an individual basis either exclusively or contemporaneously with group participation.

Because group psychotherapy addresses itself predominantly though not exclusively, to correcting ego functioning, it can be used with patients whose difficulties arise from weakened ego structure such as mild neurotics, borderline schizophrenics, and certain types of character disorders.[1] However, the point must be re-emphasized that where there is a serious libido distortion and the *vita sexualis* is pathologic, libidinal transference upon a therapist which has to be worked through is essential. In this connection it would, perhaps, be helpful if we review the term "working through" in its dynamic meaning since it is repeatedly used in discussions of psychotherapy.

Working through is the phrase applied to verbal cogitation and mental reflection during a therapeutic interview around a focal point of difficulty in the life, feeling or thought of a patient. It involves the consideration of a problem from every relevant angle—all the experiences, thoughts and affects associated with it. The fact that the problem or situation is viewed with some degree of objectivity through the help of the therapist and fellow patients leads to dissolution of inhibitions and defenses that have hitherto operated as ego-alien elements in the psychic economy of the patient. Because the difficulty can be viewed as an alien presence first through the mirroring of others, and later because of one's own increased flexibility, the light of understanding is thrown upon fears, hate, anxiety and conflicts that have lurked in the dark corners of the preconscious and the unconscious. Attitudes, values, and feelings that have been held in disturbing abeyance through inadequate repression can be brought to the surface. Working through, therefore, means that feelings and fears that the ego had been unable or unwilling to face and deal with, are brought to the surface and understood in a more rational light. The fact that this material can be verbalized and examined indicates increased strength of the ego, for now the ego no longer has to use defensive mechanisms of denial, evasion and conflictual inhibition. It

[1] For a detailed discussion of this, see Slavson (1955).

can now bring thoughts and feelings to the surface and deal with the resulting anxiety.

In this, patients must at first be helped, for few are able to accomplish it by themselves. Since the ego is itself involved in the evasive process, it requires the help of others to face guilt and anxiety-evoking facts and fancies. It is this what is meant by the term "ego support." Thus a strengthened ego results through these and other means involved in the process of psychotherapy. The patient's overt behavior, or lack of it, as well as his covert and latent feelings and intent become accessible to the contemplation of the ego and, therefore, available also to its control through either less conflictual acceptance of them, through less disturbing inhibitions, or through more secure powers.

Again it must be noted that in instances where the libidinal inter-ferences or biological lacks are too great, the ego cannot be made avail-able for such corrective measures. However, where the problem is predominantly one of ego involvement, groups can be very effective.

Transference toward fellow patients is usually less charged with hostile and libidinal affect, and patients feel more supported by peers than by a parental figure. They expect less and are less fearful of the aggression from peers than from a parent substitute in the person of the therapist. Universality of problems, i.e., the discovery that others are in the same straits and are struggling with the same problems which are helpfully shared, not only gives each support and emotional clarity, but reduces guilt, feelings of being bizarre and different, and diminishes anxiety—all of which makes possible substituting more mature responses for the infantile reactions and defensive patterns to which one had to resort in the past. The difficulties of the many make up half of our own consolation. The decreased sense of guilt and uniqueness, and the dimin-ished anxiety make it possible to accept one's hostility and negative urges and attitudes and to live with them more comfortably. This frees the ego energies that had been absorbed in dealing with them for more construc-tive effort. Hostility can now be better controlled, external pressures managed, and the capacity for object relations enhanced. Because of the limited ego energies available to deal with problems one acts in an im-patient, cruel and irascible manner. With more energy available as con-flicts are eliminated, one can respond more appropriately as a member of a family, occupational and social groups and of society generally. The unmistakable improvement in physical appearance, bodily carriage, work productivity and social deportment, and the more self-accepting attitudes that result from the release of ego energies, proceed from a change in the total personality, that is, a balance in the psychic forces in which the ego plays a major role.

However, it must always be kept in mind that the human personality does not function segmentally. The integrative dynamics of the personality are such that when any one area is affected or changed, other areas and functions undergo change as well. The personality functions as a totality and when either ego or libido is altered, the other sustains modifications as well.

Many who come for treatment are confused in or are in conflict with their "biological destiny." The group is singularly suited to correct these and to reinforce their function. The examination of roles as parents, children, husbands and wives, homemakers and providers, helps in this regard, but of equal, if not greater, importance are the identifications established in groups that aid this corrective process. As a result there is an observable enhancement in discharging the appropriate roles in these relationships, and in many instances, frigid women were able to achieve sexual climax, and minor sexual disorders in men had been eliminated. An even larger number of patients who had been unable to enjoy sex reported improvement in this area.

Patients who come for treatment have libidinized or cathected objects too intensely or insufficiently. Corrected object relationships, as they slowly and often painfully emerge in treatment, reduce the intensity of the cathexis through the process of "cathexis displacement" (Slavson, 1952). The earlier objects of cathexis that have been the cause of problems and conflict are diminished in their importance. The multiple transferences toward therapist and the fellow members, and the transference toward the group as a whole aid this process, for some of the libido becomes invested in them. It is safe to hypothesize that the therapist, whether male or female, symbolizes in groups the father figure, while the group as an entity represents the mother image. It is from the group that patients expect and demand protection, kindliness, understanding, and support, as they did from their mothers. When these are not forthcoming, or when the group becomes antagonistic to a patient, he usually leaves, either physically or emotionally, as he had left his mother who had not been kind to him. Although individuals in a group may become antagonistic and punitive, the group as a whole cannot become rejecting. When it does the patient feels himself unwanted, and unless he is motivated by masochistic needs, he will quit.

Thus, the group, as an entity, becomes the recipient of object cathexis as well as the therapist and individual members. As a result the earlier cathected objects become less libidinized, and the individual is freed for more constructive, self-expanding aims and functions. At the same time the ego is released to deal with negative aspects of the affected relationships. The net result of freed libidinal resources, whether they be sexual or nonsexual, is a better general adaptation to object relationships and, therefore, also inner harmony. However, it must be reiterated that serious distortions in the libido may not in all cases be accessible to group psychotherapy with its diluted transferences, but as will be seen in the various chapters of this volume, this is achieved in varying degrees with the less disturbed.

All groups evolve a code which is not always formulated but is rather more often tacit, creating a microculture which usually reflects the larger culture or the macroculture. This phenomenon I have described as "the primary group code."

Because the present volume deals with analytic group psychotherapy and its various adaptations and derivative techniques, it is appropriate at this point to give a brief outline of what analytic group psychotherapy is. The term is applied to the type of group psychotherapy in which both the content and the process in a group are similar to or derivative from psychoanalysis. Analytic group psychotherapy employs transference, catharsis, and interpretation of latent content and dream analysis that lead to insight. In addition, it offers possibilities for reality testing in a group setting and guides patients toward sublimations of negative, primitive, infantile, and anarchic drives. As in individual psychoanalysis, the therapist in analytic groups is aware of the latent content of the patients' communications; he deals with infantile sexuality, the unconscious, the basic hostility of man's nature and the resulting guilts, and accepts the inherent intrapsychic conflict between the id and superego and its effect in determining of character, personality and pathology.

The practice of analytic group psychotherapy bases itself on clinical categories and psychiatric diagnosis. The selection of patients for various types of therapy groups, as well, relies on diagnostic categories, which I have attempted to describe in my paper on "Criteria for Selection and Rejection of Patients for Various Types of Group Psychotherapy" (1955). The fact that in group psychotherapy it becomes necessary to expand or modify the original psychoanalytic concepts and add others, since a group presents special situations, does not in any way alter the basic principles nor the theoretic relations that inherently exist between the pure form of analytic group psychotherapy and psychoanalysis. However, despite the theoretic and historic relation between them, experience has shown that considerable modifications in psychoanalytic practice had to be made in groups. This is partly due to the fact that we are dealing with a group instead of an individual patient. The effect patients have upon each other, their interpersonal reactions and the infectiousness and intensification of emotion are peculiar to groups. Another element that determines the use of groups in psychotherapy is the particular needs of patients for whom other types of therapy are not suitable because of specific organic, personality and ego deficiencies.

Because of these variables in patients' needs and accessibility, a multiplicity of types of psychotherapy had been evolved, which are further modified and elaborated by practitioners because of their own personality, educational and background bias and predilection. We have to assume that there are personality factors involved in the acceptance, rejection or modification of a technique as well as conceptual differences. It is inevitable that even where agreement exists on assumption and theory, there should also be variation in applying these to practice because of individual differences. However, as long as the assumptions are sound, practice can be modified without injury to patients—provided, of course, the therapist is well trained and experienced and is aware of what he is doing. With a therapist who possesses adequate and soundly oriented knowledge of psychodynamics, psychopathology and psychotherapy, individual modifications or adaptations of techniques are not fraught with danger, as it is sometimes assumed. However, where basic assumptions are faulty, much tragedy can result.

The varieties of group practices fall within three categories: activity group therapy, analytic group psychotherapy, and directive group therapy. These have been described in some detail in a paper published in 1954. These techniques have been employed by the contributors to the present volume as they were indicated for specific groups of patients or clinical entities. Although with very few exceptions the treatment of choice was one form of analytic group psychotherapy or another, in some instances therapists have found it necessary to use directive techniques including didactic methods, such as lecturing, and the authoritarian approach with some deteriorated patients. Most have used free association, however. With children and psychotics the use of activity therapy is described.

One other point should be stressed in considering the content of this volume. Frequently, the term group psychotherapy or group therapy is applied to work with large numbers of patients, twenty and even more. Obviously, no psychotherapy, as we understand it, can be done with so large a number. The intimacy of the communications, the emotional proximity and accessibility is vitiated by large numbers. The maximum number of a true psychoanalytically oriented psychotherapy group should not exceed eight patients or perhaps ten. In larger numbers, one is faced with a mass rather than a group, and instead of analytic psychotherapy, directive therapies must be employed. I have described therapies with large numbers as mass therapy (Slavson, 1946). While many mass "therapies" are current, their permanent or lasting effectiveness must be questioned. At best, they nurture dependence upon a person, a set of ideas, or a system of autosuggestion. They demand from the individual that he give up his autonomy and ally himself, unify or submerge with an idea, a belief or a faith. The best known mass therapies in the Western world are Christian Science and Alcoholics Anonymous. From the point of view of our definition, these cannot be considered true therapy. However, in man's search for salvation and for means of overcoming his feelings of fear, anxiety and isolation, they have a place in our society, but it is essential that the difference between them and clinical psychotherapy be kept clearly in mind.

BIBLIOGRAPHY

Slavson, S. R. (1946), Fields and Objectives of Group Therapy. In: *Current Therapies of Personality Disorders,* ed. B. Glueck. New York: Grune & Stratton.
—— (1952), *Child Psychotherapy.* New York: Columbia University Press.
—— (1954), A Contribution to a Systematic Theory of Group Psychotherapy. *Int. J. Group Psychother.,* 4:3-29.
—— (1955), Criteria for Selection and Rejection of Patients for Various Types of Group Psychotherapy. *Int. J. Group Psychother.,* 5:3-30.

Chapter II

MENTAL HOSPITALS

•

A mental hospital is an institution for the care and treatment of the mentally ill, and the character of the institution depends largely on whether the emphasis is laid on custodial care or on treatment of the patients. In the first half of the last century, "care" meant the welfare of the patient, but toward the end of the century care came to have a different meaning, viz., the care of the patient in such a way that he did no harm to himself or to the public. One has only to read the standard works on the organization and management of "lunatic asylums" by Connolly (1847) and Mercier (1894), to realize the change that had taken place. Connolly lays emphasis on freedom, no restraint, occupation, recreation and mixed entertainments. Mercier, fifty years later, lays emphasis on suicide, on violence, the dangers arising from razors, knives and scissors, sharp points and means of suspension; the dangers arising from issuing patients braces, handkerchiefs, garters, boot laces and ties, and the dangers that may arise from the intermingling of the sexes. It was in this atmosphere that the locksmiths flourished and devised the elaborate keys, capable of giving one, two or three turns, according to the rank of the possessor. The one-time asylums for the protection of the mentally afflicted became prisons for the protection of the public from the lunatic who, only too often, had been made dangerous by the methods used to care for him. This influence still survives, for such methods die hard.

It is not unnatural that many doctors rebelled against this state of affairs and endeavored to model mental hospitals on the lines of general hospitals in which they received their medical training. They brought in nurses who had been trained in general nursing and argued that mental illness was an illness like any other, and should be treated on similar lines. The standard of bedside nursing was as a result improved, operating rooms were built, X-ray departments and pathological laboratories were established, and visiting surgeons and other specialists were appointed. All this was to the good, but unfortunately some of the more active doctors and new matrons, full of enthusiasm for general hospital methods, failed to preserve many of the good features of the older "asylums." Occupational therapy, which had been flourishing during the first half of the nineteenth century, sank to an all-time low level in the 1920's. It became necessary for our psychiatrists to travel to Holland and Germany to learn again the advantages of occupational therapy and to introduce a new type of worker, the occupational therapist.

Mental illness is not just like any other form of illness. It is completely different, if only for the fact that most of the patients are physically healthy, there being fewer than 10 per cent of the average mental hospital population in bed, and of these the majority are merely suffering from the effects of old age.

To many, the mental hospital appears to be a kind of halfway house between a prison and a general hospital with some of the worst features of both and the best features of neither. Great progress has been made in clinical psychiatry in recent years, but no comparable advances will be made in administrative psychiatry and in improving the background of treatment or the atmosphere in which treatment takes place, until we break out on new lines and cease aping the general hospital. Neither must the hospital be organized for the benefit of the very small number of potentially dangerous patients (fewer than one per cent) to the detriment of the overwhelming majority of the less disturbed.

The mentally ill are extremely sensitive, and great pains need be taken not to do anything that widens the gap between them and their fellow creatures. The etiology of mental illness in a certain individual is usually of a complex nature, depending on the interaction of intrinsic and extrinsic factors. Physical, psychological and constitutional factors may predispose the individual to develop the illness; economic and social factors may precipitate it. But whatever the ultimate cause, mental illness in its turn always leads to a disturbance in social relationships.

As there is always present an interaction between processes affecting an individual's social relationships and his intrapsychic processes, his happiness must ultimately depend to a large degree on his ability to relate himself to his social environment. If he is unable to establish satisfactory relationships, he will gradually lose self-confidence, become dispirited, feel himself misunderstood, slowly withdraw more and more from the group into his own shell, and he may turn his back completely on the world of reality which he feels is either indifferent toward him or even hostile. He will then derive most of his satisfactions from regressing into his own world of fantasy. A neurotic will fight to retain some contact with his social environment and with reality. He may be unable to do so satisfactorily, feel unhappy, and may not participate in the life of his community to the full limits of his abilities. While the neurotic may thus show undersocialization and underparticipation, the psychotic may completely renounce any participation whatsoever.

Thus, mental illness always leads to loneliness, subjectively as well as objectively. The sufferer's family and friends will first look upon him as an odd person; gradually they may become alarmed as they cannot "manage" him any longer, or feel that he is becoming "dangerous," and they may suggest hospitalization. Even now there exists in the minds of many people the idea that once a patient enters a mental hospital he has lost his freedom for good, and as they think of the "asylum" as a place of permanent sequestration, sufferers from mental illness may not come to seek help at a stage early enough for recovery and effective resocialization.

On the other hand, with the development and recognition of the function of the mental hospital as a place of treatment or of reconstruction of personality and of resocialization, and with the spread of outpatient services, more and more patients will enter mental hospitals as voluntary patients at relatively early phases of their illness. At Warlingham Park Hospital up to 90 per cent of recent admissions were "voluntary," and a large percentage of these left after a stay of only a few weeks or months. At the same time there will always be a certain number of patients who will have to spend the rest of their lives in a hospital, and it is the duty of the mental hospital to do its best for them.

In the same way as the standard of a country's civilization may be assessed by its treatment of its relatively helpless minorities, so a mental hospital may be judged by the way it treats its chronic patients. There will naturally have to be different aims of treatment for these two large groups of patients. Treatment and re-education in the one group may aim at full resocialization of the individual, at enabling him to take his place outside the hospital again. In the less fortunate second group the goal will have to be a much more limited one: to enable the patient to make for himself as happy and contented a life as possible within the hospital community. In both these types of patients, however, resocialization will be an essential aim, and group therapy in the widest sense of the word, including direct psychotherapy and occupational and recreational therapy, is the most practicable and satisfactory way of dealing with this task.

Apart from overcoming the difficulty of catering for a disproportionately large number of patients, with a limited team of doctors, there are many advantages of group therapy over individual therapy. The setting of group therapy is a much less artificial one and less remote from lifelike conditions. Furthermore, individual therapy as well as other specific therapies can only occupy a relatively short segment of the patient's time in a hospital. It is of the utmost importance that his whole day should be well planned and occupied usefully. In these groups the patient has the opportunity, perhaps for the first time in his life, of gaining a feeling of belonging, of security, of confidence, and an increase in self-esteem and happiness. Living, working, enjoying life, discussing problems side by side with others who have more or less similar difficulties, gradually lead to a lessening of feelings of isolation and loneliness, increase interest and participation, and alter attitudes from egocentricity to greater altruism and community-mindedness.

Stimulation by interaction of thought and feeling with others increasingly improves one's "social ego," and as all these activities take place in a completely free atmosphere, the patient's sense of freedom leads to a heightened feeling of responsibility. The intermingling of the sexes in occupational, recreational and discussion groups, too, makes the hospital experience more like real life and helps remove the feeling of being cloistered and living "apart" from the rest of the world.

Group psychotherapy with psychotic patients was carried out in American mental hospitals by Lazell in 1918 (1921, 1930), and later by Marsh (1931), Moreno (1946), Schroeder (1936), Wender (1936, 1953) and others in the early 30's, but, as far back as 1904, Mrs. Meyer organized occupational and recreational therapy in New York mental hospitals, and "lured the wallflowers into folk dancing as a form of group therapy" (Lieff, 1948).

By 1945, the introduction of group psychotherapy into mental state hospitals was "still in its initial stages" and "only relatively few papers" about it had been published, though "some practical attempts have been made to cope with this rather deficient situation where group psychotherapy would truly come fully into its own" (Meiers, 1946).

However, since the late 1940's, group therapy has been increasingly employed in mental hospitals in many parts of the world. In 1950, 61 per cent of the state mental hospitals in New York, and over 50 per cent of all state mental hospitals in the United States, employed some form of group therapy (Geller, 1950). The method was much less used in Europe (Merguet, 1950; Pakesch, 1950; Shentoub et al., 1950; Tosquelles, 1950; Rümke, 1951; and Teirich, 1951). Although considerable interest was shown in American experience with group therapy at the Mental Health Congress in Paris in 1950 (Hulse, 1951), there were at that time countries like Sweden where, apparently, no group therapy was carried out in mental hospitals (Bernstein, 1951; Israel, 1951). As far as England is concerned, Menninger (1946) was impressed by "the skillful use of the principle of group psychology and group dependency in therapeutic programmes" and by the fact that "they [group therapy programmes] are not as yet the preoccupation or method of preference in the leading psychiatric hospitals of America, whereas they actually are in England." Yet, in 1947, there were "still few [British] hospitals where it can be said that full opportunities are offered to patients as . . . members of groups for indoor and outdoor activities . . ." (Annual Report of the Board of Control, 1947), and in 1948, only three of sixteen mental hospitals surveyed (Pratt, 1948) used group therapy. However, as in the United States, where Geller's investigation showed that group therapy programs in psychiatric hospitals were gradually expanding, so also in England (Leading Article, Brit. Med. J., 1946; Annual Reports of the Board of Control, 1947, 1948, 1950) where Bierer (1940) and Kraupl (1947) and, in a slightly different setting, the psychiatrists involved in the Northfield experiment (Bion, 1946) were among the first to employ the method in mental hospitals, it has gained increased recognition.

The majority of psychiatric hospitals employing group practices chiefly use discussion or lecture techniques, as evidenced by the replies to Geller's questionnaire (1950a), and by a special committee report to the World Federation for Mental Health (1952).

However, quite a number of authors have recently described or suggested a more extensive employment of group methods, involving at times occupational and recreational forms of group therapy, and occasionally including the staff as well as patients; e.g., Carmichael, Dreyfus and Kline (1948), Evseef (1948), Geller (1950b), Gosline (1951), Hamilton (1946, 1953), Pelzman and Bellsmith, Schneidmuhl (1951), Wender and Stein (1953) in the United States, Nicole (1949) in England and Sivadon (1949) in France. Group therapy has also been widely employed in neurosis centers (Jones, 1952a), in Australia, England and South Africa, and at day hospitals in Canada and England, and occasionally also in general hospitals (Frank, 1952; Hadden, 1951).

The importance of group activities, as far as both inpatient and outpatient services of the "community mental hospital" are concerned, has been stressed at the last meeting of the Expert Committee on Mental Health of the World Health Organization (1953): "Activity . . . one of the most important characteristics of the therapeutic community . . .

can, in fact, become a range of occupational and psycho-therapeutic group-activities in some of which each patient should participate."

Rose and Butler (1954) described in detail what seems to be an effective technique of play group therapy with psychotic adolescent girls and Slavson (1950) outlined a diverse program of group activities including group psychotherapy for psychotic patients.

Warlingham Park Hospital is fifty years old. There are 1,050 beds, with a full-time staff of thirteen doctors. The total admissions during the first nine months of this year numbered 658. The medical staff do practically the whole of the psychiatry, including child guidance, for a town with a population of 250,000. There are about fifty outpatient sessions a week. The size of the catchment (referral) area and the amount of outpatient work result in practically all admissions being seen by a member of the staff. Some of the patients have been attending the outpatient "social clubs," or have been having individual or group psychotherapy before admission. Others were offered these after discharge. In view of this it is not surprising that for over sixteen years the voluntary admission rate has been over 90 per cent. At present there is also a small experimental unit for neurotics outside the Lunacy and Mental Treatment Acts.

A patient entering a mental hospital for the first time is beset by many fears and misapprehensions. It is, therefore, important from the start to allay these and to help him orient himself in his new surroundings. As a first step toward gaining the patient's confidence, he receives, within twenty-four hours of entering the hospital, a personal letter signed by the Medical Superintendent as well as a booklet which is a guide to the hospital. It is the task of the chaplain, or of another patient, to take the new patient for a tour of the hospital as soon as he is out of bed.

Every Wednesday morning all new patients are seen as a group by the senior officers of the hospital, including the Medical Superintendent, Matron, Chief Male Nurse and Secretary. A film dealing with mental health, such as those produced by the Canadian Film Board on Mental Mechanisms, is shown, after which coffee and biscuits are served. This is followed by a short discussion on the film. Each patient is asked to give his reactions to the hospital and to state what things he would do better if he had the job for a week of the Medical Superintendent, the Secretary, the Chief Male Nurse or the Matron. It is seldom that a week passes without at least one suggestion from a patient that can be put into effect.

These group discussions have proved invaluable to the patients. They help give them a feeling of acceptance and of participation, but have been of even greater value to the senior staff, who are always amazed to find how much they can learn from patients. The meetings end with a brief talk by the Medical Superintendent on the aims and purposes of the hospital, its organization, grouping of patients, and on the standard of behavior expected of them. These first group meetings go a long way toward dispelling the new arrivals' vague fears and suspicions and in preparing them for contributing their share in their recovery.

It is our practice to ensure that every patient is a member of at least one group. These groups may be based on common cultural interests, such as art or music, on treatment, such as the insulin group, or on the nature of the mental disability, such as the alcoholic or psychopathic group.

Even the most deteriorated patients derive much benefit from groups. The completely self-absorbed, lonely, pitiful figures who used to huddle in a corner of a ward might not only have been in the final stages of their progressive illness, but might partly be the products of the hospital atmosphere itself. Being left to their own devices with complete absence of stimulation by social contact may ultimately lead to complete intellectual and emotional impoverishment and to the disappearance of every residuum of personal pride and of any innate or acquired gregarious tendencies and attitudes.

At Warlingham Park Hospital the seriously deteriorated patients are put into *habit-training groups* (see Table 1). These are small groups, each under the supervision of a nurse who supervises its activities *all day long*. Constant repetition of the patient's activities aims at making these a habit, so that in time he may be promoted to a less deteriorated group. Eventually some cases of wet and dirty patients are able to look after their personal hygiene without supervision. Similarly, patients who, if left to themselves, become completely passive and immobile, benefit by being put into *occupational groups* carrying out simple tasks, such as wheel barrow parties and other open-air working groups.

Work in occupational groups also serves to dissipate energy in actively disturbed patients and replaces in a more constructive way the locked wards. At Warlingham Park Hospital only two of the wards are locked,[1] and the number of violent patients can be counted on the fingers of one hand. Constant distrust of the patient, and the deprivation of all his liberty and personal belongings, will make him rebellious against authority. A trusting, friendly attitude in an atmosphere of freedom removes his need to rebel.

Obviously, occupational therapists can cater only for a relatively small

[1] These two wards have been unlocked since November 1954, so that since then Warlingham Park Hospital has got no locked wards.

proportion of the hospital population. It is, therefore important that all nurses should be interested in this type of therapy, which is carried on not only in the special occupational departments but also on all wards. The more intelligent and less affected patients can be very helpful, aiding themselves in the process, by acting as group leaders to chronic patients, such as in knitting parties of elderly female patients. It has also been found that the mixing of the sexes, for example in the occupational therapy department, leads to marked improvement of behavior in some acutely disturbed patients. In this connection it must not be forgotten that a patient's attitude naturally depends to a large degree on the attitude of other patients, as well as the nursing, the nonnursing, and nonmedical staffs. For the patient, the ward nurses, his fellow patients on the ward and the cook may be much more important figures than the doctor. It is, therefore, important that the nonprofessional staff of the hospital should also be considered as a part of the therapeutic team and help in the creation of a wholesome hospital "climate" and "culture."

It was found that many of the complaints and suggestions at the Wednesday morning conferences dealt with food. It was, therefore, decided to have a special group every Tuesday afternoon, to discuss food. This group consisted of patients representing each ward, the Chef and the Deputy Supplies Officer who acts as the Catering Officer. They discussed freely any nonmedical problems concerning the arrangement, quality, etc., of meals, and offered criticisms and suggestions for improvement.

The *food conference* is one example of a group in which members of different wards participate together in a project affecting the whole community. While naturally the feeling of belonging and the spirit of loyalty is most marked among members of a more or less closely knit group, patients are encouraged to appreciate the fact that they are members of larger groups, beyond their own particular group, e.g., the ward they live in and the whole hospital community. They are thus encouraged to take pride in contributing toward the welfare of larger groups and the community as a whole.

Of the greatest importance to the patient during his stay in the hospital is the management of his ward and his relationships with the staff and fellow patients. He may belong to a group centered in the ward, such as an art or music group, but the members of such groups can never mean as much to him, or influence him to the same extent for better or for worse, as those among whom he eats and sleeps and leads his daily life. Many patients, when they leave the hospital, are unable to give the name of the doctor of their ward, but we have yet to find the recovered patient who is unable to give the name of his Ward Sister or Charge Nurse. This is only natural when one considers that even the patient who is undergoing intensive individual psychotherapy (and there are not many of them) seldom sees the doctor for more than four or five hours a week, while the long-stay patient may have to be satisfied with ten minutes twice a year. This is in marked contrast with the nursing staff, who are in the ward all day. If these facts were more generally realized, more attention would be paid to nurse-patient relationships and ward management. Good ward management is an important, if not the most important, single factor in sound mental hospital administration.

We have attempted to solve this problem by means of (1) the division of the patients in each ward into groups (Table 2). We found that a nurse can deal much more effectively with twelve patients specially assigned to her than four free-floating nurses can with forty-eight patients; (2) the planning of the lives of the patients in each group for each day of the week and every hour of the day; and (3) a weekly *ward discussion meeting* attended by doctors, nurses and patients with the aim of breaking down the barriers between doctors, nurses and patients, the releasing of tensions, and the engendering of a feeling of participation and responsibility.

The attitude of the nursing staff is obviously of the greatest importance; tension among them will communicate itself very quickly to the patients, and it is essential that the nurse is made to feel that he is one of the most important members of the therapeutic team. Nurses often feel suspicious that their security is being threatened by direct communication and exchange between doctor and patients, and the best way to allay these fears and suspicions is by making them active participants of ward groups and as far as possible also of other group meetings. Apart from this, there are special conferences held weekly where smaller groups of the nursing staff discuss psychological problems with a doctor, and where the idea of a modern mental hospital as a therapeutic community is freely discussed. The nursing staff often feel much safer in the old hierarchic system. Where the doctor is safely isolated from direct contact with patients through the intermediary nurse, there is a greater feeling of security. This is a very real factor that has to be taken into account in any progressive change in the modern mental hospital. *Nurses' discussion groups* help to dissipate tensions of this kind and encourage pride in the nursing staff in being members of the therapeutic team.

Recreational groups and *social clubs* also cut across the boundaries of special groups and ward communities. There is also a *Good Companions Club* in the hospital, run by a committee of patients under the supervision of a doctor. They are responsible for arranging entertainments. *Cultural groups,* such as music and art groups, are comprised of patients from different wards, neurotics and psychotics harmoniously participating in these activities. The hospital's weekly magazine, the *Warlingham Parker,* is a communal enterprise, as are the patients' weekly variety performances, the patients' orchestra, football and cricket teams, etc. All of these activities help to evoke a feeling of belonging and of being an accepted member of the hospital family as a whole, beyond the narrow limits of their own specific groups.

Among the patients that are helped by these groups, a few deserve special mention. There is the psychopathic group. One would not expect psychopaths to develop loyalty feelings, but they seem to take to one another, perhaps because of a common grudge against authority. According to Slavson (1947), they do not form suitable material for group therapy. There is at present no really satisfactory treatment for their condition, but an attempt is made here to treat them together in a group by means of a program based on intensive occupational therapy, physical exercise and group discussions.

The treatment of alcoholic patients is based on a combination of hospital group therapy and the Alcoholics Anonymous program, supplemented, in individual cases, by physical methods of therapy. The alcoholics live in a separate ward, form their own working parties, have daily discussions with a doctor, social worker or ward charge nurse, attend A.A. meetings outside the hospital and have formed their own A.A. group inside the hospital (Table 3). The group discussions deal with alcoholism from both its main aspects, viewing it as a manifestation of an underlying maladjustment of the whole personality, and as an illness per se. Thus, personality problems, discussions and psychodramatic presentations of life histories take place alongside with debates centered around the patients' drinking histories.

A *Neurosis Unit* (Pinel House) which, under an experimental scheme, comprises up to twenty patients of both sexes, admitted without any statutory formalities, outside the Lunacy and Mental Treatment Acts, for a stay of not more than two months, forms the most closely knit example of community life within the hospital (Table 4). They live in a small building divided into two blocks, one for the male patients and one for the female. They are to a large extent responsible for the organization of their own occupations and recreation and have at least two group discussions each day, one with and one without a doctor present. Every patient is expected to write his life history and to read it out in front of the whole group; sometimes it is acted out in the form of a psychodrama. The members of this unit develop a very high *esprit de corps* and considerable empathy is shown during the reading of a group member's history. It is remarkable that the whole unit is run with the help of only two nurses. They, however, play a very important role in the unit by establishing close relationships with the patients, observing them all day long at close range and thus being of great help in supplementing the doctor's impressions gained during the group psychotherapy sessions.

Group discussions as carried out at Warlingham Park Hospital are of a very varied nature, depending on the type of patients as well as on the inclinations of the therapist, and ranging from didactic lecture methods to repressional-inspirational and analytically orientated groups. In the main, however, the approach is a dynamically orientated eclectic one. As the same patient is often treated by various doctors at the same time it is important that the doctors meet often to discuss their mutual findings and impressions. *Staff conferences* are therefore held frequently to co-ordinate their efforts. All doctors meet the Medical Superintendent each morning, the Matron and the Chief Male Nurse also being present, to discuss current problems. The doctors on both sides of the hospital, male and female, meet in addition twice weekly to see all new admissions and to discuss their treatment. In this way no patient gets "lost." At another weekly conference the whole medical staff meets to discuss the case of one patient. Once a month the cases of all patients admitted in that month of previous years, who are still in the hospital, are reviewed.

At all times it is pointed out to the patients that hospital care is often merely the first step in the whole program of their reintegration into society, and that they will have to continue their rehabilitation efforts after discharge. The alcoholics, for example, are strongly encouraged to attend A.A. meetings regularly as well as group psychotherapy sessions at the hospital after they have left the hospital. Several outpatient groups are run especially for ex-patients of the Neurosis Unit.

While still in the hospital, patients are encouraged to attend from time to time the *outpatients' clubs* held in Croydon, so that they may more easily make a habit of attending them regularly after their discharge until such time as they feel sufficiently confident to carry on without further support. There exist different clubs of this kind, run by outpatients under the guidance of a doctor or social worker. One of these clubs is run exclusively for the benefit of elderly people of over sixty-five, who often have no other social contacts. Some of the older patients, who have no relatives with whom they could live, but who are quite capable of looking after themselves with a minimum of supervision, are housed in a very comfortable country house some distance away from the hospital; all the activities there are carried out by the patients, (some fifty-five in number) largely on their own responsibility, under the supervision of one nurse.

Apart from outpatient clubs there is a considerable number of *outpatient group activities* going on. Outpatient group sessions are held in the hospital's outpatient clinics that meet in the various general hospitals of the town. Former patients are encouraged to attend these sessions for a while after their discharge from the hospital, along with other outpatients who have never been admitted to the hospital itself. The outpatient groups held in the child guidance clinic are conducted by doctors in collaboration with social workers. They comprise groups for children of all ages (including activity groups, groups centered around fantasy games, painting groups) as well as discussion groups for mothers.

Miss X, a milliner, age 38 years, admitted June, 1953, from the Outpatient Department, with a variety of complaints among which were tenseness, palpitations, fear that she had thrombosis, awareness of her breathing, and difficulty in carrying out certain tasks. She was diagnosed as psychoneurotic. Her sister stated that the patient had recently been very depressed, though she had not complained of depression; that she had not been eating and had become "terribly thin." She thought her sister's illness was due to the death from coronary thrombosis of their mother in February, 1953, of whom she, like the rest of her family, had been very fond.

The patient stated that her trouble had started at the age of 14, when she "became aware" of herself and thought she might become "mental," a fear that had persisted ever since. The "tensed-up feeling," palpitations and the idea that she had thrombosis came on following her mother's death.

The patient was the youngest of three surviving children. She described her childhood as happy, though her mother was always of a worrying nature, always complaining of her heart, and there were frequent quarrels between the parents. According to the sister, the patient had been a normal, happy child, who got on well at school and with her work, and was very energetic and conscientious. Since her mother's death the patient had lived with her father.

In the hospital, the patient showed herself to be a pleasant, intelligent person. She participated fully in the community life of the group and in their discussions. She read out her life story in front of the group without being unduly embarrassed. She made good progress, was discharged after two months and, as is customary with members of the neurotic group, attended for several months the outpatient discussion groups and the social club, after which she said that she felt fit enough to stand on her own feet without the support of these groups. She seemed contented at home and at work when seen in February, 1954, and was asked to write a short description of her illness and current state of mind of which the following is an extract.

> Having been conditioned to fear from childhood on by my mother against men, sex, childbirth, marriage, etc., I suppose it was natural for me to develop a "fear complex" at puberty. For over twenty years I endured blind panics, fear, etc., but didn't tell anybody, as I thought I was "mental."
>
> The shock of my mother's death and the emotion pent-up over the years brought on anxiety coupled with violent vomiting every day for three months, to such an extent that I sought the help of a psychiatrist, who advised a group psychotherapy course lasting eight weeks.
>
> "Group Therapy" sounds strange. The first fortnight you cannot possibly see how this treatment is going to be of any benefit to you, but gradually in these group therapy meetings one finds one's underlying troubles coming to light.
>
> Once knowing what all the fears, the rejection and nonacceptance of the circumstances of our daily life are all about, it is then up to us to accept our responsibilities, to make alterations if necessary and if it is to our benefit, and to begin to reason and make friends with our subconscious mind which is causing all the internal conflicts.

C. D., a simple schizophrenic, was admitted in 1938 at the age of 21 years and assigned to the "habit-training group." Both parents had died in mental hospitals and the patient, who was the youngest of five children, was brought up from the age of eight, when his father died, by the latter's friend, also at one time a patient in a mental hospital, and his wife. They were a problem family, and two of the patient's brothers were known delinquents.

As a child the patient made average progress at school. At home he was said to be irritable, negativistic and obstinate, though otherwise normal, but at the age of 19 years he became solitary and morose, neglected himself, and at times became quarrelsome, interfering and violent. The other people in the house were afraid of him, and at the age of 21 years he was admitted to the hospital. He was found to be simple and childish, at times restless, subject to impulsive outbursts, was delusional, resistive, uncooperative and negativistic.

A series of insulin shocks produced no appreciable change in his condition, and he gradually became more deteriorated.

When first put into the habit-training group, he was grossly deteri-orated, sometimes threw his food on to the floor, needed to be spoon-fed, washed and dressed, was incontinent of both urine and feces, would stay put in the same place all day and showed little interest in his sur-roundings. He was subject to impulsive outbursts when he would kick, bite and scratch the nursing staff. He would not walk or do anything to cooperate with the staff and his fellow patients. After two months' strenu-ous efforts on the part of the nurses he began to show some improvement and accompanied his group on a walk around the hospital grounds. From that time on he became more sociable and amenable to group routines, sat at the table with his fellow patients and fed himself, tried to dress himself but at first needed a good deal of assistance.

After two years he was transferred to another ward where he soon became a very competent ward worker. Since then he has worked in the gardens, and among his present tasks he delivers the evening papers to the various wards. Although still hallucinating and delusional, he leads a useful life within the hospital, and each year he goes away with other patients for a fortnight's holiday by the sea, where he is largely left with-out supervision and can eat in a public restaurant without seeming notice-ably different in behavior from other customers. He has no relatives with whom he can stay, but he has frequently been out for week-end visits to friends who are either ex-patients or relatives of ex-patients.

A. B., a business man, age 43 years, was admitted as an alcoholic in April, 1952, from the psychiatric observation ward at the local general hospital. He was fairly clear mentally on admission; he stated that he was not very fond of drink and never took more than two to three pints of beer at a time. He did not think he was in need of treatment but was prepared to accept it in order to please his brother, according to whom he always carried a flask in his pocket which smelt as if it contained a mixture of sherry and methylated spirits.

The day following admission he developed a typical attack of de-lirium tremens, was delusional, visually hallucinated, restless and violent, continually trying to fight imaginary policemen. The attack cleared up after about ten days, and the patient joined the alcoholics' group and was given a short course of modified insulin to improve his physical con-dition. He took an active part in the discussion groups and gained con-siderable insight into his drinking problems.

Although not completely confident, he had acquired a much healthier attitude toward alcohol when discharged in November, 1952, and kept in touch with the hospital group as well as Alcoholics Anonymous.

Following a domestic upheaval he applied for readmission in April, 1953, and left after a fortnight feeling that he had acquired enough self-confidence to tackle a delicate and difficult domestic situation. Since then he has regularly attended hospital groups as well as A.A. meetings, has resumed successful control of his business, has remarried, is happy, and has apparently achieved contented sobriety.

At our request he sent us, in May, 1954,[2] a life history and a report on his present condition, extracts from which are given below:

. . . My childhood was quite happy . . . I was the second of three sons . . . I had love and affection lavished on me . . . After leaving school I entered business with my father . . . I suffered great grief when my father died. I was then 28 . . . I married at 26 and was very happy . . . Until the war started I was an occasional social drinker, but when the air raids began to be heavy I found myself relying on alcohol for moral support, temporary relief and escape from my fears and worries . . . I sustained quite a severe mental shock when, in 1944, a flying bomb all but ruined my house in which I had taken great pride. After this incident I drank more heavily than before.

. . . My wife died suddenly when I was 32. That was the greatest blow of my life . . . I found my need for alcohol steadily increasing and I made little or no attempt to control my desire for it. Drinking became paramount in my life and the craving for it became like an inevitable avalanche . . . I find it hard to write or even to remember many of the sordid details during the four years following my wife's death . . . there were many cunning, artful, deceitful things . . . I was taken to the hospital in a pitiful mental and physical condition . . . However, after months of hospital treatment I became quite fit. I regard my recovery as almost miraculous, for which I have to thank several factors, i.e., hospital treatment, group therapy, tolerance and understanding from my family, and, last but not least, my membership of A.A., meetings of which I attend whenever possible . . . I have lived an absolutely sober life for 1½ years. I have remarried . . . My interests in my home, gardening, business and other normal occupations have returned . . .

The aim of modern treatment is to keep the patients in a social pattern, at the same time preserving their identity, and, where they have failed to conform to that pattern in ordinary life, to teach them the art of living with themselves and with others, to give and to take, to understand other people's troubles as well as their own, and thus restore them to normal mental and social contacts with their fellow men. Membership of a group enjoying the organized freedom of a mental hospital, acceptance by the group and full participation in the daily life of the hospital,

[2] This patient has maintained sobriety and progressive improvement in all spheres of adjustment up to the present time (October, 1955).

have much to contribute toward the resocialization of those whose loneliness has been such as to make them need hospital care.

Group therapy both within the hospital itself as well as in an outpatient setting, can contribute to the resocialization and reintegration into the community of the mentally ill, and by improving their ability to form interpersonal relationships, can materially increase interpersonal harmony and inner happiness.

BIBLIOGRAPHY

Alonzo, A. M. (1948), Discussion of "Advances in Group and Individual Therapy." Proceedings of the International Conference on Medical Psychotherapy. Int. Congress on Mental Health, London.

Annual Reports of the Board of Control to the Lord Chancellor, for the Years 1947, 1948, 1950. London: H.M.'s Stationery Office.

Bernstein, L. (1951), Group Therapy in Sweden. *Int J. Group Psychother., 1*:85.

Bierer, J. (1940), Psychotherapy in Mental Hospital Practice. *J. Ment. Sci., 86*:928.

—— (1942), Group Psychotherapy. *Brit. Med. J., 1*:214.

—— (1948), Modern Social and Group Therapy. In: *Modern Trends in Psychological Medicine,* ed. N. G. Harris. London: Butterworth.

Bion, R. W. (1946), The Leaderless Group Project. *Bull. Menninger Clin., 10*:77-81.

Bridger, H. (1946), The Northfield Experiment. *Bull. Menninger Clin., 10*:71-76.

Connolly, J. (1847), *Construction and Government of Lunatic Asylums.* London: J. & A. Churchill Ltd.

Cruvant, B. A. (1953), The Function of the "Administrative Group" in a Mental Hospital Group Therapy Program. *Am. J. Psychiat., 110*:342-346.

Dreikurs, R., and Corsini, R. (1954), Twenty Years of Group Psychotherapy. *Am. J. Psychiat., 110*:567-575.

Dreyfus, A. and Kline, N. S. (1948), Group Psychotherapy in Veterans Administration Hospitals. *Am. J. Psychiat., 104*:618.

Evseef, G. S. (1948), Group Psychotherapy in the State Hospital. *Dis. Nerv. Syst., 9*:214.

Expert Committee on Mental Health, Third Report (1953). World Health Organization, Techn. Rep. Ser. 1953, 73. Geneva.

Foulkes, S. H. (1946), Principles and Practice of Group Therapy. *Bull. Menninger Clin., 10*:85-89.

—— (1948), *Introduction to Group-Analytic Psychotherapy.* New York: Grune & Stratton.

Frank, J. D. (1952), The Effects of Interpatient and Group Influences in a General Hospital. *Int. J. Group Psychother., 2*:127-138.

Geller, J. J. (1950a), Current Status of Group Psychotherapy Practices in the State Hospitals for Mental Disease. *Group Psychother., 3*:231-240.

—— (1950b), Proposed Plan for Institutional Group Psychotherapy. *Psychiat. Quart. Suppl., 24*:270-275.

Gosline, E. (1951), A Report on the Application of Group Psychotherapy at Utica State Hospitals. *Psychiat. Quart. Suppl., 25*:65-75.

"Group Psychotherapy" (1949). Leading Article, *Brit. Med. J., 1*:227-228.

Group Psychotherapy in Institutions (1952). Section V of a Report to the World Federation for Mental Health by a Commission under the Chairmanship of S. R. Slavson. *Int. J. Group Psychother., 2*:274-279.

Hadden, S. B. (1951), Group Psychotherapy in General Hospitals. *Int. J. Group Psychother., 1*:31-36.

Table 1

<u>HABIT TRAINING GROUPS</u>

5	6	7
The time-table must be strictly adhered to so that by constant repetition it becomes habit-forming. Written reports are made on Sunday.	These patients have moved up from No. 5, and it is the duty of the nurse to maintain personal hygiene and report on any patient with faulty habits.	These patients have moved up from No. 6 and should be ready for transfer to other wards.
7 a.m. to 7.30 a.m. — Patients dress assisted by nurse. Toilet, etc.	Daily time-table kept as far as possible	1. The nurse in charge of the group will report to the Head Gardener every day except Sunday. Times 10.30 and 2.30.
7.30 to 8 a.m. — Nurse to breakfast	<u>Monday</u> 10.30 — Sweeping bus shelter, main drive from gates to centre.	2. Special attention to feet and nails during bathing
8 a.m. — Patients' breakfast under supervision. Own tables	<u>Tuesday</u> — Sweeping canteen path to Nurses' Home	3. Report to Charge of ward. Work and progress of each patient.
8.30 a.m. — Toilet	<u>Wednes-day</u> — Ward gardens – G.1, H.1, J.1 wards, Cinema, visiting Ward gardens	
9 a.m. to 10.15 a.m. — Ward cleaning	<u>Thurs-day</u>	
10.30 a.m. — Walk in grounds. Dress inspection by Charge Nurse	<u>Friday</u> Walk	
11.45 a.m. — Return. Slippers. Toilet	<u>Satur-day</u> Sweeping from Church to cricket field	
1 p.m. — Dinner		
1.45 p.m. — Toilet. Hand over to nurse coming on duty		
2.30 p.m. — Walking party, cinema Wednesday and Saturday		
5 p.m. — Tea		
5.30 p.m. to 8 p.m. — Games, etc.		
8 p.m. — Toilet		
8.30 p.m. — Bed with instructions to night nurse		

Table 2

J.1 WARD – GROUP THERAPY

Group A.	Group B.5	Group B.6	Group B.7	Group B.12	Not Grouped	G.P.I.s	E.P.s
Ward workers	Habit Training	Instructional H.T.	Group transfers to other wards	Occupation Room	Nil		
Cr.	Ba.	Co.	An.	Pa.		Fl.	Al.
Li.	Ba.	Co.	Al.	Sp.		Po.	An.
Lo.	Bo.	Co.	Fu.	Sm.		Th.	Be.
Pr.	Br.	Da.	Fo.	Sp.		Wa.	Bu.
Pe.	Go.	Do.	Ha.				Co.
Sa.	Le.	Ro.	La.	C.5 Gardeners			Fo.
Th.	Ni.	Sm.	To.	Bu.			Li.
	Po.	St.	Fl.	Co.			Lo.
	Sa.	St.	Be.	Cu.			Pe.
	Wa.		+ Ward Occupational Therapy	Ev.			St.
			Ho.	Hu.			Sa.
			Kn.	Wa.			Wa.
			Po.		Student nurse i/c No. 7 Group		
			Mo.				
			Ro.				
			Wo.				
7	10	9	15	4		4	12
				6			
Charge Nurse	Staff Nurse	Staff Nurse					

WARD TOTAL 51

Table 3

GROUP THERAPY

ALCOHOLIC GROUP

SUNDAY	MONDAY	TUESDAY	WEDNESDAY	THURSDAY	FRIDAY	SATURDAY
9.30 a.m. to 11.30 a.m. Church Service	9 a.m. to 12.30 p.m. Occupational Therapy (gardens, offices, Male Occ.etc.)	9 a.m. to 11 a.m. Occupational Therapy	9 a.m. to 12.30 p.m. Occupational Therapy	9 a.m. to 11 a.m. Occupational Therapy	9 a.m. to 11.30 a.m. Occupational Therapy	9 a.m. to 10.45 a.m. Occupational Therapy
2 p.m. to 4 p.m. Visiting	2 p.m. to 4 p.m. As above	11 a.m. to 12.30 p.m. Group conference with Dr. G. and Ward Charge Nurse	2 p.m. to 4 p.m. Visiting	11 a.m. to 12.30 p.m. Group conference with Dr. G. and Ward Charge Nurse	11.45 a.m. to 12.45 p.m. Group Psychotherapy with Dr. S.	11 a.m. to 12.30 p.m. Group Conference with Dr. G.
4 p.m. to 5 p.m. Relatives' Group meeting with Social Worker	6 p.m. to 10 p.m. A.A. Group Meeting at Croydon	2 p.m. to 4 p.m. Occupational Therapy	6 p.m. to 11 p.m. A.A. Group meeting at Tunbridge Wells twice monthly	2 p.m. to 3.30 p.m. Conference with Social Worker	2 p.m. to 4 p.m. Occupational Therapy	1.30 p.m. to 5 p.m. Parole
6 p.m. to 8 p.m. A.A. meeting in Board Room attended by relatives and members of various A.A. Groups		6.30 p.m. to 8.30 p.m. Dance		6.30 p.m. to 8.30 p.m. Dance	6 p.m. to 10 p.m. A.A. Group Meeting at Croydon	6.30 p.m. to 8.30 p.m. Cinema
				6 p.m. to 11 p.m. A.A. Meeting at Guildford once a month		

Table 4

PINEL HOUSE
TIMETABLE OF GROUPS

ALL GROUPS ASSIST WITH WARD WORK

DAY	MORNING	AFTERNOON	EVENING
SUNDAY	10.30 a.m. Matins all groups	2.30 p.m. Visiting all groups 4 p.m. to 5 p.m. Whole group discussion without doctor	
MONDAY	8.30 a.m. to 10 a.m. Ward work, all groups 10.15 a.m. to 12 noon Male Patients Gardening, preparing room for Occupational Therapy. Female Patients Making lampshades	2 p.m. General Conference 4 to 5 p.m. Whole Group discussion	7.30 p.m. to 10 p.m. All groups attend Good Companions Club, Park Lane, Croydon
TUESDAY	8.30 a.m. to 10 a.m. All groups, ward work 10.15 a.m. to 12 noon Group B. Occupation Group A, Dr. M's Treatment Group	2 p.m. All groups Psychodrama 4 p.m. to 5 p.m. Whole Group discussion	6 p.m. to 9 p.m. All groups – table tennis, darts, cards
WEDNESDAY	8.30 a.m. to 10 a.m. All groups, ward work 10.15 a.m. to 12 noon All groups, occupation as on Monday	2.30 p.m. All groups, Visiting 4 p.m. to 5 p.m. Whole Group discussion	6.30 p.m. to 8.30 p.m. Cinema, all groups
THURSDAY	8.30 a.m. to 10 a.m. All groups, ward work 11 a.m. to 12 noon Group B, Dr. M's Treatment Group	2 p.m. All groups, Art Class 4 p.m. to 5 p.m. Whole Group discussion	6.30 p.m. to 8.30 p.m. Dance, all groups

Table 4

(Continued)

PINEL HOUSE

TIMETABLE OF GROUPS

FRIDAY	8.30 a.m. to 10 a.m.	All groups, ward work	2 p.m. All groups, Art Class
	11.15 a.m. to 12 noon	Group B, occupation as above. Group A, Dr. G.'s Treatment Group	4 p.m. to 5 p.m. Whole Group discussion
			6 p.m. to 9 p.m. All groups – table tennis, darts and cards
SATURDAY	8.30 a.m. to 10 a.m.	All groups, ward work	2 p.m. <u>Patients not on week-end leave</u> Ward games, discussions
	10.15 a.m. to 12 noon	Group A – occupation	4 p.m. to 5 p.m. Whole Group discussion
	11 a.m. to 12 noon	Group B – Dr. G.'s Treatment Group	6.30 p.m. to 8.30 p.m. Cinema, all groups

Hamilton, D. M. (1946), The Psychiatric Hospital as a Cultural Pattern. In: *Current Therapy of Personality Disorders,* ed. B. Glueck. New York: Grune & Stratton.

—— (1953), Cultural Treatment in a Psychiatric Hospital. *Int. J. Group Psychother., 3:*204-209.

Hulse, W. C. (1950), Group Psychotherapy and the First International Congress on Psychiatry. *Group Psychother., 3:*250-252.

—— (1951), International Aspects of Group Psychotherapy. *Int. J. Group Psychother., 1:*172-177.

Israel, J. (1951), Group Therapy in Sweden. *Int. J. Group Psychother., 1:*84-85.

Jones, M. (1952a), *Rehabilitation in Psychiatry.* World Health Organization. WHO/ Ment./30.

—— (1952b), *Social Psychiatry. A Study of Therapeutic Communities.* London: Tavistock Publications.

Klapman, J. W. (1948), *Group Psychotherapy. Theory and Practice.* London: Wm. Heinemann.

Kraupl, F. (1947), Emotional Interplay and Dominant Personalities in Therapeutic Groups. Observations on Combined Schizophrenic-Neurotic Groups. *J. Ment. Sci., 93:*613-630.

Lazell, E. W. (1921), The Group Treatment of Dementia Praecox. *Psychoanal. Rev., 8:*168-179.

—— (1930), Group Psychic Treatment of Dementia Praecox by Lectures in Mental Reeducation. *U. S. Vet. Bureau Med. Bull., 6:*733-747.

Lieff, A. (1948), *The Commonsense Psychiatry of Dr. Adolf Meyer.* New York: McGraw-Hill.

Main, T. F. (1946) , The Hospital as a Therapeutic Institution. *Bull. Menninger Clin., 10:*66-70.

Marsh, L. C. (1931), Group Treatment of Psychoses by Psychological Equivalent of the Revival. *Ment. Hyg., 17:*396-416.

—— (1933), Experiment in Group Treatment of Patients at Worcester State Hospital. *Ment. Hyg., 17:*396-416.

Martin, D. V.; Glatt, M. M.; Weeks, K. F. (1954), An Experimental Unit for the Community Treatment of Neurosis (to be published).

Meiers, J. I. (1946), Historical Survey. Origins and Development of Group Psychotherapy. In: *Group Psychotherapy. A Symposium,* ed. J. L. Moreno. New York: Beacon House.

Menninger, K. (1946). Foreword. *Bull. Menninger Clin., 10:*65.

Mercier, C. A. (1894), *Lunatic Asylums. Organisation and Management.* London: Charles Griffin.

Merguet, H. (1950), Discussion on Group Psychotherapy. International Congress of Psychiatry, Paris, 1950.

Moreno, J. L. (1932), Group Psychotherapy, Theory and Practice. *Group Psychother., 3:*142-188, 1950.

—— ed. (1946), *Group Psychotherapy, A Symposium.* New York: Beacon House.

Nicole, J. E. (1949), Psychiatric Rehabilitation in Hospital. *Practitioner, 163:*533-540.

Pakesch, E. (1950), Contributions to Group-Psychotherapy. International Congress of Paris, 1950 (mimeographed).

Pelzman, O. and Bellsmith, E. B. (1949), A Group Therapy Service in a Psychiatric Hospital: The Place of Social Service in the Program. *Psychiat. Quart. Suppl., 32:*332-344.

Powdermaker, F. B. and Frank, J. D. (1953), *Group Psychotherapy, Studies in Methodology of Research and Therapy.* Cambridge, Mass.: Harvard University Press.

Pratt, D. (1948), *Public Mental Hospitals in England. A Survey.* Philadelphia: National Mental Health Foundation.

Querido, A. (1936), *Home Care of the Mental Patient.* London: Humphrey Milford.

Rees, T. P. and Glatt, M. M. (1954), Group Therapy in Chronic Alcoholism (to be published).

—— —— (1954), The Organisation of a Community Mental Hospital (to be published).

Reiter, P. J. (1952), Differential Reactions of Men and Women Patients to Group Psychotherapy. *Int. J. Group Psychother.*, 2:103-110.

Rose, D. M.; Butler, C. M.; Eaton, F. L. (1954), Play Group Therapy with Psychotic Adolescent Girls. *Int. J. Group Psychother.*, 4:303-311.

Rümke, H. C. (1951), Group Psychotherapy in Utrecht, Holland. *Int. J. Group Psychother.*, 1:374-376.

Schilder, P. (1951), *Psychotherapy*. London: Routledge and Kegan Paul.

Schneidmuhl, A. M. (1951), Group Psychotherapy Program at the Spring Grove State Hospital. *Group Psychother.*, 4:41-55.

Schroeder, M. G. (1936), Group Psychotherapy in State Hospital. *Elgin State Hosp.*, 2:174-178.

Shentoub, S.; Desclaux, P.; Soulairac, A. (1950), Etude du comportement d'enfants caractériélles, au cours d'une psychothérapie dans un établissement hospitalier fermé. *Journal du Premier Congrès Mondial de Psychiatrie 5*, Paris 1950.

Sivadon, P. (1949), Le Centre de Traitement et de Readaptation sociale de Ville— Evrard. *Annales Médico-Psychologiques, 1*:166-169.

Slavson, S. R. (1947), *The Practice of Group Psychotherapy*. New York: International Universities Press.

—— (1950), *Analytic Group Psychotherapy*. New York: Columbia University Press.

—— (1952), Discussion of paper by Cameron, K.: Group Approach to Inpatient Adolescents. *Am. J. Psychiat.*, 109:660-661, 1953.

—— (1954), A Contribution to a Systematic Theory of Group Psychotherapy. *Int. J. Group Psychother.*, 4:3-29.

Stengel, E. (1948), The Application of Psychoanalytic Principles to the Hospital In-Patient. *J. Ment. Sci.*, 94:773-781.

Teirich, H. R. (1951), Schools Rather than Hospitals. *Group Psychother.*, 4:77-79.

—— (1951), Group Psychotherapy in Austria. *Group Psychother.*, 4:107-111.

Tosquelles, F. (1950), Psychothérapie de groupe dans un hôpital psychiatrique. *Journal du Premier Congrès Mondial de Psychiatrie 7*, Paris 1950.

Wender, L. (1936), Dynamics of Group Psychotherapy and Its Application. *J. Nerv. & Ment. Dis.*, 84:54-60.

—— and Stein, A. (1953), The Utilization of Group Psychotherapy in the Social Integration of Patients. *Int. J. Group Psychother.*, 3:210-218; 3:320-329.

Zanker, A. and Mitchell, S. D. (1948), The Use of Music in Group Therapy. *J. Ment. Sci.*, 94:737-748.

Chapter III

PSYCHOSOMATIC DISORDERS

•

From the very outset, group psychotherapy has been used in the treatment of psychosomatic disorders. The first report that dealt with this subject, that of Pratt (1906), described the use of this method in improving the emotional attitude of patients with tuberculosis. Despite the successful utilization of group psychotherapy in the treatment of psychosomatic illness, relatively little use was made of it in the treatment of such conditions until very recently.[1]

Part of this failure must be attributed to the fact that until recently neither group psychotherapy nor the concept of psychosomatic disorders were given much recognition. Although Hippocrates had sensed the unity of psyche and soma, the subsequent mechanistic approach of medicine to disease (which reached its peak in the nineteenth century) separated the patient into a body and a psyche. Similarly, in psychotherapy, although some of the dynamic factors involved in group psychotherapy were long known, the approach to mental illness that occupied the attention of psychotherapists was the individual one. Beginning with the 1920's and then gathering momentum in the 1930's, unifying concepts appeared which led to the acceptance, in the 1940's, of the psychosomatic and the group-psychotherapeutic concepts.

The psychosomatic concept of disease has served to emphasize the very universally recognized clinical fact that each and every disease affects the *whole* person as regards both the psyche and the soma. There is no somatic illness that does not to some degree, however fleetingly,

[1] Prior to 1940, there were published only twelve articles that dealt with group psychotherapy in psychosomatic disorders. Of these, six were by Pratt on the treatment of tuberculosis by the "class method." See Pratt (1922) and Thomas (1943) for reviews of the literature prior to 1940.

40

affect the sick person's emotional and mental well-being; there is no mental or emotional disturbance that does not have its somatic repercussions. In a strict sense, therefore, one should not speak of a "psychosomatic disease." However, it is generally recognized today, as stated by Ebaugh (1954), "that the nature of certain disorders can be fully appreciated only when the role of underlying emotional disturbances or psychological happenings is investigated in addition to physical disturbances or somatic happenings."

A more precise definition of psychosomatic illness is stated by Margolin and Kaufman (1948). Their lengthy but complete definition of psychosomatic medicine broadens the concept of the psychosomatic disorder to include *all the factors* leading to this syndrome. In summarizing this broadened concept, Kaufman (1953a) cites Dr. Paul Klemperer, pathologist to the Mount Sinai Hospital in New York.

There has been a very fundamental change in biological concepts . . . relating to health and disease; one no longer looked for a single etiological factor as the only cause of disease; in reality it was necessary to have a knowledge of the phylogenesis and ontogenesis of the individual in order to be able to understand what was happening to him at any given moment; a knowledge of the total individual included his psyche in terms of his endowment and life experiences; one must think in terms of multiple factors and psychogenesis does not imply the single factor in a total reaction but is one of the factors in a total picture.

These considerations indicate the modern understanding of psychosomatic disease, namely an illness in which a disturbance of the psychic adjustment of the individual operates as one of the major etiologic factors producing the illness, and this occurs in an individual whose past history, personality and present emotional situation contribute to the occurrence of the illness, the form and course it takes, to the response to treatment and to the final outcome of the illness.

With this in mind, it is possible to indicate that while all disease is psychosomatic, certain syndromes more clearly adhere to the above criteria than do others. Duodenal ulcer, certain types of ileitis and colitis, especially mucous colitis and ulcerative colitis, are commonly considered psychosomatic syndromes of the gastrointestinal system. In the cardiovascular system, the effort syndrome, essential hypertension, coronary thrombosis and certain cases of cerebral hemorrhage are considered to be psychosomatic in nature. Other syndromes designated as psychosomatic are rheumatoid arthritis, hyperthyroidism, diabetes mellitus, obesity, myxedema, migraine, certain cases of anemia, many skin conditions especially alopecia areata, pruritus, urticaria and neurodermatitis, certain cases of conjunctivitis and blepharitis, certain types of rhinitis and some cases of bronchitis, and most cases of bronchial asthma. This list which includes all sorts of conditions affecting every system of the body could be extended, but these are the disorders in which it is generally recognized at the present time that the psychic reaction of the individual, including the factors noted above, play a major etiologic role.

No precise knowledge exists as to exactly how emotional tensions in a certain kind of individual with a special kind of life history lead to one kind of pathological somatic response in one instance and to a different type of somatic manifestation in another. It is becoming apparent that certain factors play a large, if not a major, role among the many that have to do with the appearance of these disorders. These factors may be grouped under two principal headings: (1) the developmental experiences of the individual; and (2) the unconscious emotional activity characteristic of the individual. Margolin (1953) and Alexander (1950) have, in somewhat different ways, developed hypotheses concerning the factors entering into the production of psychosomatic disorders, and in the articles cited, they review the literature and give summaries of their own formulations. In their papers, they summarize some of the recent views concerning the etiology of psychosomatic disease: the role of personality structure, the conditioned reflex theory, the specificity of the conflict hypothesis, and the action of decompensated psychophysiologic moods and affective states. While the two factors noted above are considered especially important, both authors stress that they are only two of a multiplicity of influences operating in a constantly changing fashion to produce effects which themselves constantly change. Kaufman (1953b) and Grinker (1954) also stress the importance of developmental and unconscious factors and even more strongly emphasize that only a consideration of all the elements involved will enable one to achieve the understanding necessary for effective treatment of psychosomatic disorders.

These views can be summarized as follows: The chief activity of the individual, both psychic and somatic, is to maintain homeostasis, the external and internal environment most favorable, i.e., least stressful, to the individual. While certain predispositions (constitutional factors) may to a greater or lesser extent influence the way an individual does this, the major determinants are his developmental experiences. In these, a variety of factors cause the individual to establish certain characteristic mental, emotional, and physical reaction patterns which enable him to adjust to the stresses of his environment, both internal and external, so as to achieve "homeostasis." These characteristic reactions, which essentially represent the way in which the ego has developed in order to maintain the equilibrium between internal and external stresses, constitute the personality of the individual. At any time, stresses may appear which necessitate of the individual certain adjustments in order to continue functioning at the most favorable level. These stresses may be internal or external and of greater or lesser duration.

The individual may continue this new adjustment for a longer or shorter period and the adjustment may be in the nature of progress forward to a better solution, or a compromise, or a regression to a less desirable but less threatening solution. Stresses acting over shorter periods and capable of being dealt with in a progressive fashion aid in the more complete development of the individual. Stresses that are prolonged and are too great for the individual to handle adequately lead to compromise or regressive solutions which may fixate the development of the individual or distort or deform it so that permanent defects are left.

Where such defects are chiefly in the emotional and mental spheres, a neurosis or psychosis, overt or latent results[2]; the earlier the severe stress appears in the life of the individual, the more serious and widespread are the resultant defects. Where the stress occurs in a susceptible individual whose physiological response is affected as well as the emotional and mental response, the result is one of the psychosomatic disorders. Again, the earlier and the more prolonged this grave stress appears, the more profound its effects; the later and less sustained the stress is, the less serious is the psychosomatic disorder.

Ludwig (1952), in describing the psychotherapy of rheumatoid arthritis, gives a tentative formulation of the important factors involved. He emphasizes that many of these patients showed an especially intense "symbiotic relationship" with the mother. He discusses the role of separation from any object as a severe trauma, together with the poor tolerance for any frustrating experience, especially relating to any object loss, and the mobilization of primary destructive drives with the specific defense reaction. He believes that there is a close relationship between psychosis and rheumatoid arthritis and that the somatic symptoms of arthritis, like the overt manifestations of a psychosis, appear to operate as a restitutional mechanism. Finally, he states,

> . . . psychotherapy in this disorder must take cognizance of a number of facts: (1) affect is largely or even solely expressed through autonomic and somatic channels, with blocking of outward expression; (2) the ego is very weak, precariously situated, and fragmented, crushed be-

2 This view of the neuroses and the psychoses has recently been elaborated upon by Menninger (1954) in a comprehensive report.

tween overpowering primitive id forces, and a punitive archaic superego; (3) frustration and exposure to renewed trauma leads to violent
internal reactions and renewed exacerbations; (4) the disease itself
leads eventually to irreversible . . . physical disability, varying in
severity to complete invalidism; (5) the physical disability furnishes
marked and welcome secondary gains in gratifying passive dependent
needs. The psychotherapeutic methods and goals must vary with the
stage of the disease. Since the most frequent precipitating event seems
to be related to a separation trauma, by disruption of some vital relationship, the first task of therapy will be to attempt to restore a balance
by establishing contact with the patient . . .

The effective treatment of such complicated and profound disturbances is extremely difficult. Kaufman (1953b) reviews some of the considerations involved in the development of such forms of treatment as the
"surrogate ego role" therapy developed by George L. Engel, the "anaclitic
therapy" devised by Margolin, and the "sector psychotherapy technique"
of Felix Deutsch. Kaufman is primarily concerned with the utilization of
psychoanalytic concepts in the understanding and treatment of psychosomatic disorders, since "all psychic and somatic phenomena are in the
broadest sense a resultant of the interplay between biologic instinctual
forces, ego forces, superego forces and reality demands." After reviewing
various concepts dealing with the use of psychoanalysis as a method of
treatment, he makes the point that the psychoanalytic concept of psychic
illness views it as the result of gentically and dynamically determined
conflicts. This also enables us to understand a complicated illness like a
psychosomatic disorder as well as the fact that treatment, such as psychoanalysis, directed as it is toward alleviating these conflicts by self-mastery,
is a treatment truly directed at the prime etiologic factors involved.
Kaufman states that while "hypothetically psychoanalysis . . . would be
the only definitive, etiological treatment in psychosomatic illness," any
form of psychotherapy that was directed toward a "new alignment" of
intrapsychic forces would be effective since it was directed at the major
etiologic factor, the intrapsychic conflicts, and not merely toward a disappearance of symptoms. In this, he is in agreement with the views of
Margolin (1953) and Grinker (1954). Another important point about
which he is in agreement is that previously quoted from Ludwig (1952)
namely, that "the psychotherapeutic methods and goals must vary with
the stage of the disease."

These considerations indicate that one of the effective forms of psychotherapy in the treatment of psychosomatic illness would be group psychotherapy. Without going into the theory of group psychotherapy (which
is discussed elsewhere in this volume), it is possible to indicate briefly

why group psychotherapy is an effective psychotherapeutic agent directed at the conflicts between id, ego and superego, which are the chief cause of the psychosomatic disorders. The presence of the group provides immediate and effective support for the "weakened and fragmented" egos of these patients. Seeing others with the same difficulties, enables these patients to learn to verbalize conflicts which previously could not be verbalized. A more effective contact with reality is fostered through the medium of the group. Effective object relationship is encouraged by first diluting the transference through the group and then by making available, again through the group, opportunity for the development of better object relationships. The demands of the unrealistic "punitive archaic superego" are lessened by sharing guilt with the others in the group as well as by means of identification with more realistic superego attitudes in the other patients and the therapist and, most important of all, by replacing the patient's "punitive archaic superego" with more realistic and tolerant superego attitudes developed as a result of group interaction. The intensity of instinctual impulses which led to poorly tolerated conflicts is lessened by giving them effective verbal expression and by working them through in the group interaction. By lessening instinctual drives, by diminishing the demands of the superego, by supporting and strengthening the ego so that a better contact with reality is established, and by facilitating more effective object relationships, group psychotherapy helps the individual achieve a "new alignment" of intrapsychic forces so that the "psychosomatic symptom no longer is an essential part of this new equilibrium."

In the literature dealing with the use of group psychotherapy in the treatment of psychosomatic illness, very few authors indicate that their approach was based on the theoretical considerations noted above. Most workers used group psychotherapy for more pragmatic reasons. Also, the literature is, even at this date, quite limited. Beginning with the first article to appear, that of Pratt already referred to, a fairly complete survey of the literature indicates only some thirty references to the use of group psychotherapy in the treatment of psychosomatic illness.

For the sake of convenience, the literature will be reviewed in relation to the various syndromes. Articles dealing with the use of group psychotherapy in the treatment of alcoholics, drug addicts, stutterers and the aged, all of whom might be said, in a broad sense to be suffering from psychosomatic disorders, will not be reviewed since these are summarized in other sections of this volume.

The first group of articles to be reviewed deals with the treatment of conditions that are usually considered somatic but are truly psychosomatic in the broad sense of the term as previously defined. The first such condition is tuberculosis. It was in the treatment of tuberculosis that Pratt first used group psychotherapy, and he has published several reports of his work in the treatment of this disease with group psychotherapy. Marks (1952) and Knapp (1947) have also used group psychotherapy in the treatment of tuberculosis. All of the authors used a classroom, didactic technique with authoritative leadership by the physician, who gave instructions to the patients as to the medical management of this disease as well as repressive-inspirational material to help them adjust emotionally to their condition.

A second group of articles deals with use of group psychotherapy in treatment of a variety of conditions which, again, are usually designated as somatic disorders, but which are now considered psychosomatic disorders. A series of reports by Cruikshank and Cowen (1948) describe the use of group psychotherapy with physically handicapped children. Milman (1952) used group psychotherapy with the parents of physically disabled children. Rubenstein (1945), aware of the anxiety and other emotional tensions among preadolescents and adolescents hospitalized on an orthopedic ward, used group psychotherapy to help the patients deal with these tensions.

There are several reports of the use of group psychotherapy in the treatment of diseases of the central nervous system, a group of conditions again usually considered organic but which, broadly speaking, are psychosomatic in their effects. Blackman (1950) treated a group of aphasic patients with group psychotherapy and found it to be successful in helping patients overcome their anxiety, their sense of isolation and in strengthening their egos to cope more effectively with their handicap. Day et al. (1953) found group psychotherapy in the treatment of multiple sclerosis to be of considerable benefit. Several workers used group psychotherapy in the treatment of epileptics. Deutsch and Zimmerman (1948) found that group psychotherapy helped epileptics by reducing the emotional tensions that led to seizures. DeFries and Browder (1952) also found similar beneficial effects from the use of group psychotherapy with epileptic children. Randall and Rogers (1950) used group psychotherapy with good results in selected groups of epileptics.

Turning now to that group of disorders that are more specifically regarded as psychosomatic in terms of the definition previously given, the first group of papers to be considered report the successful use of group psychotherapy in several of these conditions. Pratt (1922, 1946), in two articles summarizing his own work and that of his associates, reports the successful treatment of mixed groups of patients through the use of his "classroom technique." These included cases of diabetes mellitus, rheumatism, neuritis, sciatica, and cardiac disease. Hadden (1942), using mixed groups and a technique similar to that of Pratt, found group psychotherapy to be of benefit to patients with diabetes mellitus and neurosyphilis. Thomas (1943), in a review of the literature, concluded that it was helpful in such conditions as peptic ulcer and hypertension, and that psychosomatic conditions, as well as the neuroses, "offer the most fruitful field for group psychotherapy." Dubo (1951) believes that group psychotherapy had a specific usefulness on a pediatric ward in the treatment of such conditions as diabetes, allergic states, rheumatic heart disease and eczema.

As regards specific psychosomatic disorders, there are several reports concerning the use of group psychotherapy in the treatment of obesity. Harvey and Simmons (1953), Chapman (1951), and Grant (1950), recognized the need to help obese patients deal with their emotional attitudes, and used group psychotherapy with several groups of obese patients. They found it helpful to a significant degree. Kotkov (1951, 1953) also used group psychotherapy successfully in the treatment of obese patients and states that the relationship to the therapist is important in this form of therapy. Schwartz and Goodman (1952) utilized group psychotherapy with good results in the treatment of obesity in elderly diabetic patients.

Baruch and Miller (1946, 1947) employed group psychotherapy in treating patients with allergic disorders, including asthma, hay fever, migraine and dermatitis. They found that it helped patients overcome inhibitions, release aggression and other emotions.

The successful use of the "class method" of group psychotherapy in the treatment of essential hypertension was reported by Buck (1937).

Chappell and his associates (1932) used group psychotherapy in the treatment of peptic ulcer because they felt that anxiety and emotional tension contributed to the persistence of symptoms and that patients needed to be instructed in the control of "worry" and in the management of their disease. Selesnick (1950) treated a group of about twenty-five patients hospitalized because of peptic ulcer with group psychotherapy alone as contrasted with a control group of about the same number of patients who were treated medically. A significantly greater amount of improvement occurred in the patients treated with the group psychotherapy than among those receiving medical treatment only.

In a paper reporting the use of group psychotherapy in the treatment of dermatitis, Klein (1949) gives a comprehensive evaluation of psychic malfunctions involved in the etiology of dermatitis, and describes how group psychotherapy was employed as a method of treatment directed toward those emotional conflicts.

Over a period of years, the present writer has been using group psychotherapy in the treatment of a number of specific psychosomatic disorders. From these experiences it has been possible to evaluate the effectiveness of group psychotherapy in the treatment of these conditions.

All the work was done in the Psychiatric Ward and the Psychiatric Outpatient Department of a general hospital.[3] In a previous report (Stein et al., 1952) the author and his colleagues describe the circumstances that led to the use of group psychotherapy. The first group consisted of thirteen chronic menopausal patients and was set up in 1945 when it was recognized that the patients, who seemed to utilize the clinic for social contacts with other patients, had persistent complaints related to emotional factors. A few years later a group for peptic ulcer patients was begun with the aim of helping the patients bring out and "work through" the similar patterns of oral and aggressive drives underlying this psychosomatic illness. A year later, an experimental group of patients with other psychosomatic disorders was set up to investigate some of the conditions under which they could best be treated in group psychotherapy. In the following year, two other groups were formed from the patients coming to the Follow-Up Clinic of the Psychiatric Ward. All of these patients had psychosomatic conditions and because of the difficulty they experienced in individual treatment and the fact that they spontaneously formed groups in the waiting room, it was decided to utilize these spontaneous formations.

The experiences and the results obtained with these groups are summarized as follows:

The Menopausal Group. These patients had multiple somatic complaints. They all had rigid personalities with obsessional traits, and marked guilt over their symptoms and consequently felt rather isolated socially. Group psychotherapy quickly helped the patients to overcome their sense of guilt and isolation, the group providing support for the patients so that they became able to verbalize many of their hostile feelings. All of the members of this group improved.

The first group from the Follow-Up Clinic consisted of five women and two men and included patients with ulcerative colitis, asthma, neurodermatitis and peptic ulcer. All had rigid, constricted personalities with anxiety and hysterical and/or obsessive traits. The group sessions helped these patients find support among the members of the group and aided

[3] The Mount Sinai Hospital, New York, N. Y.

them in overcoming their negative attitudes toward individual treatment which was combined with group psychotherapy. They were able to verbalize freely, especially their feelings of hostility. Of the seven patients, one remained unimproved, three were slightly improved, and three were considerably improved.

The second group organized in the Psychiatric Follow-Up Clinic consisted of five women and included patients with neurodermatitis, ulcerative colitis and migraine. These were patients with infantile, dependent personalities and rigid characterological defenses. Group psychotherapy was found to be most useful in drawing the patients together in more positive attitudes toward their psychotherapy, both individual and group, and specifically seemed to aid in making the relationship to the therapist a more acceptable and less threatening one. All of the patients in this group gradually improved.

The remaining two groups consisted of the *peptic ulcer group* and the *experimental group of patients with varied psychosomatic conditions.* The work with these groups will be described later.

The experience with these groups resulted in observations concerning certain of the dynamic factors involved and these have been described in the report cited previously. It was found that when group psychotherapy is used in a general hospital, the fact that the treatment is given in such a setting becomes one of the focal points for the dynamic factors in the treatment. While the need for more effective treatment is, consciously, one of the drives that animates, if this term may be used, the doctors and the hospital as well as the patient, it is obviously of greatest importance to the patient. The patients had indicated further needs more specifically related to underlying emotional factors. This was especially true in the menopausal and the experimental groups, although all groups showed it to some extent. In various ways, as by persistence or alteration of somatic symptoms, a need for a shift in the emphasis of the treatment toward the psychogenic side was evidenced and the patients responded when this shift was made. Similarly, the necessity for additional support in the psychotherapeutic process was shown by the patients. This was noted in the two follow-up groups and to a lesser degree in the others. In the two follow-up groups the constriction of the personalities and the severity of the underlying psychiatric condition was such as to prevent the patients from progressing in individual therapy. In the group, through such mechanisms as identification and the development of a "group ego" or ego ideal, they found the support necessary to help them face their guilt over their impulsive drives and to overcome their fear of the symbolic figure of the therapist.

The hospital serves as a focal point for several emotionally charged relationships which differ in their conscious and unconscious aspects. Consciously, the hospital is a place where the patient goes when he needs help for somatic symptoms. Unconsciously, he relates himself to the hospital often as if it represented some emotionally important figure and the patients usually identify with it. It seems most often to be regarded as a sort of mother figure, but the "transference to the hospital," as Reider (1953) has called it, may include other figures important to the patient.

Such emotional relationships to a personified hospital play an important part in the dynamics of group psychotherapy in this setting. They determine to a considerable extent the initial attitudes of the patients in the group. Negative attitudes focused on the hospital in this way markedly increase the resistance in the group. On the other hand, positive attitudes toward the hospital greatly facilitate the work of the group and often to a very surprising degree. Group formations occur very quickly as do the necessary patient-to-patient and patient-to-therapist emotional relationships which provide the energy for the group.

Based on our experience, it was felt that the work with group psychotherapy should be continued and extended in two ways: (1) investigation should be continued into the nature of group psychotherapy, especially as regards the dynamic factors involved; and (2) group psychotherapy should be used to study and treat other psychosomatic conditions such as ulcerative colitis, essential hypertension and rheumatoid arthritis.

The *peptic ulcer group* was organized in 1948 with the idea that group psychotherapy may be especially useful in a group of patients with a similar psychosomatic illness. Based on present-day concepts of the etiologic factors of peptic ulcer, it was thought that these patients might have similar patterns of chronic emotional tension related to poorly tolerated oral and aggressive drives and that group psychotherapy might have special effectiveness in bringing out and helping the patients work through such tensions.

A group of patients, both male and female, with chronic peptic ulcers was assembled. The size of the group varied from four to ten; six to seven patients were usually present at the sessions. The technique used was that of psychoanalytically oriented group psychotherapy. The spontaneous productions of the patients formed the basis for the group sessions, with the therapist participating only to help the discussion move in the direction that would bring out the underlying tensions.

All of the patients in the group had rather rigid and constricted personalities with severe underlying chronic neuroses. Despite this, the group was drawn together quickly because they all had the same illness and because they recognized the similarity of their emotional difficulties. The establishment of positive relationships with the therapist and among themselves provided very real support for the patients. They first revealed and worked through their guilt over having symptoms. They then expressed resentment over not being cared for and finally recognized their strong dependent needs. The group's attitudes were at first rigid and intolerant; later they gradually changed and became more flexible and understanding.

The group met for sixteen months. Of the ten patients who attended during this period, one remained unimproved, one slightly improved, three were moderately improved and the remaining five were improved with no recurrence of ulcer symptoms during a two-year follow-up period. Details of the work and results with this group are to be reported elsewhere (Stein et al., 1955).

Since the patients in this group were followed up for a period of two years, there was an opportunity to check on the effectiveness or lack of effectiveness of group psychotherapy. Two brief case histories will be given to illustrate this. The first case is that of a woman who showed definite improvement as a result of group psychotherapy. The second case is that of a man who had not improved through treatment.

D. D., a married woman with two children, was 37 years old at the time of admission to the group and had a typical duodenal ulcer by X-ray. Her ulcer symptoms had begun one and a half years previously, six months after the death of an older sister who was "like a mother." In addition to her ulcer symptoms, she had frequent headaches and often was depressed. She was next to the youngest of seven siblings and came from a lower income group. Both parents were rather neurotic and strict, especially the mother, and the patient had turned to her oldest sister for the affection and attention she could not get from her mother. She had always been hard-working and conscientious. In her twenties, she had married a rather passive man who worked as a taxi driver at night and slept during the day so that he was not much of a figure in the home. The patient was outwardly aggressive and independent, with a rigid, compulsive character, but underneath she was immature, dependent and emotionally labile.

In the group sessions, this patient at first was aggressive and dominating and voiced, for herself and the group, a rigid intolerant attitude toward her illness. Gradually, with the aid of the group, her guilt over her illness lessened and she was able to join with the others in expressing her resentment over not being cared for, blaming her husband for his ineffectiveness and expressing hostility to her children because of their demands on her. She then was helped to reveal her grief over the death of the older sister, to whom she had clung, and she became aware of her very marked dependent needs. She brought out her intolerant and over-protective attitude toward the children, her resentment of her husband, her social isolation and her inability to get for herself any kind of satis-faction or comfort. In the group sessions, the therapist and the patients helped her see this and work out effective solutions.

Two years after the termination of the group sessions, she was symp-tom-free as far as the ulcer was concerned, her depression had lifted, and she was much less tense and rigid. Her attitude to her family was more flexible and tolerant and she had been able to begin going out socially, to take a vacation, etc.

J. R. was a 40-year-old single man with a history of ulcer symptoms of seven years' duration. X-rays at that time revealed a typical duodenal ulcer. He had had a vagotomy three years previous to the group treat-ment without any benefit.

The patient was a short, slight, somewhat eunichoid man who was the youngest of three siblings. He had been born when his parents were in their forties. The parents were of the old school, especially the father who pounded at the patient the idea of hard work and self-sufficiency, while the mother was too busy with her household duties to give the patient much attention. The patient had worked fairly successfully at routine jobs but had little social life and apparently no sexual outlets. The death of his father seven years ago, which was followed by his mother becoming severely ill with hypertension, led to the onset of the patient's ulcer symptoms.

In the group, this patient had little to say but would make some com-ment when addressed directly. He never ventured any positive statement and followed or repeated the ideas of the others. At one point, the therapist and the group aided him to express some of his resentment toward his father but he quickly retreated from this.

Two years after the group psychotherapy had been terminated, this patient was unimproved. His ulcer and other symptoms persisted, he was still attending many hospital clinics, and his life pattern continued to be quite constricted. Obviously, the deep-seated character neurosis of this patient had not been affected by the group treatment; it may be that he could not give up his psychosomatic defensive pattern since it protected him against a more severe psychiatric illness.

The *experimental group* was set up in 1949 to investigate the effect of the type of patient on the psychotherapeutic functioning of the group.

The most effective procedure to initiate such a study was deemed to be setting up a group of entirely unselected patients. Accordingly, the first twelve patients on the list of those waiting to be admitted to the psychiatric clinic were formed into a group.

There were six men and six women in the group with the ages ranging from 28 to 50 years. The psychosomatic conditions included asthma, ulcerative colitis, anginal syndrome, retinitis, myalgias, etc. All of the patients had defective personalities with severe underlying psychiatric disorders varying from chronic schizophrenia through severe characterological neuroses to chronic anxiety states and recurrent depressions.

From the very beginning the patients, with only one exception, participated actively; in this respect there was no difficulty in having such a heterogeneous group. However, in a relatively short while, it became apparent that the resistance of the group was marked and the group formations occurred in relation to this. The resistance was to the idea that their somatic complaints had psychogenic causes, and this united the patients together strongly in aggressive attitudes toward the therapist. The need to defend themselves against their underlying conflicts seemed to be the only need this mixed group of patients had in common. When in the course of the treatment this became clear to them, the group work lost a great deal of impetus, and the patients used this understanding in a negative fashion so that the therapeutic value of the group was in danger of being dissipated. However, because of the positive relationship to the therapist, the group was enabled to continue as a group and to verbalize some of the tensions that had been expressed previously by somatization.

The mixed character of the group, both as regards the sexes and the nature of the underlying psychophysiologic regressions, interfered with the establishment of sufficiently positive relationships between the patients to give them the support necessary to bring out conflicts over dependency strivings, aggressive impulses and sexual disturbances about which there was a great deal of guilt present. A much longer period of time in treatment may have enabled this group of very sick patients to accomplish more of this.

The group was treated for a period of ten months with the following results: one patient dropped out after three sessions; the others came fairly regularly. Of the remaining eleven, three were unimproved, four were slightly improved, two improved moderately and two showed fairly definite improvement.

The work with this group confirmed the principle that groups of patients who are to be treated intensively by group psychotherapy must be selected according to whether the nature of their underlying unconscious emotional conflicts will enable them to establish the relationships necessary for effective participation. In this group, the underlying conflicts differed too much and in some instances were opposed so that the patients had too much tension and hostility to develop effective supportive relationships with each other. In addition, the group had begun its work with an initial negative attitude based on the patients' resentment of being considered psychiatric cases. Such a negative attitude, as was already pointed out, greatly affects group psychotherapy.

Several considerations led to the introduction of *group psychotherapy on the psychiatric ward* where the patients lived as a group and shared similar daily routines. Manifestations of emotional attitudes shared by the patients were quite evident often in a negative fashion, and it was thought that group psychotherapy could utilize these attitudes and perhaps channel energies into more therapeutically useful outlets. Since the severe psychosomatic illness of the patients on the ward stemmed from the inability of their inadequate egos to cope with severe emotional stress with resultant regression and diminished contact with reality, it was thought that group psychotherapy, for reasons already cited, might have a very specific usefulness for them.

Difficulties that had been anticipated concerning the relationship of individual to group psychotherapy were dealt with, and coordination of the two forms of therapy was maintained by a regular series of conferences between the group and the individual therapists. Observations indicated that the group tended to supplement and aid individual therapy. The relationship between the patient and the therapist in the group developed more easily and was different from and less difficult for the patient to accept than in individual therapy. The material brought up in the group sessions was different from that produced in the individual treatment. Group psychotherapy was helpful in the development of a better attitude in the patients in relation to the ward routine. The treatment enabled the patients to bring out and work through problems related to psychosomatic difficulties, sexual problems and family relationships, and aided them to begin the development of more realistic and effective approaches to these, especially at the time of their discharge from the ward.

The *use of group psychotherapy in the treatment of a group of patients with ulcerative colitis and ileostomies* will be referred to briefly. The group consists of six women, ranging in age from 22 to 44 years, all of whom had very severe ulcerative colitis for periods ranging from six months to twelve years prior to the time of having their ileostomy. At the time the group was started (October, 1953), the patients had had their ileostomies from one to three years. Two of the patients, in addition to the ileostomies, had also had abdominoperineal resections of their diseased colons. All of them had been gravely ill prior to their operation. Following this, their physical health improved markedly, but all of them had recurrent intestinal symptoms and all of them were troubled by persistent emotional tensions. The group was formed by offering to the members of a club composed of people who had ileostomies the opportunity to participate in group psychotherapy.

The women were all intelligent and capable and had made good adjustments to the management of their disease and functioned fairly well in the routine of their daily living. However, they were all severely ill from the psychiatric standpoint and had rigid personalities of the narcissistic type. Some tended to be withdrawn, while others were quite aggressive; all showed varying degrees of ambivalence. Despite their superficially good adjustment, they were all quite immature and at times rather infantile and had many very unrealistic attitudes. Ego integration was impaired in one patient to a rather marked degree, and object relationships tended to be poor in all of them. All showed excessive emotional reactions with poor tolerance of these.

The work with this group is continuing and no definite conclusions can be drawn at this time. However, it can be said that these severely traumatized and, from the psychiatric point of view, very ill patients have been able to form a psychotherapeutic group that is functioning very effectively. Even at this point, definite improvement has resulted from group psychotherapy.

The dynamic factors in a group such as this are both interesting and complicated and their elucidation must await completion of this project. One point should be stressed, however. Despite the voluntary formation of the group, at the beginning all of the patients were ambivalent and anxious about psychotherapy. This was especially true of two of the patients who had been in individual psychotherapy previously which was completely unsuccessful. These two patients indicated they had been almost intolerably tense in individual treatment and had felt overwhelmed and defenseless. In the group psychotherapy, the presence of others and the different relationship to the therapist lessened the tension and the threat so markedly that they were able to participate in the treatment.

The importance of this for patients with psychosomatic illness cannot be overestimated. Any type of individual psychotherapy is too threatening for such patients so that most treatment has to be directed toward symptom alleviation. Group psychotherapy, because it diminishes the threat, provides support and facilitates the ready formation of positive relationships within the group and especially with the therapist, enables these patients to participate in the psychotherapeutic process. Group psychotherapy, therefore, has a unique value in the treatment of psychosomatic illnesses. It is perhaps the only form of psychotherapy that can be readily tolerated by very sick people during the severe stage of their illness.

In addition, group psychotherapy, as the experiences recorded here have demonstrated, does have specific usefulness in treating some of the more disabling psychophysiologic regressive tendencies. Through the group relationships support is provided for defective egos so that ego integration is aided. The realistic atmosphere of the group corrects the distorting effect of diminished contact with reality. The conflicts stemming from the demands of the "punitive archaic superego" are alleviated by the development of more realistic and tolerant superego attitudes. Through identification with the therapist and the other patients and through the operation of the corrective reality factor in the group, the patients are relatively quickly enabled to learn how to deal more effectively with excessive emotional reactions.

In conclusion, then, it can be stated quite definitely that experience with the use of group psychotherapy in the treatment of psychosomatic diseases has amply demonstrated its effectiveness, which is also in accord with the theoretical formulations relative to psychosomatic disorders and psychotherapy. The psychosomatic illness arises from the attempt of a susceptible individual to achieve equilibrium under stress by means of a psychophysiologic regression. Effective treatment has to be directed at obtaining a new alignment of intrapsychic forces so that the psychophysiological regression expressed in psychosomatic illness is no longer necessary. Group psychotherapy is directed toward such a new alignment.

BIBLIOGRAPHY

Alexander, F. (1950), Fundamental Principles of the Psychosomatic Approach. *Psychosomatic Medicine*. New York: Norton.

Baruch, D. W. and Miller, H. (1946) Group and Individual Psychotherapy as an Adjunct in the Treatment of Allergy. *J. Consult. Psychol.*, *10*:281-284.

—— (1947), Interview Group Psychotherapy with Allergy Patients. In: *The Practice of Group Therapy*, ed. S. R. Slavson. New York: International Universities Press.

Blackman, N. (1950) Group Psychotherapy with Aphasics. *J. Nerv. & Ment. Dis.*, *111*:154-163.

Buck, R. W. (1937), Class Method in Treatment of Essential Hypertension. *Ann. Int. Med.*, *11*:514-518.

Chapman, A. L. (1951), Weight Control—Simplified Concept. *Public Health Reports,* 66:725-731.

Chappell, M. N.; Stephano, J. J.; Rogerson, J. S.; Pike, F. H. (1932), Value of Group Psychological Procedures in Treatment of Peptic Ulcer. *Am. J. Dig. Dis. & Nutrition,* 3:813-817.

Cruikshank, W. M. and Cowen, F. L. (1948a), Group Therapy with Physically Handicapped Children. I. Report of Study. *J. Educ. Psychol.,* 39:193-215

—— (1948b), Group Therapy with Physically Handicapped Children. II. Evaluation. *J. Educ. Psychol.,* 39:281-297.

Day, M.; Day, E.; Hermann, R. (1953), Group Therapy of Patients with Multiple Sclerosis, A Preliminary Report. *Arch. Neurol. & Psychiat.,* 69:193-196.

DeFries, Z. and Browder, S. (1952), Group Therapy with Epileptic Children and Their Mothers. *Bull. N.Y.A.M.,* 28:235-240.

Deutsch, A. L. and Zimmerman, J. (1948), Group Psychotherapy as Adjunct Treatment of Epileptic Patients. *Am. J. Psychiat.,* 104:783-785.

Dubo, S. (1951), Opportunities for Group Therapy in a Pediatric Service. *Int. J. Group Psychother.,* 1:235-242.

Ebaugh, F. G. (1954), Psychosomatic Medicine: A Review. *Int. Forum,* 2:73-76. (Contained in Therapeutic Notes 61, No. 5, May 1954, issued by Parke, Davis and Co., Detroit, Michigan.)

Grant, M. (1951), The Group Approach for Weight Control. *Group Psychother.,* 4:156-165.

—— and Rosenthal, J. (1950), Group Psychotherapy for Weight Control. *Mass. Health J., 31*:89.

Grinker, R. R. and Robbins, F. R. (1954), The Field Concept of Psychosomatic Medicine. *Psychosomatic Case Book.* New York: Blakiston.

Hadden, S. B. (1942), Treatment of the Neuroses by Class Technic. *Ann. Int. Med., 16*:33.

Harvey, H. I. and Simmons, W. D. (1953), Weight Reduction: A Study of the Group Method, Preliminary Report. *Am. J. Med. Sc., 225*:623-625.

Kaufman, M. R. (1953a), An Integration of the Psychosomatic Viewpoint in Medicine. *J. Mt. Sinai Hosp., 20*:247-256.

—— (1953b), Problems of Therapy. In: *The Psychosomatic Concept in Psychoanalysis,* ed. F. Deutsch. New York: International Universities Press.

Klein, H. S. (1949), Psychogenic Factors in Dermatitis and Their Treatment by Group Therapy. *Brit. J. Med. Psychol., 22*:32-52.

Knapp, J. L. (1947), Psychotherapy in the Treatment of Tuberculosis Patients. *West. Va. Med. J., 43*:12-15.

Kotkov, B. (1951), Experiences in Group Psychotherapy with the Obese. *Int. Rec. Med., 164*:566-576.

—— (1953), Experiences in Group Psychotherapy with the Obese. *Psychosom. Med., 15*:243-251.

Ludwig, A. D. (1952), Psychotherapy of Rheumatoid Arthritis. *Bull. Am. Psychoanal. Assn., 8*:177-179.

Margolin, R. J. and Rose, C. L. (1951), A Dynamic Group Experience in a Military Hospital Paraplegic Unit. *Milt. Surgeon, 109*:712-720.

Margolin, S. G. (1953), Genetic and Dynamic Psychophysiological Determinants of Pathophysiological Processes. In: *The Psychosomatic Concept in Psychoanalysis,* ed. F. Deutsch. New York: International Universities Press.

—— and Kaufman, M. R. (1948), What is Psychosomatic Medicine? *Med. Clin. North Am.,* New York Number, May, 1948.

Marks, J. B. (1952), Special Problems in Group Work with Tuberculosis Patients. *Int. J. Group Psychother., 2*:150-158.

Menninger, K. A. (1954), Psychological Aspects of the Organism Under Stress. *J. Am. Psychoanal. Assn., 2*:67-106; 280-310.

Milman, D. H. (1952), Psychologic Aspects of Pediatrics; Group Therapy with Parents: An Approach to the Rehabilitation of Physically Disabled Children. *J. Ped.,* *41*:113-116.

Pratt, J. H. (1906), The Home Sanatorium Treatment of Consumption. *Johns Hopkins Hosp. Bull., 17*:140-158.

—— (1922), Principles of Class Treatment and Their Application to Various Chronic Diseases. *Hosp. Soc. Serv., 6*:401-411.

—— (1946), The Group Method in the Treatment of Psychosomatic Disorders. *Psychodrama Monograph, 19*:85-93. New York: Beacon House.

Randall, G. C. and Rogers, W. C. (1950), Group Therapy for Epileptics. *Am. J. Psychiat., 107*:422-427.

Reider, N. (1953), A Type of Transference to Institutions. *J. Hillside Hosp.,* 2:23-29.

Rubenstein, B. (1945), Therapeutic Use of Groups in an Orthopedic Hospital School. *Am. J. Orthopsychiat., 15*:662-674.

Selesnick, S. (1950), Psychotherapy in Chronic Peptic Ulcer. *Gastroenterol., 14*:364-368.

Schwartz, E. D. and Goodman, J. I. (1952), Group Therapy in Obesity in Elderly Diabetics. *Geriatrics, 7*:280-283.

Stein, A.; Lipschutz, D.; Rosen, S. R.; Mischel, E.; Sheps, J. (1952), Experimental and Specific Types of Group Psychotherapy in a General Hospital. *Int. J. Group Psychother., 2*:10-23.

—— Steinhart, R.; et al. (1955), Group Psychotherapy in the Treatment of Peptic Ulcer (in preparation).

Thomas, G. W. (1943), Group Psychotherapy: A Review of the Literature. *Psychosom. Med., 5*:166-180.

Chapter IV

ADDICTS

●

In the United States it is illegal for anyone to take addicting drugs for other than medical reasons. These medical reasons, in addition, are limited to organic states. It is also against the law to procure drugs for any but the above reasons. Consequently drug addicts, by definition, violate the law when they engage in their habit which results in the fact that most patients are to be found in prisons or the so-called "hospital prisons." This chapter will concern itself mostly with the experiences of a group of psychotherapists who worked in the hospital prison settings of Lexington, Kentucky and Ft. Worth, Texas, and one outpatient group where most of the members of the group had been treated in one of these institutions. The patients used, for the most part, heroin as their drug of choice and were predominantly between late teens and thirty-five years of age.

A drug addict can be defined as a person who has an uncontrollable craving for the physical and psychological effects of narcotic drugs. Needs of different patients differ, but all use drugs either to escape from the realities of living or to be enabled by the drug to function to some extent in a world of reality. This definition encompasses a loose psychiatric classification rather than being limited only to persons who are "organically addicted" to a specific drug.

Prior to the work undertaken by the present author most of the research work on addiction at Lexington had been limited to the organic effects of the various drugs. Although the publications on drug addiction had been rather extensive, most of them were concerned wtih studies as to the sites and mechanisms of action of the various drugs. The few papers on addiction of a psychiatric nature were limited to a classificatory system. With the addition of a psychoanalytically trained group therapist, emphasis was shifted to group and individual psychotherapy of the drug addicts.

It is the opinion of this author that the fact that most of the addicts at these hospitals are "serving time" is an important factor in understanding why the patients had not been treated psychiatrically. Although the hospitals are directed by physicians, a large part of its administration is under the United States Bureau of Prisons. It is therefore inevitable that a "prison culture" would permeate the hospital atmosphere. The hospital is mainly a conventional contemporary prison with emphasis on "good work habits." The success of a patient's stay is judged by his capacity to follow rules and by his ability to work consistently on the job assigned to him.

The first paper dealing with the use of group psychotherapy in the treatment of drug addicts was published by Thorpe and Smith (1953). In this paper they describe how the group psychotherapy program was organized and set up. It was first started in the admission section of the hospital with recognized value and was at first used as a forum for giving new patients information about the hospital as well as suggesting some ideas concerning their personality problems. This also helped allay fears of the hospital staff who believed that a meeting of patients in a group would result in a riot. Because of the interest displayed by the patients in the group meetings and the growing acceptance of them by some of the staff as well as their desire to extend treatment facilities, group psychotherapy was later introduced on the wards.

A "special treatment ward" was established which was made up of patients who asked for it and who, in the opinion of the psychiatrists, needed psychotherapy. The main form of psychotherapy on this ward was group psychotherapy. In this paper they also point out the difference in the culture that grew in the special treatment ward as contrasted to the usual culture in the various wards of the hospital. One of the main points of difference between the two settings was that on the treatment ward deviant behavior was subject to group discussion and exploration, whereas outside of the treatment ward deviant behavior either against the hospital rules or noncomformity with the mores of the ward was dealt with by punitive action, either by the hospital authority or the ward leader. In addition, admission to the treatment ward was on the basis of a desire for psychotherapy, whereas admission to the choice wards of the rest of the hospital was mainly on the basis of conformity—that is, patients who were "good workers" or who followed the rules.

The authors then traced the growth of the group from a conglomerate of chaotic individuals griping about how badly they were being treated, to individuals who had arrived at a consensus that they were the source of their own problem. They then progressed to a group of people who were tentatively tested and accepted by each other and by the therapist, and finally to a stage when they began to confide in each other. The authors point out that the various steps in the growth of the group are not significantly different from those observed by the authors in groups of delinquent children or psychotic patients.

At this last stage in the group process the members who appear to be the most anxious, those whom one could describe as having the most need for treatment, begin to reveal more specific information about themselves. During this period a great deal of "character analysis" on the part of the various group members appears. The group members point out to each other how they deal with one another and with the authority figures in the hospital. This is done in an attempt either to validate the story presented to the group or to point out how the patient's story appears to contradict what they observe him doing in actual life.

From this stage the group process extends in the following fashion. Here is a patient who had presented his problems of living. His problems may or may not be in accordance with what the group members observe him to do in terms of his day-to-day living within the institution. The group will then want to know why he behaves in this fashion, and whether he has behaved in this fashion before. The group becomes analytically oriented, helping the individual patient who has presented his problem to go back into his past and pick out those interpersonal relationships with significant people that may have relevance to his present difficulty.

The next phase of the group process occurs when the group member who is presenting his problem to the group begins to recognize intellectually that part of himself which he considers "the bad self," and which had been pointed out to him by the members of the group. He then accepts it as a valid part of himself and explores with the help of others why he came to be the sort of person that he is. If he rejects the thesis of the group, then why has he such a need to reject the "bad" part of himself?

In the groups in which these phenomena had occurred the members of the group usually connected the problem of addiction with the "bad self." The members seem to feel that the need to take drugs and the craving for the sense of well-being they achieve through drugs is one way of handling anxiety caused by the denial of the "bad self." It might be mentioned at this time that the group members usually try to elicit from some of the participants a rather detailed history of certain aspects of their addiction. They attempt to find out why there is a need to take drugs; whether it is to enable one to deal with himself and others or to "block out" certain difficulties. The group then attempts to relate the problems of the individual patient to his particular way of dealing with drugs. Both therapists deal with the addiction of the patient as another symptom of maladjustment. They attempt to treat the patient, not his symptoms.

Both authors note that during the group process, traditions begin to be established. These are used with a purpose by the group during periods of extreme stress and anxiety as a base line for continued group action. They enable the group to work through resistances to treatment or to face and evaluate group transference phenomena. Groups often regress under the strain of "resistance" or "transference feeling" to a point where tradition can be used to help the group continue therapy. This is especially true of groups made up of members with a common living situation. These traditions are as follows: (1) The problem exists within the individual and not necessarily with society. (2) The group does not judge or punish behavior; the group examines and explores behavior. (3) The use of drugs is only a symptom; the real problem is the person. (4) The past is related to the present and the future. (5) Upon investigating differences between patient and personnel, the latter's effect is dissociated, while the patient's conduct is explored. (6) Differences on the ward are to be brought into the group. That is the reason for the group's existence. (7) The more you participate in the group, the more you get out of it. (8) Leaders on the ward can, and should, be questioned as to their motivation. (9) The group works with differences. It is not a "mutual admiration society."

The authors then go into how important it is to have the group sessions for the professional and nonprofessional workers who have contact with the patient. They point out how important it is to treat with respect the differences of opinion between the therapists and some of the hospital staff. They also point out how some of the professional differences can be worked through in groups for the staff.

Osberg and Berliner (1954) describe their work in the United States Public Health Hospital at Ft. Worth, Texas. Both authors carry administrative as well as therapeutic responsibilities and see no conflict between the two roles. They rather feel that this dual role has some therapeutic advantages with patients with character disorders, since one of their primary objectives is to help patients become aware that the equation "authority equals hostility" is not necessarily valid. The addict is basically a passive, dependent person who engages in the hospital in various "security operations" the goal of which is to keep the group from focusing on the primary business at hand. Patients who do not attend the groups regularly are seen individually to find out why regular attendance at group sessions was difficult for them. This helped some patients who had had difficulty in adjusting to a group process to get back into the group and work through their problems. Patients use various "testing procedures" to find out whether the therapist is going to become so anxious by the revelation of themselves that he would not be able to deal with them.

At first patients talk about addiction as a pleasure-seeking device, but soon recognize that narcotics are related to their intolerable feelings, especially feelings of inadequacy, threats to their self-esteem and their need to restore self-assurance. Discussions are centered on adjustment to the hospital with marked feelings of deprivation, of emptiness, of self-contempt, of deep pessimism and of feelings that one was safest and less vulnerable when alone. A young, extremely hostile, but ever smiling schizoid nego expressed his feelings of isolation when he took drugs as follows: "I don't want to be touched. I don't want to be talked to. I want to be left alone. On drugs I have hatred all the time." The release of such feelings of hostility through the pressure of the group was obviously too disturbing for him, for he did not return for several sessions. Patients also recognize a "therapeutic goal" in taking drugs through decreasing feelings of inadequacy and they verbalized it thus: "It's like medicine when you're sick. It isn't that you forget your worries, they just don't mean as much to you any more." A patient expressed it as follows: "Drugs give you control over yourself. My thoughts don't bother me as much."

Most patients complained that hospitalization abrogated their "rights to self-determination," enhanced their feelings of dependency and helplessness and, interestingly enough, related these to their mothers. Many felt their fathers had been ineffectual and that they were tied to their mothers. Mothers were often characterized as being "my only love," but also were described as being restricting and, often by implication, seductive.

Patients persistently dwelled on the euphoric feelings associated with narcotics and thought they were "being let down" by the hospital. It was as though the patients were indulging in "verbal fixes" because the hospital had disappointed them just as when they were on the outside and reverted to drugs because of their sense of disappointment with the real world.

Osberg and Berliner (1954) report that specific sexual experiences rarely became the subject of group discussion except when used for shock value. The patients did, however, discuss their interpersonal relationships with women and attempted to evaluate them. Women were pictured as objects of narcissistic gratification, "to be used" by them before they had an opportunity to use them. Mother was prominent in any expression of feelings about the opposite sex. Procuring was presented as an effective way of both using and controlling women and appeared to be a way of perpetuating the hostile relationship with mother. Many patients acknowledged having experienced overt homosexual relationships, but this did not appear to be a fixed pattern so much as an ineffectual way of avoiding heterosexuality. The addicts were found to be seriously disturbed individuals with marked inability to sustain satisfactory interpersonal relationships. They appeared basically angry and deprived, with intense needs for reassurance about sexual identity and maturity and unable to tolerate tension or to internalize conflicts. Many acted out their narcissistic strivings in the institution. In the group they insisted that they were "men," called each other "man" and tested the therapist. Fantasies of hostility appeared to be equated immediately with overt aggressive action. They appeared to embrace stereotypes.

In an unpublished paper Thorpe and Rath describe the treatment of drug addicts in groups in an outpatient setting. The sessions were, for about a year, held in an apartment in East Harlem in New York City. The group met twice a week for two-hour sessions. Both therapists were present as well as an observer, who was a member of the police force, a psychologist by training. In the course of the year, approximately fifty patients attended the group, all of whom came voluntarily. Most knew one of the therapists in Lexington while some were referred by the courts or other therapists. The group was made up of an active core who came regularly, and a peripheral segment who came intermittently. The latter appeared to be unable to deal with the anxiety evoked in the sessions, but felt a need to continue their contact with the group and the therapist and kept up with the progress of the group by talking to the more regular members between sessions. Patients would call the therapist and give some excuse for not attending. The third and the smallest segment of the group were those who came once or twice and did not return.

The focus of the therapists was on the patient as a whole and not on his addiction per se. It was the therapist's experience that both the patients and their families attempted to alter this emphasis. The parents of the patients invariably would attempt to manipulate the therapist by pointing out that there was no improvement in the patient, that he was back on the use of drugs, or that the patient was stealing to obtain drugs. They presented this information with the expectation that the therapist would do something magical to change the situation. The patients themselves attempted to manipulate the therapist in various ways, such as, "I am hooked, what are you going to do for me?" They would get themselves arrested and turn to the therapist for legal help; they attempted to seduce the therapist into getting jobs; some also sought to monopolize the therapist by attempting to engage him for individual treatment or by refusing to pay the fee for the group sessions.

This became an important problem in the early stages of the group's existence. Some either categorically refused to pay a fee, others would promise to pay and never did. These strategies were, of course, part of their transference feelings. They seemed to be saying, "I can only work with you if you are my friend; and if you are my friend, you won't charge fees for the service." If fees were involved, it was a professional relationship, and therefore unacceptable. This was related to the patient's fantasy attitudes toward their mothers. They related to their mothers also in an infantile, dependent manner; all their needs must be met; mother must never make any demands; she must never in a sense take away the breast.

Early transference feelings manifested themselves in the group also in other ways: (1) the above-mentioned testing operation using the fees; (2) attempts on the part of certain patients to get the therapist "to do something" for him, to get him a lawyer, to help him find a hospital where he could "kick his habit," or to help him in his relationship with his parents; (3) although it was an accepted rule that no drugs or "hot goods" were to be brought to the clinic, periodically certain patients would bring them. All these maneuvers seemed to be attempts to find out more about the therapist and how he was going to relate to him as a person. The patients were so accustomed to being rejected and being treated disrespectfully that they had to find out in the very beginning whether the therapist would react to them as their parents did. At this time, the patients seemed to have very little awareness of how they were activating rejection.

Another way in which early transference feelings would manifest themselves was the following: certain patients would suddenly attempt to have the doctor commit himself to taking them on as individual patients. This was related to their need for more magic, and a reluctance to share the doctor with the rest of the group. These attempts were handled by referring the question back to the group. However, toward the end of the group program two or three patients had been seen individually. In every instance, however, the group was aware of this and had agreed that the particular patients had a need for, and should be seen for individual help in addition to the group.

Early resistances that manifested themselves in the group were: (a) *The problem was hopeless.* The patients presented their addiction in a hopeless fashion. Nothing could be done about it; nobody understood it; they didn't understand it themselves. "Society doesn't understand me, and will not approve of them, and they can do nothing about it," was the general attitude. In brief, it was a denial of the therapists' formulation that they were interested and could be helpful. (b) *Absences.* How was the therapist going to handle this? "Is he going to miss me? Is he going to demand my presence all the time as a requirement for treatment?" (c) *Silences.* This manifested itself usually when the therapist refused to engage in magical operations with the patients, such as to give them an immediate answer that would solve all their problems, or the therapist's refusal to treat them individually. (d) *"I'm hooked."* Certain patients would use this in the group as an attempt to shift the emphasis from an exploration of themselves to a discussion of drugs. This was derived from the way they had related to their families. To the latter, the drug was connected with the "bad self." The patients appeared to be saying, "If I can get rid of this bad self, everybody will love me." The group would interfere with this process, and point out to the patient what he was doing. (e) *Lateness.* This was characteristic of certain group members who would usually come late, sometimes only one or two minutes before the group ended. They would demonstrate a great deal of annoyance because the rest of the group insisted on breaking up on time. The group's interpretation of this was that these patients really wanted to work out their problems, but that it was too anxiety-provoking for them. They engaged in a magical maneuver: if they came late not much would happen to them, and yet they could maintain the fantasy that they were in treatment. (f) *Emphasis on the stupidity of "squares."* The usual connotation of the word "square" was that anybody who didn't take drugs, anybody who went to work at nine o'clock and worked until five, who conformed to the hospital culture and got any happiness out of the world, was deluded. It became quite clear that in addition to contempt, there was a great deal of envy among the patients. As the group progressed in treatment, "squares" were to be understood and emulated rather than considered with contempt. (g) *Change of group membership.* The idea expressed here is "I can't cop out with strangers."

All patients talked about their ambivalence toward their parents. All the patients lived at home, hated it, felt that they hated their parents, felt that their parents did not understand them, and yet they could not make a change. They could not quite give up the idea that they would not be accepted for what they were. Yet, remaining at home, they experienced constant rejection. These data pointed to an unresolved oedipal situation. However, to succeed, was to win mother from father, and this, too, would be disastrous. Addiction seemed to be a compromise. They could maintain their narcissistic dreams of monopolizing mother, and yet in reality father would have her.

Father was seen as a punitive demanding person, the man who represented the culture, who set the rules and insisted on the patient assuming responsibility. Part of the inability to leave home was related to a need to monopolize mother's attention, and to compete with the father. The mothers felt that the boys were not understood; that there was some magical way to help them. The fathers felt disgusted with them, insisted on their leaving home, and evaluated the patients as being "no good."

The patients reported that the only time they could relate to their parents was when they were taking drugs. The parents of the patients usually alternated between telling them to get out and begging them to stay home, even at the price of supplying the boy with drugs.

The dependency feelings of the patients were reflected in the type of jobs they obtained. The jobs were always far below their abilities. They assumed no responsibility and nothing was expected of them. This extended also to the group where they could not assume responsibility for being on time, paying a fee, or considering that the therapist may have some needs of his, too.

Their relationship with women was an extension of their relationship with their mothers. The woman that would attract them would be one who would "go on the turf" (work as a prostitute) for them and supply their need for drugs. This woman who would make no demands on them, would understand them, and, ideally, would "take off" (take an injection) with them. As soon as their women were addicted, however, there was great competition between the two for drugs.

The patients' needs that were satisfied by the use of heroin were multiple. It was first of all a predictable method of achieving "peace." As the patients said, "We have it made, Doc, because whenever we get 'bugged,' we know there is one way we can get peace at once." The rest of the world has to fight unpleasant situations and deal with the anxiety thus provoked. A certain number of the patients felt they could deal with life, with people and the demands people made on them when they were "high." They all took drugs in order to function and recognized their difficulties, their personal isolation and their low sense of self-esteem.

Another time that the drug became very necessary was when a "hassle" (fight) was impending. This usually had to do with a situation with mother in which they felt they could not win. Sometimes it had to do with being found out by mother, and heroin appeared to be the drug of choice in dealing with this anxiety. When they were "clean" (free of drugs), the feeling that they were not getting what they needed from mother would induce them to "joy-pop" (intermittent injection of drug). This in turn, would re-create the old situation of being a "bad boy." Anxiety and guilt would follow that mother would find out. To be "found out" by mother means something special to the addict: he has forced mother to make a choice between father and him. This inability to cope with the oedipal situation causes him to be "hooked" (addicted). The period of "being hooked" is punishment for his unconscious incestuous wishes. Following this he is ready to "kick his habit" (withdraw from drugs), that is, give up mother and "be clean."

The need to be accepted and the need to be rejected, constitute the life pattern of the addict. Some of the patients felt so keenly about these ideas that they needed the drug at any time during the 24 hours. Others took heroin to create a dream world. These took drugs in large amounts and would go "on the nod" (a peculiar half-sleep as a result of large doses of the drug). They would cease to function and engage in dreams in which they were the center of attention, invariably accomplishing great things. They needed to make friends but closeness was too threatening. They chose other "junkies" (addicts) who would respect their loneliness. When the group was exploring the relationship between Sarah and Ernest, Sarah said, "I like Ernest because I can be with him and be alone."

There is an expressed mixture of envy and contempt for the rest of the world. Sexual life is unorthodox and there appeared no overt interest in women or men; sexuality seemed to dissolve in the hypodermic. Father and mother are not clearly defined. Genitality is fragmented and in the process of regression: the father is with breasts and the mother is phallic. The erogenous zones appear to be the mouth and the skin. The drug is felt as food and warmth. To be relieved of responsibility and to be completely taken care of is the ideal situation to the addict. Even jail was on occasion a blessing. In jail the addicts relived some of their early family experiences where one could express rage against being deprived and at the same time have one's needs satisfied, and the authority to tell you how to live.

There seemed to be two major types of addicts. One type took drugs to go "on the nod," create a dream world, and avoid reality. The other used drugs in order to be able to deal with reality and function in our culture. Clinical data from the group and data from projective tests seemed to indicate that a frank psychosis was averted by the use of drugs, especially in the first group. Marked depression characterized the second group, whereas the first group appeared allied to the schizophrenic reaction type.

All manner of associated neurotic patterns and symptoms came into play when the patients were removed from drugs. It should be mentioned, in addition, that a fair number of these patients had overt psychotic breaks, often taking the form of paranoid schizophrenia. One of the most valid studies of the personality of the drug addict has been made by John Fort (1954). He states:

> There was always a considerable degree of immaturity in these patients. . . . Most of our patients were friendly, cooperative individuals who tended to be rather passive and submissive in their early relationships with the therapist. On the other hand, they showed little emotion initially and were frankly skeptical and pessimistic about the hope of getting a cure. The average young heroin addict tended to be introverted, sensitive, quiet and interested in artistic manners. The interest in music was especially impressive. A large percentage were jazz musicians, a few classical musicians. Many of the others had spent a large part of their young lives around jazz spots. . . .
> The family background revealed the presence of an overprotective domineering mother, and usually no father figure or occasionally a distant punitive one. We believe the drug addict has shown an "attempt at cure," in trying drugs, but has, at least in part, usually failed, and shown regression to oral levels of satisfaction. There is an accompanying sadistic and masochistic system in which aggressive feelings are turned both against themselves and against society. A paranoid system is built up in which the drug itself is of primary importance and is endowed with magical properties—perhaps of both suicidal, self-destruction and destruction of the internalized, feminine object, which is both loved and hated (mostly the latter). The question is posed as to whether the drug used may thus prevent melancholia, and also preserve the person present from the necessity of setting up a complete paranoid system.

Basically, opiate drugs prevent the external carrying out of aggressive acts (as opposed to alcohol). The same problem, in a way, seems to face the potential addict which faces the potential schizophrenic. So enormous do the hostile, destructive drives seem to him, that the patient is unbearably frightened by them. Turning them inward can be accomplished by the drug addict through the relatively simple mechanism of using a drug which is relatively simpler than interpersonal reactions. He can, as it were, with one short act, accomplish the destruction of the external world, his own destruction, and achieve a libidinal goal with real orgastic pleasure. Such phantasmagoria of psychic effects can in fact be observed in many young drug addicts. We have repeatedly seen in our young patients, a revolt against what they consider the competitive, striving aspects of American society. This revolt also included a move against accepted authority, their parents, their orthodox church, and the ideal of success. The risk was not, however, a successful or happy revolt as it represented a cover for aggressive feelings, a sort of passive aggression against the parents.

This author's experience with the treatment of drug addicts on an outpatient plan, indicated very strongly the need for inpatient care during acute phases. An inpatient setting would have the double function of withdrawing the patients physically from drugs as well as providing a therapeutic milieu where they can begin working on their difficulties while still in the hospital. It is this author's opinion that the most useful tool for the beginning exploration of an addict's problems is a group. Ideally the outpatient setting where the patients would meet for their groups should be the same physical location as that where they had been inpatient. This arrangement would provide a continuum in the treatment.

Since a sizable part of the treatment of an addict should be done in an institutional setting, some attention ought be paid to the various types of group processes that have been observed. The author has had experience with five types of group organization:

1. Individual patients referred by the institution to the group therapist. Under this heading belong also those individuals who are sent for treatment against their will to a group already functioning.

2. A group formed of individual patients chosen by the group therapist for treatment in a group.

3. A group of individuals who come of their own volition to the therapist asking for treatment in a group, provided that the therapist excludes other patients.

4. The group situation that arises when a therapist comes into the living area of patients and begins group therapy without the patients having requested it.

5. A group of patients who volunteer, and were chosen for group therapy, and are placed in a special treatment ward, the intent of which is to provide an adequate therapeutic climate for psychotherapy.

Each of these group organizations has certain consequences for the therapist. In general it is very important for the group therapist to explore his own countertransference feelings. Unless these are explored and dealt with, the group invariably disintegrates. In the first type of group (where patients are sent to the therapist for treatment) it is important that the therapist and the institution arrive at a consensus as to whom they want to treat, otherwise the therapist may find himself with a group of patients who he feels do not warrant treatment, but where he needs to prove to the institutional administration that he does group therapy. It is also important that communication be established between the group therapist and the institution so that the administrative personnel can have some idea of what they can expect as the group process unfolds. It would appear that in many institutions the group therapy programs are dedicated mainly to the therapist's need to demonstrate, through his groups, how inadequately the institutions are conducted by the administrative personnel.

The second type of group (where patients are chosen by the therapist for treatment in a group) is characterized largely by the fact that the therapist feels comfortable in the group of patients whom he has himself chosen. There is danger here that such a group may become a mutual admiration society where the therapist is unaware that he had selected patients who would agree with him. In such groups patients may be afraid to reveal their true selves for fear of excommunication from the group unless they meet with the therapist's approval. This may also be an area where the therapist's hostility to the institution may manifest itself. For example, the therapist may pick patients who the institution personnel may feel should not be treated. Certainly if the selection of patients on the part of the therapist differs considerably from the notions of the institution as to who should be treated, this point should be explored by the therapist. For example, in an institution that prefers to ignore overt homosexuality within its walls, the therapist may suddenly find himself extraordinarily interested in treating a group of homosexuals. He should, therefore, explore whether he is trying to work out his own feelings in this area or whether he is unconsciously attempting to make the institution personnel anxious by forcing them to recognize what they prefer to overlook.

The third type of group (where patients present themselves as a group asking for treatment) usually ask that anybody else but themselves be excluded. This is rather rare and would appear to be the result of the fact that some of the patients desire treatment, but do not dare ask for it openly. They use the group as a shield. In addition, this group presents itself as if its members knew each other and were comfortable with one another. In most instances, the group members relate to each other in a somewhat peripheral fashion. It is as though the only basis for the group's organization is the unconscious understanding among the group members: "I will not notice the bad part of you if you will do the same for me." If this type of group is launched, it is most important that the therapist make it clear that he is not altogether in agreement with the idea, but that they may form a good nucleus. When it later becomes apparent that the therapist's prediction has been correct, it can be used productively in the group setting.

An example of this phenomenon is the group of the antisocial leaders of the wards of a prison hospital who visited this group therapist in his office. These were inmates of a hospital prison type of institution who pretty much set the tone of their ward and enforced conformity to these antisocial norms through the power of their own "gang." If an attendant, for example, wished to have something done on his ward, he would go to one of these leaders who would then, in exchange for something from the attendant, translate this to the other inmates of the ward. This group told the therapist that they had been watching group therapy, that they did not feel it could be of any use to them, but were willing to "give it a try" provided that the group therapist saw them as a special group. It was quite clear that they were attempting again to bargain with the therapist as they bargained with the other authorities. The therapist felt that part of their intent was to get treatment. The therapist told them that he would not agree to seeing them as a "special" group; that he was not in agreement with the basis of their relationship with each other, but that he would be glad to meet with them as a group and see if they could work together. After about a month, it became clear to them that their sense of uniqueness from the rest of the inmates was not real. Of its own volition the group decided to disband and to join other existing groups. It would appear that, in the course of the month, they were able to work through their defense of uniqueness and exclusiveness. The therapist's formulation in the beginning seemed to help considerably in bringing about this result.

The fourth type of group situation (where the therapist initiates therapy by going into the living area of patients) should be initiated only by group therapists who are uniquely skilled. In this instance, the therapist leaves the comfort of his milieu and goes forth into the patient's milieu. He has to deal with strong overt hostile feelings against his attempts to disturb their equilibrium. In addition he will have to deal with the hostility and indifference of the administrative personnel in charge of the ward or day room. They unconsciously sense that his arrival in their domain will require certain changes in their way of life, too. In this type of group, the therapist at once is the focus of attention. His every movement is an object of scrutiny. He is "on the spot," as it were. The physical setting on wards is such that if patients wish to make the therapist uncomfortable, all they have to do is to wander off to the other end of the room and leave him in his corner; in addition, a great many interfering activities are going on at the same time. There are usually radios playing, people are wandering in and out, and the subprofessional staff are in the vicinity. The therapist is conscious of whether or not the attendant, psychiatric aide or nurse approve of him, or whether he is being treated with condescension by the staff. Before the therapist attempts to conduct this type of group, it is necessary that he get together with the psychiatric aides and nurses on the wards. He must attempt to give them an understanding of the group process so they may be "on his team" rather than against him when the group is started.

The last type of therapy group (where patients volunteer and are chosen for group therapy and live in a special treatment ward) appears to be the most useful form of group therapy in an institutional setting. The cultural tone of a treatment ward is more tolerant with people who are "different," whether this difference is one of color, aggressive conduct, homosexual behavior, or mental illness. These differences in character and behavior are not necessarily approved, but are tolerated by fellow patients and form the content of group discussions. A deviant member of a "regular ward" of a hospital may be punished by other ward members for behavior not in keeping with the rules, but on a treatment ward such behavior is brought to the group for scrutiny and analysis.

Another difference noted between the treatment ward and the other wards is that on the latter asocial or antisocial behavior usually has static value, whereas on the treatment ward behavior that is more prosocial and more in accord with living on the outside is accepted as the norm. The patient who is "getting better" becomes the group leader resulting in prosocial leadership for the group. It was the experience of this author that the patients who had worked through their hostility to authority and who had developed sufficient security to accept prosocial norms emerged on the treatment ward as the leaders. These leaders differed from those of the other wards in that they would not attempt to seduce or bargain with authority and assumed more personal responsibility for their behavior in the treatment ward. In the therapy group on the treatment ward, the men were interested in exploring their role in any difficulties between themselves and authority. On the other wards of the hospital there was no discussion of difficulties. The ward leader invariably enforced his norms through the threat of his own antisocial gang and related to the authority such as attendants by the device of bargaining. The antisocial leader of the ward offered the attendant conformity on the part of other inmates in exchange for specific privileges for himself and his antisocial gang. This sort of behavior was not tolerated on the treatment ward.

On a treatment ward the group seemed to progress therapeutically much more easily. The patients were able to discuss their transference feelings much more openly and with less anxiety. They were able to face their resistances to treatment quicker and to deal with them more logically and adequately. A minimal amount of time was spent on purposeless "gripes," the goal of which was to resist therapy. The patients quickly entered into the discussions of the way they dealt with each other on the ward and how this could be pertinent to their lives in the past and to the problems that brought them to the hospital in the first place.

It would appear from the foregoing that group psychotherapy is a valid therapeutic medium in the treatment of drug addicts as well as a possible research tool to gather information about the dynamics of addiction and addicts. In addition, it appears that there are limited clinical data to support the current feeling of hopelessness in the psychiatric treatment of addicts. It seems clear that psychiatric facilities for drug addicts should be expanded and that possibly the ideal facility for them would be a combination of inpatient and outpatient treatment center in their own communities. Certainly the culture of the institution where addicts are treated is very important in the individual prognosis. The contemporary "hospital prison" arrangement has a dual disadvantage. It encourages the dependency of the addict by the very nature of the institution, and its punitive and repressive aspects give him an opening to engage in power struggles with the institution as a means of avoiding treatment and of recognizing his problems. However, properly managed, inpatient treatment of addicts is definitely indicated. Further, in this author's opinion, there are little clinical data to justify the practice of segregating addicts from other psychiatric patients.

BIBLIOGRAPHY

Chapman, K. W.; Isabell, H.; Vogel, V. H. (1948), Present Status of Narcotic Addiction. *J. A. M. A., 138*:1019-1026.

Felix, R. H. (1944), An Appraisal of the Personality Types of the Addict. *Am. J. Psychiat., 100*:462-467.

Fenichel, O. (1945), *The Psychoanalytic Theory of Neurosis.* Chap. XVI. New York: Norton.

Fort, J. P., Jr. (1954), Heroin Addiction Among Young Men. *Psychiatry, 17*:251-259.

Glover, E. (1932a), Common Problems in Psycho-Analysis and Anthropology: Drug Ritual and Addiction. *Brit. J. Med. Psychol., 12*:109-131.

—— (1932b), On the Aetiology of Drug Addiction. *Int. J. Psychoanal., 13*:328.

Himmelsbach, C. K. (1942), Clinical Study of Drug Addictions: Physical Dependence, Withdrawal and Recovery. *Arch. Int. Med., 69*:766-776.

Isabell, H. (1950), Manifestations and Treatment of Addiction to Narcotic Drugs and Barbiturates. *Med. Clin. N. Am., 34*:425-438.

Karpman, B. (1948), The Myth of the Psychopathic Personality. *Am. J. Psychiat.,* *104*:1-11.

Knight, R. P. (1937a), The Dynamics and Treatment of Chronic Alcohol Addiction. *Bull. Menninger Clin., 1*:2-13.

—— (1937b), The Psychodynamics of Chronic Alcoholism. *J. Nerv. & Ment. Dis., 86*:1-8.

Kolb, L. (1925a), Types and Characteristics of Drug Addicts. *Ment. Hyg., 9*:300-313.

—— (1925b), Pleasure and Deterioration from Narcotic Addiction. *Ment. Hyg., 9*:699.

—— and Ossenport, W. F. (1938), The Treatment of Drug Addicts at the Lexington Hospital. *South. Med. J., 31*:914-922.

Mandel, G. (1951), *Flee the Angry Strangers.* New York: Putnam.

Rado, S. (1926), The Psychic Effects of Intoxicants: An Attempt to Evolve a Psychoanalytic Theory of Morbid Craving. *Int. J. Psychoanal., 7*:396-413.

—— (1933), The Psychoanalysis of Pharmocothymia. *Psychoanal. Quart., 2*:1-23.

Rivers, L. (1950), The Heroin Addicts. *Neurotica, 7*:41-46.

Simmel, E. (1930), Zum Problem von Zwang und Sucht. *Bericht über den V. allgemeinen ärtzlichen Kongress für Psychotherapie in Baden-Baden.*

—— (1948), Alcoholism and Addiction. *Psychoanal. Quart., 17*:6-31.

Slavson, S. R. (1943), *An Introduction to Group Therapy.* New York: International Universities Press, 1952.

—— (1947), *The Practice of Group Therapy.* New York: International Universities Press.

Thorpe, J. J. and Smith, B. (1953), Phases of Group Development in the Treatment of Drug Addicts. *Int. J. Group Psychother., 3*:66-78.

Wiker, A. (1942), A Psychodynamic Study of a Patient During Experimental Self-Regulated Re-Addiction to Morphine.

Zimmering, P.; Toolan, J.; Safrin, R.; Wortis, B. (1951), Heroin Addiction in Adolescent Boys. *J. Nerv. & Ment. Dis., 114*:1-12.

—— —— —— —— (1952), Drug Addiction in Relation to Problems of Adolescence. *Am. J. Psychiat., 109*:272-278.

Chapter V

ALCOHOLICS

•

Alcoholism may be defined as an uncontrollable craving for alcohol, leading to its excessive use (Haggard and Jellinek, 1942). Characteristically, the tendency for this craving becomes the regnant need of the individual, which progressively comes to dominate his motivative patterns. It is not the quantity of alcohol consumed but rather the role which it occupies in the individual's adjustment to life that marks him as an addict. Gradually over a period of years the need to drink becomes more and more uncontrollable. A Chinese saying puts this appropriately: "The man takes the drink; the drink takes the drink; the drink takes the man."

For a long time religious and social agencies tried to combat "drunkenness." The 18th Amendment (prohibition) bears mute witness to the vigor of this attempt and the magnitude of the problem. Yet neither the law nor the church have been really effective. Such pioneer movements as the Salvation Army, the Washingtonians,[1] and other temperance groups have helped many, but the problem has remained unsolved. Scientific and medical interest has only recently been aroused. Whereas the older movements were concerned with the evils of alcohol, recent concern is only with alcoholism and does not imply any commitments for or against the use of alcohol per se.

The approach and the attitude toward alcoholism and the alcoholic have undergone considerable change. Research and treatment have started to be substituted for contempt and punishment. In 1930 a Department for Special Studies on Alcoholism was established at Yale University in the

[1] In 1840 a Baltimore group of ex-alcoholics organized themselves, as the Washingtonians, to help alcoholics. They looked on alcoholism as a sickness and their membership soon reached a quarter million. The movement declined, and the Washingtonian Hospital in Boston is all that survives.

Laboratory of Applied Physiology. There biochemists, physiologists, psychiatrists, psychologists, sociologists, economists, and social workers began to make surveys and to seek scientific answers relative to the effects of alcohol and the causes of alcoholism.

In 1940 the *Quarterly Journal of Studies on Alcohol* was launched and at the same time a center was created where all books and articles on the subject were registered, thereby making information available for people interested in this field. The founding of this research center helped make alcoholism a problem to be viewed in the same manner as other medical problems.

In 1943 the Yale Center for Alcohol Studies was established at Yale University. At the time of its foundation this school was greeted in some quarters with contempt and irony. Nevertheless, this school, in cooperation with the Yale Plan Clinics, has been operating ever since and its attendance has steadily increased. It is attended by physicians, research scientists, psychologists, social workers, and members of allied professions who are given an opportunity to become acquainted with various aspects of alcoholism. Their comprehensive summer sessions have also been very successful. The *Quarterly Journal of Studies on Alcohol* of 1952 includes a survey of activities in research, education and therapy, covering the years 1941-51 (Bacon, 1952a).

In 1944 the National Committee for Education on Alcoholism was established in connection with Yale University (Mann, 1950). Through the activities of this committee other local committees have been brought into existence. One of the first, and most active, local committees was established in Boston and was successful in arousing interest and cooperation on a community level (Whitney, 1953). This committee has developed educational campaigns, gives regular radio programs, and has established close cooperation with industry. Courses and series of lectures have been arranged and incorporated in the curricula of some universities.

In addition to these programs organized through private initiative, state programs have developed in most states. These are closely adapted to local needs, and are concerned with the social problem caused by large numbers of alcoholics as well as with subsidizing treatment centers. They are based on the growing awareness that it is better for the state to treat the alcoholic than to confine and punish him. From a fiscal viewpoint jailing the alcoholic costs the community money, whereas through treatment he may not only cease to be a public burden, but may become a productive member of society.

A very important phase in the approach and treatment of alcoholism came about through the efforts of alcoholics themselves. The formation in 1934 of Alcoholics Anonymous (A.A.) and its rapid growth are among the most dramatic developments in the fight against alcoholism. The movement developed as a spontaneous group phenomenon, originating among lay people at approximately the same time group therapy was taking root as a new psychotherapeutic technique in 1934 (Slavson, 1943, 1947).

A.A. was founded by two alcoholics—one a physician, the other an engineer. Its underlying program and philosophy are the outcome of a "spiritual revelation" experienced by one of these men.[2] The teachings and principles of this organization have spread so widely that today there are in the United States organized A.A. chapters in almost every community, large or small. The movement is still growing and gaining momentum; its fundamental doctrines have varied very little since A.A. was founded. The basic philosophies and the initial theory are: Surrender to a power greater than yourself; the 24-hour plan; the 12-step work; first things first; easy does it; etc. They have become so well known that it seems unnecessary to elaborate on them here.[3]

Alcohol is a drug with a wide variety of effects on the human organism. The most important one from our viewpoint is its action on neural tissue. It acts as a central nervous system depressant (Salter, 1952). However, its peculiarity is such that the higher centers, the seats of learning and integration, are affected first. Clinically, in low dosage it may seem like a stimulant, which is due to the release of inhibition as the higher centers are affected. Its effect will depend upon the basic personality of the individual; thus some become aggressive, others elated, still others, depressed. Alcohol also has analgesic properties, its potency being between morphine and codeine.

From a technical viewpoint it may be questioned whether physiological addiction to alcohol exists or whether alcohol addiction is in fact a habituation phenomenon. Drugs such as morphine are metabolized differently in the addict than in the nonaddict. It is highly probable that they acquire a new metabolic function in the organism of the addict. Thus decerebrate animals can be addicted to morphine and will show withdrawal symptoms. This is not the case with alcohol where the metabolic pathways seem to be the same in the "addict" as in the normal (Newman and Card, 1937). On the other hand neural tissue develops tolerance to alcohol in animals as well as humans after exposure to moderate con-

[2] Cf. *Alcoholics Anonymous* (1939).
[3] Cf. the A.A.'s Monthly, *Grapevine*, and *Alcoholics Anonymous* (1952). For a detailed analysis of A.A., see Bales (1944) and Thompson (1952).

centrations for a considerable period, the same concentration leading to less evidence of neural impairment (Salter, 1952).

The great popularity of alcohol is probably due to the depressant effect on the higher centers, leading to release of tension. This effect may be demonstrated experimentally on cats. Masserman (1944) has shown that moderate amounts of alcohol will lessen the "anxiety" evidenced by cats in anxiety-provoking situations. Other drugs have similar effects, i.e., hashish, mescaline, marijuana, etc. None of these, however, has enjoyed such universal usage through the ages and throughout the world. The capacity of alcohol to reduce anxiety serves a positive function for the individual. Horton (1943) states: "Anxiety is so universal and constant an experience that any means of alleviating this burden of pain must be valued."

Any activity, once it becomes an integral part of a culture, will acquire new meanings. Drinking also serves social needs quite apart from tension reduction. For instance, alcohol lends glamour to festive occasions, champagne as conspicuous consumption, the toast as a tribute, the college beer party as a means of furthering social solidarity. Alcohol consumption and addiction must be considered from two points of view. The incidence of alcoholism in a given culture can be understood in terms of cultural factors, but why any particular individual becomes addicted can be understood only in terms of his individual make-up.

Before discussing the various psychological and sociological factors one must consider the constitutional predisposition which undoubtedly plays a role in determining who shall and who shall not become an alcoholic. Early writers made much of the "hereditary taint" and felt that individuals are born with the predisposition which will eventually make them alcoholics. They point to the large proportion of alcoholics who come from families where one or both parents have been problem drinkers. Modern writers have been more impressed by environmental influence and have tried to account for addiction on the basis of early experience and the needs which alcohol serves in the individual. They have felt that it would be only natural that children of alcoholics, being subject to early conditioning in the use of alcohol, should show a high incidence themselves. Here, as in other fields, the controversy of heredity versus environment has not yet been resolved. It seems safe to assume, however, that both factors are of significance. We agree with some of the more recent writers who feel that a nonspecific predisposition to become addicted plays a significant role, while the environment must provide the suitable matrix for such a predisposition to become focalized about alcohol.

Many workers have tried to find a hormonal basis for the predisposition to become addicted. Almost every hormone has at one time or another been under suspicion. Insulin (Clark et al., 1941) and the cortical steroids (Smith, 1949, 1950) especially have been the subjects of much research. Up until now no conclusive evidence has been brought to light which establishes that such a hormonal basis does in fact exist.

The incidence of alcoholism varies greatly in different societies. To clarify this aspect Bales's analysis (1946) has proven most helpful. Since alcohol is a means of reducing tension the incidence of addiction will be influenced by "the degree to which the culture operates to bring about acute needs for adjustment of inner tension in its members." All other factors being constant, an increasing amount of addiction should be encountered with an increase of tension among members of a culture.[4]

"The degree to which the culture provides suitable substitutive means of satisfaction" (Bales, 1946) will decide whether tension reduction is accomplished by alcohol primarily or in other ways. The Peyote cult among the Plains Indians and opium among the Orientals are good examples to the point. Finally whether the attitude toward drinking positively suggests drinking to the individual as a means of relieving his inner tension or whether such a thought arouses a strong "counteranxiety" will be a significant determinant. The attitudes prevalent in various cultures toward drinking are classified by Bales (1946) into four basic types. (1) Abstinence (usually for religious reasons, viz., Moslems); (2) ritual attitude toward drinking (alcohol considered sacred and plays role in religious ceremony, viz., Orthodox Judaism); (3) convivial attitude (alcohol used for purposes of social solidarity, facilitating friendship, in social intercourse); (4) utilitarian attitude (medicinal or business reasons, viz., salesman drinking with customer).

The significance of the attitude toward drinking is demonstrated by the relatively high incidence of alcoholism among bar attendants, waiters, and distillery employees (Bowman and Jellinek, 1941). Moslems and Orthodox Jews are groups who, due to their religious orientation (abstinence and ritualism), show a virtual absence of alcoholism. Among the Moslems hashish has long been a substitutive means of satisfaction and among Jews drug addiction shows a high incidence.

A variety of psychological theories has been put forward to explain why a particular person becomes alcoholic whereas another does not. A considerable number of psychoanalytic studies have dealt with this problem and have arrived at an almost equal number of etiological factors.

4 Thomas (1925) shows the incidence of suicide, crime and alcoholism fluctuating with the business cycle, which illustrates this point.

There has been a tendency to draw far-reaching conclusions on the basis of one case or a very small number of them.

Freud's original hypothesis related alcohol addiction to repressed homosexuality. According to him alcohol addiction is psychodynamically a defense almost parallel to that of paranoid delusions. Drinking in the company of men may provide the alcoholic with emotional satisfaction not provided by his wife. Freud gives the example of the patient whose love for his drinking companions, unacceptable to his superego, is unconsciously projected onto his wife. He then suspects his wife's relationship with the men to whom he himself has felt attracted. Several analysts have accorded latent homosexuality a major etiological role (Read, 1920; Juliusberger, 1916; Tabori, 1933). Glover (1928), on the other hand, negates the importance of this factor. Abraham (1926) states that alcoholism is an actual replacement of sexual gratification. Tausk, Sachs, Rado and Davidson state, according to Bowman and Jellinek (1941), that there is no gratification and therefore the addict has to continue to try again and again until drinking, analogous to "forepleasure," becomes an end in itself. Menninger (1938) puts forth the view that alcoholism is a form of self-destruction used to defend against a more serious form of suicide. Simmel (1929) was impressed with the significance of the castration anxiety in the alcoholic and suggests that the alcoholic is compelled to regress to an oral means of satisfying his libido, drinking being especially related to the oral-sadistic phase. Bromberg and Schilder (1933) also discuss the importance of castration anxiety in this connection. Goitein (1942), on the basis of one patient, expresses the viewpoint that alcohol addiction is a symptom of neurosis; citing his case with anorexia, he concludes that the sex drive is displaced to the gastric sphere where it is resisted by not eating and gratified by periodic drinking bouts. It is implied that this mechanism may be basic to much of the excessive drinking found among prostitutes. A unified psychoanalytic theory based on a sufficient number of cases is not as yet available.

Other psychological theories have been equally inconclusive. Strecker (1941) believes the alcoholic to be an introvert and socially inadequate; he drinks to overcome this, while the extrovert may drink to heighten the pleasures of reality. It is the introvert, according to him, who is more in danger of becoming addicted. Thompson (1948) points to the tendency of neurotic personalities to drink heavily because otherwise their inhibitions prevent them from fulfilling their desires. Lolli (1949) says addiction is an expression of lopsided mental growth coming from unsatisfactory family constellations. The drinker longs for infantile comfort, warmth, coddling, liquid filling the stomach. These desires, not fully satisfied by alcohol, lead to more psychological discomfort and compel him to continue drinking, analogous to the rhythm of hunger and sleep in early life.

Martensen-Larson (1954) recently has presented an interesting hypothesis wherein he places weight on the apparent frequency of the older of two siblings, born less than two years apart, to become addicted. The psychological trauma in early life of having the mother lose interest for the sake of the younger sibling with the resultant unsuccessful competition leads to a passive inadequate personality structure, especially prone to addiction (Martensen-Larsen, 1954).

There are no uniform dynamics of alcoholism. Therefore it seems to be a more fruitful approach to distinguish different types of alcoholics. In our opinion there is no typical personality pattern of the alcoholic patient. Various authors have described a number of distinct types of drinkers; thus distinctions are made between primary and secondary addiction (Thompson et al., 1948). The primary type suffers from addiction with his first use of alcohol. The addiction arises from the individual's make-up and is influenced but little by external factors. In the secondary type alcoholism is a symptom of an underlying mental disorder, i.e., neurosis, depression, or schizophrenia. Schaefer (1954), on the basis of an obverse factor analysis, arrives at five basic types: a schizoid personality, a relatively normal personality, an uncontrolled personality with an anxiety reaction to stress and frustration, an emotionally unstable personality, and a psychoneurotic personality with pronounced sexual conflicts and feelings of inadequacy. Whether the classifications thus far proposed are definitive or whether we may eventually arrive at different categories on the basis of more extensive studies remains to be seen.

It is clear that alcohol does not serve the same function in every individual. Rather, it serves a variety of functions, and the relative significance of these will vary with individuals. On the other hand, addicts also show certain uniform characteristics. These seem related to the prolonged use of alcohol. By this we mean not primarily the physical effects of the drug, but its psychological impact. The availability of a ready pseudo solution for any conflict that arises seems a major factor in the almost uniform immaturity encountered among alcoholics. In every form of insight psychotherapy it is required of the patient that he tolerate a certain amount of anxiety. The availability of alcohol makes it possible for a patient to avoid to a large extent any strong feelings of anxiety. While the patient drinks, he may be able to think and talk about very promising material. This, as a rule, is of little therapeutic significance, however. When he is sober between bouts, he is so overwhelmed by feelings of remorse and guilt about his drinking that it is almost impossible to deal with the underlying problems. It appears to us that any psychotherapeutic treatment of an alcoholic patient can only take place when sobriety has been achieved for some time.

Few reports have appeared in the literature pertaining to group therapy with alcoholics. We shall review briefly some of these. Heath (1945) reports on group sessions with alcoholics closely patterned after A.A. principles. The patient was encouraged to believe in a power greater than himself which can help him control his drinking and he is given intellectual insight into some of his rationalizations. The importance of the alcoholic's wish to be helped is stressed. Heath emphasizes the alcoholic's need to feel important, and believes that this need must be satisfied if a rehabilitation program is to be effective.

McCarthy (1946) reports on group therapy in progress at the Yale Plan Clinic. Each group meets for approximately six months. The smallest group was six men and the largest varied from nine to sixteen members. Attendance was voluntary, and the atmosphere informal. Psychopaths and neurotics with symptoms of acute anxiety were excluded from membership. Three objectives were stressed at the meetings: (1) to stimulate the patient to understand that his problem is not unique and eliminate the defensive will to isolation; (2) to facilitate intellectual grasp of the problem of alcoholism as it involves the individual's behavior pattern and the dynamics which appear to underly the excessive use of alcohol; and (3) to gain emotional release through group participation.

Friedland, Pfeffer and Wortis (1941) distinguished between neurotic alcoholics and psychopaths or other types. They state that only the group of neurotic alcoholics should be selected for treatment and suggest groups of five to six people of the same sex. They emphasize that group therapy is of specific value with alcoholics because it involves a less dangerous transference to the therapist and stimulates the patients to remain sober by mutual encouragement. Patients tend to support each other against the therapist and to divert their feelings from him toward each other.

Brunner-Orne, Iddings, and Rodrigues (1951) reported the use of group therapy in an experimental court clinic for alcoholics. Patients were referred by the court and had their choice of attending clinic or serving sentence. The purpose of the clinic was to investigate whether the alcoholic's initial desire to be cured was necessary in order for him to be helped. The clinic was held weekly on the premises of the court. Each new member was given a thorough physical examination and a personal interview with the psychiatrist. Then he joined the group. A combination of permissive "directive" and "nondirective" therapy was used in group sessions, discussions focusing on a specific topic each week. Environmental and social problems were investigated at the clinic. Every patient referred was accepted. It was found that although patients first attended sessions under coercion, they were soon made to feel that they were coming of their own free will. Gradually genuine interest in the group emerged and active participation soon followed. The study seems to indicate that it is not always necessary for the alcoholic patient to enter a treatment program of his own free will in order to render it helpful.

Allison (1952), using a nondirective approach in a state hospital, reported that it created an atmosphere in which each group member could take the initiative in his own thinking. This facilitated a more objective viewing of group defense mechanisms and a regulation of the individuality of each patient's problem. He pointed out certain disadvantages in this technique, such as heterogeneity of the alcoholic population and a lack of group cohesion and integration due to a changing patient population.

Myerson (1953) reported on his work with "Skid Row" alcoholics in Boston. This group, previously given up for lost, thoroughly depleted of all resources, has required a different approach. Antabuse is administered to all patients as a routine. The patients are admitted to the Long Island Hospital and live there. The principal therapy is individual; however, the group lives together and thorough interaction takes place. This interaction is encouraged and attempts are made to strengthen the group feeling. As soon as possible, attempts are made to find positions in the community for the patients. Special arrangements have been made to enable them to continue residing at the hospital. Giving the patients the feeling of receiving something for nothing is avoided and as soon as possible they contribute financially toward their treatment.[5] The results with this group, despite all odds, have been promising and the work has been continued.

Stewart (1954b) reports on group therapy with alcoholic patients in the Crichton Royal Mental Hospital in Scotland. Alcoholics were housed in a separate building and while private interviews were readily available, group therapy has proven equally effective, if not superior. He emphasizes the importance of empathy which exists in the group relationship. Voluntary and informal meetings were held in the lounge with rotating chairmen. Meetings were held on the average three times a week and attendance varied at the meetings. Identification of group members with

5 Part-time protective environment in working parole systems was introduced by Dr. J. Thiemann (1944) at the Washingtonian Hospital in Boston, Mass.

each other is felt to be a basic healing element. This identification was more pronounced between group members than in face-to-face therapy with the psychiatrist. In another paper, Stewart (1954a) deals with the ethical aspects of group therapy and points out in detail what psychotherapy can do for the alcoholic patient by teaching him how to understand himself. He has adapted ten phases from Haggard's and Jellinek's (1942) "Phases of Alcohol Addiction" for use in analyzing the etiological aspects in alcoholism and group therapy.

Martensen-Larson (1954), in reviewing group therapy with alcoholics, describes the work in Denmark where group therapy has recently been introduced in alcoholic clinics. It is used in conjunction with Antabuse. Much ingenuity and manipulation are exercised. The approach is very permissive: patients are accepted in the group even when they are intoxicated, and attendance by relatives and wives is encouraged. The rule of insight is emphasized, and it is felt that group acceptance is a major factor in treatment. An interesting technique employed is the two-person group. A new patient passing through a crisis is confronted with another who went through a similar stage. This type of session is often the preface to a larger group meeting. The author states: "Increased catalysis often takes place as a result of pre-warmed two participants." There is some screening of patients, and severely regressed individuals are given extensive individual therapy before they join the group. An attempt is made to extend the group's activities beyond the confines of the clinic. Social get-togethers are encouraged. Joshua Bierer (1940) in England, has pioneered in establishing such groups.

At the 10th Annual Meeting of the American Group Psychotherapy Association, 1953, the authors presented a paper on "Directive Group Therapy in the Treatment of Alcoholics," on which we have elaborated here. In our approach we have been influenced by a number of considerations. The failure of psychoanalytic procedures to cure alcoholics is well known, and it is emphasized that a special type of situation is required to make the alcoholic patient available for psychotherapy. We have found that once sobriety has been achieved, analytically oriented therapy is desirable and in many cases necessary. However, sobriety is a prerequisite to the treatment of underlying personality problems which may have etiological significance. Furthermore, we are dealing with a phenomenon which, once it has become established, loses a great deal of its connection with the original conflict. Conditioning takes place, and the patient organizes his diet and his everyday life around alcohol. Alcoholism becomes, to borrow Allport's (1937) phrase, "functionally autonomous." This aspect of the problem may be of major importance for the success of therapy.

In our group therapy we constantly remind ourselves that the patient has tried to stop drinking before we see him. His friends, relatives, minister and physician will have vividly portrayed the dangers and "evils" of drinking, but this has not helped. We therefore avoid vigorously any moralizing or lecturing and rather than minimizing the difficulties of remaining sober, we tend to point out that a long, hard road lies ahead. We recognize that alcohol has come to occupy a major portion of the patient's thinking, and that drinking has consumed much of his time. Substitutive behavior and purpose are essential if sobriety is to be maintained. By the time we see the patient his social, physical, and psychological resources have been exhausted, necessitating a threefold approach to the problem. He must be treated physically for his immediate condition and this can often best be accomplished by short-term hospitalization. Not only does this facilitate rapid physical recovery, but people regain their self-respect more quickly in the protective, friendly hospital atmosphere where they are treated with sympathy and understanding. In this way we can break the vicious cycle of a deteriorating social, moral, and economic position associated with intense guilt feelings while sobering up, which again force the alcoholic to continue drinking. Individual and group therapy can be optimally initiated at this time. When the patient is in a hospital he can admit more easily that he is "sick" without loss of self-respect. He finds treatment for his total condition and can accept psychotherapy in this setting, whereas it may have been unacceptable before (Brunner-Orne, 1955). Many patients who have been unable to accede to A.A.'s requirement that they confess their alcoholism, have by this method been successfully introduced to group therapy.

Antabuse, the Danish drug, which is incompatible with alcohol, has proven a valuable adjunct in treatment. It is especially valuable as an aid because the patient who takes it regularly cannot drink for a number of days after he stops taking the drug. This prevents a momentary impulse from initiating a new "binge." The patient who decides he wishes to drink must stop taking the drug and if during the succeeding day or two he changes his mind, he has only to resume taking his pill. The patient who takes Antabuse voluntarily—and we believe this is the only justified way of administration—still retains the feeling of control which he loses in such treatments as conditioned reflex or confinement.

Our therapeutic efforts are guided by the fact that no specific treatment methods for alcoholism have been found, despite research and progress. Group therapy is a recent approach which, in our opinion, has become an integral part of treatment programs for alcoholics. There are two tasks that can best be accomplished by group therapy. First, we try to make the alcoholic currently abstinent. Directive group therapy in a permissive setting is in many ways ideally suited for problems where conscious effort on the part of the patient is desirable. A high degree of active participation by the patient is also essential. The second and equally important therapeutic effort is directed toward giving patients substitutive emotional satisfactions. It is necessary for patients to feel secure so that they can tolerate anxiety without resorting to drinking, yet not be forced to develop symptoms. The permissive setting of the therapy as well as the support of the group help a great deal in this respect.

The fact that support coupled with a relatively direct approach to the problem will frequently succeed in bringing about sobriety, is evidenced in the spectacular success of A.A. Our method is, however, somewhat different from that of A.A. While we encourage our patients to attend A.A., we ourselves rigorously avoid becoming involved in moral or spiritual questions, preferring to treat the problem from a medical and psychological aspect. We consider it important that a patient should regard our work not as a "conversion cure," but rather as medical attempts based upon scientific principles. In this way we are able to supplement A.A., and A.A. in turn is able to supplement our work. It will be seen that there is some overlapping in the dynamics of these therapeutic processes. The patient, however, perceives us in a different light from A.A. Whether this is more acceptable to him depends on the individual. The widespread public acceptance of "medical science" is probably a great help to us.

The technique which we employ is as follows: A topic for the day is proposed by the therapist (group leader). A typical example of this is "What function does alcohol serve?" or "What does alcohol do for the individual who drinks?" The group leader then explains that obviously anything we do has a reason. If people drink alcohol, there must be something that it does for them. What does one get out of drinking? What's the point of it? Why? After a short introduction of this topic, members of the group are encouraged to point out what alcohol does for each individual. Responses vary. A salesman, for example, says: "When I take a couple of drinks before I go on the road, I don't get embarrassed meeting strangers or having to barge in on strangers." Another patient said: "I don't get along with my mother-in-law and I have a fight with my wife about it. So I go out and get drunk. Then I don't care." From a housewife: "I stay home alone all day long, with my housework. A few drinks make me feel better and then I feel up to it."

The group leader comments as little as possible at this time. He rather encourages free discussion of the topic. The responses are interpreted either by the leader or by other members of the group. The interpretations, however, are not in terms of the individual's dynamics but rather are focused on general mechanisms. Thus, the group leader may point out to the salesman that alcohol, in his case, increases his self-confidence. For the husband it releases tension. The housewife might be told by a group member that she is using alcohol to escape boredom and loneliness. While the leader actively encourages discussion, he also tries to prevent any patient from monopolizing the group by telling the full story of his life in the masochistic, self-recriminatory story fashion which is so characteristic of the alcoholic. This is done by keeping the group goal-oriented.

We have found that the tendency to exhibitionism, if permitted to flourish excessively, does not help the patient who is telling the story and causes the rest of the group to lose interest and leave the field. Actually, the leader is not required to do much because group members are quick to perceive excessive wandering and direct the trend back to the topic.

After a discussion has illuminated as many facets of a question as possible, the leader sums up and enumerates the factors covered, and then directs the discussion further. A brief remark is made, such as, "If alcohol does so many things for so many people, why should we attempt to stop drinking?" In other words: "Why are we here?"

The members of the group then discuss this topic with which they are so well acquainted. They are quick to point out such things as: "My doctor says, one more drink and I'm done." "When I get drunk I get awful nasty. My wife won't have me in the house as long as I keep drinking." "I can't keep a job and I can't go on like this." It is interesting to note that most of the reasons given represent external pressures. Even statements dealing with the physical state of the body are perceived by the patients as something which is forced upon them. In the latter cases, however, the patients give the reasons and the group discusses them, helping the internalization of the essentially external pressures to stop drinking. When a discussion seems to reach the point of diminishing returns, the leader sums up the points brought up by the various group members, having refrained as much as possible from commenting during the discussion.

He then raises the question: "If alcohol serves as many functions as we have discussed, and if we can't keep on drinking, what about the things alcohol did for us? It must have done something important for us, or we wouldn't have become compulsive drinkers. Now we can't drink any more. What can we do to make this easier? Giving up alcohol isn't just a question of staying away from the bottle. If we can't find other things to take the place of alcohol, we will never be able to give it up."

With such an introduction, the group leader then has directed the group's effort toward the finding of substitutive behavior patterns. This then becomes the task of the day.

Members of the group quickly begin to realize that no one substitute will do the many things which alcohol did, and they will begin to split up the functions. A typical example of this is the social problem which many of our patients encounter. They go to a party and everybody drinks. What can they do about it? Such a problem, when brought up, may be handled in a somewhat different manner.

The group leader's orientation is that of the specialist and, in this case, the leader presents in rough outline experiments done on the effects of drugs on college students. It was found that the same amount of alcohol which did not affect people very strongly when given intravenously without their knowledge, would get them quite "high" if taken orally. Further, they would get quite "high" on grape juice if they believed it contained alcohol. Thus, one sees that the effect of the drug in amounts usually consumed is to a great extent the result of the individual's belief that he is drinking.[6] The group leader, having presented these data, leaves them with the group for consideration. The ensuing discussions enabled many of our patients to become "the life of the party" on ginger-ale or any soft drink.

Another topic invariably brought up is the problem of boredom. Many alcoholics spend several hours a day drinking. When they become abstinent they suddenly find they have time on their hands and do not know what to do with it. Many solutions are proposed by different members, and through an interchange of ideas workable suggestions of practical help to the individual patient are brought out.

The release of tension, certainly a major problem, is another example, and here suggestions from the group include going down to the "Y" for a workout, changing jobs, acquiring hobbies, or going to church. Again, not all solutions fit all patients, but most get valuable suggestions from these discussions, not to mention the fact that discussion itself releases tension. When the time is up the group leader summarizes briefly the conclusions arrived at by the group and emphasizes the important points brought out.

The question arises whether this form of therapy is actually therapy in a strict sense of the term. While we believe that the total effect of this process is therapeutic, this form of therapy itself is not modeled along lines of individual therapy. Our group essentially is not a therapeutic

6 Personal communication from Michael von Felsinger. Unpublished research conducted at the Massachusetts General Hospital.

group, but a "work group." The group as a whole is trying to work on the problem of alcoholism. Each member of the group must feel that not only is he curing himself but above all is working together with the other members of the group on a common problem. This "work group" approach is very effective in causing patients to act upon the material which they have discussed. Not only is it more readily accepted than straight lecturing, but understood also at a deeper level. The studies by Kurt Lewin (1947) show very clearly how membership in a group, working together on a common problem, will be extremely effective in inducing rather profound changes in the attitudes of the individuals comprising the group. Powdermaker and Frank (1953) in their report on research in mostly psychoanalytically oriented group therapy, mention: "A group when insecure and resistant to therapy may seek mutual support by finding a topic around which most or all of its members can rally. This releases tension sufficiently for therapy to progress."

In essence, then, our group is a "work group" oriented around the task of finding solutions to the problems of the alcoholic. In the attempt to find these solutions, the goal of the group—sobriety—is effectively introjected by the members, and the fact that sobriety is a goal which can be achieved takes on a new and more intimately personal meaning.

In part, the sessions also convey some elements of dynamic psychology to the members of the group. This is not done at a high conceptual level, but rather at a level which the individual members can utilize in their efforts at adjustment to the world. We do not believe that this is the essential, or the most dynamic, part of the therapy. However, it is frequently of great value to the individual and, above all, it makes therapy acceptable to him.

The important dynamics of the therapeutic process as we see them may be conceptualized in the following terms: (1) The group provides substitute emotional satisfactions to the patient. (2) The feeling of psychological isolation so characteristic of alcoholics is materially decreased. (3) It is made possible for the patient to accept the fact that he is an alcoholic, and that there are other "nice" people who share this problem. (4) The patient is forewarned by the group against many of the rationalizations which are so popular with alcoholics. (5) The fact that group conclusions arrived at by free discussion exert a potent effect on the individual is well known and is utilized in prompting the idea that sobriety is not only desirable but attainable.

Our policy to encourage group members to bring husbands, wives and relatives to the sessions helps the nonalcoholic in his understanding and handling of the alcoholic with whom he is living. An important part of "clinic dynamics" occurs while patients gather and sit around waiting. They talk informally and discuss the events of the meeting the week before, and have an opportunity to consolidate the material at their level. The insight some patients display during these casual conversations is surprising. We have found that these periods yield very important therapeutic results. Frequently it is far more acceptable to patients to be helped with a problem by someone of their own group rather than by a "doctor." While usually no "new" material is brought out at these spontaneous discussions, the working through process is greatly facilitated by them.

Recently we have begun to use "Autogenes Training" in our group sessions. This technique, developed by Schultze (1950), and currently championed by Kretschmer (1949) in Germany, has been used extensively abroad. It is a means of teaching the patient to relax. This is done by the practice of a graduated set of exercises, first in the group and secondly at home. It is of particular value with alcoholics who suffer from tension states and those with a tendency toward autonomic crises. The following brief case histories are examples of results obtained by the method described.

Miss E. B., 52 years of age, is the oldest of seven children. Her father, aged 81, a retired steel worker, has been blind for the last ten years. Her mother died when the patient was fourteen years old. The patient could not finish high school but devoted her time to bringing up the younger siblings.

Medical History: Noncontributory.

Alcoholic History: The patient started drinking about ten years ago when her siblings were married and she was left alone with her father. She took increasing amounts of alcohol and became quite seclusive, drinking in solitude. She was treated as an outpatient with several individual interviews supplemented by group sessions which her sisters were invited to attend. This patient responded well to treatment and was able to remain sober and to build up interests and self-confidence. During group meetings the "active dependency reaction" was discussed which helped the patient's sisters to understand her condition and to realize that she had neglected to satisfy her own needs because she had accepted the role of mother substitute for the rest of the family. The members of the family began to understand and cooperate, which in turn encouraged the patient to regain her self-respect and incentive. Her physical and emotional condition had improved. Her appearance changed from a disheveled, unhappy, rejected person who was entirely lost, to a well-groomed, animated, happier person, looking considerably younger. We feel that this patient was helped not only by group discussions, but that the education and cooperation of her family were essential for her improvement.

Mr. G. E. C., 34 years of age, was one of seven boys born to his father's first wife. The father, aged 63, is still alive. The mother died of tuberculosis when the patient was 15 years old. He and his siblings were cared for in a shelter while the mother was sick, although his father was a good provider and not addicted to alcohol. Six months after the patient's mother died, his father married a widow with three children of her own. The patient was unhappy about this stepmother and enlisted in the army instead of finishing high school. He got along with his father but not with the stepmother. Of patient's brothers, one was killed in an automobile accident at the age of 5; one is in a state hospital suffering from alcoholism. Another brother has also been hospitalized in a state hospital because of alcoholism. The youngest is in prison because he could not be handled in the same hospital. The patient married at the age of 23. His wife is the same age. She is earning a good salary. They have no children.

Medical History: Noncontributory.

Alcoholic History: The patient has been drinking since 1940 but has grown worse during the last two years. During drinking bouts the patient becomes abusive to his wife. In 1952 he was admitted to a state hospital for ten days. Recently he took $100.00 from his wife's pocketbook and pawned some silver worth $400.00, then took his wife's car and drove to Canada where he was involved in an accident. While he was gone, his wife gave up their apartment and went to live with her family.

After a short hospitalization, the patient was introduced to group sessions. He attended meetings regularly. His wife also attended some of these sessions. At first the patient was timid, but his wife took the active part. Through group participation it became evident that her dominating attitude was overshadowing her husband. During a general discussion the competition element among family members, including husbands and wives, was brought up. Gradually the patient began to take a more active part in the discussions and made many valid and pertinent contributions. His wife finally gave up her domineering and patronizing attitude and began to accept her husband as an equal.

Instead of separating, they decided to live with her family until he showed some improvement. After several months they bought a new car, acquired a home of their own and their marriage gives the patient security as well as something to work for. The couple can have no children as the wife has had a hysterectomy. We feel that this patient benefited more from management in the group than from individual or group insight therapy. He had two relapses, but quickly overcame them. At this point we want to emphasize the importance of explaining to the patient and family members that relapses do not mean all efforts were in vain, but that they serve a purpose and very often reveal areas that have not been reached before. Relapses bring them to light where they can be interpreted and resolved.

We feel that in the treatment of alcoholism group therapy is a valuable tool. It is not a substitute for individual treatment; rather it serves a different function. Within the scope of an over-all treatment plan it often serves to make the initial therapeutic approach possible, helping to bring about at least temporary sobriety. Once this is achieved personality growth can take place. Group therapy may also help the patient to a better understanding of his problem, of his environment, and of himself.

BIBLIOGRAPHY

Abraham, K. (1926), The Psychological Relation between Sexuality and Alcoholism. *Int. J. Psychoanal.*, 7:2-10.
Alcoholics Anonymous (1939), New York: The Works Co.
—— (1952), Twelve Steps and Twelve Traditions. New York: Alcoholics Anonymous Publ. Co.
Allison, S. G. (1952), Nondirective Group Therapy of Alcoholics in a State Hospital. *Quart. J. Stud. Alc.*, 13:596-602.
Allport, G. W. (1937), *Personality: A Psychological Interpretation.* New York: Henry Holt Co.
Bacon, S. D. (1952a), Alcoholism, 1941-1951. A Survey of Activities in Research, Education and Therapy. *Quart. J. Stud. Alc.*, 13:453-461.
—— (1952b), Alcoholism, 1941-1951. A Survey of Activities in Research, Education and Therapy; Introduction. *Quart. J. Stud. Alc.*, 13:421-425.
Bales, R. F. (1944), The Therapeutic Role of Alcoholics Anonymous as Seen by a Sociologist. *Quart. J. Stud. Alc.*, 5:267-279.
—— (1946), Cultural Differences in Rates of Alcoholism. *Quart. J. Stud. Alc.*, 6:480-499.
Bierer, J. (1940), *Therapeutic Social Clubs.* London: H. K. Lewis & Co., Ltd.
Bowman, K. M. and Jellinek, E. M. (1941), Alcohol Addiction and Its Treatment. *Quart. J. Stud. Alc.*, 2:98-172.
Bromberg, W. and Schilder, P. (1933), Psychologic Consideration in Alcohol Hallucinations, Castration and Dismembering Motives. *Int. J. Psychoanal.*, 14:206.
Brunner-Orne, M. (1955), Treatment and Rehabilitation of Alcohol Addicts in a General Hospital Setting. *J. Am. Med. Women's Assn.*, 10:193-194.
—— Iddings, J. F. T.; Rodrigues, J. (1951), A Court Clinic for Alcoholics. *Quart. J. Stud. Alc.*, 12:592-601.
—— and Orne, M. T. (1953), Directive Group Therapy in the Treatment of Alcoholics: Technique and Rationale. Paper presented 10th Annual Conference American Group Psychotherapy Association, New York.
—— —— (1954), Directive Group Therapy in the Treatment of Alcoholics: Technique and Rationale. *Int. J. Group Psychother.*, 4:293-302.
Buhler, C. and Lefever, D. W. (1948), *A Rorschach Study on the Psychological Characteristics of Alcoholics.* New Haven: Hillhouse Press.

Clark, B. B.; Morrisey, R. W.; Fazekas, J. F.; Welch, C. S. (1941), The Role of Insulin and the Liver in Alcohol Metabolism. *Quart. J. Stud. Alc.*, 1:663-684.

Freud, S. (1922), *Group Psychology and the Analysis of the Ego.* New York: Boni & Liveright.

Glover, E. (1928), The Etiology of Alcoholism. *Proc. Roy. Soc. Med.*, 21:45-50.

Goitein, P. L. (1942), The Potential Prostitute: The Role of Anorexia in the Defense against Prostitution Desires. *J. Crim. Psychopath.,* 3:359-367.

Haggard, H. W. and Jellinek, E. M. (1942), *Alcohol Explored.* New York: Doubleday, Doran and Co.

Heath, R. G. (1945), Group Psychotherapy of Alcohol Addiction. *Quart. J. Stud. Alc.*, 5:555-563.

Henderson, R. M. and Straus, R. (1952), Alcoholism, 1941-1951; A Survey of Activities in Research, Education and Therapy. Programs on Alcoholism in the United States. *Quart. J. Stud. Alc.*, 12:472-496.

Horton, D. (1943), Functions of Alcohol in Primitive Societies. *Quart. J. Stud. Alc.*, 4:299-311.

Jellinek, E. M. (1952), Phases of Alcohol Addiction. *Quart. J. Stud. Alc.*, 13:682.

Juliusburger, O. (1916), Alcoholismus und Psychosexualität. *Ztschr. f. Sexualwissenschaften*, 2:357-366.

Keller, M. and Efron, V. (1952), Alcoholism, 1941-1951; A Survey of Activities in Research, Education and Therapy. Sources of Scientific Information. *Quart. J. Stud. Alc.,* 12:444-453.

Kretschmer, R. (1949), *Psychotherapeutische Studien.* Stuttgart: Georg Thieme.

Lerner, A. (1953), An Exploratory Approach in Group Counselling with Male Alcoholic Inmates in a City Jail. *Quart. J. Stud. Alc.,* 14:427-468.

Lester, D. and Greenberg, L. A. (1952), Alcoholism, 1941-1951. A Survey of Activities in Research, Education and Therapy: The States of Physiological Knowledge. *Quart. J. Stud. Alc.,* 13:444-453.

Lewin, K. (1947), Group Decision and Social Change. *Readings in Social Psychology.* New York: Henry Holt.

Lippit, R. and White, R. K. (1947), An Experimental Study of Leadership and Group Life. *Readings in Social Psychology.* New York: Henry Holt.

Lolli, G. (1949), The Addictive Drinker. *Quart. J. Stud. Alc.,* 10:404-414.

—— (1952), Alcoholism, 1941-1951. A Survey of Activities in Research, Education and Therapy. *Quart. J. Stud. Alc.,* 13:461-472.

Mann, M. (1950), *Primer on Alcoholism.* New York: Rinehart.

Martensen-Larsen, O. (1954), Personal Communication.

McCarthy, R. (1946), Group Therapy in an Outpatient Clinic for the Treatment of Alcoholism. *Quart. J. Stud. Alc.,* 7:98-110.

—— (1949), Transcriptions of Three Sessions of Group Therapy on Alcoholism. *Quart. J. Stud. Alc.,* 10:63-108; 217-250.

—— (1952), Alcoholism, 1941-1951. A Survey of Activities in Research, Education and Therapy; Activities of State Departments of Education Concerning Instruction about Alcohol. *Quart. J. Stud. Alc.,* 13:496-512.

Masserman, J. H. (1944), Experimental Neurosis and Group Aggression. *Am. J. Orthopsychiat.,* 14:636-693.

Menninger, K. A. (1938), *Man Against Himself.* New York: Harcourt, Brace.

Myerson, D. J. (1953), An Approach to the "Skid Row" Problem in Boston. *New Eng. J. Med.,* 249:646-649.

Newman, H. and Card, J. (1937), Duration of Acquired Tolerance to Ethyl Alcohol. *J. Pharmacol. & Exp. Therapeutics,* 59:249-252.

Pfeffer, A. Z.; Friedland, P.; Wortis, H. (1949), Group Psychotherapy with Alcoholics, Preliminary Report. *Quart. J. Stud. Alc.,* 1:217-251.

Powdermaker, F. B., and Frank, J. D. (1953), *Group Psychotherapy—Studies in Methodology of Research and Therapy.* Cambridge: Harvard University Press.

Read, S. C. (1920), Psychopathology of Alcoholism and Some So-called Alcoholic Psychosis. *J. Ment. Sci.*, *66*:233.

Salter, W. T. (1952), *A Textbook of Pharmacology*. Philadelphia: Saunders.

Schaefer, E. (1954), Personality Structure of Alcoholics in Outpatient Psychotherapy. *Quart. J. Stud. Alc.*, *15*:304-320.

Schultze, J. H. (1950), *Das Autogene Training*. Stuttgart: George Thieme.

Simmel, E. (1929), Psychoanalytic Treatment in a Sanatorium. *Int. J. Psycho-Anal.*, *10*:83.

Slavson, S. R. (1943), *An Introduction to Group Therapy*. New York: International Universities Press, 1951.

—— (1940), Group Therapy. *Ment. Hyg.*, *28*:414-422.

—— (1947), *The Practice of Group Therapy*. New York: International Universities Press.

Smith, J. J. (1949), A Medical Approach to Problem Drinking. *Quart. J. Stud. Alc.*, *10*:251-257.

—— (1950), The Treatment of Acute Alcoholic States with ACTH and Adrenal-Cortical Hormones. *Quart. J. Stud. Alc.*, *11*:190-198.

Stewart, D. A. (1954a), Ethical Aspects of Group Therapy of Alcoholics. *Quart. J. Stud. Alc.*, *15*:288-304.

—— (1954b), Empathy in the Group Therapy of Alcoholics. *Quart. J. Stud. Alc.*, *15*:74-111.

Strecker, E. A. (1941), Chronic Alcoholism; A Psychological Survey. *Quart. J. Stud. Alc.*, *2*:12-17.

Tabori, J. (1933), Ueber die seelischen Hintergründe des Alkoholismus. *Psychoanalytische Praxis, 3*:10-19.

Thiemann, J. (1944) , Part-time Protective Environment as an Adjuvant in Therapy for Alcohol Addiction. *New Eng. J. Med.*, *231*:9-11.

Thomas, D. S. (1943), Alcoholism and Mental Disorders. *Quart. J. Stud. Alc.*, *3*:65-78.

Thompson, C. E. et al. (1948), Characteristics of Alcoholics. *Am. J. Psychol.*, *3*:363.

Thompson, G. S. (1952), An Experience of a Nonalcoholic in Alcoholics Anonymous Leadership. *Quart. J. Stud. Alc.*, *13*:271-296.

Whitney, E. D. (1953), Socio-Economic Aspects of Alcoholism. Paper presented at the 18th Annual Meeting of the Industrial Hygiene Foundation.

Wortis, H.; Sillman, L. R.; Halpern, F. (1946), *Studies of Compulsive Drinkers*. New Haven: Hillhouse Press.

Chapter VI

STUTTERERS

•

Stuttering and stammering, disturbances in the rhythmic flow of speech, are characterized by intermittent hesitations, prolongations, repetitions, and/or stoppages of sounds, syllables, or words. It is a dramatic disorder of our principal medium of social contact.

The etiology and treatment of stuttering has plagued mankind from time immemorial. It appears that no class of people in any period of recorded history has been spared this affliction. Archeological excavation in the biblical town of Beth Shemish uncovered a clay tablet inscribed with the prayer: "Oh God, cut through the backbone of my stammering." Moses was "slow of speech and of a slow tongue" (Exodus 4:10) and required his brother Aaron's assistance in his talks with Pharaoh. The prophet Isaiah (Isaiah 32:4) prayed that "the tongue of the stammerer shall be ready to speak plainly." Herodotus, the "Father of History," recorded the Oracle's recommendation of a trip south to Lybia for relief of stuttering. Demosthenes, the Greek orator, treated his stuttering with the aid of a mirror and pebbles in his mouth. In more recent years King Charles I, Charles Lamb, Charles Darwin, and the late King George VI, are among the famous people who have stammered. Among the 1,500,000 stutterers in the United States today, there is a ratio of four males to every female stutterer.

Aristotle localized the defect in stuttering to the tongue and for a long time treatment was focused on that organ. Galen cauterized the tongue and Hippocrates recommended the application of healing oils to the throat and neck. A great variety of surgical techniques, innumerable drugs, grotesque mechanical devices, distracting movements like arm swinging, and even witchcraft have been employed. Currently, breathing

and/or speech exercises and psychological measures varying from suggestion to hypnosis to psychoanalysis are the accepted modes of therapy.

Objective evaluation of the different treatments is an impossible task
for several reasons. The proponents of all theories claim some measure of
success with their own methods but adequate controlled studies are not
in evidence. This is not intended as a criticism of the diligent workers in
this field. There are two very obvious factors inherent in the syndrome
that interfere with evaluating results. One is the propensity for temporary
remissions of the symptom for no discernible reason or in conjunction
with minor incidental environmental alterations. Another problem in
recording the outcome of therapy is that some individuals who no longer
observably stutter, seek treatment ostensibly for this nonexistent symptom.
We shall discuss our understanding of this phenomenon subsequently.
The literature devoted to speech correction is noted for the rarity of
reported cures of adult stutterers. In fact, it is not difficult to locate pessi-
mistic cliches like "once a stutterer always a stutterer" in the journals and
texts.

The diversity of methods of treatment is a product of the multitude of
ideas about the cause of stuttering. Etiological theories range from those
impugning an inherited constitutional predisposition or neurophysio-
logical instability (diminished unilateral cerebral dominance, delayed
myelinization, or a biochemical imbalance) to psychological difficulties.
Considerable research along neurological, electroencephalographic, biochemical, metabolic, and dietary lines have produced few positive findings
and none that have been generally accepted as significant. The bulk of
the positive findings have been a product of psychological investigation.
The nature of these often seem to depend on the orientation of their
respective proponents.

Educators have been inclined to consider stuttering as a learned bad
habit originating in the natural hesitations of the child's early efforts at
verbalization. The so-called "semantogenic" theory says that when these
normal hesitations are labeled abnormal by significant adults in the child's
environment, stuttering ensues. Some psychologists believe that the stutterer lacks the visual and auditory imagery ostensibly necessary for normal
speech. Others have advanced the theory of a conditioned inhibition
following a traumatic experience. Psychiatrists, among others, have considered stuttering to be expressive of a basic personality problem.
Psychoanalytic investigators have gone deeper and labeled it a pregenital
conversion because, as Fenichel (1945) so succinctly stated it, "The unconscious impulse expressed in the symptoms are pregenital: while the symp-

tomatology is of the nature of conversion, the patient's mental structure corresponds to that of a compulsion neurotic."

It is generally recognized that man almost invariably wants to consider his afflictions as being of a somatic origin and thereby in no way his own "responsibility." When this is coupled with the fact that many of the investigators in this field refer to themselves as stutterers,[1] it is somewhat amazing that rapidly increasing support has been forthcoming for psychogenic hypotheses. An indication of this is the American Medical Association's (1952) official nomenclature wherein stuttering is classified under personality disorders "of psychogenic origin or without clearly defined tangible cause or structural change."

Stammerers have been treated in groups for years. Leary (1950) summarized it by saying that "association with other patients is helpful for the will to get well is contagious and the spirit of mutual understanding is powerful." However, groups of stutterers meeting primarily for psychotherapeutic purposes has been a rarity. Rhythmic speech exercises in a group or choral reading based on Barber's (1939) observation that reading in unison decreases the amount of stuttering, have been far more common. Not infrequently such groups have engaged in discussions about the social problems emanating ostensibly from their speech disability and the means of coping with it.

The therapy described by Backus and Dunn (1947) endeavors to teach new speech patterns in devised situations in which different members of the group play various social roles. Lemert and Van Riper (1944) employed psychodramatic techniques which they cryptically called "reversing traditional psychiatric treatment." Apparently the stuttering itself attracted the bulk of their attention. They described it as follows: "When the stutterers first enter the clinic, no attempt is made to force them to repress or eliminate blocks. Instead they must intensify them. While this as well as other psychodramatic methods give rich emotional release, its most beneficial effect is to point out the ultimate goal of treatment. By deliberately varying and manipulating his symptoms the individual gradually brings them under greater and greater control until they are emptied of the bulk of their pathological emotion and can be accepted in life situations." Lemert and Van Riper called their treatment "cathartic" and apparently extended it to the utilization of "real life" situations in

---

[1] James S. Greene (1947), late Director, National Hospital for Speech Disorders, expressed a prevalent view when he said: "In working with stutterers, it has been found that the best therapists are those who have been speech sufferers themselves and have worked their own problem through successfully." Our experience in working through transference reactions, an example of which we shall subsequently describe, causes us to doubt the wisdom of this statement.

the community. They reported that "One girl in a candy shop has been employed to good advantage because she always responded to stuttering by an explosion of laughter." They recognized the danger inherent in their method of precipitating ego-disrupting states.

The most extensive experience with group psychotherapy for stutterers is that of the staff of the National Hospital for Speech Disorders founded by the late Dr. James Sonnett Greene. According to the present Medical Director, Dr. Lynwood Heaver (1954), group psychotherapy has been used in the treatment of stutterers for thirty years at their hospital. Greene's (1935, 1939, 1942, and 1947) approach was a truly electic one. In 1935 he called it "open door" psychiatry. He described the patient consulting with the doctor in a large room with the door open so that the physician could call in other patients who happened to be passing. He felt this diminished the distorted importance the patient attached to his own problems. He reasoned that since stutterers were afraid of social contacts "we reverse the situation by bringing society to the stutterer." This was enhanced by automatic membership in clubs devoted to debating, dramatics, etc. In 1942 Greene clearly stated that "group therapy is the most important factor in the treatment of the stutterer." His efforts were directed toward having "the patient realize his biologic limitations and to effect a harmonious compromise between those limitations and the demands of the everyday environment." In 1947 he recommended exposing each patient to several different groups and several different therapists. This was accomplished by graduating patients from smaller "low pressure" groups to larger advanced ones, gradually increasing the environmental pressure in proportion to the patient's growing ability to withstand it. Greene strongly recommended that the therapist should frequently restate (presumably to the patient) the basic goal: "to treat the personality as a whole and not the symptom." At the same time he said: "speech re-education, carried out in the group medium is introduced to give the patient an opportunity to 'act against his symptom' and to prove to him that in a state of emotional equilibrium he can verbalize normally. Thus, by repeatedly and successfully facing the situation toward which he has had most anxiety, he gradually breaks down his fear response to it."

Glasner and Dahl (1952) consider group therapy for the mothers a vital part of their successful prophylactic program for preschool age stutterers. Conrad and Peacher (1954) have utilized psychodrama in their work with prepubertal and adolescent patients. They were very gratified with the results of analytically oriented interview group psychotherapy for the mothers of the stuttering youngsters. Their description of the psychology of the mothers of stutterers corresponds to that of Glauber's (1952).

We (1954) have attempted to describe the atmosphere of utter despair that prevails in initially meeting a group of adult male stutterers in psychoanalytically oriented group psychotherapy. In our experience this reaction has not been limited to this virtually self-selective group.[2] The majority of the patients (there were initially eleven but it soon dropped to seven, at which number it became stabilized), had received various types of treatment for their speech difficulties over the years. They were told that self-understanding was the goal of our weekly one-and-one-half-hour meetings and that this understanding might favorably affect their stuttering. The patients were asked to express themselves without reservation.

At the outset the members of the group were extremely tense and anxious. They did not know what to expect, and were reluctant to say anything other than some labored words about their symptom. The atmosphere of pessimism was most depressing. All felt that nothing could be done for them and repeatedly said that stuttering was an unbearable tragedy ruining their lives.

From the very beginning this group of strangers formed a cohesive band that seemed to look upon the psychotherapist as an outsider who could not possibly understand their problem. The picture presented was one of a long-suffering, persecuted minority group. Their concept of how stuttering could be overcome by the individual was striking in its uniformity: they all expressed the opinion that the symptom should be dealt with violently. They felt if they were strong, they could force themselves to stop stuttering by means of "cutting it out" and "ripping it away." They said they were unable to accomplish this only because they "lacked the strength," had "no guts," or were "too inferior."

The psychotherapist tried to encourage the group, but this seemed to cause the men to become more resentful. The therapist found himself fighting to extend a ray of hope to the group. He offered the interpretation that each was prejudiced against himself, and perhaps, if as individuals each could accept and be proud of himself, including his stuttering, that would be his first step toward overcoming it. The group

2 The group was organized by Georgianna M. Peacher, Ph.D., Speech Consultant in the Department of Psychiatry, Temple University School of Medicine and Hospital. The authors would again like to express their appreciation to Dr. Peacher for encouraging this undertaking and for the interest she has shown in its progress. Without her cooperation this study would not have been possible.

reacted as a unit, saying that this substantiated their feeling that the psychotherapist did not understand them at all.

Most interpretations at first dealt with this transference problem. Feeling themselves different from other people and believing others to be critical and intolerant of them, they banded together cohesively. Not only did they feel different from the therapist but also reacted as though they were inferior to him. He attempted to get the group to reveal their feelings; however, they remained rather sullen and lacked spontaneity. The absence of the usual social amenities, such as saying "hello" and "good-by," was very obvious.

After approximately three months the pathological transference reaction reached a climax and the men were able to talk about their difficulty. With vehemence they said it was the fault of the psychotherapist. Some said it was because he was older than they; that he did not stutter; that they felt as though he were a teacher. Others said that he was trying to be a boss or overseer. Their unreasonable attitude, approaching absurdity, caused the group to realize that their behavior was unjustified. The unreality of their attitude was discusssed with them in terms of a transference reaction. The psychotherapist pointed out that he had never wanted to take the lead and had pleaded with them, to no avail, to take the initiative. However, they had forced him into an authoritative position. It was their usual way of reacting to people whom they felt were older or were in authority. They immediately realized the validity of these statements and supplied confirmatory associations in discussing their reactions to teachers, bosses, etc.

We also recognized that despite their resentment toward authority, the patients were very quick to take a back seat and let someone else be boss; but at the same time each and every one of them was eager to be the boss. This had been evident in the therapeutic situation in that whenever the psychotherapist refused to be placed in the role of a leader, one of the group would set himself up as one. As a rule this new self-appointed leader endeavored to emulate the psychotherapist. As this had been discussed from time to time, all recognized it; and after this one hectic session, the transference problem was never again particularly troublesome. From that point on the patients said "hello" and "good-by" to the therapist. The spontaneity of the group increased, and there was a gradual working through of their conflicts.

The psychotherapist could have selected the simplest path and completely ignored the transference problem. But he chose to use it as the focal point of treatment. This was accomplished by repeatedly confronting the men with their reactions, their hesitancies, their tensions, and their fear and distaste for talking. In the earliest phase of treatment when the above-described transference problem was at its height, this was carried to the extreme by pointing out to them that in view of their perseveration on their symptom it would be appropriate to call them "Mr. Stutterer."

At this point, in a nonanalytic treatment the psychotherapist might have spared no efforts to make the patients feel at ease by ignoring their manifestations of hostility, and being friendly. He could have shaken hands with them, encouraged them, supplied food to them, etc. This would have relegated to the background the pathological reaction manifested in the early phase of therapy. However, such suppression of the transference problem would have deprived us of our best therapeutic device. The persistence of the individual men in treatment, the stability of the group, and the eventual beneficial results speak for the achievement of this method of treatment.

With the gradual working through of the spontaneous transference reaction, we had an increasingly greater opportunity to study and interpret dynamics. Early in treatment, paradoxical as it may seem, our patients manifested a universal effort to conform to what they perceived as authority. In the third session several of the men said they had been trying to find pride in their stuttering but were having difficulty in doing so. There was also evidence that they were trying to memorize by rote what had transpired in the sessions. The psychotherapist interpreted this and discussed blind conforming with the group. This led to a group discussion about being easily influenced. There was an obvious tendency for each man to speak in terms of the group rather than as an individual. This was evident from the outset as manifested by their use of the words "we" and "us" rather than "I" and "me." It was only on rare occasions that a patient would take exception to another group member's speaking about his individual problems in this collective manner. This rather consistent tendency to universalize was pointed out repeatedly by the therapist.

As early as the third session spontaneous discussion of dreams appeared as one of the men dated the onset of his stuttering to a fall on the spine at the age of 13 years. Following this he had recurrent dreams of falling over Niagara Falls which he said were not at all frightening. After this initial recollection by one of their number a succession of dreams was reported voluntarily by others. Most of these dreams were recurrent and dated back to childhood. Each dream reported seemed to stimulate others in the group to relate a similar type of dream.

One patient said that when he was five years old he had a dream that he still has occasionally where he sees his mother as a towering monster that frightens him a great deal. This particular man had previously said that he conformed so easily because his home had been such a happy one. Another reported the following recurrent dream. "I am crawling through a tunnel that has water on the floor. The tunnel gets smaller and smaller and I am just barely able to squeeze out at the end. When I come out, I walk into sunlight, air, and a large crowd of people. There is a train on the tracks about a hundred yards away. I am about to board that train and leave, but somebody is following me and that is very unpleasant."

The group's associations related to escape, sex, and hiding. The psychotherapist contributed thoughts about the birth fantasy and also pointed out the similarity in all of the dreams, namely, the theme of a threatening mother figure. At this point the man who had reported the tunnel dream suddenly remembered another one in which he was being smothered and not able to breathe. The apparently similar themes in the successive dreams reported in this early session impressed us with the rather marked suggestibility in the group.[3]

In the early sessions when one man stuttered, a deadly silence would descend upon all the others. No one would dare to try to supply the blocked word, even though it might have been very obvious. This was highlighted and discussed. On one such occasion when the group was in a friendly mood, a word was supplied to a man. He accepted the word but said sadly, "I don't like having something taken out of my mouth. It is as though you are taking the word away from me." The interpretation was made that the intention had been to give him something, i.e., to supply the missing word and there was no desire to take something away from him. Much later when a man stuttered, the group did not become rigidly tense. With increasing frequency, they tried to make things easier for the man having difficulty by supplying the words.

One gains the impression that the stutterer has formed an object relation to the spoken word, as though words represent an internalized object —the mother. The stutterer is in conflict as to whether or not he should give up the internalized object. It is as though the word is a part of the stutterer that he dreads losing. The stutterer's relationship to his words suggests the symbiotic relationship of mother and child described by Glauber (1952).

As treatment progressed, it became clear that to these men the organ of speech was more important than anything else in life. One man carried this so far as to unfavorably compare himself as a stutterer with deaf and

---

[3] We recognize this may be also a manifestation of a group function as well as a reflection of the homogeneity of our group.

dumb people. Granting the value of good speech, we nevertheless felt that our patients invested far more importance in their speech than reality warranted. In subsequent discussions the patients themselves equated their overvaluation of perfect speech with the importance one invests in a phallus. The stutterer feels himself to be castrated but unconsciously displaces this feeling of castration to the disturbance in his speech.[4] This was clearly brought out by one of our patients who said he was fearful that he might stop stuttering. If this should happen, he felt he would be an entirely different person. He made it clear that this feeling was not to be compared with one of a person who has a plastic operation on his nose to remove a defect. The change that loss of stuttering would bring about in him would be much more radical and total. Other patients confirmed this feeling. It was as though the stuttering represented a defective person rather than a circumscribed defect so that the stutterer does not feel complete unto himself. It suggests the symbiotic relationship mentioned above.

It was in this same hour that the patients spoke spontaneously of castration fantasies. One man spoke of his tonsillectomy, another of a broken arm, and another of his fear of broken twigs. These were all brought out as first childhood memories. The stutterer libidinizes his speech in a manner that most other people libidinize the phallus. This phenomenon had been described many times in the literature (Bryan, 1922, 1925; Fluegel, 1925; Jones, 1926; Lewin, 1933). It seemed clear to us that stuttering represented castration. This probably explains why one who no longer stutters keeps seeking treatment for his alleged stuttering. It is really not relief from stuttering that he seeks.

It has long been recognized that speech is a sensitive reflector of emotional states (Brody, 1943). A bashful person loses his tongue; amazement leaves one speechless; an angry person bites his tongue; a tongue-tied lover is not unusual; and one hardly expects a person in a state of sexual excitement to emote smoothly. The stutterer, to a much greater degree than the average person, uses his speech to express emotion. In a way the patients in our group resemble average people in various emotional states whose speech had been affected. It is as though the stutterer has lost sight of the primary purpose of speech, namely, the communication of meanings.

It is commonly known that emotions influence respiration (Alexander and Saul, 1940). A surprise leaves one breathless; people get a "load off their chests," and then, after "sighing in relief," are able to "breathe

---

4 It was remindful of Moses' reference in Exodus (6:30) to his speech defect as "uncircumcised lips."

easily." Smooth respiration is required for smooth speech. Disturbance in respiration is intimately related to the stutterer's disturbed relationship to words. Functioning respiration is newly introduced to the organism immediately or almost immediately after it passes through the birth canal. It is commonly thought of as being synonymous with an existence separate from the mother. Respiration is stimulated by the powerful process of birth and is often assisted by other strong stimuli, such as a slap or medication. Since speech for the stutterer expresses a relationship with the mother, the respiration of the stutterer inevitably is affected. The stutterer appears to be fixated at an oral-respiratory stage of libidinal development.

Abraham (1924) described some neurotics that used speech primarily as a mode of projecting affects that they fear to express at the same time that they insist on forcing them out. It can be compared to the child who regressively expresses defiance by refusing to surrender his overvalued feces in response to his mother's request (Spring, 1935).

We are impressed with certain similarities between the respiratory and anal stages (Binger, 1937; Greenacre, 1952). The anal zone is the only erogenous area where the associated product (feces) is erotized along with the mucous membrane. This is markedly different from the oral and genital stages of development when the products of the respective zones are invested with relatively little importance. Our patients, in their libidinization of respiration, erotized not only functioning respiration and the vocal apparatus, but also the product, speech, was highly significant. There is much to indicate that the parents of stutterers have been too interested in the speech of their children.

Discussion about feelings of obligation, overconscientiousness, feelings of guilt, and self-consciousness were the most frequent topics in our group. The men were constantly striving to live up to the demands of the ego ideal and felt uneasy whenever they fell short of this ideal. We were impressed that the outstanding conflict that disturbed each and every man of our group was a severe superego. Despite the early negative group transference reaction, each man had extreme difficulty in expressing hostility. They were obedient, submissive people who, without exception, characterized themselves as having been "very good children." Their superficial hostile attitude was a reaction formation against passivity.

In conclusion, all the ramifications of the etiology of stuttering are not thoroughly understood. Therefore, treatment rests on an empirical basis, and the results are difficult to evaluate. The only area in which an opportunity for basic change is afforded the patient is via the medium of psychological therapy. Our experience with group psychotherapy has convinced us that stuttering results when a forbidden feeling approaches verbal expression. The symptom of stuttering represents the expression of, the defense against, and the punishment for, forbidden affects. The stutterer feels free of castration anxiety since he already has mutilated himself. He feels free of separation anxiety because he holds onto his overvalued words. The stutterer should be helped to tolerate a more direct expression of his feelings. Then speech would no longer be treated as though it were a vehicle for forbidden affects. Under such circumstances there would be no need to cut off the offending part. This would enable the production of an easy, free, smooth flow of speech which of necessity would be correlated with rhythmic respiration. The stutterer could again breathe easily and accept and enjoy his independent existence. Group psychotherapy is of value in achieving this.

BIBLIOGRAPHY

Abraham, K. (1924), The Influence of Oral Eroticism on Character Formation. *Selected Papers on Psycho-Analysis*. London: Hogarth Press, 1949.

Alexander, F. and Saul, L. (1940), Respiration and Personality. A Preliminary Report. *Psychosom. Med.*, 2:110-119.

American Medical Association (1952), *Standard Nomenclature of Disease and Operations, 4th Edition*. New York: The Blakiston Company.

Backus, O. L. and Dunn, H. M. (1947), Intensive Group Therapy in Speech Rehabilitation. *J. Speech Dis.*, 12:39-60.

Barber, V. (1939), Studies in the Psychology of Stuttering: XV. Chorus Reading as a Distraction in Stuttering. *J. Speech Dis.*, 4:371-383.

Binger, C. (1937), The Psychobiology of Breathing. *Ann. Int. Med.*, 11:195-208.

Brody, M. W. (1943), Neurotic Manifestations of the Voice. *Psychoanal. Quart.*, 12:371-380.

—— and Harrison, S. I. (1954), Group Psychotherapy with Male Stutterers. *Int. J. Group Psychother.*, 4:154-162.

Bryan, D. (1922), A Note on the Tongue. *Int. J. Psychoanal.*, 3:481-482.

—— (1925), Speech and Castration; Two Unusual Analytic Hours. *Int. J. Psychoanal.*, 6:317-323.

Conrad, S. W. and Peacher, G. M. (1954), Personal Communication.

Fenichel, O. (1945). *The Psychoanalytic Theory of Neurosis*. New York: Norton.

Fluegel, J. C. (1925), A Note on the Phallic Significance of the Tongue and Speech. *Int. J. Psychoanal.*, 6:209-215.

Glasner, P. J. and Dahl, M. F. (1952), Stuttering—A Prophylactic Program for its Control. *Am. J. Pub. Health*, 42:1111.

Glauber, I. P. (1952), Dynamic Therapy for the Stutterer. In: *Specialized Techniques in Psychotherapy*. New York: Basic Books.

Greenacre, P. (1952). *Trauma, Growth, and Personality*. New York: Norton.

Greene, J. S. (1935), Treatment of the Stutter Type Personality in a Medical-Social Clinic. *J.A.M.A.*, 104:2239-2242.

—— (1939), Speech and Voice Disorders. *Med. World*, 57:719-722.

—— (1942), Stuttering: A Psychosomatic Disorder. *N. Y. State J. Med.*, 42:1561-1564.

—— (1947), Interview Group Psychotherapy for Speech Disorders. In: *The Practice of Group Therapy*, ed. S. R. Slavson. New York: International Universities Press.

Heaver, L. (1954), Personal communication.

Jones, E. (1926), Deprivation of the Senses as a Castration Symbol. *Int. J. Psychoanal.*, 7:236-237.

Lemert, E. M. and van Riper, C. (1944), The Use of Psychodrama in the Treatment of Speech Defects. *Sociometry*, 7:190-195.

Lewin, B. D. (1933), The Body as Phallus. *Psychoanal. Quart.*, 2:24-47.

Spring, W. J. (1935), Words and Masses: A Pictorial Contribution to the Psychology of Stammering. *Psychoanal. Quart.*, 4:244-258.

Chapter VII

ALLERGIES

•

The allergic diseases are a group of clinical syndromes. The most important are bronchial asthma, hay fever, allergic eczema, urticaria, and gastrointestinal allergy. Although different physiological systems are involved in these various syndromes, as, for example, the lower respiratory tract in bronchial asthma, the upper respiratory tract in hay fever, the skin in eczema and urticaria, and the gastrointestinal tract in gastrointestinal allergy, it is generally accepted that all the allergic syndromes have in common the same underlying physical pattern.

In individuals suffering from allergic diseases there is usually demonstrable a physical allergic constitution. It is evidenced by the presence of reagins (allergic antibodies), by eosinophilia, and by a genetically significant family history. Individuals possessing such an allergic constitution show an abnormal susceptibility to allergic sensitization by ordinary protein substances in the diet and in the environment. Once sensitized to these substances, exposure to them, whether by inhalation, ingestion or injection, may precipitate one or several allergic syndromes.

Allergic syndromes, however, may also be induced, prolonged, aggravated or made intractible by emotional factors. Furthermore, regardless of the physiological system involved, these emotional factors have in common the same underlying psychodynamic pattern.

By psychoanalytic technique, Eduardo Weiss (1922), French and Alexander (1941), Fenichel (1945), and others have shown that the asthmatic is generally a passive dependent individual. Foremost among the component factors in his psychological make-up is the sense of having been deprived of maternal love and affection early in life. Miller and Baruch (1950a) have confirmed this observation, not only in individuals suffering from asthma but in those suffering from other allergic diseases as well. In a study of emotional traumata precipitating various types of allergic syndromes in a group of allergic children, it became evident that regardless of the disease syndrome, all the patients had taken the trauma preceding its onset essentially as the loss of maternal love. That this feeling was usually on a realistic basis of actual maternal rejection was shown by further study. For example, in a statistical analysis of rejection as expressed by the mothers of 100 allergic children, 97 per cent gave overt evidence of rejection. In 96 of the cases, the rejection was present before the first onset of symptoms, and in two thirds of the cases it appeared to have preceded the child's birth (Miller and Baruch, 1951).

That this emotional trauma, moreover, brought in its wake inordinate affect hunger became clear also in these investigations and in subsequent observations by Miller and Baruch of 354 allergic patients psychologically studied.[1] In diagnostic and therapeutic sessions, in both children and adults, and in patients suffering from all types of allergic diseases, affect hunger has appeared universally as a dynamic entity. Along with this, as residual of the earlier oral deprivation emanating out of the original maternal rejection, an intense fear of further rejection usually persists. In addition, with affect hunger as a basic stimulus, hostility is universally generated. Almost as frequently, however, the allergic patient has great difficulty in facing and in bringing out his hostility, especially the hostility he feels toward his parents, and most particularly toward the mother.

To comprehend the significance of this fact, in the psychodynamic pattern of the allergic which is important in its implications for therapy, the means by which the allergic handles his hostility needs to be more clearly seen. Toward this end come data from a study comparing a group of 90 allergic with a control group of nonallergic children (Miller and Baruch, 1950b). Differences in the two groups became manifest when hostility to parents was analyzed in terms of its direction, or vector, the object or target against which it was aimed, and the energy output characterizing its expression.

One way of expressing hostility toward parents is for it to come out directly without subterfuge or hiding. In temper tantrums, in defiance and in name calling, for instance, the fight is openly against the parent. The vector of the hostility is outward from the self. The target is frankly the parent. This can be termed *direct hostility*. Another way of expressing hostility is by indirection. In bed wetting, refusal of food, whining and untidiness, for instance, the vector is still outward, the target is still the

[1] This is in line with what Margolin (1954) has found to be true in the asthmatics observed during anaclitic therapy.

parents but the hostility is unavowed. This can be termed *indirect hostility*. Still another way of expressing hostility is by displacement. In teasing or hitting other children, in cruelty to animals and in destruction of property, as examples, the vector of the hostile expression is still outward away from the self, but the manifest target is changed. Such expression can be identified as *displaced hostility*. A final way of expressing hostility is to turn it *against the self*. Self-condemnation, accident proneness, ideas of suicide, nail biting, head banging and the like are examples of this.[2] Here the vector has changed. The direction is no longer *out* but *in*. The manifest target has also changed. It is no longer an external object but is now the self.

When the group of allergic children was compared with the nonallergic control, marked contrasts were evident in relation to these various means of expressing hostility. The expression of *direct hostility* to the parents, and particularly to the mother, was the most difficult for the allergic patients to bring out. Only 20 per cent of the allergics manifested this direct type of hostile behavior in contrast to 83 per cent of the nonallergics (critical ratio = 9.4).[3]

Although the expression of *indirect hostility* by the allergics was more common (45 per cent evidenced it), it was still significantly less frequent than in the nonallergics who manifested it in 100 per cent of the cases studied (critical ratio = 10.3).

Displaced hostility was somewhat more readily expressed by the allergics, 63 per cent employing this method. But even this number bore significant contrast with the nonallergics' 100 per cent (critical ratio = 7.2).

However, when *hostility against the self* was compared in the two groups, there was a striking reversal in the data: 55 per cent of the allergic children evidenced behavioral symptoms of hostility against the self as opposed to 28 per cent of the nonallergics (critical ratio = 3.3). In other words, the allergics turned their hostility inward, back on themselves, to a significantly greater extent. In the light of these data their somatic symptoms could be recognized as a part of the pattern of turning hostility back on themselves.

From the above statistical comparison it becomes clear that dynamic forces are operative in the inhibition of the outward expression of hostility in the allergic child to a significantly greater degree than in the

2 In the statistical part of the study cited here, the allergic symptoms were not tabulated or counted as hostility against self, not only because they were inherent in the sample but also because one purpose of the study was to explore how frequently in other respects the organism tended to injure itself.

3 In samples of 50 or more, if the critical ratio is approximately 2.6 or above, the probability is less than 1 in 100 that the difference could have occurred by chance.

nonallergic. This was evidenced also in the degree of affect with which hostility was expressed, that is in the amount of energy mobilized for its expression. The allergic child "blocks" his hostility. In most instances he is what his parents term a "good child." He is nonaggressive, timid and clinging. In diagnostic play sessions he brings out hostility with reluctance or withholds it entirely. Evidence of such blocking was found in 92 per cent of the allergic children studied. In contrast it was seen in only 17 per cent of the nonallergic controls (critical ratio = 12.8). Of the allergic children, 25 per cent showed no overt evidence of hostility at all.

In short, the allergic child does not dare to express his hostile feelings to the same extent or as freely as does the nonallergic child. He more commonly generates guilt and anxiety in relation to his hostility and more frequently is in conflict about its expression. Furthermore, although projectively he may evidence the presence of hostile feelings toward the mother in particular, he cannot bring this out as *direct hostility,* frankly shown or stated, admitting the mother as the object or target. He must utilize various defenses instead.

In the writers' work with adult allergic patients, the same psycho-dynamic pattern has been discernible. In hypnotherapy Harold Rosen obtained a similar picture.[4] He found that persistent affect hunger was present and that great hostility directed especially toward the mother was also present. The latter came out with tremendous intensity during hypnosis but in waking states was blocked. This blocking of hostility may be taken as a measure of the intensity of the fear of further rejection. It mitigates against solid, satisfying relationships and keeps alive the affect hunger. This in turn stimulates more hostility against which indirect expression, displacement, repression, and inversion against the self are characteristic defenses. This psychodynamic pattern, as has been stated, is a basic one in all the allergic syndromes. It points to problems which are inherent in any psychotherapy with allergics.

To summarize then, in terms of the psychodynamic pattern, psycho-therapy with the allergic patient involves four major necessities: (1) to deal with the patient's affect hunger; (2) to deal with the patient's fear of rejection; (3) to reduce the anxiety that makes the patient block the expression and even the awareness of the anger within him; (4) to help the patient release his anger so that it brings harm neither to others nor to himself, and to lead him eventually to recognize the actual and true object of his anger without unrealistic anxiety so loaded as to pre-cipitate his disease.

4 Reported in a paper presented at the American College of Allergists. Miami, Florida, 1954. See also Rosen (1953).

In terms of achieving the above necessities, group therapy with allergic patients has certain inherent values. Some of these are unique; some it shares with individual therapy; others facilitate individual therapy. There are also dangers in the group process which must be guarded against.

In dealing with the allergic patient's affect hunger, the group has particular value. The visibly sick patient entering the group is, ordinarily, met with less resistance than a "stranger" whose suffering is not so evident. Characteristically the first reaction of the group toward him is that of sympathy and concern over his physical symptoms, and the patient usually equates this reaction in his fantasy to the affection he has always craved. Thus, initially, the group feeds the patient's affect hunger in a manner similar perhaps to that in which the activity group feeds the child's "social hunger." As a result the patient feels in his initial response to the group that psychotherapy has something positive to offer him. In view of his particular emotional pattern, this feeling holds especial importance. It counteracts his fear of being rejected and, at the beginning of therapy, gives him enough to go on so that he need not back away.

Obviously in such a state of affairs, there is also the inherent danger of prolonging the patient's neurosis for the secondary gains he achieves. But, since the group process is a dynamic one, the initial sympathy and concern over symptoms does not remain static. With the help of the therapist, the physical symptoms are gradually seen as having emotional meanings. Then, undue and unrealistic sympathy is usually reorganized on more of a reality basis. In its place comes an acceptance of the patient as a fellow group member, or, in other words, as a person who has emotional problems similar to those of others in the group. This in its turn assigns him an entity in the group and helps to integrate him into it.

The patient then begins to see that he can get response from group members without resorting to his physical symptoms. In fact he gets more response as he discloses what he feels. He senses a kind of group solidarity, albeit unconscious, of respect for the person who has courage to show himself as he really is. After repeated signs of this in the group, he begins to seek an answer to his affect hunger, not as heretofore in sympathy, which prolongs dependence, but in the more vigorous and vital nourishment that acceptance brings. In other words, he gradually comes to distinguish between the invalidity of symptom-focused sympathy as a sign of affection and the validity of emotional acceptance that accords him as a person greater dignity and worth.

Along with occasions where the group accepts his feelings, come occasions when the group furnishes him with active support and direct commendation, approval and affection on a reality basis. There are such remarks, for instance, as "The hives you came in with this afternoon disappeared as soon as you stopped pretending. Not a sign of them now!" "Your skin's so much better than it was six months ago!" Or, "What you did there surely took lots of guts. You stood right up for your rights! And you used to be such a sheep."

However, what appears to hold utmost significance to the allergic patient does not lie in the response that he gets fron one or another of the group members. It transcends such individual response. It has to do with the response of group-as-a-whole and with the entity with which he endows the group-as-a-whole, an entity that is greater than any of its separate parts (Foulkes, 1950). The group-as-a-whole is not merely a cluster of individuals. It is *his* group, *his* home, as it were, and more even. It seems to personify for him the good mother for whom he has always wished. This fits in with the concept of the group as "mother" suggested by Berne (1954).

Because the group is a group and not any one person, and because it is different from any one person, it is easier to keep its identity separated from the threat which the allergic has felt in his contacts with any and all persons. To him, now, this impersonalized mother figure of group-as-a whole offers a haven he has never had. The intimacy which Erikson (1950) stresses as a human need is experienced. In consequence, the patient's sense of isolation decreases and his ego is fortified to move ahead.

As a result he can gradually develop a capacity to subject his persistent feelings of rejection to the test of reality. Heretofore he has never done this. Instead, he has characteristically denied, on the conscious level, the deep sense of being rejected which he has felt unconsciously. Such denial in turn has intensified his anxiety. For as long as the feeling of being rejected remains unconscious, he encapsulates with it a fantasy of himself as a helpless infant; and he keeps with it, too, all the threats that accompany an infant's being deserted by its mother. He keeps alive within himself the continuous fear of further rejection too painful to face. He has constantly anticipated rejection, and he has found it often where it did not realistically exist. Every criticism and difference of opinion has spelled total rejection to him, too dangerous to face.

In the group, as he becomes amalgamated into it, the individual members naturally begin to differ and make critical comments. Sometimes these comments possess validity for him; at other times they merely represent projections and feelings that other members are displacing onto him. He sees, however, that other members do the same sort of thing to each other. And gradually, through precept, example and interpretations from both therapist and group members, he catches a glimpse of the fact that he has taken too much as total rejection. He begins a struggle to put things in their proper proportion and place. He can do this now since he has found that in spite of real or seeming rejection by individual members, the group-as-a-whole still receives him. He is not rejected by it. He still belongs.

In terms of his fear of being rejected by the therapist, the group also plays a role. When the allergic patient sees the therapist individually, his characteristic reaction at the beginning of treatment is to make a rapid positive transference. This he needs in order to feel the therapist's support when he first enters a group. Later, in treatment, as the therapist assumes a more interpretive role, the patient's fear of rejection is remobilized. However, in the group, the fear of rejection by the therapist is diluted.

It is true that the patient is apt to take as rejection, when the therapist gives his attention to other group members. But, hand in hand with this, his fear of *total* rejection grows less acute. Not only has he seen other group members stand up to or berate the therapist, but his own need to be accepted by the therapist as the all-important parent figure has been dispersed. The group-as-a-whole vies with the therapist in its importance and makes the therapist less threateningly "big." As one allergic woman expressed it, "I'm not so afraid of you in the group as I am by myself. You're not so all-important. Somehow I don't have to keep making such a good impression on you and I'm not as afraid of what you might say."

Such elements in the group process make it possible for the patient to accept interpretations more clearly, to have more courage in working things through. Thus he gradually becomes able to leave behind him his self-imposed blindness, and finally to see and face the evidence he brings in, which shows that his mother actually did reject him. He has developed sufficient ego strength to recognize that it need no longer make him an impotent, helpless, amputated infant. Nor does it need to make him anticipate rejection in every situation wherever he goes. Moreover, when he recognizes that his constant fear of rejection was based on the fear of losing infantile supplies, he begins to see also that the secondary gains he attempted to achieve through physical illness were not only inappropriate but harmful to himself. Simultaneously, as the anxiety over rejection is reduced, the patient is more able to accept the fact that he is angry. He begins to unblock the hostility that he had repressed.

In this connection, however, it must be remembered, that the mere unblocking of hostility is in itself not enough. There has been repeated evidence that symptoms decrease only when the allergic patient has developed enough ego strength to permit the expression of hostility without engendering undue, unrealistic anxiety. Furthermore, he needs to express hostility with the vector outward. He must also be able to admit who the real object of his anger is, and to bring out feelings aimed at this target directly, not circuitously through indirection, nor by displaced anger. He needs insight so that the object of his hostility is not evaded but is consciously faced (Baruch, 1952; Miller and Baruch, 1953, 1954).

Nevertheless, expressions of indirect and displaced hostility do provide stepping stones from anger turned inward to the final achievement of anger outwardly and directly expressed. The group experience gives the patient varied opportunities to move ahead gradually to this goal, although for the allergic this phase of the group experience also holds particular dangers. As with other individuals, the group stimulates the allergic patient to more outward modes of hostile expression. He hears and sees others opening up on feelings which he echoes in his unconscious and this serves as encouragement and sanction for him.

When a patient remains silent, other group members encourage him to talk. But, if his silence persists, another trend usually appears: some begin to show resentment. They say: "We expose ourselves. Why don't you?" "You think because you're sick you can get away with it." "To me, your silence is like a whip." In other words, some react to and identify that ingredient in silence which actually is hostility indirectly expressed. They react in a similar manner to physical symptoms if they continue to occur in the group. One group member once said to another: "I wish I had something I could fall back on like you do to get the center of the stage with, and cut all the rest of us out."

When such attacks come, other members may rise to protect the target of their resentment. Even so, he may still take the onslaught as too grave a rejection in which case he retreats. Then the therapist must intervene, recognizing that at such moments the allergic needs concrete confirmation that a good parent figure is present to protect him from being overwhelmed by anxiety and repressed hostility. For if they do, the allergic patient may go into such a severe exacerbation of physical symptoms as to threaten his life.[5]

On the other hand, if he has developed ego strength sufficient to counterattack, the danger subsides. It is as if he were expressing his hostility toward his "bad mother" with the good mother still present to

[5] At times such an emergency can be forestalled by arranging immediately for an individual session to provide the support of proof that the therapist is not rejecting.

protect him. He has advanced far enough so that he can handle the situation by beaming such projections onto the group-as-a-whole or onto individuals in it. At least the hostility is directly discharged and aimed at a present target and with this, the exacerbation can completely clear. Occurring under the very eyes of the therapist and other members of the group, the patient's attention may be called to it, providing a striking and convincing evidence that the exacerbation is a manifestation of hostility.

A patient may also attack members directly when they offer advice or show overconcern about his symptoms, both of which throw him back into the status of a small child with an engulfing, overprotecting mother. This in its turn can lead him into recognition that his mother's overconcern and overprotection were not really what he wanted or needed and that it engendered his resentment because it did not really represent love. Such experiences are often the basis for recalling memories of anger and resentment toward his own mother at such manifestations of overprotection as her insistence on meticulous dieting, restrictions of play, unpleasant medical attention, and complaints about the expense and bother of caring for him. Gradually these lead to insight and memories which prove his mother's rejection and activate anger directly focused on her without too great anxiety or guilt.

So far we have dealt with direct group psychotherapy of the allergic adult. Another phase of group psychotherapy in allergic diseases is group psychotherapy with parents of allergic children.[6] All that has been said concerning the psychodynamics and the resultant therapeutic indications regarding allergic patients is confirmed by the experience in group psychotherapy with parents of allergic children. One may follow each step in the psychodynamic pattern of the allergic individual by a kind of mirror image in the parent. One sees in the parent those very feelings which have activated the emotional problems seen in the allergic patient himself.

By what appears in the parent's emotional life as brought out in the group experience, the child's affect hunger is confirmed as a reaction to realistic maternal rejection. Furthermore, in psychotherapy with the mothers, there appears repeated evidence of the overprotection that comes

6 In their practice the writers have treated allergic children individually, while their parents, either the mother or both mother and father, were simultaneously either in individual therapy, in group, or in combined individual and group treatment. In some cases, therapy with the child has been omitted and only the parent or parents were treated. To date forty-one parents of allergic children have been treated as members of nonhomogeneous groups, that is not comprised solely of parents of allergic children.

in part as a reaction formation to their rejecting attitude. This is in line with a previous study where maternal overprotection was overtly definitive in 57 per cent of the mothers of allergic children in contrast to overprotection as demonstrated in 10 per cent of the mothers of nonallergic controls (critical ratio=5.5) (Miller and Baruch, 1948).

Etiologically, maternal rejection usually is a reflection of the rejection the mother herself has suffered from her own mother (Miller and Baruch, 1950c). As a result, she has retained a defensive attachment and intense hostility to her own mother and an unresolved and deeply repressed oedipal attachment to her father. Her own life stresses have created an intense affect hunger in her own psyche and an exaggerated need to appear as a good child herself. There is also present an overload of hostility to her own mother which she has ordinarily repressed.

In short, the mother of the allergic child is an immature person for whom the role of motherhood presents grave difficulties. In her immaturity she keeps seeking a good mother for herself, all the while fearing a bad mother. Onto her child she projects both the good mother and the bad mother images. Her child becomes the good mother when he serves her as a source of supply. When he is "cuddly" and close, passive and obedient, he enhances her sense of being good. It is then that she has moments of seeing him as a mother by whom she is being emotionally fed. At such moments she engulfs him, as it were, seeking more and more gratifications from him. But in this process she nullifies him as a person so that he feels virtually killed.

In addition, her own sadomasochism invariably enters and takes over. She must compulsively do too much for him and makes his dependency into too big a burden. He in his turn senses her feelings and increases his plaintive demands. Then he becomes the bad mother to her. She feels she can never satisfy him and this increases her own sense of being "bad" and makes her reject him all the more. Despite her protests, his remaining ill is a response to her unconscious animosity. Essentially then, by remaining ill, he acts out her wish.

Thus, if the child goes into therapy without the mother's simultaneous treatment, and if, through his therapy his ego is strengthened enough for him to take tentative steps away from her, she fantasies him even more as the bad mother who rejects her and makes her feel helpless, threatened and unloved. She finds herself also losing out on her own unconscious hostile aim to keep him sick, so that by one subtle means or another, she undermines his therapeutic gains. For these reasons, if for no other, work with the mother is of paramount importance in any psychological treatment of the allergic child. Unless she, herself is in therapy, she continues in her neurotic swing between a rejecting attitude and the defensive overprotection which at one and the same time represents a seeking for love and a sadomasochistic expression of her own repressed hostility.

In her life with her husband a related struggle is pursued. Ordinarily she selects for a husband the type of man on whom she can project a picture shifting between that of a nonthreatening mother and that of a father for whom she still carries strong, unconscious oedipal feelings. On his part, he also is seeking a good mother. In consequence, when he meets her, he often mistakes her demandingness as strength, her masochism as goodness. To her he gives the impression of being gentle and nondemanding. Sometimes along with this he does possess a capacity for true warmth but more often than not this must stay dormant. For, he is a passive dependent person afraid of revealing warmth, lest he betray his feminine component which he fears. In some cases he is in fact so immature that he must avoid fatherhood, even when it has been accomplished, and this leaves the mother holding an unwelcome responsibility with the father cast in the role of another burdensome child.

In other cases, the mother becomes more demanding as time goes on. Because of her own immaturity and her consequent desire to avoid motherhood, she pushes onto the father the responsibility of the child. To this he either accedes with resentment or escapes into immersion in work, in drink, or the like. In still other cases, the mother, because of the unconscious drive to prove herself a good mother and to cover up her rejection, pushes the father away from the children.

There are some families, however, in which the father spontaneously assumes a protective role, attempting to make up for his wife's failure. He is not basically rejecting, but has the desire, often unconscious, to give to his children, almost as if he were belatedly giving to himself, values he has missed. But this too ordinarily fails. Sometimes his wife's increased demands again cause resentment. Sometimes his own fear of feminine identification comes into play. Added to this, sexual adjustment is rarely good. In short, there is so much conflict in the marital situation that even where the father might be able to furnish needed warmth, it comes to naught.

In passing, it should be mentioned that the striking similarity of the parental psychodynamic patterns with those of the child's is not surprising because many of the parents of allergic children are known to be allergic themselves. Whether or not this is the case, the best prognosis has lain in therapy that reaches down into those lifelong conflicts that have produced in the parents their own affect hunger, hostility and inability to provide the love their child needs.

Sometimes, however, relief of a child's symptoms can come with more limited goals. Where pursuit of deeper therapy is not possible, more limited goals may serve as intermediate measures. These are not merely ameliorative. They are perfectly sound and valid therapeutic tasks in terms of the psychodynamic etiology of the parental attitudes, albeit they are focused on the realities surrounding the child. As they are accomplished, the child often gains some relief of physical symptoms and the parents gain some feeling of growth in themselves. These in turn have proved encouraging and have served as incentives for the parents to go deeper into their personal problems, where this is feasible.

One such measure has been to work on an immediate reality basis to alleviate the mother's compulsive overprotection as evidenced in her need to keep on assuming unnecessarily burdensome responsibilities with the child. In the group this has been done by the therapist's calling attention to some of the unnecessary or inadvisable aspects of the child's care. Ordinarily members of the group are quick to follow in citing illogical or needlessly arduous procedures. The therapist's willingness here to step into an authoritarian role is often crucial. When properly timed, a categorical statement from him as to steps which are medically unnecessary has given immediate relief. It is as if he has stepped into the role of good mother who is advising a daughter with firm kindness that she need no longer burden herself quite so much.

A second reality measure lies in freeing the father, if he is warm enough, to help sufficiently with the care of the child so that neither parent needs to feel too burdened. This has been done in individual counseling sessions or in either group or individual therapy sessions with the father while therapy with the mother proceeded.

A boy of three serves as a case in point. He suffered from anorexia and asthma. Food would poison him, he said. He was also terrified of his bath. He would dream repeatedly of a poison-lady coming to drown him. Psychotherapy with the child and both parents was initiated. During its course, the fact emerged that it was neither the food nor the water but rather his mother's unlovingness that engendered the child's basic fear. Through her psychotherapy the mother sought to overcome this. Meanwhile, until she could develop more responsiveness, the father was encouraged to take over the morning and evening meals and the bathing. With his therapist's sanction he proved himself glad and able to step in and do with a good deal of natural warmth what he had thought was not a father's job. As a result of this emotional feeding, the child's overabundant anger diminished to where it grew more normal and could be handled in a healthy fashion. Both the anorexia and the asthma improved.

This brings us to the third immediate reality measure that has shown itself to be advantageous. It is focused on helping the parents to become more accepting of the child's hostility, to abet the child in discharging it verbally or in other harmless channels directly avowing the person who engendered it.

The three-year-old asthmatic boy cited above serves as further example here. At 9:30 one morning the father phoned his therapist. He reported that he and the mother had gone out the previous evening. When they returned at 10, they found the child wheezing. He said, "Nobody loves me." During the night this continued. After the phone call in the morning, the father returned to the child, as the therapist had suggested, and said, "You feel nobody loves you and that naturally makes you mad."

The child said, wheezing, "Be quiet. I'm not mad. Be quiet."

The father said, "It won't make me mad. You can tell me whatever you want to do."

With this the child yelled all of a sudden, "I want to kill you. I'd like to lasso you and choke you round your neck. And I'd like to cut open mother's stomach and hit Mommy and everybody with a baseball bat."

Within forty-five minutes the father phoned that the wheezing had stopped.

In relation to parents becoming able to accept the child's hostility, the group has proven especially helpful. In the group, as has been recognized, the parent comes to see the normalcy and universality of hostility so that the child's hostility directed toward him, or her, comes to hold less threat.

With these reality measures of reducing overt overprotectiveness, of increasing emotional feeding, and of abetting and accepting the child's direct hostility—the parent is often more ready to move on. However, in cases where the hostile wish to keep the child ill is too strong, the reality measures obviously fail.

In any event, as may have been recognized, all of this creates a difficult problem in countertransference. The parent's initial reason for entering therapy is to help the child. Realistically if the child is to be helped, the psychodynamics of his disease must be kept in focus. But if this focus takes precedence over the parent's own needs when the therapist is working with a parent, then the parent is bound to see the therapist as the mother who rejects him. In all contacts with the parent, it is essential for the therapist to feel with and to relate himself to the parent's own needs and to tie in with validity whatever he does or says in terms of these.

To illustrate what has been said, case reports and excerpts from group sessions are quoted below. They illustrate some of the points in relation to the psychodynamics and psychotherapeutics in groups both with allergic patients directly, and with the parents of allergic children.

Case 1: A man of 38, suffering from hay fever, brought a picture which he had painted into a group previously described by Miller and Baruch (1952). The picture showed a baby in a crib, the black figure of a man lying face down in the foreground and a gold-colored woman sitting with a bowl on her knees. Two hands towered up behind the head of the crib and at the foot of the crib a huge mouth bared its teeth. Immediately members of the group began associating to the painting as to a dream. A 40-year-old male asthmatic who had always overemphasized the importance of intellect in himself to cover his emotions said, "The baby has advanced intelligence. Its head is so big. It wants to tell people what it wants and knows but nobody pays any attention . . . [Note the affect hunger and feeling of rejection] . . . It's trapped . . . [The mother engulfing him with her overprotectiveness—a common feeling, as has been seen, among allergics] It wants to get out because it has intellect but it doesn't have strength. The side of the bed is down" . . . [indicating the dependent attitude and the feeling of passivity so characteristic].

A 34-year-old asthmatic remarked, "On every side of me is rejection. My parents then, my wife now. No ears on the child. I'm still trying to close off hostility and rejection around me but I'm conscious of it and it won't work" . . . [manifesting the beginning of insight and acceptance of the fact that he was rejected by mother and wife—both of whom actually did reject him].

A 40-year-old asthmatic woman remarked, "The big mouth is the baby too. She's making a loud noise crying like I wanted to but couldn't". . . [recognizing her block].

The man who had painted the picture began associating, "The baby's mouth is empty and hungry. And his hands are clutched." Then he, too, blocked and could say no more, and in his anxiety he began to sigh deeply.

The next day in an individual session he said, "I did get so frightened I got short of breath. I was very affected by the reactions of the group to my picture last night" . . . [The unexpected "emotional feeding" by the group had touched him deeply, as though the group represented a feeding mother to him. This was corroborated, by the associated material which followed.] "I realize," he went on, "I want warmth so badly I get hay fever when it's cold. I want someone who will really accept me fully with a bosom that is warm and welcoming. Why couldn't she have done it, my mother, even for a little while? . . . And now I want my wife to stroke my head and let me lie in her arms and not make me get up and wash dishes. . . . That baby in the bed is starving and freezing to death while the golden mother just sits self-centered in feeding herself, and the father is nothing more than a shadow on the floor with his back turned." [In this way he epitomized his anger at maternal rejection and implied the wish that his father might provide him with something instead. Later it became evident that his hay fever represented a wish to take in through his nose the substance he longed to get from his father.]

Case 2: L. was a vivacious, affable man of 27, who had had perennial asthma since childhood. The only time he had been clear was when he was in army service. Physical examination revealed the characteristic changes in nasal mucosa and sibilant rales in the chest. Skin tests showed him sensitive to many substances.

He had no individual therapy, but after a preliminary consultation enrolled in a continuous group which included people who were already open and free in their emotional expression. The physician served as co-leader. The group, meeting once a week for one and a half hours, was composed of allergic and nonallergic men and women.

During his first session when he heard group members bringing out hostility to parents, L. sat silent and blocked. After the session he had a severe asthma attack. However, in his second group session the sanction-ing effect of the group became obvious. He said with apparent anger, "My father has a violent temper. I can never carry any important discussion with him to a conclusion. If we have opposite points of view he gets violent about it." A few minutes later, L. again became anxious. He started making excuses for his father and attempted to deny the anger he had expressed. Again he had severe asthma.

During several sessions following this, the same pattern was repeated. He released hostile feelings; then blocked them. Gradually, however, with the help of therapist and group members he became aware of what he was doing. He described it by saying, "I keep catching myself and shutting my-self off." Gradually, too, he brought out that he had always felt a longing for greater response, understanding and acceptance from his parents than he had ever been able to obtain. His mother, however, had given him more care, attention and response when he was sick than when he was well.

In his sixth session with the group he let his resentment come out more openly. He spoke of his mother's "intolerance"; she had failed to understand him; she had embarrassed him in front of others. He finally avowed that he hated her. Then again he felt anxious and had to add quickly that in spite of all this he really did love and admire her. During the week that followed, his anxiety apparently mounted. He had asthma on and off all week.

He came to the next group session looking dejected. Things had not been good; he had been blocked in everything; he had not even been able to work. When talk of hostility commenced, he started wheezing. He got up from the floor where he was sitting with several other group members and took a chair. He sat there tensely, the wheezing increased until he was struggling for breath.

The group's reception of his spectacular attack was interesting. Summing up their attitude, they appeared to appreciate that this was a psychosomatic expression of the man's difficulty, and that their role was to accept the emotions involved. They identified with his troubled feelings rather than with his symptoms. In effect, through this episode they established for him a sense of the group as a haven. "I feel as if it's my home, here," he declared.

From this time on, release came much more freely. He identified with other group members in their expressions of hostility. He related his childish mischief and a persistent eating problem to having been deprived as a child. A great discovery came with the emotional conviction that his refusal of food dated back to too harsh weaning and was evidence of childish resentment. He said of his mother, "She was cruel and broke me too harshly; just threw the bottles out and I couldn't eat well till I was sixteen."

Along with the freer release and the apparent reduction in guilt, his asthmatic attacks cleared. As time went on it became evident to him that the group accepted not only his hostility but his anxiety and the fact that it was hard not to block feelings which made a person feel unworthy or ashamed. Remarks from others revealed feelings similar to his own: "It was hard for me to bring things out in the beginning," and "It still is." It showed our patient that he was not alone in his plight.

Among other things, the foregoing case illustrates one serious danger that needs to be guarded against in group psychotherapy with allergic patients. When the allergic goes into an open group that is already established and free in expressing hostility, too much anxiety may be mobilized. The impact comes too fast and without the cushion of any established positive transference to fall back on. Overwhelmed by anxiety, a patient may go into dangerously severe attacks or may be so frightened that he drops out. To counteract this, it has been found that entry into a group is best postponed until there have been a sufficient number of individual sessions for a positive transference to the therapist to have been formed. Then, depending on the case, individual work can be discontinued as the transference to the group grows.

Case 3: E. was a stocky, fluffy-haired girl of 23. She had a scaly flushed skin identified by the allergist as disseminated neurodermite, a form of allergy. This condition had been present since childhood, had not improved with medical treatment, but had in fact been getting worse. She was shy and worried over her parents "overpowering her." Ample evidence of the latter was present in this case.

Her mother, for instance, acompanied her to a preliminary interview with the psychotherapist and took over the interview until the therapist indicated the wish to talk with the girl alone. The father called for her after each group session. The mother phoned repeatedly complaining that her daughter was sleeping only six hours a night. Would the therapist please insist on her sleeping eight hours. (The patient had had several individual sessions at regular intervals, and then went into the group with the understanding that she could ask for individual sessions as she wished.)

During her first five group sessions, the patient sat with an immobile, expressionless face and did not open her mouth. At the close of the sixth session she remarked, "I feel we're closer and freer than we were at the beginning."

In the seventh session she started to talk very slowly and with a kind of jerky halting. She complained that her parents had not let her have the music lessons she had wanted. Then she said, "They both try to take too much care of me. They don't think I'm grown up. They try to keep me a baby." The therapist wondered if she would act out her problem in some psychodramatic scenes, which she did in an inhibited way, portraying an argument with her older sister and her parents blaming her for again losing a job.

Meanwhile she heard other members of the group voicing their feelings with increasing freedom. She heard of hostility that dated back into childhood. Another of the allergic patients, for instance, told of the "murderous" feelings he had had toward his father. "I was going to gas him. I was going to poison him. I figured out sixteen thousand ways to kill him." She witnessed the constant acceptance with which these feelings were received by the therapist and the growing acceptance of the group-as-a-whole. Moreover, she saw group members expressing animosity to each other, and, with the therapist's help, working it through—still maintaining acceptance of and liking for each other.

She heard other feelings voiced which are not ordinarily admitted—feelings of childhood sexuality, shame over bed wetting, elimination and masturbation, birth fantasies, and so on. She found herself also voicing her feelings more freely, first with a rather peevish sort of annoyance over her parents' forever "managing things" for her and "keeping her from getting out and doing things" on her own, and then with more downright, direct and open avowal of resentment and revolt.

On the reality side, she managed to get her father to stop calling for her after the group sessions. In her fifteenth session, she mentioned having smoked for the first time in front of her family. Up to that time, she said, she had locked herself in the bathroom—"away from criticism." But the other evening "I went right ahead and smoked that cigarette right at the table . . . I felt like I'd done something." One of the men remarked how she had changed in manner, and also how her skin had cleared. She smiled and said, "I was like this" putting on a cringing air. "I wouldn't let out a peep."

In her eighteenth session she talked of having told her mother off. "And," she said, "she seems a lot better. Things have been a lot better for me all around." Later, she said "I don't care any more whether she accepts me or rejects me." [In spite of the exaggerated protest, she was able, at least, to face that rejection was possible.]

Apparently the patient's increased self-confidence carried over into her work. Whereas she had not been able to hold a job heretofore, she now reported a raise in salary.

In her twenty-first session she came in obviously upset. There was a noticeable recurrence of the skin condition. She commented on needing the group to talk with and then came out with the fact that she had had sex relations. "I had an affair," she said. "I was sorry afterward. . . It was the first time. . . You think . . . oh, gee, what have I done? . . . I thought it would be fun, but afterward I wondered . . . I was disappointed. I said to myself, Is that all there is to it? I thought there was something extra special."

Other women in the group, both married and single, spoke of having felt the same way. With the group's acceptance behind her, E. was able to voice her more basic anxiety. She said, "I was told nobody would marry me." Her feelings were again accepted and collectivized in the discussion that followed. Furthermore, some of the men crystallized that what they wanted was not virginity per se but a good total relationship. She seemed somewhat relieved but asked if she could have an individual session with the therapist. During this interview, she rehashed the experience, commenting, "Gee, it helped to hear those other women and to hear those men say you didn't have to be a virgin." [The group-as-a-whole had served in the role of the good mother who accepted as natural her wish for physical gratification.]

At the following group session her confidence seemed to have returned. Her skin again was clear.

Up to the date of reporting, she had attended twenty-four group sessions and had had the one extra individual conference after entry into the group. She felt "less shy," "more successful," that she could put herself across better and that she was freer of her parents. Her personality and bearing showed this. Her physician stated that her allergy was "markedly improved."

Case 4: The following briefly describes Mrs. S., a woman of 24, who attended a group consisting of eight mothers. Her child, a little girl of three, was asthmatic. In the group sessions, the characteristic psychodynamic pattern in parents of allergic children was clearly revealed.

Ordinarily Mrs. S. covered up her feelings with an air of flippancy. However, one day in the group when she spoke of her 3-year-old asthmatic girl, she suddenly gave way to a strong onrush of feeling. "I actually felt I could kill her!" she exclaimed. "I wanted to throw her against the wall and bash her brains out" [thus bringing out and facing her feelings of rejection to her child].

Her own mother had died during Mrs. S.'s adolescence. Her death made it especially difficult for Mrs. S. to admit the ambivalence toward her which gradually came out in the therapy group. She would say of her mother, "She really never loved me. She would punish me terribly. She'd tell me all the time not to be bad. I was afraid to do anything" [indicating her feelings of having been a rejected child herself].

With her father, she recalled some intimate scenes. She recounted, with excited embarrassment, that after her mother died, she had shown herself off to him in her slip and he had fondled her breasts. On several occasions she climbed into bed with him. "I wanted him to hold me like I'd always wanted my mother to and she wouldn't!"

When her father remarried, she resented her stepmother and ran away to the home of the man whom she subsequently married. Obviously putting him in the place both of father and mother, she sought to have him take care of her. (He once said in an interview: "I've been a father to her. I've had a rough time being a boy friend and a father both and a mother, too, sometimes.") As would be expected, their sexual adjustment was poor. She never experienced orgasm.

In the therapy group, the death wishes she had expressed in the beginning toward her child were ultimately related to her death wishes toward her mother. In spite of rejecting her child, however, she would not let her husband have anything to do with the child's care. When he demanded that he had a right to take part in it, she would pack up and leave home, taking the child along, only to return when the care of her daughter grew too burdensome for her. In this unstable environment, the child could gain adequate love from neither parent and felt lost and insecure.

As for accepting hostility from the child, this to her was too condemning. It held too grave a proof of her rejection. However, as she progressed, she was able to be more honest with herself and could let the child be more honest, too. She could also let the care of the child become less burdened by excessive perfectionistic standards and by the necessity to shove the father out and do all by herself.

BIBLIOGRAPHY

Baruch, D. W. (1952), *One Litle Boy*. New York: Julian Press.

Berne, E. (1954), Discussion of Transference and Countertransference in Group Psychotherapy. First Conference of the Western Group Psychotherapy Association. Berkeley, California.

Erikson, E. H. (1950), *Childhood and Society*. New York: Norton.

Fenichel, O. (1945), *The Psychoanalytic Theory of Neurosis*. New York: Norton.

Foulkes, S. H. (1950), Group Therapy. *Brit. J. Med. Psychol.*, *23*:199.

French, T. M. and Alexander, F. (1941), *Psychogenic Factors in Bronchial Asthma* (Part I). Washington: Psychosomatic Medicine, Monograph IV. National Research Council.

Margolin, S. G. (1954), Psychotherapeutic Principles in Psychosomatic Practice. In: *Recent Developments in Psychosomatic Medicine,* ed. E. D. Wittkower and R. A. Cleghorn. Philadelphia: J. B. Lippincott.

Miller, H. and Baruch, D. W. (1948), Psychosomatic Studies of Children with Allergic Manifestations. I. Maternal Rejection. *Psychosom. Med.*, *10*:275-278.

—— —— (1950a), Emotional Traumata Preceding the Onset of Allergic Symptoms in a Group of Children. *Ann. Allergy*, *8*:100-107.

—— —— (1950b), A Study of Hostility in Allergic Children. *Am. J. Orthopsychiat.*, *20*:506-519.

—— —— (1950c), Marital Adjustments in the Parents of Allergic Children. *Ann. Allergy*, *8*:754-760.

—— —— (1951), The Patient, The Allergist and Emotions. *Proceedings First International Congress for Allergy, Zurich*, *1*:834-838. Basel: Karger.

—— —— (1952), Some Paintings by Allergic Patients in Group Psychotherapy and Their Dynamic Implications in the Practice of Allergy. *Int. Arch. Allergy & Applied Immunol.*, *1*:60-71.

—— —— (1953), Psychotherapy in Acute Attacks of Bronchial Asthma. *Ann. Allergy,* *11*:438-444.

—— —— (1954), Bronchial Asthma Unrelated to Positive Skin Reactions. Presented at Tenth Annual Meeting, American Academy of Allergy, Houston.

Rosen, H. (1953), *Hypnotherapy in Clinical Psychiatry.* New York: Julian Press.

Weiss, E. (1922), Psychoanalyse eines Falles von nervösen Asthma. *Int. Ztsch. Psychoanal., 8*:440-455.

Chapter VIII

GERIATRICS

•

It is the unusual event in medicine to find a single therapeutic agent that recommends itself as appropriately, offers supplies for as many needs, and manages the total person as felicitously as does group psychotherapy in the relief of the emotional disorders of later maturity. Group treatment for the aged simultaneously offers counteractants for neurotic symptoms, improved social status, betterment of family relations, a mode of liberating emotional energy, channels for sublimating libidinal investments, and reflects all this in increments of physiological welfare. Yet, while accomplishing such a multitude of benefits, group therapy presents a high order of specificity in each area of need among the older age category of patients.

At the outset the admonition must be made that there is no curative system for *dementia vera* of senility, a condition of sometimes complete psychological disorganization consequent upon advanced cerebral degenerative changes. The crucial point in the entire matter of psychotherapy with late mature patients is the problem of distinguishing between dementia and the more predominantly psychological indispositions of aging. For the sake of establishing a frame of reference it is well to regard the nondementing mental disorders and those associated with nonadvanced organic central nervous system alterations as *psychopathological senescence*. This includes the following major groupings as employed by the present writer:

A. Simple Senility
 1. Mildly depressed ⎫
 2. Perplexed   ⎬ with insight
 3. Confused   ⎭
 4. Stoical

B. Psychoses of the Senium
   1. Melancholic and agitated
   2. Anaclitic
   3. Paranoid
   4. Schizophrenoid
   5. Delirioid
C. Late Senescent Neuroses
   Severe forms of all the known psychoneuroses and character disorders flourishing prominently in very late maturity.
D. Senile Character (Hostile and Embittered)
   The constricted, morose, irritable, contentious, indolent, and withdrawn personality occurring as a behavioral complex often unrelated to presenescent personality as socially observed.
E. Psychoses with Cerebral Arteriosclerosis
   These range from acute remitting disorders to chronic and progressive ones practically indistinguishable from senile psychoses and dementias.
F. Other Psychiatric and Neurological Conditions Occurring in the Senium
   This category includes the gamut of other psychoses, such as manic-depressive, schizophrenia, paranoid condition, etc., as well as a wide variety of organic afflictions, including operated brain tumors, head injury syndrome, epileptic and choreatic personality changes, etc.

Since a greater degree of reversibility of the disorder will be found in the more purely psychological illnesses of age, and since not infrequently patients with dementing disorders and those with nondementing psychoses resemble each other in the acute phases, it is of some value to employ the following criterion areas for the selection of patients:

1. Psychopathological elderly patients are on the whole significantly younger than the demented seniles.

2. There is a greater degree of interpretable and meaningful variations of transference relationships in psychopathological senescence than is found in the organic dementias. The latter are characterized to a more marked degree by systematic psychological recession, euphoria, irritability, and lack of object relationships.

3. Psychopathological senescents generate feelings of empathy and affection among attending personnel. Demented seniles evoke "mothering" and "nursing" impulses.

4. Trials at therapy as a rule bring response more quickly in the psy-

chopathological group. In them improvement is greater and more enduring than among the demented aged.

Continued personality growth is very likely possible throughout most of life, except that, as the psychic institutions of the ego continue on an upward developmental course, they encounter a point or level of interruption or interference. The main obstacles in the path of continued ego development along the route of later maturation are: (1) lifelong neurotic ego involvements; (2) sociological attitudes toward aging; (3) intrapsychic regression in response to stress; (4) degeneration of the organ of the mind (brain). Any or all of these items may be the major factor in the psychological disturbance of a particular person.

In addition to the decremental changes of physiological involution that are themselves causes of disagreeable sensations and anguish, there are at least four other areas of psychic stress that may affect the aging ego:

1. The unconscious neurotic mainstream of defensive mechanisms, that have underlain the lifelong formation of character traits, disposition, and behavior, becomes uncovered in later maturity and penetrates the ego weakened by psychophysiological exhaustion.

2. Cultural and family attitudes toward the aging and the aged are colored by a high order of ambivalence. Traditionally the positive component is exaggerated and oversentimentalized. Such attitudes as annoyance, impatience, tolerance, and exclusion highlight the rejection component. Culture exposes the older person to increasing amounts of setting-aside, neglect, and discard.

3. Residues of the emotional conflicts of infancy and childhood as well as the intrapsychically internalized elder-rejecting attitudes of culture escape from repression in late senescence and are turned against the host-ego, thus eventuating in self-rejection.

4. The later periods of life are characterized by a progressive reduction in the circle of available friendly objects. As a consequence there occurs an increasing diminution in opportunities for libidinal interchange.

The mass of blows to narcissism and the emotional deprivations which the aged ego cannot long endure produce the ensuing fairly universal sequence of psychological events:

(1) cultural rejection; (2) self-rejection; (3) anxiety and intrapsychic panic state; (4) psychophysiological exhaustion and enfeeblement; (5) psychosexual regression; (6) withdrawal of object interest (isolation); (7) restitutive phenomena with enhancement of pathological mechanisms; (8) autistic and dereistic preoccupation. These are the stages in the development of a psychosis. The complete series of steps in the development of the severe emotional disturbances which lead to physiological breakdown

if unimpeded are seen clinically as follows: (1) disillusionment; (2) partial neurotic surrender; (3) senescent melancholy; (4) attempted reorganization; (5) secondary surrender; (6) senescent decline; (7) emotional regression; (8) combined (physiological and psychological) recession.

Intrapsychic Configurations. The late senescent, embattled by a variety of rejections and affective impoverishments, is witnessed clinically to develop a progressive loss of self-confidence, diminution in the feeling of usefulness, reduced self-esteem, and a feeling of growing insecurity. There then follows a profound sense of loneliness. Due to shattered and crumbling defenses, the senescent experiences terrifying anxiety and intrapsychic panic. As his search for narcissistic support and reinforcement from the external environment goes ungratified and his frenetic attempts at internal repair progress to exhaustion, the older patient redirects his interest and attention away from extrapsychic reality and discovers in the deeper recesses of his own ego a multitude of internalized object images from out of his own past. Old pleasures are revitalized as the aged patient invests his libido in such ancient memory objects. However, a complication occurs unexpectedly. The recathected old memory objects have attached to themselves hitherto repressed infantile and childish misperceptions, errors, and misconceptions as well as associated appropriate mixed affects. As a consequence, the procession toward awareness of particular memory complexes produces mercurial and lightning-like changes in mood. External reality simultaneously makes demands upon attention. Libidinal interest, vacillating as it were between conflicting endopsychic and extrapsychic elements, eventuates in confusion, perplexity, and waning alertness. Remaining ego resources become concentrated toward repairing defenses and bringing order out of chaos. Further fatigue and enfeeblement ensue.

For the purpose of conserving mental energy and achieving some pleasure, the aged mind yields to the pressure of the tide of the unconscious. Hackneyed and outmoded defensive systems are resurrected against a deluge of primitive ideational and affective memory systems. The now impotent ego capitulates to the superior force of newly energized unconscious memories and proceeds to organize them into a new psychic structure—the dereistic sphere of fantasy. The more completely the ego is absorbed in this process, the more gratification the patient experiences. The dereistic mental construction consists of three areas: a reliving of old experiences, delusional misinterpretation of external reality, and a denial of death coupled with fantastic concepts of immortality.

Psychophysiological interrelationships are such that in the disturbed aged, whose indisposition is partly consequent upon physiological recession, the sick ego seems to have an undesirable effect on somatic integrity and further degeneration is introduced and hastened. The unimpeded vicious cycle thus established can only result in total decline and death.

The Symptoms of Psychopathological Senescence. Diagnostic accuracy dictates the choice of a therapy. This is no less true of the emotional disorders of aging in which a knowledge of the origin of symptoms and a conceptual etiological scheme must lie at the foundations of a treatment regimen.

The *confusion* that is so commonly seen among the aged is due to fragmentation of the ego and the intrusion into consciousness of unconscious irrelevancies. *Perplexity* is the outcome of libidinal interest vacillating through a cycle composed of memories emerging from repression, rudiments of normal ego, and perceptions of external reality. *Disorientation* is the logical consequence of the return of libidinal interest to timeless unconscious recollections, a mélange of memory objects, and historical situational associations.

Loneliness develops out of loss of real objects. This improves greatly when fantasy objects take over supremacy, in which case the sense of satisfaction is due to regression to primary narcissism and to magic hallucinatory omnipotence. *Judgment* falters partly as a consequence of the loss of objects, because the deprivation of real objects removes the sense of responsibility that is normally associated with targets for affection. In addition, diminishing judgmental functioning is based on a reversion to dependency accompanied by anaclitic suggestibility. The delusional transformations of dereism further entangle and modify the capacity for discrimination and discernment.

At least five factors may contribute to the *memory impairment* of late senescence: (1) block-outs caused by cerebral deterioration and probable interruption in the transmission of memory engrams; (2) redirection of attention from recollection to the reconstruction of defenses against anxiety; (3) disruption of ego structures with resulting discontinuity of memory traces; (4) hyperacute interest in archaic memories lacking currency; and (5) lack of a reality-inspired motive for remembering.

The *mood changes* of psychopathological senescence depend largely upon the level of regression and recession to which intrapsychic structures have eroded as well as the factor of kaleidoscopic memory complexes. In practically every late senescent the onset of the emotional turmoil is characterized by a *depression*. The melancholy spirits are due to: (1) turning of hatred toward internalized objects mistaken for the self; (2) turning of cultural and family attitudes of rejection against the ego; and (3) a return to orgiastic masochism touched off by feelings of disappointment, regret, and self-reproach associated with a fear that imminent death will prevent expiation of guilts and undoing of mistakes.

There is a multitude of other behavioral elements such as *wandering* (acting out), *irritability* (temper tantrums), *restlessness* (fantasied rejuvenescence), and *insomnia* (warded-off death) etc., which grow out of the altered psychic state. They are as a rule symbolic and representative of patients' needs. In a majority of instances it is an error to regard them as haphazard expressions of organic damage.

Rationale for Group Psychotherapy with the Aged. It is an error to regard senility as second childhood. It is, rather, *childhood in reverse* combined with certain psychophysiological processes found only in great age. A subtle difference in the management of the aged person is implied as contrasting with the treatment of children. Treating the aged patient as children are traditionally treated, practically guarantees therapeutic failure. To overlook the possibilities for transferences, to neglect the memory traces of adult sexuality, to disregard the vestiges of a former reasoning, judicious, and responsible ego, denies any therapy the goal of personality rehabilitation and reintegration.

The preponderance of aged patients for whom group psychotherapy has much to offer is comprised of those suffering from numerous variations of the senile psychoses. Therefore the following discussion will be directed mainly toward the major psychological process.

Those elements of the ego that remain unaffected by the psychotic process and continue to exercise the function of self-awareness come into conflict with the derealistic components of the psychotic ego. This is fortunate for the treatment of senile psychosis, because it is to the areas of unaltered ego that external reality may make its appeals. It is apparent that the greater there is a loss of the self-scrutinizing and self-critical faculties of the ego, the deeper is the regression, the greater is the implication of the ego in the psychotic organization, and the lesser is the probability of response to a system of therapy.

Of unmistakable importance is the recognition that the psychological disturbances of late maturity are almost exactly analogous to those at other age levels with but two added features: cultural rejection and psychophysiological recession. The senile psychosis is a dream state in the partly conscious aged ego in which the particular systems of distortion of endo- and exopsychic perceptions are in accord with the person's neurotic residues from childhood, and in keeping with the need to deal with environmental elder-discarding.

The combination of the following major events constitutes the prime sources of suffering summating into psychopathological senescence: a rejecting milieu; neurotic narcissistic and masochistic predisposition; isolation and loneliness; regression and recession; the employment of overdetermined pathological defensive systems. It is clearly seen that a major proportion of the factors contributing to senescent behavioral alterations consists of psychological components even in the face of physiological decline.

A certain degree of reversibility is inherent in psychological factors because (1) they are based on object relationships which have in themselves an order of variability; (2) emotional energy is in a constant state of flux and can be channeled as necessity dictates; (3) the psychic systems always seek modes of relieving tension; (4) the compulsion to repeat past and learned modes of performance tends to re-establish familiar patterns of behavior from which the organism has departed; (5) the mere process of living at any age level requires inexorable and continuous psychic accommodation to changing internal and external realities. However, pathological psychic mechanisms do not reverse themselves automatically. The favorable alteration of sick defenses among the aged can be achieved only in a setting that ministers at once to every need.

Individual psychotherapy is very useful with the aged and is often the treatment of choice, but it requires augmentation by other items in a total program. Individual treatment is a very limited social event that lacks elements germane to group treatment.

The reconstitution and rehabilitation of the emotionally ill aged necessitate the following minimum of constituents of treatment:

1. *Environmental manipulation.* The elderly psychotic must be removed from the environment that rejects him. His subsequent care requires an institutional setting in which a high order of elder-acceptance has been developed through (a) indoctrination of personnel; (b) appropriate architecture and furnishings; and (c) a relaxed, therapeutic atmosphere *in which "mothering" and "nursing" are avoided.*

2. *Activity.* Movement, moderate excitement, and participation are a *sine qua non* in the management of the elderly in order to counteract idleness and stagnation. Where there is no impedence to vegetative inactivity, further regression is the inevitable outcome.

3. *Resocialization Opportunities.* It must always be remembered that the aged psychotic's withdrawal is from the social and group reality of which he was long an integral part. For all of the neurotic components, his is a social ego. Even in the rudimentary form to which his ego is reduced there are relics of cultural, aesthetic, and responsible values which are the acquisition of acculturation. Opportunities for multiple

object relationships reawaken such value systems and help return them to accustomed prominence.

4. *Psychotherapy*. As employed among psychopathological senescents, psychotherapy means (a) rerepression or compartmentalization of dereistic fantasy systems; (b) an appeal to adult capacities for affection and sexuality; (c) reanimation of reflective judgment; (d) intellectual stimulation; (e) exercise of reasoning faculties of mind; and (f) the reconstruction of memory sets. In order that all this be accomplished, the treatment regimen requires the availability of a routine for the establishment of space-time guideposts; appropriate objects for choice and identification; companions for mutual assistance; a social setting for stimulation, externalization, and lateralization of affects; a group structure for interaction of emotional systems; and trained leaders for observation and interpretation of psychological dynamisms.

Group psychotherapy, by virtue of its unique combination of social and therapeutic factors, presents a high order of specificity in refurbishing the supplies needed by the deprived, rejected, and regressed elderly patient. Therapeutic intervention assists in the resolution of depressive affects, increases alertness, diminishes confusion, improves orientation, and replenishes many memory hiati, all this being reflected in improved social relationships and physiological welfare. Since the average age of institutionalized senile psychotics is in the neighborhood of seventy-two and life expectancy at that level is about eight years, it is apparent that a good response to group psychotherapy offers the elderly patient a potential of several years of pleasurable living. Indeed, a fair number of such patients live well into the ninth decade.

One of the factors not to be overlooked is the tremendous morale effect group psychotherapy of the aged may have upon their families. The knowledge that the elder is receiving active treatment, that there is a likelihood of improvement, and a possibility of some return to self-sufficiency, often is a palpable mental hygiene factor among the offspring whose guilt and ambivalence threaten their own emotional welfare.

Historical Backgrounds. Activity, membership, socialization, and participation in groups have long been recognized as having value in the emotional rehabilitation of the aged. Newstetter (1939), Trecker (1948), and Wilson and Ryland (1948), authorities in this field, have summarized the factors and contributions that relate to it in separate publications. A recent book by Kaplan (1953) defines *social group work* with older people and delineates the preparation and indoctrination of the worker in such a way that the relationship of this province of interest to group psychotherapy is unmistakable. The following excerpt from Kaplan's treatise highlights that relationship: "He [the group worker] must have a basic philosophy of respect for the individual; he must understand the behavior of people; he should be aware of the interpersonal relationships between the members of the group; he must be able to use this awareness in a consciously controlled manner" (p. 31). However, to group workers the working knowledge of personality structure and the psychological needs of the older individual are of value because they lie at the foundations of fitting recreational systems to personality types.

Group counseling, as outlined by Mathiasen (1953), has been employed for some years by industries, unions, universities, church groups, welfare agencies and others in the preparation of the aging and elderly for the exigencies of retirement. Golden Age clubs and their counterparts have employed the principles inherent in group participation for over a decade. A good deal of the psychology of aging groups was recorded in the now classic publications of Dr. Lillian J. Martin in the early 1920's.

In recent years such investigators as Lawton (1951), Grotjahn (1951), Clow (1953), Goldfarb (1953), Stieglitz (1946), Meerloo (1953), Hollender (1951), Wayne (1953), Ginsburg (1953), and Kubie and Landau (1953), have added considerably to the comprehension of the emotional needs of aged people as well as therapeutic measures designed to meet these needs. The present author and many colleagues to whom he is indebted have been unable to uncover in the literature a scientific communication dealing precisely with the specific qualities of group psychotherapy as employed with the emotionally disturbed aged. Early in 1950, coincident with the opening of a modern geriatric unit in a large state hospital, it became apparent that the extraordinarily large number of newly admitted patients over 65 and the manifold psychiatric problems they presented necessitated a new therapeutic approach; one that was applicable to groups, practical to administer, and harmonious with a philosophy and scientific concept of aging. Much of the following is taken from the first report on *gerontologic group psychotherapy* presented before the Philadelphia Psychiatric Society in October, 1952 and published April, 1953 in the *International Journal of Group Psychotherapy*.

The Psychopathology of Later Maturity. The widespread tendency to compare the disorders of the senium with the developmental aspects of childhood makes it imperative that the differences be thoroughly understood. In the following section the contrasting elements are exposed and identified. Additionally, some of the ways the leader has of suiting his therapeutic intentions to patients' particular needs are discussed briefly. Note that the inexact term *senile* is used here for the general group of troubled aged merely for the purpose of simplifying communication.

Some of the elements to be discussed are dependency, isolation, psychophysiological exhaustion, fantasies, regression, empathy, and identification.

The child is, of course, fundamentally a *dependent* person who is progressively acquainted with independence. To him a state of independence is new, untried, desirable, but perilous. His rebellion against dependence is a renunciation of helplessness with progressive efforts toward centripetal and centrifugal mastery. He is grudgingly dependent through necessity only so long as his native resources are in a state of evolving.

The aged person, on the other hand, has already tasted of independence and self-sufficiency, but his self-dependency has become seriously threatened by the diminution of effectiveness of his resources and defenses. He is thus precipitated into a state of hostile, but anxious and fearful dependence. He clings tenaciously to support, and the more authoritative the support, the more blissfully dependent he becomes. Thus his ego dwells almost exclusively in the person of the potent leader who is in a position to use his power for good or for disaster. The senile person can be reinstated to some degree of independence only when the authority progressively divests himself of authority, removes from himself the fiction of omnipotence, and gradually levels himself toward an area of mutuality with the patient.

The child comes from *isolation* and helplessness and progressively renounces and repudiates his private strivings in an effort to please the society of the family group whose acceptance he desires. He thus progressively fits himself into group cooperation. The alternative to group cooperation is exclusion and isolation, which he fears. Through fear of loneliness and hunger for participation and social contact he accepts cultural restrictions on his individualistic drives and realizes the reward of belonging.

The senile person contrasts strongly, since he has come from social life to a state of isolation. Although therapy proves that he has a secret longing for group participation, his conscious attitude toward society is essentially hostile, because it is there that he perceives a collective unfriendliness. Society is his tormentor, a vast potent force with which he is powerless to cope, and which has set him aside, denied his importance, and neglected him. The senile person can be assisted out of his isolation only by creating for him an attractive group situation into which it is once again profitable to integrate himself.

For the child available energy is boundless and his horizons for conquest unlimited. No goal is too great for his incalculable ambition; no obstacle too imposing for his indomitable will. Psychic elasticity allows the child to rebound from most hurts, and he repeats his efforts untiringly to reach that future which for him is a foregone success.

The senile state contrasts strikingly here, for the aged person conserves his energy supplies dwindling through *psychophysiological exhaustion,* pleads sullenly for guidance, fears the future with a desperation that blinds him to realities, and hence he makes no preparations, but waits instead for a magical state of transition to immortality. This longing for death is an almost conscious belief in rebirth, a renewal of energy and a return of potency. Emotional re-education must be directed within a framework of realistic limitations. Those illusions the senile nurtures cannot be destroyed, since they are gratifying and sustaining. Instead they must be compartmentalized. To encourage compartmentalization every effort must be made to avoid challenging fantasies and delusions, since, if the patient senses that his notions are under attack, he mobilizes much precious mental energy to defend his viewpoint. Skillful evasion of these topics allows such ideation to become walled off, reduces the affective charge otherwise held captive, and releases much psychic energy for reality activities.

The child finds ample compensation for unrewarding reality in the formation of *fantasies* and illusions. Such fantasy formation in the child becomes progressively reality-oriented, and his future strivings become efforts to make realities out of his illusions. Such fantasies become the very substance of ambition.

The senile, however, is in a general state of disillusionment. Hitherto unrealized wishes convey no hope of being fulfilled now. His lifelong dream world of love, peace, and perfection is shattered. He is no longer interested in accomplishing anything, and he loses curiosity and excitement in the manifold activities and attitudes of the world around him. This reflects his diminishing ability to identify with others. Many of his fantasies pertain to regrets over past errors, usually minor. To overcome this he must be encouraged to regain an energetic thought life filled with ambitious fantasies and to enjoy again vicariously the exploits of others. This is afforded him in group life with opportunities to share experiences. A spirit of good-natured competitiveness is thus reawakened.

The back-steps of childhood or *regression* are transitory events in the developing, but unstable, ego. The pleasures the child receives from such periods of regression are canceled out by the greater rewards available to him for psychosocial advancement. The precept of the family group and the greater peripheral society pose a challenge to the child and evoke a desire to imitate and emulate. Thus transient unlearning of elements of integrated social behavior in the child usually presents no difficulties.

The loss or decrease of utility of defense mechanisms in the aged is the product of a unitary interweaving of biophysiological and psychological factors of a decremental character. The resulting alteration of repressive forces permits a host of long-concealed infantile patterns and unadorned instinct-representative attitudes to invade consciousness. The unaided impoverished ego is powerless to cope with this flood of primitive affects and uses regression as a compromise. A series of regressive stages is discernible in senility which, without assistance, eventuates in continuous loss of ego integration, which is witnessed in the progressive loss of social faculties and self-mastery. The social disillusionment and feeling of rejection in the aged diminish the urgency of cultural values, and, having lost their attractiveness, they no longer stimulate a desire for conformity and adaptation. Therefore a strict, but flexible, set of routines must be scheduled for the senile in a newly conceived group setting in which the reality of time-honored conventions gradually resumes significance and in which *activity* becomes the bulwark against catastrophic stagnation. In a setting of acceptance, interested care, and creative participation, old values regain their importance, hunger for social relationships returns, regression is halted, and an urge to contribute to group cohesion emerges.

The point hardly needs reiteration that *identification* is a fundamental factor in the child's ego development. It is probably one of the most important civilizing and socializing mechanisms in the acculturation of the person. Although in its primary form identification is selfish and aggressive, it assumes in the course of maturation a progressive humanitarian quality of understanding of the feelings of others. It is this empathic capacity which gives human conflicts a universal appeal and enables people to form groups in which problems and pleasures alike may be mutually appreciated and shared.

Perhaps nowhere, not even in the other psychoses and neuroses, is there to be found a greater degree of loneliness than in senility. A society which is perceived as exclusive can hardly be regarded as a mass object for identification. Additionally, the senile condition with its physiological decline and threat to psychological defenses is virtually a chronic panic state wherein the ego is much too preoccupied with its own alarm reaction to allow for much externally directed interest. Consequently the capacity for identification is enormously decreased. On this account the potential for group formation would seem to be so greatly diminished and the quantity of narcissistic self-concern to be so increased as to prevent any degree of relationship from developing sufficiently to yield a setting for modification of attitudes. The one factor, however, that outweighs this is the senile's great dependency needs and almost religious aggrandizement of authority. By assuming at the outset the false mantle of a demigod and distributing his beneficence among a group of seniles, the therapist can stimulate a good deal of rivalry among the members, become the target for a number of individual transferences, and by eventually shedding these allow identifications and group identity to take place. When group identity develops, a potent morale factor is introduced which allows for lateralization of transferences. The lacework of transferences within the group becomes the vehicle for further affect externalization and empathic capacities are revitalized. A chain reaction of increasing socialization ensues.

In addition to the characteristics of senility, some of which have been mentioned above, each aged patient possesses a great agglomeration of individualistic traits, conditionings, and attributes, the behavioral products of mechanisms. The intense anxiety generated by the senile alarm state causes the more dominant mechanisms to become overdetermined and used to excess. Thus in pathological later maturity the person becomes both a prototype of the senile and a caricature of himself. Therefore, his therapeutic requirements are twofold: (1) *needs characteristic of his group which are met by the group process, and* (2) *individual neurotic needs which require interpretive therapy.*

Indications for Group Psychotherapy. As of the time this is being written the present author has partaken in the treatment of many groups and several hundred patients over a period of four and a half years devoted to gerontologic psychiatric studies. However, the following discussion concerns the problems that were encountered in meeting the needs of the aged patients as they were experienced in the original, pilot effort. The solutions to such difficulties are also described. This is being done on the assumption that therapists desiring to initiate an analogous therapeutic program in their own provinces of professional activity will experience similar problems. The group reported upon here is not a random sampling of aged women from among 330 available in one building of a mental hospital. Some selection was exercised on the basis of intuitive clinical criteria. These criteria may be divided into positive (indications for group participation) and negative (contraindications for group participation), somewhat after the manner of Slavson (1950).

Positive Criteria: (1) expressed desire to join the group; (2) appearance of relative alertness; (3) a fair degree of good personal hygiene; (4) ability to understand English; (5) ability to walk or be wheeled to meeting room; (6) at least a minimal range of affects; (7) evidence of some degree of adult adjustment prior to entrance into senile state; (8) capacity for evoking interest and affection from nursing and attendant personnel; (9) sardonic hostility.

Negative Criteria: (1) dementia; (2) advanced physical debility; (3) systematized and chronic paranoid thought life; (4) manic behavior; (5) intense chronic hostility with assaultiveness; (6) unremitting bowel and bladder incontinence; (7) advanced deafness; (8) monothematic hypochondriasis; (9) undirected restlessness with inability to sit still; (10) unwillingness to participate; (11) inability to understand English.

At the outset twenty-five women were asked to form a group. While this is an unusually large number of patients for group psychotherapy, it was deemed advisable on the basis of experience with the aged. There is insufficient interaction among small groups of older people. One patient, a 54-year-old schizophrenic, who had obtained a very gratifying remission in two years of group psychotherapy with a group of middle-aged psychotics, was used as a cadreman nucleus around whom the group was formed. Membership remained open. The group met twice weekly for one-hour sessions. Within three weeks of the inception of the group, a very large number of other patients requested admission into the group. The number who enrolled by the end of the first two months was nearly one hundred. Each meeting was attended by forty to sixty members. Of the fifty-one patients reported in this paper, forty attended regularly.

Announcement of the next meeting was made at each session, bulletins were posted at the nurses' stations, and nurses and patients collected the members before each session. The more alert patients spontaneously made themselves responsible for bringing the more confused and disoriented to the meetings.

The patients were arranged in semicircles before a table in a tastefully decorated day hall. The partially deaf and/or blind women were encouraged to take front seats. Wheel chair patients flanked the group. The patients voted to welcome visitors, consequently hardly any meeting was devoid of an interested audience. Word of the procedure spread rapidly throughout the hospital with the result that several patients from other buildings, having ground privileges, attended first as onlookers and, later, as active participants. The presence of visitors and younger patients had a catalytic effect on the group. The participation in group by the visitors was encouraged by the members.

At the beginning the group leader was the male ward physician. After six months this was changed to dual, male and female, leadership. The female leader was a ward nurse who had auditioned the group meetings before. She was given some didactic orientation in group psychotherapy and had herself participated for seven months in intensive analytic group psychotherapy with other young nurses. "Auxiliary leaders" emerged months later from among the patients and organized themselves into a hostess committee, education committee, membership committee, entertainment committee, and committees for functions on special occasions.

A formal air was developed because of the prestige position of the leaders (at the table) and the amphitheater atmosphere. This was occasioned by exigency, but did not seem to be the factor hindering the development of group identity. At the outset two rules were established in a casual way by the leader: (1) that violent physical acting out was unwelcome, and (2) that the group was to be bound by the ethical principle of privileged communication.

The Group Process. For several months the group was discouragingly quiet. The members waited dependently and helplessly for "lectures from the doctor." Efforts to stimulate animated discussions were seemingly futile. There seemed to be no real group formation and such conversations as did take place were "gripe" releases between individuals and the therapist. A pall of gloom charged with slight expectancy hung over the group and was punctuated by stifled laughter in response to an occasional witticism from the leader who found that deft, but good-humored sarcasm was the most effective stimulant. The patients seemed to enjoy being scapegoated. When, for example, 75-year-old Frances, a self-recriminatory, dour, passively suicidal feeding problem, who, whenever she deigned to speak, was bitterly and crisply sarcastic, was told by the leader: "You are an impossible old curmudgeon," she laughed uproariously, perhaps for the first time in years. This marked a turning point in her ability to verbalize.

The development of group solidarity was very slow in showing itself. The one factor that seemed generally appreciated and contributed to the continuation of group meeting was the leader's patience and perseverance. He spoke of activities available to patients, individual forms of ward behavior, the general policies and programs of a mental hospital, the history of the institution, the values of hygienic routines, and current topics of interest. He chided diffident members into answering personal questions and welcomed any amount of complaining, guaranteeing that any *bona fide* gripe would be corrected, whenever possible.

The first noticeable effect of group therapy was a pronounced change in atmosphere throughout the building. A morale factor, very difficult to describe, was emerging. The traditional atmosphere of pessimism, inactivity, stagnation, and futility began to be dissipated. Even patients not enrolled in the group showed increased alertness and activity. The factor of contagion was obviously in operation and in a few months relatives and visitors commented on the welcome change which was discernible in off-the-ward visits. When dual leadership was introduced, conventional psychotherapy took place. The seventh and eighth months witnessed the evolution of group identity. Interest in the group became keen. Strong affectional ties sprang up among patients and cliques of patients. Discussions in the meetings often became heated arguments to which even the habitually quiet patients contributed by taking sides.

Buoyed-up spirits continued to effervesce in the wards. Petty altercations broke out in the dormitories which were usually temporarily settled by the lusty voice of some newly energized woman shouting: "Save it for group therapy!" Interest in hitherto neglected recreations was revived and attendance at occupational therapy, the library, ward movies, and card tables increased. The ladies seemed suddenly to become intensely interested in shampoos, rinses and permanent waves at the beauty salon. Many patients refused to go to group meetings in institutional clothing and began to vie with one another in donning their much-valued gowns and fineries. The group leaders abetted all this by complimenting the well-dressed members publicly.

The topics of parties, picnics, dances, and group sings often were raised during sessions and were accompanied by offers to finance the special events and by detailed planning. When these plans came to fruition and, at the members' request, male patients of the same general categories arrived as invited, the differences between the sparkling group therapy ladies and the lusterless men was almost comically striking.

After about the twelfth month of therapy the subjective personality of the building had changed utterly and with it its reputation. Throughout the hospital requests were received by staff members for transfers to this building. It was generally regarded as a reward and a promotion to be admitted there. It had lost its "ward" and "mental" connotations and was regarded as a desirable "home." Visitors were surprised to find it was a building with a number, the remark often being made that they thought it had some commemorative name.

Early in the group process an effort was made and sustained for a few months to encourage free association, uninhibited public expression, and mutual interpretations. While this was not without its successes, it was found that the rotation method of calling on as many members as possible and questioning them about some few biographical items was more stimulating, yielded fewer embarrassing silent periods, and kept the group alert. Much later an educational element was introduced with members volunteering to prepare ten- to twenty-minute presentations of subjects of group and seasonal interest. Since it was found expedient to use almost every method of group approach at one time or another, the process came to be known as "opportunistic group therapy."

Probably the most important factor was the mechanism of *universalization*. It required the self-effacing boldness of intrepid catalysts in revealing their own hidden longings, fears, doubts, hates, and dreams to give emotional conflicts a human familiarity which afforded the more reluctant patients a common meeting ground for self-expression. The leaders always took an active part in helping patients piece together incomplete memories. Where opportunities for group insight were missed by the members, the leaders arrested group movement until the point was worked through. The female co-leader was often extremely helpful in giving a feminine point of view. She occasionally led the group alone and the variations in leadership atmosphere stimulated much response. In one group meeting a patient said to the male therapist, "Last Tuesday when you weren't here, we had a wonderful time with Miss ——. We talked about dresses and shoes and things women like. You're always making us try to understand ourselves." To this another aged woman, coming immediately to the aid of the presumedly injured physician, replied, "They're both important."

Contrasting with traditional individual and group psychotherapy, an aura of serious effort was not regarded as a *sine qua non*. Every opportunity for light-hearted fun and laughter was exploited to the fullest. There was never any danger that frolic would supplant the main goals. Depressed patients often teased other depressed patients for their ruminations with the surprising result that instead of taking offense, the victims tried to join in the fun after a few feeble efforts to protect their anxious notions.

Mutual support and protectiveness were outstanding dynamisms as the group progressed. When the leader purposely selected a member for scapegoating, antagonism to the therapist from the group was evoked. He patiently listened to protracted nonsensical and delusional utterances. When a disorganized patient faltered in expressing herself, others hastened to help her. An overabundance of egocentricity always brought out group antipathy. Once, when 78-year-old Henrietta, a chronic paranoid woman, had just finished a prolonged self-directed eulogy, 76-year-old Louise, a paranoid, arteriosclerotic Parkinsonian and former school teacher said, "I'll bet you can't talk about something for five minutes without saying 'I.' How about trying it, all of us, and we'll pay a penny to the kitty for each 'I.'" Henrietta accepted the challenge, but was saved from losing a small fortune by the leader's intervention. This had a long-enduring therapeutic effect, however, since the others became aware of their own numberless self-references.

The following case histories have been selected because each illustrates some diagnostic, prognostic, or therapeutic variation.

Case I., E. M. This married woman, born in Ireland, was 65 at the time of admission to the state hospital in November, 1948. All her life she had been healthy and happy. Following several years of employment as an elite domestic, at the age of 44 she married a widower with two children. She was described as obstinate, quick-tempered, but able to give and take jokes. She was thorough and neat. Nothing of her childhood was known to informants. Her admission to the hospital was occasioned by her being "nervous, worrying about money, agitated, depressed. Upset about her memory, her health, her husband, and her finances." She asked of the admitting physician, "Did you ever feel like you had sinned?" For two years of hospitalization she remained restless, anxious, retarded, depressed, and even too frightened to accept privileges. She began attending group psychotherapy September, 1950. There her memory showed spotty impairment, but, except for her melancholic mood, most of her mental faculties were fairly intact. Her transference in therapy was classified as predominantly negative, hostile-depressed. Her improvement in group psychotherapy was steady and very slow. By early 1951 she was able to accept increasing freedoms. Later in 1951 she became cautiously cheerful. In early 1952 she began making home visits. She was a passive participant in group psychotherapy at the beginning, but months later she started talking about her childhood and living experiences. As her diffidence fell away she proceeded to demonstrate a fairly remarkable understanding of human nature and helped others gain insights as she prospered. Her transference turned warm and friendly as time passed. In early fall, 1952, her psychological tests and evaluations showed normal mood, memory, and capabilities. She left the hospital in October, 1952. Interim reports reveal that she is leading a normal community life and has been working as a domestic in order to help with the family finances. Her husband described her very recently as "even better than when she left the hospital."

Case II, M. L.[1] When admitted in 1944 at age 70 this short, very stout woman was said to have shown signs of mental illness since 1937. She complained that a neighbor placed a copperhead snake in her bed and that other snakes inhabited the cellar. She heard voices giving her

[1] This patient's behavior is described in somewhat greater detail in "Group Psychotherapy with Institutionalized Senile Women" (Linden, 1953).

commands she had to follow. Restless and disturbed at night, she remained in bed all day. There was no informant acquainted with her early history. She had been living as something of a recluse for several years. On examination she showed evidence of preservation of intellect and most psychological modalities except in the areas of mental illness. During about seven years of hospitalization the patient was a noisy and militant ward tyrant. Embittered, seclusive, paranoid, and argumentative, she was disliked by patients and personnel. In August, 1950, she wrote to her ward physician, "Perhaps it would interest you to know that I am a Freemail with Mail eyes. You should see the X-ray pictures taken of me. One doctor thinks I have two hearts. If one lets go the other would take over. I only feel one beating. But I have just about two of everything else inside. Two sets of intestines and two stomachs, one inactive and glad of it for it is hard to supply one stomach let alone two. I am such a medical freak." In group psychotherapy this patient's keen intellect became a pivotal reference point. Her comprehensions of others' needs were precise, accurate, and searching. She recounted her own dreams, hallucinations, and delusions and gave valuable associations which led to insight formation and a good deal of working through. A dramatic turning point took place in therapy one day when she suddenly confessed to the group that she was a frustrated spinster whose sexual longings were always disappointed and that "even today, and you may not believe it because I'm 79, I have hopes that the right man will come along and marry me." Unable to leave the hospital permanently because of physical limitations due to obesity, M. is now a charming, affable, cheerful and cooperative woman whose letters are coherent and without a shred of dereistic fantasy. She has been in group psychotherapy continuously since fall, 1950. No manifestations of psychosis are present. A volunteer visitor has taken a liking to the patient and has had M. to her home for many visits up to five days in length. The patient is now 80 years old.

Case III, E. L. L. This 86-year-old widow was admitted in June, 1952 with the following commitment statements, "This patient shows loss of memory for recent events and confusion. She is uncertain whether or not she owns property, is unable to tell the street address where she lives and how long she has lived there." She believed that her relatives were being substituted by strangers. Quarrelsome, periodically agitated, and careless and untidy in personal hygiene, the patient developed the notion that everyone was against her. Psychological tests showed the impairments common to "senility." By July, 1952 the patient was described as wizened and enfeebled. Following her entrance into group psychotherapy in March, 1953 (delayed because of hospital treatment for several physical ailments) Mrs. L. became very effective as a ward worker, gained weight, and became noticeably robust and cheerful. This was due in no small measure to her medical and surgical treatment. However, in group participation she became progressively oriented, filled in many memory hiati, and frequently volunteered recitations, whereas earlier she had been very shy, perplexed, and withdrawn. At the present time this patient's daughter is considering removing her 88-year-old mother to her home. The patient is now nearly fully oriented and alert. Bowel and bladder incontinence, which were present the first nine months of hospital stay, have been absent completely since April, 1953.

Case IV, L. B. (A therapeutic failure). In October, 1944 this 77-year-old negro spinster was admitted from a county home where she had lived for fifteen years. A relatively short time before admission the patient was brought to jail for larceny and disorderly conduct. She had stolen a purse from a store and entered a home while the occupants were away. She seemed pleasant and cooperative, gave her age as "32," thought the year was variously 1876, 1882, etc. Later, when asked her age, she said she was born either in July or in the year of March. She said the interview date was either Tuesday or April. Her affect was flat throughout her hospital stay. She didn't care about anything, was seclusive, confused, incoherent, and her memory was grossly impaired. She remained fairly neat about her person and participated mechanically in ward chores. This patient was a pet of nurse and attendant personnel, and she was enrolled in group psychotherapy in Summer, 1951. She attended regularly for two years. Her treatment in addition consisted of many well-indicated medical and surgical procedures as well as a variety of replenishing and stimulating medications. Except for the slightest improvement in work efficiency, to date this 87-year-old woman, who looks much younger, is precisely as she was ten years ago.

Case V, F. R. This elderly widow is a remarkable case. 65 in 1941, when she was admitted, she spent nearly twelve miserable years in a bitter, hostile, passively suicidal rut depression. She was self-isolated, self-recriminatory, unconsolably vituperative and hotly sarcastic. Institutional life was for her an empty unpleasantness. She showed enthusiasm and ambition only for death. She was placed on a stimulating drug routine (oral Metrazol(R) and B vitamins) and after two months, when she was sufficiently alert and apparently hungry for social contacts, she was coerced into attending group psychotherapy. There she showed a pseudo-rejecting transference and in a few months she became affable, jocular, teasing, and beneficently wily. She actually fell deeply in love with the male therapist, asked to kiss him, and twittered and blushed like a virginal adolescent whenever he came near. She gained weight, became much more agile, and proved to be a witty raconteur in group meetings. Her emotional interplay with the other participants in a web of positive transference efforts to gain the therapist's favor was an unsurpassed experience for all observers. Mrs. R. developed a tranquility and good humor she had not known for a sixth of her life. She would walk about the building singing and saying encouraging things to other patients. Many months later she died of a known heart ailment only after she had proved conclusively that group psychotherapy with the aged is a potent therapeutic agent. Her passing was an occasion for mourning among all the patients and personnel who had known her through the therapeutic period.

Case VI, M. C. This brief presentation is to demonstrate a patient's continued adjustment after disposition from the hospital following group treatment. This spinster-lady is now 73. She was diagnosed as a psychotic with cerebral arteriosclerosis. Neat, tidy, talkative, overly sentimental and emotionally labile, she minimized her difficulties in circumstantial chatter when admitted in December, 1950. After three months of group psychotherapy in which she revealed her many real prehospitalization difficulties, she left the hospital to live as a pensioner in a hotel. During the past three years she has augmented her income considerably as a much-sought-after baby sitter.

Case VII, S. R. (Success and failure). This widow, now 74, born in Holland, is most likely a presbyophrenic. She had had a hard life, replete with many setbacks, but had always retained a brave and cheerful disposition. At 70 she showed signs of advancing dementia and on hospitalization she was incontinent, restless, silly, and good-naturedly meddlesome. She always gave the misleading impression of knowing what was going on, but was actually very much out of contact. She was placed in group psychotherapy as an experiment. Language barrier was intensified by senile reversion to historical type. In spite of every contrary factor this patient responded to therapy. Her ability to sit still increased in time from less than one minute to over an hour; attention span increased from a few seconds to about fifteen minutes. Her incontinence became rare and her physical condition improved markedly. These changes occurred progressively during two years of treatment following which the patient's daughter died of injuries received in an automobile accident. When the patient was informed of this, her response was appropriate shock, tears, and grief. Subsequently she deteriorated rapidly despite further therapeutic efforts and she is now a senile vegetable.

Space does not permit the presentation of many more interesting cases, some with prefrontal lobotomies, some with operated brain tumors, a Huntington's chorea, a chronic paranoid condition with almost complete recovery at age 83, etc. However, perhaps the foregoing patient histories give some indication of the value of gerontologic group psychotherapy.

Some group work has also been done with aged men in the same institution by other therapists. However, the effort has not been carefully standardized nor followed through sufficiently long in order to draw conclusions. The feeling is entertained that men would respond much as the women do, but that there is a much greater amount of organic deterioration in the former by the time they get hospitalized.

Results of Gerontologic Group Psychotherapy. It is found that the response to group psychotherapy is quite distinctly commensurate with the nature of the emotional transferences manifested by aged patients. However, a consideration of transference is a technical and detailed area that would suffer from an attempt to condense it in this brief account. The reader is therefore urged to avail himself of the sources of information to be found in the reading list at the end of this chapter, particularly the communications dealing directly wtih transference in the aged.

Improvement among the geriatric group is more a measure of comparison between a patient's behavior before and after group psychotherapy than an estimate of approach to community normality. A disorganized, disoriented, confused, and sensorially clouded patient who becomes relatively alert, oriented, reasonable and able to care for himself, and a melancholic, self-recriminating, hostile, and seclusive, but exactly oriented patient who becomes cheerful, optimistic, conversational, and cooperative with group treatment are both to be regarded as much improved, yet there is a marked qualitative difference. For one, tempestuousness and emotional instability moving toward greater cooperativeness, fellowship and tranquility is improvement, while for another considerable benefit from group participation is seen in petulant, querulous, provocative, and demanding behavior being modified into a relatively mature form of affability, altruism, and self-sufficiency.

In general a very high order of improvement can be expected from these patients with group treatment for the many reasons already enumerated. When the dementias, neurasthenias, casehardened character neuroses, extremely chronic psychotics, mental defectives, and other severe organic afflictions are weeded out, the remaining late senescents will probably show some degree of favorable response in over 60 per cent of the cases. When the selection of cases for presentation in this chapter was being done, it was actually difficult to find cases that could be regarded as complete failures.

Aged persons who have led intellectually active lives do particularly well in group psychotherapy, although on the whole they do very poorly in retirement. It is probable that about 40 per cent or better, of aged patients selected for group management can be restored to nearly full pre-illness duties in retirement. About 8 to 10 per cent can become partially or wholly self-sustaining.

Conclusions. Group psychotherapy in the rehabilitation and emotional reintegration of the disturbed aged is a valuable and specific method of treatment. While its therapeutic goals are somewhat less demanding than at other age levels, its potential contribution to the welfare of a very large number of people is beyond question. It should be distinguished clearly from nonclinical group management systems, for although it does contain some educative, suppressive, and inspirational elements, its major focus is upon meeting the exact psychological needs of each individual in the group with exact therapeutic vectors.

Group psychotherapy with the aged is being employed increasingly in many institutions throughout the country. Considered in terms of relief of suffering alone it is well worth the effort it entails. But its promise is greater than that. It affords an area of study which may confirm or amend present psychiatric concepts, thus indirectly benefiting younger age groups. It may help to demonstrate that there is a potential for mental development continuously through life even into the later years. And it may contribute to that very necessary long-term culture-wide endeavor directed toward returning to the elders a measure of veneration to the end that even the sunset of life may contain an invigorating social reward. It is quite likely that when human existence becomes meaningful at its every turning, then many of the now extant forms of so-called senility will be relics of the past.

BIBLIOGRAPHY

Clow, H. (1953), Individualizing the Care of the Aging. *Am. J. Psychiat.*, *110*:460-464.
Ginsburg, R. (1953), Geriatric Ward Psychiatry—Techniques in the Psychological Management of Elderly Psychotics. *Am. J. Psychiat.*, *110*:296-300.
Goldfarb, A. I. (1953), Recommendations for Psychiatric Care in a Home for the Aged. *J. Gerontol.*, *8*:343-347.
Grotjahn, M. (1951), Some Analytic Observations about the Process of Growing Old. In: *Psychoanalysis and the Social Sciences*, *3*:301-312. New York: International Universities Press.
Hamilton, G. V. (1942), Changes in Personality and Psychosexual Phenomena with Age. *Problems of Ageing*, *2*:310-331. Baltimore: Williams and Wilkins.

Hollender, M. (1951), Role of the Psychiatrist in Homes for the Aged. *Geriatrics,* 6:243.

Kaplan, J. (1953), *A Social Program for Older People.* Minneapolis: The University of Minnesota Press.

Kubie, S. H. and Landau, G. (1953), *Group Work With the Aged.* New York: International Universities Press.

Lawton, G. (1951), *Aging Successfully.* New York: Columbia University Press.

Linden, M. E. (1953), Group Psychotherapy with Institutionalized Senile Women. *Int. J. Group Psychother.,* 3:150-170.

—— (1954), Significance of Dual Leadership in Gerontologic Group Psychotherapy. Studies in Gerontologic Human Relations III. *Int. J. Group Psychother.,* 4:262-273.

—— (1955), Transference in Gerontologic Group Psychotherapy. Studies in Gerontologic Human Relations IV. *Int. J. Group Psychother.,* 5:61-79.

—— and D. Courtney (1953), The Human Life Cycle and its Interruptions: A Psychologic Hypothesis. Studies in Gerontologic Human Relations I. *Am. J. Psychiat., 109*:906-915.

Madden, J. J.; Luhan, J. A.; Kaplan, L. A.; Manfred, H. M. (1952), Nondementing Psychoses in Older Persons. *J.A.M.A., 150*:1567-1570.

Mathiasen, G. (1953), *Pre-Retirement and Retirement Aid and Counseling* (Pamphlet). New York: National Social Welfare Assembly.

Meerloo, J. A. M. (1953), Contribution of Psychoanalysis to the Problems of the Aged. In: *Psychoanalysis and Social Work,* ed. M. Heiman. New York: International Universities Press.

Newstetter, W. (1939), Social Group Work. *Social Work Year Book.* New York: Russell Sage Foundation.

Slavson, S. R. (1950), *Analytic Group Psychotherapy with Children, Adolescents and Adults.* New York: Columbia University Press.

Stern, K.; Smith, J. M.; Frank, M. (1953), Mechanisms of Transference and Counter Transference in Psychotherapeutic and Social Work with the Aged. *J. Gerontol., 8*:328-332.

Stieglitz, E. J. (1946), *The Second Forty Years.* Philadelphia: Lippincott.

Trecker, H. B. (1948), *Social Group Work; Principles and Practices.* New York: Women's Press.

Wayne, G. J. (1953), Modified Psychoanalytic Therapy in Senescence. *Psychoanal. Rev., 40*:99-116.

Wilson, G. and Ryland, G. (1948), *Social Group Work Practice.* Boston: Houghton Mifflin.

Chapter IX

MOTHERS

●

The close psychological relationship between children's behavior and their parents' unconscious conflicts and attitudes has long been known. Even the most normal parents have their emotional blind spots resulting from unconscious conflicts. These are involuntarily reflected in their attitudes toward the members of their families and become the very warp and woof of the way they bring up their children. Just as normal child behavior develops from the soil of well-integrated parental emotions and satisfactorily solved conflicts, so problem behavior in children derives from the parents' neurotically resolved unconscious conflicts.

The history of the child guidance movement and child psychiatry has increasingly revealed the necessity of not merely recognizing this relationship but also dealing with it therapeutically. It has frequently happened that the best therapeutic efforts on behalf of the children have been vitiated because too little was done with the parents. Experience has shown that parents who bring a child for help with a particular problem find an excuse to remove the child from treatment just when that problem is in process of modification.

A case in point is the little boy who was brought for treatment because he was too submissive and quiet. After a few months he became able to use aggressive measures experimentally. Understandably he began where it was easiest for him, with his younger sister. Immediately the parents complained bitterly, and it required several hours to help them give up their violent disapproval at the slightest sign of the boy's aggression. Even then the parents succeeded only in avoiding outbursts. The more subtle expressions of disapproval continued, for only analysis of the fear of their own aggressive impulses could have reached the roots of this attitude and thus have freed their son. This could be done, however, only within the framework of a treatment relationship.

Even if parental interference or the child's removal from treatment have been circumvented, the successfully treated child cannot easily withstand the effect of returning to the same neurotic environment which caused his difficulties in the first place. He is often prey to its undermining effect and falls ill once more as a result of renewed emotional pressures. Only treatment of the parents will enable them to tolerate and freely cooperate with the child's therapist and, in the end, make the changes in the child's emotional environment so essential to his continued welfare.

But parents seldom seek treatment for themselves and since the demand for help by really anxious and disturbed people was greater than the supply of adequately trained and skilled therapists, it was a long time before any systematic attempt was made to treat parents. Child guidance clinics tested various approaches to the problem. Parents were seen occasionally by the child's therapist; social workers saw mothers regularly with the aim of relieving pressure rather than to treat them. The sickest mothers were put into individual treatment. Finally in the late 1930's a solution was found to this pressing problem. Psychotherapy was applied to *groups* of mothers of disturbed children.

The literature on psychotherapy with mothers' groups seems to have made its first appearance in about 1939. This followed on an extended period of interest in group work with rather vague unarticulated therapeutic aspects. The Brooklyn Child Guidance Center, for example, ran both children's and mothers' groups in 1937, but the aims, the method, the goals, and expectations were not yet clarified.

Gabriel (1939) reports on "an experiment in group treatment" in which she limits herself to dealing with matters concerning the parent-child relationships and avoids the mother's own deeper problems. The mothers in such groups, conducted by the Jewish Board of Guardians, were not treated as patients in their own right. Amster, Gabriel, Kolodney, and others under the direction of S. R. Slavson all worked with mothers applying a kind of attitude group therapy to mothers, whose children were under treatment.

Durkin (1939), in an article on a children's group, mentioned meetings with the mothers as a group and suggested the possibility that mothers might be treated by the same method (John Levy's relationship therapy) that she had used with the children's group. This was attempted the following year at the Brooklyn Child Guidance Center where Durkin, Glatzer, and Hirsch all started mothers' groups. Their method was different from that of Gabriel (1939) in that they dealt directly with the problems of the mothers. The rationale was that if the mothers' own unconscious conflicts could be solved by group treatment, their children's problems would be alleviated and the children's treatment could proceed unhampered. The results were considered sufficiently effective so that group therapy for mothers was adopted as a regular part of the clinic services. They were described by Durkin, Glatzer and Hirsch (1944). These authors concluded that direct treatment can be carried out effectively with small groups; that results in terms of modified personality and behavior patterns take place in about the same way and to the same extent as in individual therapy; that simultaneous treatment of mothers' and children's groups is particularly effective since therapeutic movement occurs at both ends of the relationship at once; and that group treatment for mothers saves valuable time for the clinic and solves the problem of the parents' interference with the children's treatment. Their work was evaluated by Lowrey (1954).

Following through on the point of view presented by Gabriel (1939), Amster (1944) published a report on the mothers' groups. She attempted to treat each mother by using specific material presented by her and help her understand her child's needs and the confusion in her feelings and in relationships to her offspring. Amster also attempted to work with the group as a unit by using specific material to secure elaboration and release of feeling and help them develop understanding of such concepts as aggression, compliance, love hunger, what the child experiences in growing up, etc. She found that the members of the group expressed their feelings toward one another and toward her.

In these reports from both child guidance centers, we see the early methods being expanded and the foundations laid for a psychoanalytically oriented group method. And this is exactly what happened. S. R. Slavson gave the name "analytic group psychotherapy" to this new development. In the following decade, Durkin, Glatzer and Hirsch joined the staff of the New Rochelle Child Guidance Center and under the leadership of Dr. Geraldine Pederson-Krag, and Dr. Mark Kanzer, further developed their method until, in its present form, it must be classed as analytic group psychotherapy. During this period Durkin and Glatzer published a series of papers presenting clinical data and showing in specific detail how the method worked and how it was developing. Together they wrote the "Role of the Therapist" (Durkin and Glatzer, 1945), showing the dynamic interrelationship between concomitant mothers' and children's groups. Glatzer (1947) in an article on selection of mothers for groups stressed the need for heterogeneity, especially as to personality. In papers on transference (Glatzer, 1952) and on resistance (Glatzer, 1953), she shows the change from the old relationship therapy to analytic group psychotherapy. The same holds true of Durkin's articles on the "Theory and Practice of Group Psychotherapy" (1948), and on the "Analysis of Character Traits in Group Psychotherapy" (1951).

A parallel development took place in the work with mothers at the Jewish Board of Guardians under the leadership of Slavson. The changes are evident in an article by Spotnitz and Gabriel (1950), and one by Gabriel and Halpert (1952). Spotnitz and Gabriel (1950) state: "The object was to modify their parental attitudes as they rose from their own emotional difficulties . . . resistance and defenses hampered the telling of their life stories . . . The group gave these women an opportunity to relive past emotionally crippling experiences . . . When they gained courage to express criticism of the therapist they were freer to express hostility to their children after which their attitudes to their children were modified . . . working out their sibling rivalry in the group, they were better able to understand and handle their children's rivalry problems." Slavson's classification, analytic group psychotherapy, also applies to this work.

Meanwhile Slavson trained workers to go on with the older approach which limited the therapist's work to dealing with child-parent relationships, refining and developing it to a more thoroughly thought-out method which he calls "child-centered group guidance of parents," and which is employed with less neurotic parents who can be reached by a more conscious, rational approach. He is on the point of publishing a book on this method.

These two approaches, the analytic and the guidance, are the two main lines of development in group therapy for mothers. They have come into rather widespread use. Most of the reports given in the literature deal with the therapeutic guidance approach which seems to have been more widely adopted for use with mothers than analytic group psychotherapy.

One series of such reports deals with therapeutic guidance work done with special groups of mothers. For example, Peck et al. (1949) report on work done with the mothers of schizophrenic children; Millman (1951) on work with groups of parents of cerebral palsied and poliomyelitic children; Bauer and Gurevitz (1952) on groups with parents of schizophrenics; DeFries and Browder (1952) on work with the parents of epileptic children. These authors stress that better understanding of the problems of their children and a more realistic handling of them resulted from group discussions by the parents than it was possible to achieve by working with the parents individually.

Another series of articles reports on discussion groups with mothers, all with limitations in the degree and depth of treatment. Lloyd (1950) describes group interviews in which the focus is on the children rather than on the mothers in a parent child relationship. Lulow (1951) used groups to help parents bring up children with some knowledge of themselves together with an understanding of the children's behavior. Barnes (1952) reports on parent study groups around the problems of the preschool child, in connection with a nursery school. These are discussion rather than therapy groups.

Somewhere midway between the analytic and the guidance approach seems to stand the work of Bross (1952) in the group psychotherapy unit of the Flower Fifth Avenue Hospital, who reports that individual therapy is alternated with group therapy. Children and mothers are seen by the same psychiatrist. The children are selected on the basis of their willingness to participate in group discussions, the parents must attend groups if their children are to be treated. The therapist's attitude is permissive, and the members are encouraged to become individuals in their own right and to develop a feeling of importance and relatedness. Neither the mothers nor the children are treated as patients. The results consist in "extensive modification of the feelings and attitudes to themselves and to people in general, and a more harmonious home environment."

Fabian, Crampton, and Holden (1951) described group treatment of preschool children and their mothers. They find that "by virtue of interaction of the patient's identifications and interpretations of their interrelations it is possible to reach the deeper layers in a shorter time than in other therapies. Depth treatment, however, is with the individual in the group rather than by the group, because the individual members of a group do not function uniformly." Bross (1952) and Fabian et al. (1951) seem to be doing direct therapy with the mothers, but not analytic group psychotherapy as defined by Slavson.

Mothers' groups present a special problem. As we have seen, it soon became clear that the mothers who present themselves to a child guidance center do not want and are often unwilling to accept treatment for themselves. Diagnostically these mothers tend to suffer from neurotic personality disorders rather than full-blown psychoneuroses. Although every type of neurotic or psychotic problem may eventually present itself among the prospective group members, experience shows that there is a decided preponderance of character difficulties without much overt symptomatology. What symptoms there are and those neurotic character traits that are causing the difficulties, are likely to be ego-syntonic.

The women have generally coped satisfactorily with their conflicts during their premarital lives. Their careers have often absorbed a good deal of their hostile aggression and guilt. In many cases they have married men whose neurotic trends are complementary to their own and have thus kept a precarious neurotic balance intact. It is only as the results of their unconscious conflicts appear in their children's behavior that the balance is upset.[1] They reason therefore that it is only the children who are difficult; they do not want help for themselves. They do not experience much personal anxiety; it is externalized and seen only in relation to the children's behavior.

All these factors determine the goal in the first weeks of analytic group psychotherapy with mothers. The group therapist must first of all arouse in them some need for help, some inkling of their own relationship to the children's problems, some anxiety. He must lead them to a realization of the ego-alien quality of the character traits and behavior patterns which they have regarded as acceptable and even desirable in themselves.

At first glance it seems an almost impossible task to effect this change: to make parents accept themselves as patients. But experience shows that it is not as difficult as it seems. The parents do have unconscious guilt which can be tapped to serve as motivation for treatment. It is not really that they have no anxiety but that they have externalized and tried to deny it. They blamed their children but when they could not cope with them, they did come for help. At that point anxiety is near the surface and becomes the therapist's entering wedge. The opening weeks of treatment must be spent in capitalizing on this situation in order to put the mothers' groups on a therapeutic basis. This requires considerable skill.

The question as to which mothers should be put into therapy groups has received a variety of answers. Large agencies have worked out a careful scheme to solve this problem (Glatzer, 1947). Smaller institutions and therapists in private practice had to be less selective. This latter necessity has taught us that almost all mothers can be helped in groups. Selection is left to the clinical judgment of the therapist who sees the prospective patients first and rules out those for whom group therapy seems contraindicated. Certain rules of thumb have developed from this process. Mothers who are in some way apt to be in the public eye because of their own or their husband's activities should not be expected to expose their personal problems before others in the same community. Schizoid and psychopathic mothers may benefit from group treatment, but they cannot

---

1 Some children, of course, play into the neuroses in such a way that they remain satisfied. These parents do not seek treatment but their children are likely to be needing help years later as adult neurotics or psychotics.

be said to be helpful to the group, so that it seems best not to chance hampering the work of the group.

Extremely emotionally deprived women, usually orally regressed and narcissistic, may be too sensitive to rivalry to gain from group treatment unless it can be combined with individual interviews. For the rest it has been our experience that all mothers can gain from group treatment. Scientific proof as to what optimal conditions should be is not available. Hulse (1948), who has had opportunity to select from a wide range of prospective group patients, has said that he feels that the clinical judgment of the therapist is the only essential basis for selection.

Closely related to this problem is that of the constitution of groups. Here, too, there has been a wide variety of opinions, none of them scientifically established as yet. It may, I believe, be fairly said, that most clinicians hold that heterogeneity is a sound criterion for group composition. However, each therapist seems to make his own exceptions. Some make up groups that are homogeneous as to the nature of the psychological problems, taking, for example, only psychosomatic cases, or even only asthmatics. Others limit the group as to age, or as to the ages of the children of the patients; still others, as to education or socioeconomic status, and so on. By necessity I, too, make exceptions. My mothers groups are sexually homogeneous because it is so difficult to get fathers to come in the daytime. On the whole, though, I believe that heterogeneity in every possible area is desirable, because it stimulates dynamic interaction.

Durkin (1951) indicates that heterogeneity in character structure is the most important criterion. It is almost a *sine qua non* for dynamic group interaction. Ego defenses tend to vary with character structure and it is these ego defenses that form the dynamic matrix of group interaction. For example, it is known that repression is the most common defense mechanism in the hysteric character, reaction formation is in anal character, and so on. Patients with one kind of defense tend to have blind spots for that defense in others, and that they therefore bolster up one another's resistances. These observations have been borne out experimentally by Glatzer (1954) in an unpublished Ph.D. Thesis. She reported on studies of two parallel groups, one of which consisted entirely of hysterics, another of compulsives. In a follow-up study also unpublished she mixed the two groups. The results show decisively that the hysterics did better than the compulsives, but that both did much better when the two were mixed.

We must return now to the important problem of how to make *patients* of our relatively unwilling *clients*. Since this is equivalent to the laying of the foundation without which therapy cannot succeed, we must deal with it more specifically than we have done so far. Let us examine the process in some detail.

Let us visualize the setting of a group of mothers at their first meeting. They have been interviewed at least once individually to determine if group therapy is indicated for them. They have acceded to our request to come to the first group session. They are seated in an informal circle and are waiting to see what will happen. In their minds there is a curious and contradictory mixture of cynical misgiving and hope of omnipotent aid. Not knowing exactly what is in store for them, they inevitably have the idea that they will talk about their children in much the same way as they talk to their neighbors with the added advantage that someone in authority will tell them what to do.

From the beginning the group therapist must work toward changing this socioeducational goal of theirs into a therapeutic one. He may decide to focus on their heretofore unrecognized anxiety, by indicating that children's problems are derived from their parents' emotional difficulties. Many mothers have already experienced a sense of guilt and respond to this explanation by being willing to accept what the therapist seems to offer, that is, a chance to "talk it out." Occasionally a mother will be sufficiently anxious to reveal some emotions immediately. If so, the therapist will convey his understanding and acceptance and help her to talk about herself. Such a situation will make a strong impact on the whole group toward accepting treatment.

Often, however, there is no immediate reaction, and the therapist must wait for material which he can use specifically to connect the children's problems with those of the mothers. For example, the therapist's recognition of the value put by a mother on honesty, cleanliness, education, may lead her to reveal her conflict in this area. The therapist will then gradually help her understand the defensive nature of these attitudes and the way in which her child had reacted to them. If the matter is handled with due regard for the patient's narcissism, she feels that she is understood and a positive transference results within the framework of which treatment can proceed for her. This helps others gradually to participate as a result of group contagion.

Most mothers, however, talk somewhat repetitiously about their children's behavior during the early sessions. The therapist listens passively to the discussions and is alert to their underlying feelings. As soon as he thinks they can accept it, he may call attention to these feelings. Soon the tone of the whole discussion shifts from factual description of the children's behavior to the mothers' feelings about their children. They then have taken one step toward accepting their role as patients.

Meanwhile the intragroup identifications and transferences also begin to take shape. Furthermore, the consistent emphasis on feelings, many of which have been heretofore avoided, because they are not in harmony with the amenities of social life, establishes the unique emotional climate of the therapeutic group. In this way the women begin to be aware that something is happening to them which they did not expect and that they are getting some relief from this process even if they do not know why. They then begin to feel safe in letting down some formerly rigid defenses. Gradually they begin to talk of their feelings toward husbands, siblings, and parents. This period has a certain cathartic value and at the same time prepares the way for later insight.

Another means of establishing the therapist-patient relation in the group stems from the manner in which requests for advice are met. Advice is always demanded, yet the therapist rarely provides it. He must withhold it without rebuff, at the same time that he brings into the open emotional reactions to the withholding procedure. The therapist may, for example, say, "I know you will be disappointed, but we have found that in the long run advice does not really help. Suppose you talk about it and I will listen. Together we will try to find out what is causing your trouble. When that happens I believe you will know what to do yourself." Because this handling of the demands for advice implies the therapist's confidence in his method, without implying omnipotence it gives the patient confidence too, even though she demurs. There may be further repercussions with which the therapist must be ready to deal. For example, another member of the group may provide the desired advice, implying perhaps that to her the therapist seems a depriving person for whose omissions she will make up. Whatever the meaning of her reaction, the therapist must find a way of bringing it into the open too at the appropriate time and without letting her feel criticized.

Meanwhile the therapist will have been on watch for signs of interpersonal feelings among the members or to the therapist which may or may not have transference significance. Among the first of such feelings toward himself may be the patients' doubts of or perhaps hope for omnipotence in the therapist. Bringing these masked feelings into the open, will keep transference resistance at a minimum. Once they are discussed, however, additional feeling will come to the fore. Some will tend to interpret any comment directed toward them as criticism. They are those who have probably had critical and rejecting parents, and in this way they begin to develop a negative transference which, too, must be discussed freely before too strong resistances set in.

The order in which the therapist applies these techniques is a matter of clinical judgment and experience. The therapist must sense the patient's need. There would be no use in trying to help Mrs. X become aware of her resentment to her child before her resentment to the therapist for not giving her advice was handled. Mobilizing Mrs. Y's guilt about her son's predicament may be a *sine qua non* for *her* therapy, while such a move would frighten Mrs. Z out of returning to the group. One woman may be unable to comprehend a clarification of her underlying feelings to her mother before a positive relationship to the therapist was established; another patient might be brought to a positive relationship with the therapist by the sympathetic understanding implied in just such a comment. The course to be taken depends on how close to the surface unacceptable feelings lie. Obviously the group situation presents a more complex picture in this respect than does individual treatment. It is for this reason that only therapists skilled in individual psychotherapy should attempt to do group psychotherapy.

Once a mother's group is put on a therapeutic basis, treatment proceeds much as it would with any group of neurotic adults. The surface content will differ somewhat, of course. It will begin with a good deal of stress on the parents' relationships with their children and then gradually move on to other family relationships. Marital relationships for example are more likely to play a more prominent role than they would in a group of young unmarried neurotic adults, or of people with professional problems. Frigidity is obviously more likely to be discussed than the inability to acquire a mate. But as the underlying content is revealed, the same psychodynamics that appear in any group of neurotic adults become apparent. Problems concerning instinctual drives, superego pressures, and ego defense measures must be dealt with as usual. The degree and level will depend on the skill and training of the therapist and the capacity of the patients for insight and change. Gradually much that was formerly warded off is brought into consciousness; the anxiety surrounding it is reduced and it becomes integrated into a modified personality structure. A new equilibrium of intrapsychic forces is achieved.

Of special significance in the psychodynamics of mothers are the problems which grow out of the deep interplay between the unconscious of the mother and that of the child. Only a few significant studies of this subject have been made but they demonstrate its importance in the therapy of mothers and children. Mahler (1949) refers to "typical characteristic, and fairly constant correlations between parental attitudes and specific emotional constellation in cases of the motor syndrome called tic disease." Sperling (1945) says that the symptoms of neurotic children often represent their responses to the mother's unconscious wishes as though they were carrying out orders. She explains it as "a result of the extraordinary sensitivity of the child to the behavior of the mother in a continuation of the phase of preverbal communication which these children seem to have preserved to a high degree." My own observations seem to reveal at least one definite trend in this unconscious relationship. The child often seems to act out the mother's unconscious wishes while defying her carefully established defenses. Johnson et al. (1954) show how the antisocial child acts out repressed drives of his mother.

Material relating to this dynamic interaction may begin to come up in the early days of treatment when the mothers are still presenting descriptions of their children's behavior and their own reactions to it. It may be implied in the very emphasis the mothers themselves put on those ego-syntonic character traits we have already mentioned. We often hear a mother (with strong reaction formations) say in the early months of treatment, "How could this have happened to me? Here is John, lying and stealing, and I have always been so honest and stressed the importance of the truth in word and action." Likewise overly clean mothers are only too apt to be struggling with children who are incorrigibly messy or obsessed with a need to use obscene language. Mothers with oral conflicts often produce feeding problems. Frequently erudite, intellectual mothers cannot understand why they should "happen" to have a child with learning difficulties, yet the very fact that the mother has established counterphobic or reactive defenses against her voyeurism and perhaps also her oral cravings in epistomophilic fashion seems often to lead to strong conflicts in these areas in her offspring.

It is in this way that we are able to take the first steps in resolving the unconscious interconnections between the neuroses of the mother and the child. Putting together all the pieces of this complicated puzzle requires a long period of analyzing, one by one, the mother's defenses and tracing them back to their origins. Usually it will involve the patient's problems with her own parents and siblings. Because of its complexity it may not be fully accomplished until the very end of treatment.

The ego defenses built up by mothers against their own unacceptable instinctual drives find expression in characteristic behavior which is applied not only in relation to their own children but with other persons as well. It is not surprising, therefore, that evidences of this appear in their relationships to group members and the therapist. Indeed, the essential framework for the analysis of feelings, attitudes, and patterns of behavior will be that of the intragroup and patient-therapist transference relationships. It is in these group transferences that irrationalities, blocking, and other signs of neurotic conflict come to light. In group psychotherapy these may be dealt with on several levels. The therapist may deal with them merely by letting the interaction itself take effect; he may clarify the meaning within the existing group situation and relate it to similar situations in the present; or he may interpret the defense mechanisms involved and eventually trace them back to their genetic origins. The third method is the mark of analytic group psychotherapy. Let us take one or two examples to illustrate the manner in which parent-child conflicts can be solved in terms of intragroup transferences.

Mrs. F., whose mother was a temperamental opera singer, found it very difficult to establish a transference to the therapist because the latter lacked the outward evidences and that aura of omnipotence that she had come to look for in authority figures. After she had made several conscious attempts to imbue the therapist with such omnipotent characteristics, she revealed in a dream that she really identified her with a colored maid (Mrs. F. was a Southerner). It was only when this was recognized and related to the fact that Mrs. F.'s mother had seemed an omnipotent figure that she could form any kind of working relationship with the therapist. For a long while she turned much more confidently to a woman in the group whose basic problems were actually derived from fantasies of omnipotence that frequently clashed with reality. Meanwhile Mrs. F. complained that her daughter looked up to her too much. The girl seemed to think everything "mama" did was perfect and could not seem to establish independent ways of thinking or acting for herself. Mrs. F. could not understand her daughter's attitude because she had so often told the girl that grownups could be as mistaken as children (her ego defense).

Having unconsciously endowed her mother and mother substitutes with omnipotence, she saw herself as being weak and consequently had never taken an authoritarian position in the home. Yet it was apparent that she acted out an unconscious identification with her mother's omnipotence, while she consciously verbalized the philosophy of democracy in the home. On the other hand, she reacted rather scornfully and sadistically toward one woman in the group, a Mrs. J., who seemed to have the most outward signs of confusion in handling her everyday affairs. It eventually developed that she had made a father transference to Mrs. J., who seemed as inept, vague, and ineffectual as her own gentle but weak father. At other times she compared this woman to her son Jeff, about whom she had great anxiety. It was not until the second year of treatment that all these pieces of the jigsaw puzzle were fitted together.

One day, Mrs. F. told the group how pleasantly surprised she was that Jeff had done rather well on his baseball team. Another woman called the group's attention to the fact that apparently she always expected her son to do badly. Why? Mrs. F. had not realized this and now suddenly saw that she considered the boy in the same light that she did her father. She now became aware for the first time that in her family women were considered strong, and men weak. She had always felt sorry for her brothers, one of whom was a ne'er-do-well, protected only by the fact that he had a good deal of money which he inherited. The other brother had had a nervous breakdown.

At this point a further understanding came to her. She had been unconsciously fearful that Jeff would turn out like this second brother who had, like Jeff, been very dependent on her. On the surface she had been very good both to the brother and to her son, although her unconscious scorn and hostility came through in subtle ways.

The reasons for her attitude toward Mrs. J. now became clear, as did her disappointment in her daughter and in the therapist for not approximating her ideal, the strong omnipotent mother. As she realized that her unconsciously determined distinction between the sexes had been irrational, her attitudes toward Mrs. J. and toward her son began to change appreciably. There were rewarding results in that her son began to show further signs of improvement in his own therapy and in school. Her attitudes toward her daughter did not begin to change until her own unconscious identification with her mother's omnipotence became conscious. This was difficult to work out because of her defensive system of democratic values, but it was eventually modified. Only then could the daughter begin to criticize her. The girl then decided on a career for herself and succeeded in winning her mother over to accepting the young man to whom she became engaged.

There was also Mrs. F., who came to treatment because she had such a difficult time with her seven-year-old daughter Connie, who was overly prone to colds and stomach upsets. As a baby, this child had been put on demand feeding by the doctor. The mother had complied but had reacted rather violently against the process. She felt drained and furious most of the time, she told us. Almost everything Mrs. F. said revealed her as an orally regressed ambivalent woman with strong masochistic tendencies. Within the group she demonstrated two main types of transference reactions. Those stronger than herself in some particular respect she turned into harsh depriving mother figures with whom she became by turns placating and furious; those who displayed weakness she seemed to identify with negatively as bad children worthy of rejection. However, anyone in the group who had any kind of physical ailment or who happened to cry aroused in Mrs. F. tender maternal feelings.

Gradually through these transference attitudes she was able to discover the reasons for her behavior and how they were related, on the one hand, to her mother and, on the other, to her little girl. She came to understand that she identified both with the depriving mother and the bad rejected child and had often felt toward the child the same way that, as a child, she had felt toward her own mother. She switched from one role to the other in staccato fashion. Almost every relationship she made suffered from this transferred ambivalence.

She would start by seeing the other person, man or woman, as the all-giving, desirable good mother, and would then try to get close to him or her (to get "in her skin" was the expression she appropriately used). If her expectations were not justified, she immediately felt rejected and began to criticize and hate the person involved just as she did her mother. If he or she complied and displayed signs of dependence, she identified them with herself as worthy of being rejected. At that point she herself would assume the harsh depriving mother role. There was only one exception and that is when they were ill or when they wept; then she took care of them. It turned out that that was the only time she herself had received affection from her mother. It was also the only time she was affectionate with Connie.

The group was alert in showing her the many times she displayed these attitudes toward group members. As she came to recognize the pattern and to trace it back to its origins in her earliest relationship to her own rejecting yet incorporating mother, she gradually modified it. She began to develop an identity and some ego strength of her own. She became less inconsistent in managing Connie, too. The child began to develop in her own right. Connie began to make fewer demands and grew emotionally much healthier.

These examples demonstrate, (1) how analysis of the unconscious relationships between mothers and their children leads to freeing the children from their parent's pressures so that they may develop ego strength, and (2) how analytic group psychotherapy with mothers operates in much the same way as with other adult neurotics, that is, by bringing unconscious material to consciousness through the analysis of transference and resistance.

Resistances in mothers' groups are also essentially the same as in any type of psychotherapy and, particularly, in group psychotherapy. This subject has been described by Wolf (1949, 1950). There are, however, two forms of resistance to which mothers groups are especially prone. During the early group sessions talking about children is a sign of task orientation. Later on when a mother in the group reverts to this topic it usually signifies resistance, which may be easily overlooked by an inexperienced therapist because of the interest he feels in the parallel progress of the patient's child. He may become anxious because he feels that an upset or a regression in the child's life is to be regarded as an important reality event, or that the child's therapist is at fault. He must check with the child's therapist of course but he must be aware that in most instances it is the mother herself who has become anxious, perhaps because of the feelings that are stirred up in treatment. Because of her anxiety the mother is apt to relate family events with a lot of feeling and so confuse the therapist.

One mother who had already reported evidences of improvement in her child, came in one day to say indignantly that "Ruthie has not made any progress at all, in fact, she is getting worse. She has not only wet the bed again but she is now refusing to go to bed and wakes up screaming several times during the night." Upon exploration the therapist found that the mother had exaggerated the facts. Such an incident had taken place, but details revealed that it had happened only once right after the last mothers group session when sex had been discussed for the first time. In discussion it became clear that the mother's anxiety had touched off the child's anxieties.

Once the therapist is aware of what dynamic meaning children may have for the mothers, he is able to make some useful shortcuts. For example, one mother always dreamed about her little girl in a superego role when she herself felt unduly burdened by guilt feelings. Another, reported "unbearably aggressive behavior" on the part of her adolescent son every time her own repressed hostility to his father was threatened. When the therapist learns the particular language of resistances of each patient, it is not difficult for him to deal with it.

The second form of resistance likely to appear in mothers groups is also disguised as "valuable" material. The group members may appear to be trying to work out their sexual problems, yet they are not making progress. They may be acting out on an oral level homosexual feelings toward one another or to the therapist. The sexually homogeneous atmosphere is conducive to such well-camouflaged resistance and since female homosexuality rests on oral basis, oral activity makes a satisfactory symbol for it yet at the same time, disguises it. Without the therapist's intervention much time may be wasted, or group tensions may be increased to such a degree that one or more members drop out and the group may be in danger of breaking up.

The results of this method of group therapy have been gratifying on several counts. Serious interference by the mothers in the treatment of their children has been almost wholly eliminated. The mothers' relationships with their children have been changed dynamically in so basic a way that when the children themselves complete treatment, they return to an emotional environment in which the neurotic factors have been greatly reduced. It has become possible then to safeguard the children's treatment. More than that, it has been possible to produce character change in the mothers. Time has been saved for guidance clinic, and the opportunity offered for treatment at relatively low rates to those who otherwise could not afford it. The necessity of making patients out of mothers who showed chiefly character neuroses with little or no motivation for treatment has produced a technique for opening treatment which is applicable to any poorly motivated neurotic patients and to character neurotics in general.

BIBLIOGRAPHY

Amster, F. (1944), Collective Psychotherapy with Mothers of Emotionally Disturbed Children. *Am. J. Orthopsychiat., 14*:44-51.

Barnes, M. (1952), The Educational and Therapeutic Implications in Working with Parent Study Groups around Problems in the Normal School Child. *Am. J. Orthopsychiat., 22.*

Buchmueller, A. D. and Gildea, M. C. (1949), A Group Therapy Project with Parents of Behavior Problem Children in Public Schools. *Am. J. Psychiat., 106*:46.

Bauer, I. and Gurevitz, S. (1952), Group Therapy with Mothers of Schizophrenic Children. *Int. J. Group Psychother., 2*:344.

Bross, R. (1952), Mothers and Children in Group Psychotherapy: A Preliminary Report. *Int. J. Group Psychother., 2*:358.

—— (1954), The Family Unit and Group Psychotherapy. *Int. J. Group Psychother., 4*:393.

DeFries and Browder (1952), Group Therapy with Epileptic Children and Their Parents. *Bull. N. Y. Acad. Sci., 28*:235.

Durkin, H. (1939), Dr. John Levy's Relationship Therapy as Applied to a Play Group. *Am. J. Orthopsychiat., 9*:583.

—— (1951), The Analysis of Character Traits in Group Therapy. *Int. J. Group Psychother., 1*:133-143.

—— (1955), *Group Psychotherapy for the Mothers of Disturbed Children.* Chicago: Charles Thomas.

—— and Glatzer, H. (1945), The Role of the Therapist in Group Relationship Therapy. *Nerv. Child, 4*:243-251.

—— —— (1948), The Theory and Practice of Group Psychotherapy. *Ann. N. Y. Acad. Sci.*

—— —— and Hirsch, J. (1944), The Therapy of Mothers in Groups. *Am. J. Orthopsychiat., 9*:583.

Fabian, A.; Crampton, J.; Holden, B. (1951), Group Therapy for Preschool Children. *Int. J. Group Psychother., 1*:37.

Gabriel, B. (1939), An Experiment in Group Treatment. *Am. J. Orthopsychiat., 9*:146.

—— and Halpert, A. (1952), The Effect of Group Therapy for Mothers on Their Children. *Int. J. Group Psychother., 2*:159.

Glatzer, H. (1947), The Selection of Mothers for Group Psychotherapy. *Am. J. Orthopsychiat., 17.*

—— (1952), The Transference of Mothers in Groups. *Am. J. Orthopsychiat., 22.*

—— (1953), Resistance of Mothers in Groups. *Am. J. Orthopsychiat., 23.*

—— and Pederson-Krag, G. (1947), Relationship Group Therapy with the Mother of a Problem Child. *The Practice of Group Psychotherapy*, ed. S. R. Slavson. New York: International Universities Press.

Hulse, W. (1948), Report on Various Experiences in Group Psychotherapy. *Jewish Soc. Serv. Quart.*, *25*.

Johnson, A.; Giffin, M.; Litin, E. (1954), Specific Factors Determining Antisocial Acting Out. *Am. J. Orthopsychiat.*, *24*:4.

Kahn, J.; Buchmueller, A. D.; Gildea, M. C. (1951), Group Therapy for Parents. *Am. J. Psychother.*, *5*:108.

Kolodney, E. (1944), Treatment of Mothers in Groups as a Supplement to Child Psychotherapy. *Ment. Hyg.*, *28*:437.

Lloyd, W. (1950), Group Work with Mothers in a Child Development Center. *Ment. Hyg.*, *34*.

Lowrey, L. (1954), Group Treatment for Mothers. *Am. J. Orthopsychiat.*, *14*:589.

Lulow, W. (1951), An Experimental Approach Toward the Prevention of Behavior Disorders in a Group of Nursery School Children. *Int. J. Group Psychother.*, *1*:144.

Mahler, M. S. (1949), Psychoanalytic Evolution of Tics. *The Psychoanalytic Study of the Child*, *3/4*:279-310. New York: International Universities Press.

Peck, H.; Rabinovitch, R.; Cramer, J. (1949), Treatment Program for Parents of Schizophrenic Children. *Am. J. Orthopsychiat.*, *19*:592.

Slavson, S. R. (1943), *Introduction to Group Therapy*. New York: International Universities Press, 1952.

Somerfield-Ziskind, E. (1949), Group Therapy. *Med. Woman J.*

Sperling, M. (1945), The Neurotic Child and His Mother. *Am. J. Orthopsychiat.*, *24*.

Spotnitz, H. and Gabriel, B. (1950), Resistance in Analytic Group Therapy: A Study of Group Therapeutic Process in Children and Mothers. *Quart. J. Child Behav.*, *2*:71-85.

Wolf, A. (1949, 1950), The Psychoanalysis of Groups. *Am. J. Psychother.*, *3*, *4*.

Chapter X

UNMARRIED MOTHERS[1]

•

For many years the unmarried mother was generally considered to be a community problem. Little attention was given her as a person with specific personality difficulties and motivations for her plight. The child born out of wedlock also presented a special problem to the mothers and to the community, being branded as legally illegitimate. In addition, there were also the difficulties attendant on the rearing and education of these children. Most of them had been placed away from home by private boarding arrangement or in foundling homes and orphan asylums. The unmarried mother carried the stigma of her transgression for the rest of her life. She was doomed to a life of an inferior and a comparative outcast. With the growth of insights into human behavior and motivations, a better understanding has emerged and with it greater tolerance and acceptance toward this particular human error and foible.

The unmarried mother is no longer eternally stigmatized and shunned and her offspring is no longer an outcast of society. The understanding is abroad that unmarried mothers, like all persons, are not governed by free will and unconditioned choice. Enlightened knowledge stemming from the newer understandings of man's behavior and motivations has mitigated public opinion. The conviction is gaining ever-wider acceptance that man acts out of inner needs, activated and conditioned by his nature

[1] The material in this chapter is drawn from a study of the socio-psychodynamics of unmarried motherhood conducted for the last three years at the Youth Consultation Service of the Diocese of New York by the authors, with the cooperation of the staff of that youth guidance agency. The study was subsidized by The Grant Foundation, Inc.

In view of the brevity of the time given to the study, many of the formulations must be viewed as tentative and subject to further investigation and validation, which the authors hope to do in the future. The formulations are offered here with the expectation that they may serve as a stimulus to other investigators.

and nurture, rather than from free choice. The unmarried mother, there-fore, as is also the case with other transgressors against the social codes, is now the object of understanding and of help, rather than ostracism.

Children born out of wedlock today are given up for adoption, taken care of by the mother or her relatives, or else placed temporarily in Foster Homes for a shorter or longer period. Caseworkers now generally believe that the girl should be helped to make her decision on the basis of her individual needs and the realities of her situation. In the Youth Consulta-tion Service Study about 50 per cent of the girls give their babies for adop-tion and only a very small number avoid making a final decision by placing the child in a Foster Home. However, the preference derived from many years of experience with numerous cases is that the children are by far better off when adopted by carefully selected childless couples, except in the instances where the unwed father and mother are genuinely in love with one another and wish to continue their relation, get married, and set up a family.

As a result of the more enlightened attitude toward these problems, it has been possible to throw the searchlight of reason and understanding upon this phenomenon so that some pertinent knowledge has come to light. In considering unmarried motherhood, it is necessary to differen-tiate between it and sexual delinquency. Because of definite conditions in our society, sexual delinquency is incomparably more prevalent than is the former, but despite the prevalence of sexual acting out, a compara-tively small percentage of the girls become unmarried mothers. Due to the knowledge and accessibility of preventives, extramarital conception is viewed as having some conscious or unconscious motivation and aim. Another fact that has a major bearing on our subject, uncovered by studies and observation, is that unmarried motherhood is not primarily conditioned by economic circumstances or social stratum. Susceptibility to it is resident in the intrapsychic structure of the girl as a compelling, though usually unconscious, need. It has also been established that what-ever impels a girl to enter the estate of unmarried motherhood proceeds from her familial relations and specific emotional states and attitudes resulting from them.

Psychodynamics of Unmarried Motherhood. The five elements that are predominantly involved in the psychosocial complex are the girl's relations with, and attitudes toward, (1) her father, (2) her mother, (3) a sibling or siblings, (4) the putative father, and (5) herself.

1. Studies reveal that in almost every case of unmarried motherhood, there has been a disturbance on the part of the girl in her relation to her

father either in a person-to-person tie or, where others had been involved in the interpersonal complex. A large number of the girls had fathers who had been too strict and rejecting (whom Young [1954] describes as "father-ridden") or had been overindulgent and seductive. In the one case they enter into a liaison with a man because he fills their emotional void, while in the other the unwed father of the child serves as a substitute; that is, the girl acts out her incestuous wishes. We have also found that some of the girls grew up in families without a father. In these instances, too, the putative father served as a substitute for him, but because the social taboo was not present in this case the putative father became the sexual object with whom the girl could act out her otherwise prohibited wishes.

The seductiveness of a father toward his daughter produces a feeling of rivalry with her husband on the part of his wife, causing her to woo the girl as well and thus overstimulate her and produce in her sexual confusion. Some of our clients had mothers who, because of their own drives, were unable to share their daughters with their husbands and had taken over the full management of the daughters' lives, thereby depriving the latter from normal relationships with their original male love objects, the fathers.

Some of the girls came from families where the mother monopolized the father and made him emotionally inacessible to the daughter. In both types of intrafamilial relations, it is understandable why a girl would seek a substitute father outside of the home and by bearing a child (incestuously) would attempt in her unconscious to complete for herself the family romance. When the unity of a girl with her father is prevented or interfered with, she invariably seeks that unity with another man. In having an out-of-wedlock child, there is also achieved the secondary gain, namely to revenge herself against her mother for the deprivation she had sustained. Actually, in these situations, the girl also identifies with the mother as well as acting out hostility toward her.

Where the mother is rejecting, rigid and cruel, the girl seeks to establish her love and security needs through the father, wth consequent exaggerations of her oedipal wishes, which she later seeks to gratify by a substitute object. This situation is frequently found where a stepmother is present in the home.

Edlin (1954) reports a case of a girl of seventeen who, as an act of retaliation, because she felt she was unloved by her domineering and ambitious mother, gave birth to a boy by a man of a different faith than her own. Her vengeful feeling was even more satisfied by the latter fact since her parents were deeply religious. Because there were no sons in this orthodox family, the father, especially, was eager to add the grandson to his menage. Four years later the girl became pregnant again and when she returned to the "shelter" for the period of the pregnancy, she emphatically declared, "This time I'm not going to give him to my mother! I'm going to keep him for my own!" One wonders whether in this instance the girl did not mean to gratify the father's unconscious craving for a son as girls sometimes do in relation to the unconscious cravings of their mothers.

One of our girls, 15 years of age, had conceived through a relationship with a very suitable fellow student in high school with whom she had had a good and affectionate relationship which she had continued after she had become pregnant. The girl was strongly attached to her father who was separated from the family. As a result of her condition, the father accepted her into his home. Thus having the baby served her fantasy to give him a child and living with him in a completed family unit. The baby served in two ways here. The girl was getting back *at* her father and getting back *to* him.

Mary, another of our clients, whose father had always wished for a son and had had two daughters instead, became pregnant at the age of 29 years, two months after her younger married sister had become pregnant. During the group discussions she frequently reiterated her wish that her child be a boy since her sister had given birth to a girl and "this would be my father's first male grandchild." As a result of the group discussions she finally told her parents about her condition which was at an advanced stage at that time. She later told the group that though her "mother was still very upset," her father "was very nice about it." We shall presently indicate other psychodynamics in this case that illustrate our general thesis.

2. Relations with mothers are almost universally negative and hostile. In a predominant number, though not in all cases that came to our attention, the attitude toward mothers was one of hostility. This is understandable since the oedipal situation which is reactivated during adolescence is nearly always an element in moral transgressions. Especially is susceptibility to unmarried motherhood present where the girl's mother was rejecting, punitive, nagging and debasing. Here, as in most instances, the girl by her act retaliates against and punishes her mother. By outraging the most cherished ideal of the latter, namely the virginity of her daughter, the latter employs a very sure and very virulent weapon of retaliation. Another motivation discernible in some girls is their wish to prove that they are as good as their persecuting parent, that they are acceptable to others and can attract and hold a man. They can get a "husband" just as the despised mother was able to do.

However, because of the psychic masochism of the girls and their low self-esteem, they frequently manage the episode by making a choice of a sexual mate so that no permanent relation would be possible, and when it is, the predominant number of the girls refuse to consummate it. Through this they defeat the mothers' wishes that their daughters "get married and settle down," among other things.

Not all of the mothers of the girls are rejecting, rigid, lacking in understanding or feelings. Many of them are immature. The immaturity of the "grandmother" is an important consideration in the nosology of unmarried motherhood, for it induces ego insufficiency in their daughters, making them susceptible to unsocial behavior. Josselyn (1953) suggests that some girls respond to the unconscious wishes of their mothers by having a child. She reports one instance where the mother had had a number of children at intervals of four to six years and whose youngest child had reached the age when he went to school, leaving the mother without a baby to nurture. It appeared that by having a baby out of wedlock, her young daughter had responded to the woman's wish to have a baby to care for. Needless to say, this child was accepted by the family as one of their own. The same author reports on a woman who had been promiscuous before her marriage and unconsciously wished that her daughter, too, lived out a similar pattern. The mother neither verbalized her wish, of which she was probably unaware anyway, nor did she openly encourage her daughter. The latter nonetheless became an unmarried mother.

A similar case has come to the attention of one of the authors (S.R.S.). A married woman, the daughter of a clergyman with two grown children, continued in her more or less promiscuous extramarital relations. Her husband, as well, frequently strayed from the path, though he did so with lesser compulsion and much lesser frequency. One of their children was a girl who was married at the age of sixteen, had her marriage annulled soon after and became promiscuous, finally ending up at the age of eighteen years as a prostitute.

One of the striking discoveries one makes in the study of the emotional reactions of unmarried mothers is their almost complete indifference toward the sexual act itself and the very rare incidence of pleasure derived from it. It would seem that for many of these girls the most important and significant aspect of the experience is the foreplay, when they are held tight and caressed as they yearned to be caressed when they were children. The girls often say that they feel "most complete" when they are carrying their babies in pregnancy. These reactions can be assumed to manifest their basic affect hunger and a strong identification with their babies, that is where the unmarried mother becomes the child, herself, and by giving to it the love, affection and protection, she feels vicariously fulfilled. However, the desire to be caressed and loved cannot entirely explain unmarried motherhood. It may account for sexual delinquency, generally. We must assume that other dynamics are present which lead specifically to fulfillment of wishes through the act of motherhood, which we shall presently discuss.

The maternal urge and its consequent vicarious gratifications that were mentioned represent a certain disharmony, since many girls who have children out of wedlock willingly give them up for adoption. Nonetheless, there is just as frequently present great hesitancy and conflict. Very few girls brazenly decide to give up their babies; there is always a period of vacillation and inner conflict. It is quite possible that material considerations and social pressures make them bow to practical necessities. There is little doubt in the minds of caseworkers and others who guided or treated these girls that the overwhelming majority of them would keep their babies if conditions favored it, which actually occurs in a large percentage of cases, especially in certain ethnic groups and races. Among Negroes, for example, nearly all illegitimate babies are accepted into the family fold with little and most often no question. Edlin (1954) reports that one third of the babies in the Jewish group that came to her attention in recent years had not been placed for adoption. No statistics are available on other racial and cultural sections of the population in the United States.

In a personal communication Ann Lambert of the Hudson Guild Guidance Service states that in her experience a predisposing factor to unmarried motherhood is the age interval between siblings. A girl between 13 and 15 whose mother gives birth to a child may become desirous herself of becoming a mother and therefore may be disposed to unmarried motherhood.

The present authors have not encountered such cases or at least have not studied them so as to uncover this fact. However, it seems plausible that this is a factor and one that should be considered in the future.

3. The attitude of parents toward the sex of their child is an etiological element, as well, though not a very frequent one. Where the girl is not welcomed or wanted by the parents because of her sex, preferring boys, or wishing they would have had a boy in the family instead of her, retaliatory impulses are evoked in the girl. To this can be added her undefined need to prove the worth of her sexuality. This she proves to herself and especially to her parents by the evidence of having a child. The preference given to brothers by parents makes a girl desirous to be-

come a boy. This desire is accompanied by diffuse feelings of anger and resentment against men and becoming an unmarried mother may therefore be an act of punishment of the putative father. She displaces upon him her antagonism toward her brother. In some instances sexual intercourse is an act of incorporating the penis which in her fantasy would make her a boy, as the parents had wished she were. As is well known, a child can also represent symbolically a penis to its mother. Having had a child and having been accepted by a man further serves to prove, and particularly to her parents, that she is a desirable person. Through this act she attempts to establish status with her parents. Among unmarried mothers there is a number who have a history of having been tomboys as youngsters as a result of the confusion in sexual identification that arises both from the attitude of parents and a desire on the part of the girls to be like their brothers.

Ellen, a 19-year-old white girl, came from a middle income family. Her mother was described as "very rigid and domineering who constantly depreciated her daughter." The father was a weak man at once submissive and resentful toward his wife. Following in his wife's footsteps, he rejected Ellen and was somewhat sadistic toward her. Ellen felt that both parents favored her 28-year-old brother and was very resentful toward all the three members of her family, but at the same time felt strongly attached to her father. Two interesting facts stand out in this case: (a) the putative father was a married man with two children, and (b) in the group discussions Ellen repeatedly expressed fear that her baby would be born defective. Apparently her guilt feelings were so intense that she was apprehensive of the punishment that would be visited on her. Her choice of a sex partner undoubtedly stems from her oedipal attachment for her father which was intensified by the unloving and punitive mother. Other contributing factors were (c) her retaliatory drive toward her rejecting parents; (d) the need to prove herself acceptable and adequate; (e) her confused sexual identification: the possible fantasy of incorporating a penis and becoming like her brother and, therefore, accepted and loved by her parents; and (f) the inevitable masochistic character that could not but result from the treatment she received at the hands of her parents.

Where a girl is not as attractive and acceptable as is her sister or sisters, she may not only act out sexually, as an assurance of her self-worth but, further, by having a child she defeats them because she can show herself as acceptable to men. Some of our girls have become unmarried mothers after a sister was married. The sister's marriage was the direct precipitating cause. Mary is one illustration of this.

Jean's family relations were quite the opposite from those of Ellen.

Here the father was stern and domineering and the mother passive and compliant. She fell in with all of her husband's wishes and actions. Jean was one of two twin girls, the only children in the family, and was very close to her sister. In fact, when she became pregnant, her sister was the only person to whom Jean imparted her secret. During the group discussions in the shelter Jean expressed the wish that she could give her child to her sister, but hesitated to do so because her brother-in-law was very strict and she would "not approve of the way in which he would bring up" her child. Because her sister had two boys Jean hoped that she would have a girl "so that there would be a granddaughter in the family." Actually Jean planned to give up her baby for adoption, but she was expressing and working through in the group discussions her wishes and fantasies of (a) placating her father, (b) raising her self-esteem in relation to her sister, (c) punishing her parents, (d) expressing her dependence.

4. The fourth category of relational attitudes that affect the unmarried mother syndrome is the girl's attitude toward the "putative" father. A number of striking features are found here. First, the girls usually choose a man who is an unlikely prospect for marriage, and frequently, it is a man whom the girls actually dislike once they had become pregnant and refuse to have anything to do with him after that. In fact, most girls do not inform the men of the pregnancy and childbirth. Edlin (1954) states: "About eighty per cent of the marriages of Lakeview girls who have kept their children have been to men other than the actual fathers" (p. 137). There are some exceptions to this but comparatively few.

Ted, a very attractive, tall, slender, professional girl with a good education became pregnant at the age of 25 years. She came from a Protestant background and a family whose head intensely desired to have a boy. He thus proceeded to treat Ted as a boy and encouraged her to participate in activities and sports as though she were one. Despite the higher social status of her family, she became involved with a man who, though very attractive, had served two prison terms and was on parole at the time she struck up a friendship with him that led her to the estate of unmarried motherhood. The sexual confusion, the masochistic trend, and the need for setting up impedimenta against marriage are all present in this case. Another element present is that the parents' strong objection to their daughter's friendship with the putative father may have intensified his attraction for her, since by her act she got even with her snobbish, supercilious, highly demanding mother who imposed her unrealistic standards of propriety and achievement on her daughter. Thus the retaliatory motive was also strong here.

Unmarried mothers also tend to choose men of a different religion than their own, and sometimes also of a different race, and married men, so as to be unable to join them in wedlock. In this respect as well, one should not overlook the possibilities of punishing the parents who may have rigid prejudices in these matters. In a study by Donnell and Glick (1952) of a group of 100 Jewish unmarried mothers, they found that one half of the putative fathers were boys and men of other religions and races, thus making marriage impossible for them. They state "that out of the 100 cases, 83 girls chose men who for one or more reasons would have been an unsuitable choice of a husband. It was interesting to note that in half of the cases studied, the putative father was non-Jewish. Not only were religious differences very marked, but many of the putative fathers were already married. In several cases there were extreme differences in age, and many of the boys in no way were adequate to supporting a wife, and several seemed to be emotionally unsuitable."

In our group discussions with more than 160 Protestant girls, only in about a third of the cases did any of them express a desire to see the putative father again or to marry him. Most frequently they were averse to continuing any kind of a relationship with the man. One rather masculine unmarried mother who came to our attention insisted on involving the father of her child in every step in the planning for hospitalization, costs, adoption and all other details. The caseworker was impressed, however, with the vehemence and hostility with which she insisted on forcing him to take part, even though this was actually not necessary. The girl's attitude and manner revealed an unmistakable punitive and hostile intent.

Another interesting fact is that a large number of the girls had had a normal and what would ordinarily seem to be a desirable relationship with a young man other than the child's father at the time they had become pregnant. It would seem as though the normal, acceptable relation and legalized motherhood was not to their liking. This may be significant in a number of ways. There may be a very strong masochistic component in the character of these girls; they seem to have an unconscious need for self-defeat and self-destruction. We suspect that the masochistic trend involves rape fantasies and the need to be forced into sexual relations. A relation in which the man would give of himself and to whom it would be necessary for the girl to give herself willingly, with a prospect of a constructive, permanent relation did not satisfy unconscious needs. The single sexual episode with the putative father, which is frequently the case, seems to have rape as its aim. In a casual relation of this kind and the circumstances under which it occurs, the element of aggression must play an important part. In a relationship of this sort, the man must take the girl much more aggressively than in marriage to which she comes with the intent to consummate, and prepared for, the sexual act.

An illustration of this enigmatic phenomenon was supplied by a young, professional woman who had spent the night in a young man's room, also a professional person. He was a quiet and unassertive person, very gentle and kind. In a conversation at breakfast when the matter of sleeping the preceding night was mentioned, the young woman exclaimed with resentment in her voice addressing her erstwhile bedmate, "If you only were more of a cave man!" By this subtle, though emphatic remark, she literally stated that had force been used, she would have submitted. That is, she wanted to be raped. A male patient once described the reaction of a virginal girl of about 28 years of age, who during the sexual act repeatedly exclaimed, "Hurt me, hurt me, hurt me." While in both instances there is the possibility that the reactions stemmed from their guilt feelings, in one case to shift the responsibility on the man, in the other to be punished for her crime, there is nonetheless discernible in these reactions a definite rape fantasy and desire for masochistic pleasure.[2]

We found that in a large number of cases, probably one half of the unmarried mother population we studied, the relation between the girl and the putative father was perfunctory. It is short lived and frequently they are casual and first acquaintances. In some instances, the episode occurs at the first meeting, after which the couple never see each other again. However, Donnell and Glick (1952) who studied Jewish unmarried mothers found that this was not the fact with that particular group. They say, "It was found that in 74 out of the 100 cases studied, the unmarried mother was well acquainted with the putative father. In several instances marriage was considered and nine of the 100 girls actually did marry the putative fathers. In only seventeen per cent of the cases could there be said that a relationship was casual." We do not find these statistics reflecting the condition in the non-Jewish, white group. It is our impression that the Donnell-Glick findings may apply also to the Negro group. If further studies demonstrate this to be the case, this fact would have special significance and may be related to the minority status of these two ethnic groups.

Despite the fact that the overwhelming majority of the girls completely rejected the putative fathers, there were a few in our groups who have entered the state of unmarried motherhood as a means of compelling them to consummate a marriage. This occurs most often when there existed a prolonged sexual relation between the two. A noteworthy fact is that the

[2] These illustrations had been culled from sources other than Youth Consultation Service files.

largest number of the fathers, while willing to carry on the liaison, rejected a permanent relation. Most of them disappear.

The striking fact about unmarried motherhood already recorded, and which is not usually true of the ordinary sex delinquent, is that few of them derive pleasure from sexual intercourse. This characteristic holds even for those girls who have repeated the sexual act. Quoting again from Donnell and Glick, on this point, "It was notable that only 5 of the 100 girls had achieved the pleasure of a sexual adjustment, while 52 stated directly that they did not enjoy intercourse and found it painful and unpleasant. Sexual relations were frequently described in such terms as 'a horrible experience' and 'disgusting.' In 43 cases, no information was obtained on this point."

It is quite possible that the absence of pleasure is due to the fact that sex intercourse was carried out under unfavorable conditions in an unrelaxed state of mind, and since in many instances it was the first such experience, full enjoyment could not be expected. No unwed mothers came to our attention who had been promiscuous, though there were a few recidivists among them. The latter got into difficulties again because their basic inner problems that precipitated the first transgression had not been overcome.

5. Relative to the general character peculiarities of unmarried mothers, our observation leads to the conclusion that by and large they have inadequate ego development, are weak, compliant and submissive. This is confirmed by other observers as reported in the literature. Our impression is that the predominant majority of the girls, at least in the Protestant, white group, have character disorders. There were among them a small number of neurotics, a negligible number of psychotics and no full-blown psychoneurotics. The Negro girls presented problems of inadequate ego development with a large representation of psychopaths and girls with masculine identifications.

In our group discussions with the girls, both white and Negro, we were impressed with the intense feelings of deprivation the girls had which were not illusory. They had been subjected to intense and early emotional and social deprivations. Many reacted to this by a superficial façade of adequacy, though they soon revealed basic weaknesses. All the girls revealed denial of parental love and an impressive number complained of difficulties in making friends and expressed a desire for friends and male companionship that would not involve them in sex relations.

We have found little guilt in our girls. Though they were perturbed by the many practical problems, they displayed no remorse or feelings of guilt either toward their parents, their unborn babies or society generally.

They rather accepted the situation and concentrated in their discussions on plans for their babies and for themselves after the delivery and surrender. The latter process and the legal entanglements as well as the possibility of being discovered in the future are their major preoccupations.

It would seem from this that the superego development of the unmarried mothers is inadequately developed as are their ego strengths. In some of the girls the identifications are defective which result in ego and superego deficiencies; in others the superego standards imposed on them had been so unrealistic and strict that they have rejected them. Our impression from the group discussions is that the girls do not recognize disagreeable feelings in themselves and that they do not think of themselves as "bad" or as "angry" or even as disturbed. This, of course, can be a typical anxiety-denying mechanism of some neurotics, but our feeling about unmarried mothers as a group is that this is not the case. Rather, because of the permissive superego and the absence of appropriate anxiety, they can be considered more as being on the side of psychopathy and not neuroses. Certainly the fact that they have acted out their problems rather than internalized them would justify this hypothesis.

There is, however, one mitigating circumstance for the unmarried mothers' self-absorption and seeming narcissism. The state of pregnancy being a biological fulfillment and a genuinely creative period, the feelings of gratification and heightened self-esteem as a woman and a person may overshadow qualms of conscience. However, the refusal to recognize their social transgression and the signficance of their act by postpartum unmarried mothers supports our observation that they fall, by and large, in the category of character disorders with psychopathic coloring.

An examination of the various intrapsychic and social factors that seem to contribute toward unmarried motherhood reveals the fact that none are present here that cannot be found in other types of personality disturbances and social maladjustments. We have, therefore, come to the conclusion that a specific combination of factors must be present. We have found confirmation of this in the brief study published by Donnell and Glick (1952). They, too, suggest such a possibility, but do not list or suggest what elements in combination would produce the favoring syndrome.

Though an authoritative statement in this regard will require further analysis and statistical validation, we suggest at this time such a syndrome. Before we do this, however, it will be necessary briefly to classify the causes or factors present in order to show, equally briefly, their dynamic interrelations. The factors present can be grouped under two headings:

(1) *predisposing* factors, and (2) *precipitating* factors.[3] In the first classification are included various intrapsychic dispositions and states and socioeconomic conditions. These are either singly or in combination always present. Sometimes, as in the cases of individual girls, there occurred a particularly disturbing episode in their lives that, on the basis of the predisposing trend, triggered the consummation of the trend. This is the precipitating factor and it may be the separation of parents, being ejected from the home and family circle, losing a loved one, and, as Josselyn (1953) suggests, the impulsion of the biological cycle when women are most responsive sexually. Precipitating factors are, however, not essential to cause unmarried motherhood. Thus the phenomenon of unmarried motherhood may be expressed by the following formula for some cases

$$U.M. = P.F. + Pr.F.$$

where U.M. represents unmarried motherhood, P.F. = predisposing factor or factors, Pr.F. = precipitating factor.

As already indicated, a precipitating factor may be essential to trigger the act in some cases, and it may be unnecessary or fortuitous in others. Most girls have children out of wedlock without experiencing a precipitating trauma; only a few do. In our opinion, however, there must be definite conditions present for a girl to become an unmarried mother. To show this relation we are suggesting that in the mass of predisposing factors there are *constants* and *variables*. By this we mean that some of these factors are present in *all* the girls who get into this plight. These are constants that are always present either in combination with others (the variables that may or may not be present) or produce the full effect on their own. Thus the following formulae are offered:

$$U.M. = C.F. + O$$
$$\text{or}$$
$$U.M. = C.F. + V.F.$$

in which C.F. = constant, V.F. = variable factors, and O = none present.

It is our belief that the intrapsychic conditions that are constant, that is, present in all unmarried mothers are *hostility, craving for affection* (affect hunger), and *masochism*. That is,

$$C.F. = \text{Hostility} + \text{Affect Hunger} + \text{Masochism}$$

To this equation variable factors may or may not be added. All the factors, only a few of which we have described, are the variables that

---

[3] Donnell and Glick (1952) have also suggested the term "precipitating factor."

contribute to and reinforce this combination of the constants. Using abbreviations of H, for hostility, A.H., for affect hunger and M, for masochism the equation is

$$U.M. = H. + A.H. + M.$$

or, where variables are present

$$U.M. = H. + A.H. + M. + V.F._1 + V.F._2 + V.F._3 + \cdots$$

$V.F._1$, $V.F._2$, $V.F._3$, etc., represent different variable factors.

Sociological Factors and Backgrounds. Writers on unmarried motherhood have been interested in a number of different facets of the problem. However, it has generally been agreed that there cannot be a problem at all except within a social group which disapproves of out-of-wedlock pregnancy (Schmideberg, 1951; Josselyn, 1953). Within this framework, public administrators, social workers, social scientists and psychologists have sought to understand what type of person becomes an unmarried mother, what is her background, what practical and psychological services she needs, what happens to the baby and how the mother reaches her decision, what kind of man becomes an unmarried father, and what are the motives behind unmarried pregnancy, in all, and in particular cultural groups within American society.

Efforts at estimating the frequency of unmarried motherhood are handicapped by the disapproval of society which leads an unknown number of girls to hide and disguise their condition or to attempt to get rid of the baby. Studies of the unmarried mother and her child are generally based on live birth registrations and applications to public and private social agencies. As a result, while a number of middle-class girls are heard of through these channels, almost nothing is known of illegitimacy in the uppermost strata of society. Estimates of frequency vary from place to place and from time to time. Mattingly (1928) says that the number of illegitimate births per 1,000 live births of white mothers increased in Cleveland from 17 in 1923 to 19 in 1926 and of colored mothers from 72 in 1923 to 80 in 1926. A Los Angeles study gave a figure for that county of 41 per 1000 live births (Dean, 1944) and in Puerto Rico in 1937, 33 per cent of all births were registered as illegitimate (U. S. Children's Bureau News Letter).

While the proportionate distribution of unmarried motherhood throughout the different social classes is impossible to determine, the largest number of studies have been concerned with girls drawn from the lower-income groups. The role of poor economic conditions in out-of-wedlock pregnancy has been discussed by a number of writers, and the general consensus appears to be that economic needs and pressures are contributory rather than primary factors in unmarried motherhood.

A number of studies have been made with regard to the age, intelligence and employment of these girls. Most writers find that unmarried motherhood is most frequent between the ages of 15 and 25 and quite rare below 15 and over 30. In a study of 500 Negro girls, Reed (1934) found 25 per cent under 19 and 76 per cent under 25. Travers (1942) discovered in a group of 164 unmarried mothers that the largest numbers fell within the 17 to 18 and 22 to 23 year age categories. Nottingham (1937) considered that almost all her group fell between the ages of 15 and 25 with an average age of 19 years. Frost (1939), in a study of 500 unmarried mothers in Detroit, calculated the most frequent age for white girls to be 19 to 20 and for Negro girls 17 to 18. Dean (1944) concurs in these findings in a study of 1,839 cases from welfare agencies where 70 per cent were 20 and over and 25 per cent under 20 years of age. Thus out-of-wedlock pregnancy may be considered largely a phenomenon of adolescence and early adulthood.

While intelligence among unmarried mothers appears to follow the normal distribution of the general population, a number of studies have found that a disproportionate number of domestic servants become unmarried mothers. For instance, Reed (1926) in a study of Negro illegitimacy in New York City found that 85 per cent were domestics as opposed to 71 per cent of all Negro women thus employed in this area. Mattingly (1928) in Cleveland in a sample of 53 white unmarried mothers found that 22 were employed in domestic service. Nottingham (1937), Frost (1939), and Laverty (1942) obtained similar results in their studies. While unmarried mothers may come from the professional groups and may have received a higher education, the largest numbers are found among girls who have not completed high school.

There is a general belief that the number of broken homes is very high in the families from which unmarried mothers come. In six studies numbering 255 unmarried mothers, 149 were found to come from families where at least one parent was out of the home (Smith, 1935; Nottingham, 1937; Laverty, 1942; Powell, 1949; Bernard, 1944; Donnell and Glick, 1952). Homes in which there is extreme friction are also prevalent and poor parent-child relationships are believed by all writers to be an important factor in unmarried motherhood.

Few writers have been concerned with the social status of the unmarried father. However, Frost (1939) found that most of the fathers in his group were between 20 and 25 years of age, that 47 per cent were single,

21 per cent married, 4 per cent divorced, and 26 per cent of unknown status. Sharpe (1940) also agrees that most of the fathers tend to be in their 20's, while Lenz (1940) found that the median age of a group of 583 putative fathers who appeared before the Erie court was 27 years. In this group 34 per cent were married. Travers (1942) believes the men to be generally 8 or 9 years older than the girls. Kasanin and Handschin (1941) also say that the putative fathers are older. Nottingham (1937) and several other writers state that the fathers tend to come from slightly higher economic levels than the girls and that the largest group are found among the skilled and semiskilled workers.

A number of writers have concerned themselves with the provision and coordination of services and special procedures relating to the mother and her child and with the community attitudes to the unwed family. The U.S. Children's Bureau has published pamphlets on adoption procedures, the confidentiality of birth records, and the services available for unmarried mothers. Judge (1951), C. Brenner (1950), Embry (1937), and Dudley (1939) emphasize the importance of coordinating services so that the unmarried mother is not sent from agency to agency but can sustain a major contact with one individual worker who will help her in her planning and give her the necessary support and guidance.

Maternity home facilities and their programs are discussed by Morlock (1946), Genrose (1939), and Blethen (1942), and in pamphlets issued by the National Committee for Service to Unmarried Mothers and the Child Welfare League of America. Several writers report on the establishment of craft and discussion groups in maternity shelters, and in a personal communication from the Florence Crittenton Home, Toledo, experiences and conclusions similar to those described in this chapter are reported.

The influence of community attitudes is also discussed. Edlin (1954) points out their influence on the decision of the girl whether or not to keep her baby. Rodriguez (1937) discusses the difficulties the unmarried minor is up against if she wishes to remain with her baby in Argentina, and Young (1954) emphasizes the role which caseworkers should play in influencing public opinion. C. Brenner (1950) examines the influence of Aid to Dependent Children on the incidence of unmarried motherhood and concludes that public assistance tends to mitigate illegitimacy because it reduces insecurity which, in his opinion, is one of the factors in unmarried parenthood.

Nondirected Group Interaction. Over the last three years at the Youth Consultation Service of the Episcopal Diocese of New York, Inc., we have carried on an experiment which also served as a demonstration and a study of the possibilities of treating and guiding unmarried mothers in groups. The purpose of this study was to see whether through this medium (a) more could be learned about the unmarried mother; (b) whether her conflicts and indecisions during pregnancy could be reduced; and (c) whether more girls can be enabled to accept and make use of treatment after delivery and after the decision with regard to the baby had been reached. Two different types of groups have been tried: (a) free discussion groups for girls living in "shelters" during the prenatal period, and (b) therapy groups for girls who were considered to need further treatment after the disposition of the baby had been made.

The former were conducted in two shelters which are different in character, one being in a small village with a capacity of 24 girls, and the other in a large city, housing 14 girls. While both shelters are interracial and nonsectarian, the girls were predominantly white Protestants. A small number of them were Negroes: only 15 of the 126 who attended the groups were Negro girls. While the girls who took part in the project were a typical group of unmarried mothers with regard to age (113 out of 126 girls fell between the ages of 15 and 26), they came from all parts of the United States and included a rather high ratio of middle-class girls with better than average education.

As do also other therapists, we have refrained from involving our pregnant girls in intensive treatment. Psychotherapy can become disturbing and anxiety-producing, and because of the need of a pregnant woman to maintain a state of good physical health and of emotional equilibrium for the best interest of the unborn child, we did not consider it advisable to expose them to intensive psychotherapy. In addition, the pregnancy state does not favor productive therapy, since the pregnant woman is both physically and psychologically preoccupied with the nurturing of the fetus that she carries. There occurs during this period a tendency toward inversion and comparative withdrawal from the world; at least, there is a diminution in the keenness of interests which are understandably displaced by preocupation with the coming event, its poignancy, its hazards, its consequences. As a matter of fact, even these do not stand out too clearly or too realistically. Instead the woman undergoes a state that approaches that of listlessness and self-absorption.

These reactions need not be encouraged or nurtured, for if they exceed permissible intensity, they may lead to morbidity. Centripetal interests should be maintained, but encouragement of self-analytical, introspective preoccupations should be avoided. However, pregnant women and especially unmarried mothers, are greatly relieved, and their health is in a better state, when they can verbalize and share with others their puzzlements, fears and fantasies. Our girls, for example, invariably brought out in the group conversations the fear of giving birth to a child with some physical defect or inadequacy, or a monstrosity, as in Ellen's case. These thoughts and apprehensions have obsessed them in privacy, and the relief concerning them and other similar topics supplied by the group and leader was unmistakable.

It is also desirable that the pregnant woman should keep in contact with reality and her mind occupied with practical problems of her life and future. Again, in unmarried mothers these are more numerous and more pressing. They, too, cause them uncertainty and anxiety. The dependencies characteristic of these girls are enhanced by their state of maternity, and caseworkers find that much of their time and effort are taken with meeting dependency needs of the girls. One value, among others, of group discussions lies in the fact that the participants act in a more independent role. They, together with others, arrive at understandings and make decisions with little or no help from a mother figure. This is more difficult, if at all possible, to achieve in individual casework, since the juxtaposition of client and worker inescapably assigns them definite roles and a clearly implied relation.

We have, therefore, modified the procedures of group psychotherapy and of group guidance and counseling for the prenatal unmarried girls, though we have used direct analytic group psychotherapy with the postnatal mothers. The process in these groups can be described as *nondirected group interaction* and consists of completely free and undirected conversations among the girls of whatever subject that interests them at any time. Thus they talk about the situation in the "shelter" where they live, express their disapproval and preferences of staff, analyze their relations with each other in the living situation at the shelter, relieve themselves of gripes as well as talk about practical problems in relation to surrendering or keeping the baby and their reintegration into the community, anonymity, jobs, marriage, confidentiality with their future husbands, attitudes of their parents, their family tensions, putative fathers and their conflicts about giving up their babies. We shall presently delineate the value of these cathartic and on occasion insightful discussions in the groups we have conducted on this plan.

The shelter groups were organized in three different ways: (1) as general groups which anyone could attend on a voluntary basis; (2) groups for Y.C.S.[4] girls only, who were also seen by different caseworkers, and (3) groups for Y.C.S. girls only, i.e., the girls were all assigned for indi-

[4] Abbreviation for Youth Consultation Service.

vidual guidance and treatment to the worker who also led the group. We have found that there are a number of advantages which may be obtained from this last arrangement. The worker already has a relationship with the girls before the group starts, knows more about the girls, and it is, therefore, easier for her to understand the significance of what they are saying. It facilitates the carry-over from group to individual interviews and makes it much easier to handle any tendency to use the groups as resistance to or escape from individual treatment. The girls also seem more at ease with their own caseworker right from the start and talk more freely at an early stage in the group. However, because of the usually small case load and geographic distribution, this plan makes for difficulties in the assignment of cases. It is, therefore, not always possible to follow it. Also, in a small shelter, it is not desirable to select some girls for special consideration, that is, belonging to a group and leaving others out. Since there is constant turnover as girls deliver their babies and leave the shelter, it is difficult to maintain a sufficient number of members in the groups when they are built around a single caseworker.

The girls were told at the outset that they could talk about anything that concerns them and could share ideas with each other. While the groups were nondirective and the girls were full of questions and talked with ease, it was necessary for the leader on occasion to stimulate discussion by asking a question which would help a specific girl to bring out what was troubling her. Apart from this, the leader's major activities were in clarifying areas of confusion and in supplying factual data on procedures with regard to hospital, birth certificates, adoption, anonymity, and community reactions.

Five distinct continuous or open groups led by four different caseworkers, had met in consultation with a group therapy specialist and several psychiatrists, during the three-year period, with a revolving membership of 126 girls. The content of the discussions was remarkably similar in all of the groups. A large part of the time was consumed in clarifying feelings about, and understanding, the possibilities and problems involved in a decision about the unborn babies. Typical of these discussions is the following:

Joan said she would like to talk about something which was constantly being asked her and which she knew they all had to answer for themselves. "Should a girl keep her baby when she was not married?" Catherine laughed self-consciously and said that was certainly a question she had asked herself many times. She said she thought a child needed a father, having herself had a very unhappy childhood because her parents had been divorced. She had seen very little of her father, and had not seen him at all during the last five years. She said somewhat defiantly that she would not be in this "fix" if she had a father. Marion said that her case was different. She had to decide about giving her baby away or keeping it on a different basis because she had a chance to marry the father of the baby but she was not ready for marriage and had not wanted to give the baby a home as long as it was possible to make another plan for it. She thought she would be getting off on the wrong foot to marry because of the baby.

Whether to care for the baby after it is born and before surrender, feelings for the father of the baby and for the girl's own parents, feelings about pregnancy and people knowing about it—have been discussed in all the groups. The girls said that through talking things over they have begun to feel more clearly about the whole situation and have then found it easier to talk to other people and to tell their parents of their plight when this seemed advisable. The girls always remarked that it was a big help to know that other people were worried and scared about the same things that they were (universalization).

We have found that groups are beneficial in a number of other ways. The girls gain support from each other by sharing and talking over their difficulties. They are helped to accept themselves and their situation and are able to reveal their feelings freely. The group discussions enrich the individual interview. There is carry-over not only from one group session to another, but also from group session to individual interview. Frequently through the group a girl, for the first time, begins to recognize that she herself has the opportunity of making the major decision that will affect her entire life.

Through the group discussions all the girls become much better informed on adoption and legal procedures which frees time from individual interviews for the discussion of other problems. Through sharing their feelings about the decisions they have made, the girls grow more sure and more confident that they are doing what is best for them as individuals and for their babies. The girls who are diffident and shy, and unable to talk freely are yet able to listen and benefit from the general dicussion (vicarious catharsis and spectator therapy).

Apprehensions around the pregnancy are much more freely ventilated in the group than in any other situation, and there is a general reduction of fear and anxiety as a result. The groups also serve to supplement the general accepting attitude of the shelter staff, and the latter report that because of the close identity they establish in the group, the girls get along better with each other and a more harmonious community living results. The girls also begin to understand their parents better and grow more accepting of them.

Those who have benefited most from the discussion groups were the timid and withdrawn who had not been able to talk up for themselves. Peggy was such a girl. Peggy was the 21-year-old daughter of a Protestant clergyman, who together with his wife, had had "very high standards." She was her father's favorite, was strongly attached to and identified with him. She struck up a friendship with an aggressive Catholic boy, and the two young people planned to get married, but the strong interference by Peggy's mother broke up the relation. Thereupon, so Peggy's story goes, the boy raped her.

Peggy presented herself in the group as a strikingly quiet, fearful and withdrawn person, with evidences of underlying severe hostility and resentment. She was, however, unable to express her hostile feelings and appeared to disapprove of others who did so. Before we describe Peggy's participation in the group it may be of value to point up the psychodynamics of her case. She obviously (a) retaliated against both her parents for their repressive treatment of her; (b) she acted out her oedipal wishes toward her father for whom she continued her infantile attachment and consequent hostility toward her mother; (c) she acted out her rape fantasy; (d) she followed up on her masochistic needs and; finally (e) she made a permanent relation with the putative father impossible by choosing one who would unavoidably be rejected by the family on religious grounds.

Peggy seemed to enjoy the group sessions and attended them regularly. Though she was at first quiet and diffident, she gradually became much friendlier. After several sessions she appeared more relaxed and able to participate in the group conversations. At one of the sessions when the girls were evaluating their own changed attitudes since coming to the "shelter" and to the group, Peggy said, "I've learned to live with all kinds of people here, and I think that I'm more tolerant now. I think I was pretty 'high hat' when I came and I don't think anyone could call me that now."

At a session after having delivered herself of her baby, Peggy said, "I didn't expect to feel differently after the baby was born because I thought I had done all my thinking ahead of time, but when I saw the baby I realized that I wanted to keep it. Now, however, I am content to relinquish it." The leader asked what had changed Peggy's mind. She replied, "Although I made my decision when I was mad right through, I think I realized from the beginning I could not keep it because I want to go back to my family, and I could not bring an illegitimate child home. Something else happened, too. I thought I was just mad at the father of the baby but I was mad at my mother, too. However, when she looked at the baby she realized how hard it would be for me to give him up. For the first time she saw the baby as a human being and would have liked to keep him. For the first time in many years she felt at one with me and perhaps this was what I was looking for."

Hence another element can be added to Peggy's motivations in becoming an unmarried mother: (f) the gain of being fully accepted (and forgiven) by her mother. Apparently the mother's affection for her "illegitimate" grandchild was transmuted in Peggy's fantasy into love for herself.

It may be helpful to categorize the factors present in this case according to our schema. They are as follows:

Predisposing Factors		Precipitating Factors
Constants	Variables	Frustration through rejection of boy friend by parents
Hostility toward parents	Oedipal wishes	
Masochism	Rape fantasy	
Striving to be accepted by parents		

For girls like Peggy the free atmosphere of the group has been the most meaningful experience in their stay at the "shelter." The few aggressive and assertive girls found it difficult to get along with the others in the common home, and as a result have curbed their boldness. They have become more in harmony with their environment. Some of the older girls who seemed to have a need to appear independent in individual casework have found it easier to accept help from the group. Girls with homosexual tendencies had been less menaced by a group than by a transference relation with an individual woman caseworker or shelter staff member and were able to talk their problems over more freely. The few girls with pronounced hostile feelings toward authority and parental figures, as a result of which they could not tolerate an individual guidance situation, have been able to attend the group and work through their confusions and basic anxieties about their babies and future plans in the common pool of the group's discussions.

Because unmarried mothers have by and large low self-esteem, the leader must be warm and accepting, and because they have great difficulty in revealing negative feelings, being predominantly compliant and submissive, the leader must be ever alert to underlying currents, help bring out what the girls really want but are afraid to say, and at the same time remain *neutral*. The situations the girls have to unravel and deal with are emotionally highly charged; the leader must at all times be aware of the psychodynamics of each member of the group and of the effect upon each girl of the content of the discussions and the resulting interpersonal reactions.

Some of the other topics the girls discussed have been: adjustment to and problems in the shelter; reactions toward the discussion group; fantasies around pregnancy; pros and cons about caring for the baby the first two weeks; feelings about giving babies for adoption; advisability of telling their parents about their pregnancies and having had babies; feeling about people knowing of, or discovering, their pregnancies; resentment against caseworkers' asking personal questions; use of private vs. agency adoption sources; attitude toward the father of the baby; christening and baptism; misgivings about their children finding out about their "real parents"; problems around naming the babies so as to conceal the mother's identity; birth certificates and the adoption papers; the child's and father's name; length of time of keeping the baby before adoption; fear of abnormalities in the babies; parenthood and proper procedures of bringing up babies; choice of and conduct in the hospital; adoptive parents, their attitude, feelings and qualifications; attitudes toward and problems of marriage in the light of previous unmarried motherhood; revealing their status to husbands; the importance of sex education; feelings about families: fathers, mothers, siblings; family tensions; causes of their plight (occasionally and brought up by specific, usually neurotic, girls).

Our estimate of the value of these group discussions is that (a) they buttress the positive rather than the deleterious trends in the girls; (b) they aid self-acceptance and correct defective self-image; (c) they supply mirror reactions so that each can gain better insight into her own conduct and responses; (d) by providing universalization of problems guilt and anxiety are reduced; (e) the groups provide mutuality and heightened sense of social relations and improve object relationships; (f) through sharing and communication, the load the ego has to carry is diminished; (g) a definite and useful body of information and knowledge results from the discussions; and (h) there is opportunity for identification with a wholesome parental figure in the person of the leader.

Postpartum Group Psychotherapy. The postpartum groups were set up as analytic groups (Slavson, 1952), and they were presented to the girls as a therapeutic means for correcting noxious intrapersonal conditions and states so that they could achieve a more satisfying life for themselves. It was thought that it would be possible through these groups to involve the girls in treatment. Most of them resisted individual psychotherapy, but were considered to be in need of further help with their personality problems.

Four such groups had been formed, and 38 girls accepted and prepared for them. Of these only 7 attended regularly and 22 did not respond. All the 7 who responded also accepted individual treatment. Only 5 of the 22 who did not come to the groups continued in individual treatment after the decision around the baby was finalized. Apparently even they were unable to participate with comfort in group situations.

Of the 7 girls who came regularly to the groups, 4 had character disorders and 3 were diagnosed as having character neuroses. They were all girls with high intelligence ratings; 4 had some college education. All related positively to their individual caseworkers as well and were aware that they had personality problems that caused them unhappiness.

It was found that the groups did better when they were homogeneous: mixed groups of Negro and white girls were less relaxed. It was more difficult for the girls to relate to each other when there was wide disparity of intellect or of social or economic status. When girls with different problems or who had made different decisions around the adoption of their babies found themselves in the same group, usually one or the other dropped out. It appeared that the postnatal unmarried mothers who gave up their babies felt guilty about their decision when they were confronted by the conversation about the babies from those who had kept them. They verbalized great longing for their offspring and curiosity about their appearance, state of health and general condition. The girls who kept their babies, on the other hand, still young, were envious of the others because they had more freedom, more money, and prettier clothes.

The reaction to the analytic groups for postnatal unmarried mothers substantiates the prediction made by one of the authors (S.R.S.) at the outset of the study that this would be the result. The mere fact of unmarried motherhood does not constitute a motivation for psychotherapy. In fact it was his opinion that, if anything, once the girls placed their babies for adoption, they would avoid all contact that would remind them of their past plight: it is an experience which they would rather see pass into limbo and not keep alive in their memories. There is some doubt in his mind whether unmarried mothers, merely by virtue of be-

coming mothers, require psychotherapy. Motherhood is a biological fulfillment. It becomes a problem only when it is consummated in a socially
disapproved manner and circumstance. It is also a problem when motherhood has secondary values and yields secondary gains rather than being
a primary purpose and a completion of the biological urge and need.
It was therefore his opinion that the girls who are psychoneurotic and
whose unmarried motherhood is part of a neurotic constellation should
and could be involved in treatment, for they suffer through their neuroses.

Unmarried mothers should, therefore, be chosen for psychotherapy
on the basis of their general pathology and psychological syndrome
(Slavson, 1955) rather than because they had become unmarried mothers.
Unmarried motherhood is no criterion for selection or grouping of patients for group therapy, beyond the fact that it is a path to the general
psychoneurotic nucleus.

Some therapists hold the view, however, that *all* unmarried mothers
require treatment and can be motivated to accept it if they are made
aware of the intrapsychic determinants of their act *while they are still
pregnant*. They hold that once delivery has occurred the possibility to
activate this awareness is greatly reduced. In our opinion this is a subject
of utmost importance for prevention of recidivism and should receive
appropriate attention. One wonders, however, how one can induce such
awareness in a pregnant girl without at the same time activating anxiety
which, we believe, should be avoided.

BIBLIOGRAPHY

Bernard, V. W. (1944), Psychodynamics of Unmarried Motherhood in Early Adolescence.
   Nerv. Child, 4:26-45.
—— (1948), Needs of Unmarried Parents and Their Children As Seen by a Psychiatrist.
   National Conference of Social Work.
Blethen, E. C. (1942), Casework Service to a Florence Crittenton Home. *Family, 23*:248-
   254.
Brenner, C. (1950), Illegitimacy and Aid to Dependent Children. *Pub. Welfare, 8*:174-
   178.
Brenner, R. (1942), What Facilities Are Essential to the Adequate Care of the Un-
   married Mother? *Proceedings of the National Conference of Social Work,* 426-439.
Clothier, F. (1943), Psychological Implications of Unmarried Parenthood. *Am. J.
   Orthopsychiat., 13*:531-549.
Dean, H. C. (1944), *Unmarried Parenthood.* Monograph of Metropolitan Los Angeles
   County Welfare Council, Publication No. 3.
De La Fontaine, E. (1948), Needs of Unmarried Parents and Their Children As Seen
   by a Caseworker. National Conference of Social Work.
Deutsch, H. (1945), Chapter on the Unmarried Mother. *Psychology of Women,* Vol. II.
   New York: Grune & Stratton.
Donnell, C. and Glick, S. J. (1952), Background Factors in 100 Cases of Jewish Un-
   married Mothers. *Jewish Soc. Sci. Quart., 29*:152-163.

UNMARRIED MOTHERS 195

Dudley, K. (1939), A Referral Service for Unmarried Mothers. *Family, 20*:200-202.
Edlin, S. B. (1954), *The Unmarried Mother in Our Society.* New York: Farrar Straus & Young.
Embry, M. (1937), Planning for the Unmarried Mother. *Child Welfare League of America Publications, 1.*
Frost, L. (1939), A Study of 500 Unmarried Mothers. *Child Welfare League of America Bull., 18* (January):3-4.
Genrose, G. (1939), The Casework Function of the Maternity Home. *Child Welfare League of America Bull., 18* (December):1-2.
Josselyn, I. M. (1953), What We Know of the Unmarried Mother. National Conference of Social Work.
Judge, J. G. (1951), Casework with the Unmarried Mother in a Family Agency. *Soc. Casework, 32*:7-15.
Kasanin, J. and Handschin, S. (1941), Psychodynamic Factors in Illegitimacy. *Am. J. Orthopsychiat., 11*:66-84.
Laverty, R. (1942), A Study of 50 Unmarried Mothers. New York School of Social Work Thesis.
Lenz, M. W. (1940), The Out-of-Wedlock Father. *The Unmarried Father.* Washington: United States Children's Bureau.
Levy, D. M. (1954), Research as a Method of Increasing Our Understanding of the Unmarried Mother. National Conference of Social Work.
Mattingly, M. (1928), *The Unmarried Mother and Her Child.* Cleveland: Western Reserve University School of Applied Social Science.
Morlock, M. (1946), *Maternity Homes for Unmarried Mothers.* Washington: United States Children's Bureau, 309.
Nottingham, R. D. (1937), Psychodynamic Factors in Illegitimacy. *Genetic Psychology Monographs, 19*:155-228.
Powell, M. (1949), Illegitimate Pregnancy in Emotionally Disturbed Girls. *Smith College Studies in Social Work, 19*:171-179.
Reed, R. (1934), *The Illegitimate Family in New York City.* New York: Research Bureau Studies No. II. Welfare Council.
—— (1926), *Negro Illegitimacy in New York City.* New York: Columbia University Press.
Rodriguez, O. (1937), Madres desamparadas. *Boletin del Instituto Internacional Americano de Proteccion a la Infancia Argentina, 10*:365.
Schmideberg, M. (1951), Psycho-social Factors in Young Unmarried Mothers. *Soc. Casework, 32*:3-7.
Sharpe, A. M. (1940), A Study of a Private Agency's Experience with 21 Unmarried Parents. New York School of Social Work Thesis.
Slavson, S. R. (1952), *Analytic Group Psychotherapy.* New York: Columbia University Press.
—— (1955), Criteria for Selection and Rejection of Patients for Various Types of Group Psychotherapy. *Int. J. Group Psychother., 5*:3-30.
Smith, E. S. (1935), A Study of 25 Adolescent Unmarried Mothers in New York City. New York: Columbia University Thesis.
Travers, V. D. (1942), One Hundred and Sixty-Four Unmarried Parents. *Child Welfare League of America Bull., 21* (May):9-10.
United States Children's Bureau (1937), *On Problems Associated with Birth Out of Wedlock.* News Letter, No. 10.
Young, L. (1954), *Out of Wedlock.* New York: McGraw-Hill.

Chapter XI

DELINQUENTS

•

The difficulties encountered in treating adolescent delinquents become apparent to those who engage in individual or group psychotherapy with these patients. The dynamic and structural nature of delinquent character development not only precludes the effectiveness of "orthodox" psychotherapy methods, but actually places these adolescents at variance or in conflict with the goals of psychotherapy. This chapter will elaborate on the origin and significance of certain problems encountered in group psychotherapy with male and female delinquents, and in doing so will also discuss procedures employed in an attempt to deal with the delinquent's unique character distortions.

The complexity of interaction processes inherent in group psychotherapy cannot be underestimated. When these complex processes are additionally complicated by character-determined uncooperativeness or dissocial attitudes, it behooves the therapist to understand the basis for these complications, so that he may constructively modify or structure the treatment situation, and thereby attempt to maintain its therapeutic effectiveness. If the therapist fails to take ino account the character problems of delinquents in favor of utilizing accepted procedures as they are generally applied to neurotics, or in favor of thinking of group psychotherapy in terms of the vague concept of *group process*, it is likely that his therapeutic efforts will result in confusion, disillusionment, and failure.

The role of group psychotherapy in the treatment of antisocial adolescents has not yet been clearly formulated. Discrepant views exist concerning its value with this type of maladjustment, and little has been reported suggesting modifications in treatment which might improve its effectiveness.

Slavson (1947a, 1950a) has stated that activity group therapy is contra-indicated for "psychopathic" youngsters, and that a "psychopath" among a group of neurotics in interview group therapy may cause a disruption of the treatment process. Redl has expressed somewhat similar views in an unpublished paper cited by Slavson (1947b).

Other studies have seen value in group psychotherapy with antisocial adolescents. Gersten (1951), in a controlled experiment utilizing psychological tests as a means of evaluation, found that group psychotherapy with institutionalized male delinquents led to an improvement in their intellectual and school functioning, together with indications of increased emotional maturity. An improvement in institutional adjustment was also reported by Thorpe and Smith (1952) following group psychotherapy with male delinquents. In analyzing the group process they observed that the delinquent goes through two phases in therapy; first, a series of "testing operations," and second, a period of "acceptance operations," both phases being initially therapist-centered and then group-centered. This writer, in an earlier paper (1952), evaluated the influence of the male character-disordered delinquent's personality on the group therapy process and concluded that modifications in technique were essential.

It was also indicated that group psychotherapy in itself did not effect a marked character improvement, although it did prove of some value in preparing these adolescents for more intensive individual treatment. Peck and Bellsmith (1954), in employing group psychotherapy with court-referred delinquents in an outpatient clinic, suggest that positive response to this form of therapy is directly related to the patient's degree of "classical neurotic pathology" and negatively related to degree of "psychopathy." The dearth of literature on the use of group therapy with antisocial adolescents is surprising in view of the magnitude of the problem of delinquency and the increasing interest in approaching this problem with psychotherapeutic techniques.[1]

In the remainder of this chapter, reference will be made to group psychotherapy with institutionalized antisocial male and female adolescents who have been categorized as character-disordered delinquents.[2]

---

[1] A survey of the use of "group therapy" in correctional institutions is presented by McCorkle (1953).

[2] In considering treatment of delinquents we have found it helpful to categorize their dissocial behavior in one of the following groups: (1) delinquency associated with intellectual retardation or organic brain pathology; (2) delinquency associated with incipient or early psychosis; (3) delinquency primarily related to neurotic conflicts (internalized conflict); (4) character-disordered delinquency (externalized conflict). The latter group is often referred to as adolescent psychopaths. However, we refrain from using this term since it has become diffuse in its diagnostic application.

Their behavior has been marked by repeated encroachment upon the moral and social values of the community and, unlike the reactions of many neurotic delinquents, they show no apparent guilt following their antisocial activity. Included in their dissocial behavior are such acts as stealing, truancy, sexual promiscuity, running away from home, and aggressive attacks upon people and objects without reasonable provocation. The extent of destructiveness manifested by these adolescents has required that they be removed from their home environment and be placed, by court order, in a treatment home to undergo a "re-educational experience."

Despite frequently encountered pessimism regarding the value of group psychotherapy with character-disordered delinquents, this type of treatment has been integrated into an over-all therapeutic program[3] with the following threefold purpose in mind. First, group therapy provides an atmosphere not encountered in individual treatment in which intellectual insight can be stimulated by others and in which reality testing can occur. The latter is of particular value in therapeutic work with delinquents. Second, the group situation proves ideal for observing and evaluating the dynamics of antisocial character development with particular reference to the individual's *alloplastic* symptom formation[4] and degree of superego development. Third, group psychotherapy often proves of value in determining the strength of newly acquired positive attitudes, since the homogeneous delinquent make-up of the group creates an unusual atmosphere of tension and stress which stimulates the manifestation of basic character defenses.

In the introduction to this chapter it was suggested that in order for group therapy to be effective with delinquents, it must be geared to deal with the specific character attitudes presented in this maladjustment. The following section will discuss briefly those aspects of this character distortion which, in the group situation, must be dealt with *en masse*.

The Antisocial Adolescent.[5] The most obvious and certainly most socially unacceptable personality trait of the character-disordered delinquent is his use of aggression to deal with his internal stress and the

[3] Our experience has shown that the most productive therapeutic work with these adolescents results from a program that includes individual and group psychotherapy combined with a planned "therapeutic" environment.

[4] *Alloplastic* symptom formation refers to an *externalization* of conflict and is aimed at restructuring the environment; it is contrasted to *autoplastic* symptoms which are *internalized* and constitute a reorganization of the self. For a discussion of this concept in relation to delinquency see Eissler (1949a), also Fenichel (1945).

[5] For a thorough analysis of the dynamics of antisocial character formation see Aichhorn (1935), Friedlander (1947), and Eissler (1949b, 1950).

pressures from his environment. This behavior pattern, which can often be traced to his early years, reflects an *externalization* of his conflicts, aimed at restructuring the environment so that it provides a state of personal emotional gratification. It is most unfortunate for those around him that this gratification is always derived from some form of aggression, which serves to lower or allay body tension (*internalized* anxiety). The delinquent's use of aggressive physical means to express instinctive needs attests to his severely impaired ego development. The fact that this type of delinquent obtains gratification from his antisocial activity creates a specific barrier in psychotherapy since the therapist is seeking, in effect, to have him forego his pleasurable aggression and to adopt a mode of behavior that results in increased psychic discomfort.

That the delinquent uses others to gratify his instinctive needs reflects his defective incorporation of social values (superego). Many of these youngsters come from homes in which parents are amoral or dissocial, or they have been raised in institutions which have not provided desirable parental figures with whom to identify. In some instances these delinquents are products of homes in which emotional detachment has been so exaggerated as to inhibit the incorporation of parental values; others are raised in family settings in which the mother or father harbor strong repressed delinquent needs which are vicariously satisfied by subtle stimulation of antisocial behavior in the child.[6] Despite the etiology of the delinquent character disorder, one factor stands out: namely, the delinquent's absence of empathy with and incorporation of social values.

The relative ease with which the delinquent's instinctive needs enter consciousness, coupled with his basic motor orientation, makes him restless and dissatisfied. His concentration ability suffers and he becomes bored with long-term projects—psychotherapy being no exception.

Psychoanalytic theory has postulated that higher levels of thought can only develop from the process of curtailing direct responsiveness to instinctive demands (Rapaport, 1951). It is for this reason that the delinquent who gives vent to his impulses is deficient in such personality traits as fantasy, creative ideational activity, introspection, and self-awareness—all derivatives of this *detour* process. This also suggests why treatment, which relies so heavily on introspective thought, is often not appropriate for antisocial adolescents.

In keeping with the pattern of thought organization noted above, one finds that the delinquent relies heavily on concrete thought in his deal-

6 Space does not permit a more comprehensive examination of the early relationships that lead to delinquent behavior. For additional background material see Eissler (1949b), Friedlander (1947), Johnson (1949), Szurek (1942).

ings with the environment. He is concerned with what takes place at the present moment. The past, and for that matter the future, are too abstract to interest him. It is this characteristic that has led others to regard the delinquent as lacking in a reasonable time-perspective (Eissler, 1950).

When the character traits described above are incorporated into a pattern of interpersonal behavior, one generally finds associated with it the attitude of omnipotence (Eissler, 1950). The delinquent's pressing need for instinct gratification, combined with his lack of respect for social values, results in repeated antisocial activity without apparent concern for the consequences. Another way of describing this reaction pattern is to say that he is indifferent to the demands of authority, whether it be at home or in the community.

Since the delinquent's opposition to the rule of authority is the immediate cause of his difficulty with society, it comes as no surprise that the basis for establishing a therapeutic relationship with him revolves around this particular interpersonal situation. It has been found to be of considerable importance in the treatment of delinquents to create a relationship in which they are dependent upon the therapist (Bromberg and Rodgers, 1946) or see him as more omnipotent than they (Eissler, 1950).[7]

In a series of papers and a recent book, Slavson described derivatives of group therapy in the social treatment of delinquents (Slavson, 1947b, 1948, 1950b, 1950c, 1954b; and Slavson and Shulman, 1936). He emphasizes the importance of the institutional environment, the interpersonal relationships of staff members and their effect on school residents, the need for carefully planned therapeutically oriented group recreational activities, grouping of residents in cottages with therapeutic intent, as well as the use of direct group psychotherapy. Slavson feels that activity group therapy should not be employed in a residential setting but that analytic group psychotherapy can be of value with certain cases. He points out that difficulties may arise in a residential treatment setting if information and feelings brought out by group members become known to others in the school.

In proceeding with an analysis of the group psychotherapy process as it applies to antisocial adolescents, it should be stressed that those character traits which have been discussed above influence all aspects of treatment, including *transference, catharsis, insight,* and *reality testing.*[8]

[7] See section on Transference.

[8] For a systematic examination of the process of group psychotherapy with elaboration on the areas cited above, see Slavson (1950a, 1954a). Slavson also includes *sublimation* as a major aspect of group psychotherapy. Since *sublimation* plays an insignificant role in interview group therapy with antisocial adolescents, it will be discussed briefly in the section on therapy goals.

It is these four areas that will be evaluated in the sections that follow.

Transference. The concept of *transference* as it is employed in the context of this chapter refers to the emotional relationships that develop between the delinquent and the group therapist,[9] and among members of the group. This definition differs from the term as it is commonly employed in psychoanalytic literature (see Fenichel, 1945, pp. 29-31).

It is axiomatic that personality improvement in psychotherapy hinges on the patient's ability to establish an adequate relationship with the therapist. Basically, the relationship must be positive and involve elements of trust and confidence. Although hostile feelings are frequently directed toward the therapist, and may even persist for periods at a time, this in no way detracts from the patient's deeper feelings of confidence in the therapist's ability to help him. A patient's potential to develop the necessary therapeutic relationship depends upon the availability in his character make-up of positive feelings which can be directed toward external objects, in this case the psychotherapist.

The idea has frequently been advanced that the character-disordered delinquent is unsuited for individual or group psychotherapy because of his narcissistic emotional orientation, his defective conscience, and his need to exploit situations for personal gain. It is true that if this type of delinquent is left to his own emotional devices he will not respond to the therapist's overtures. However, it has been found that if certain alterations are made in the therapist-patient relationship, the delinquent can often be helped to develop an emotional attachment, albeit shallow, which can then be exploited in a manner that may lead to desirable character change.

In a previous publication, this writer (Schulman, 1952) employed modifications in his approach to male delinquents in group psychotherapy that involved supplying certain of their narcissistic needs in order to encourage interest and trust in the therapist. Elements of surprise and novelty were constantly being introduced into the group therapy situation in the form of variations in activity and unexpected refreshments. Favors were dispensed with sufficient caution to avoid the stimulation of exaggerated sibling rivalry.

In using this technique with aggressive, sexually promiscuous girls, it was found that they did not respond similarly. Since their narcissistic needs were previously, to a large extent, satisfied by sexual or seductive

---

[9] In this chapter, reference will be made to the therapist's attempts to "create" a *transference* situation with the delinquent. This unusual concept of transference refers to an authority-dependency relationship that is regarded as basic in the treatment of antisocial adolescents (Bromberg and Rodgers, 1946; Eissler, 1950).

activity, it was found that they regarded the therapist's offering of alternative satisfaction an affront to their "maturity." The need to employ caution in the use of this technique with male delinquents, coupled with the fact that it is ineffective with females, led to the development of a more reliable method of establishing a meaningful tie with the antisocial adolescent. It was found that the authority-dependency relationship inherent in the process of institutionalization could be used toward this end.

Experience has shown that the delinquent's predominantly *alloplastic* orientation precludes his developing intense psychological pain and thereby eliminates one of the strongest motivations to change. It is this lack of motivation that is regarded as a major cause for failure in treating the adolescent delinquent. By placing the antisocial adolescent in a controlled environment such as a treatment home, his pattern of acting out is interrupted, creating a situation of discomfort for him. This discomfort tends to be particularly pronounced at the onset of institutionalization, and it is then that it is regarded as strategic to impress upon him the fact that the therapist has been given the responsibility to recommend when he is ready to be released.[10] Due to the adolescent's discomfort in this new environment, the therapist becomes an important person toward whom he now may begin to focus his manipulative and seductive capacities. An emotional tie is established which fortunately incorporates the dynamics that have been found to be important in treating delinquents—namely, that the therapist be regarded by the delinquent as being more omnipotent than he, and therefore a person with whom to identify. The therapist then utilizes this originally shallow relationship to establish himself as a trustworthy authority figure who will not exploit the patient.

By creating this type of relationship, one is, in many respects, reconstructing a father-child situation, the outcome of which is very unlike the delinquent's earlier life experience. In this new situation the therapist (father figure) remains consistent in his feelings, never uses the child for personal emotional gain, is honest with him, and makes meaningful the social and moral values of the community. In other words, the therapist attempts to become an ego ideal and thereby effect the development of a rudimentary superego.

Catharsis. An important aspect of analytic group psychotherapy is the airing of thoughts, attitudes, and feelings regarding current experiences and earlier life events. The various modes of expressing these personal

10 It is, of course, important that the therapist have this responsibility without equivocation.

reactions are subsumed under the term catharsis.[11] Catharsis in interview group psychotherapy occurs through verbalization except when disintegration develops in the treatment situation, resulting in physical acting out.[12] In this section, an analysis will be made of the various forms of catharsis as they are observed in interview group psychotherapy with dissocial adolescents. Included will be *free association, associative thinking, directed discussion, induced discussion, forced discussion,* and *vicarious catharsis.*[13]

Experience has demonstrated that *free association* in individual or group psychotherapy is incompatible with the character-disordered delinquent's ideational and emotional orientation (Eissler, 1950; Schulman, 1955). His fear of divulging his feelings to others, together with the fact that free association is an abstract procedure that requires an individual to produce a chain of ideas that have no predetermined goal, makes the delinquent suspicious of this technique. When asked by the therapist to discuss freely whatever comes to his mind, or to indicate what he was thinking about during a period of silence, the delinquent's invariable response is "nothing." In keeping with his characteristic reactions to stress, he becomes antagonistic if pressed by the therapist to attempt free association. It is often difficult for the delinquent to translate feelings into ideas and ideas into words. The therapist should be aware of this so that he does not become impatient with an apparently nonresponsive delinquent patient.

An examination of the delinquent's *associative thinking*—that is, communications dealing with current experiences and feelings—reveals that if permitted to structure the emotional atmosphere of the group, the male delinquents will continuously express hostility toward authority, whereas the females tend to vacillate between hostility and sexual preoccupation. In an institutional setting, the hostility is usually directed toward cottage parents, teachers, law enforcement personnel, etc. (Thorpe and Smith, 1952). Sexual fantasies of female delinquents are usually

[11] The term *catharsis*, as employed in this chapter, is not in common usage in present-day psychoanalytic literature. This is probably due to its earlier descriptive association with Breuer and Freud's (1895) hypnotic method; and its current use to describe emotional reactions during narcosynthesis (Grinker and Spiegel, 1945).

[12] The use of physical means to express emotional conflicts is not encountered frequently in interview group psychotherapy with neurotics. However, it occurs in groups of action-oriented delinquents unless controlled by the therapist (Thorpe and Smith, 1952; Schulman, 1952), and may occur with schizophrenics whose reality-testing is seriously impaired.

[13] See Slavson (1954a) for a comprehensive discussion of catharsis in group psychotherapy.

stimulated by past promiscuity, by allusions to sexual activity among staff members, or through the expression of interest in male members of the staff.

Since both male and female delinquents tend to be activity-oriented, the repetition of aggressive or sexual fantasies becomes a source of frustration unless acted upon. Weaker members of the group become recipients of the hostility (Schulman, 1952; Thorpe and Smith, 1952), whereas sexual fantasies lead to seductive attention-getting and coy "sexy" overtures. Experience has demonstrated that if either of these instinctual preoccupations is allowed to progress freely, it leads to a disintegration of the group situation which we refer to as "deterioration through perseveration." As mentioned earlier, the "scapegoat" in the group serves as the object of aggressive acting out in an attempt to alleviate the tensions generated by preoccupation with hostility, whereas the female's exaggerated discussions of past heterosexual experiences combined with current overtures toward the male therapist stimulate an undesirable competitive situation which often leads to aggression.

If the therapist allows himself to become the focus of physical acting out, whether it be aggression or some direct derivative of sexual impulses, his status in the eyes of the group is lowered, and this interferes with the development of the desired transference. The importance of forestalling physical acting out toward the therapist cannot be overstressed. If a nondirective approach is used with these patients, it leads to a disintegration of the procedure since the therapist, in accepting the delinquent's hostile emotional expressions, is in effect allying himself with the patient's instinctive drives and thereby stimulating externalization of conflict. Since our goal is to effect a curtailment of dissocial activity, *directed discussion* is frequently employed to change the tone of the session or to prevent deterioration of the group. It is only in this way that we have found it possible to maintain a therapeutic atmosphere in a group of character-disordered delinquents.

The following is a demonstration of the type of disintegration which can occur. The group is composed of five adolescent delinquent girls (9th interview).

Jane, who was unable to match the sexual experiences being discussed by the rest of the girls, swung her chair around and looked out the window. The other girls continued their naming of boy friends and comparison of photos. Anger continued to mount in Jane who then turned around and threw a pencil at the therapist. He "interpreted" this behavior to her as a sign that something was annoying her and making her angry.

This "acceptance" of her aggression acted as a catalyst, stimulating the others into physical activity. Barbara picked up a ball of clay that was lying on a table and threw it full force at the therapist. The other three girls began milling around the office. Mary, in an attempt to "get into the act," rubbed stick cologne on the therapist's suit. By the end of the session, all five girls had managed to coat the therapist with many odors of cheap cologne.

Much of what may have been gained up to this point in developing an authority-dependency relationship was aborted when the therapist "lost face" in the course of becoming a recipient of the aggressive and sexual impulses of the group members.

If aggression is directed toward the therapist, it is important for him to make it clear to the group, without countering with hostility or aggression, that this type of behavior cannot be condoned. An effective therapeutic use of such manifestation of aggression is to relate these outbursts to the delinquent's pattern of behavior that led to his institutionalization.

Experience has shown that it is desirable to curtail the development of physical acting out by recognizing this trend and reorganizing the group discussion. As suggested previously, one method of doing this is to employ directed discussion in which the therapist introduces leading questions in order to stimulate analysis of a particular subject.

At the onset of group psychotherapy the purpose of the sessions is clearly and concretely stated. The group is then allowed to structure the discussion until the therapist notes that they are preoccupied with aggression or sexual matters. The discussion is cut short and the group informed that this kind of talk is not leading to an understanding of the cause of their problems and, therefore, *How are they going to change and get out of the treatment home?* A subject for discussion is then introduced that involves some aspect of interpersonal feeling, such as being incompatible with people, love in the family, etc.; or one dealing with a clarification of what is desirable or undesirable behavior.

The following example points up the technique being discussed. The group is composed of four adolescent delinquent girls (6th interview).

The group spent much of this hour and previous hours attacking their cottage parents and griping about authority. It was obvious that this perseveration was leading to deterioration in the group situation. The therapist, at this point, commented that the group had been doing nothing but talking about how everybody is against them. He said that he knew it made them feel better to gripe about things but wondered how this type of discussion *was ever going to get them out of the treatment home.*

He emphasized that as soon as they came to know themselves[14] and could get along with people, out they would go! The therapist then suggested that since they were expressing their anger, it would be a good idea for them to examine what *really* made them mad—why they got so angry at people all the time. He then asked who would start it off. The desire to show the therapist that they "knew" themselves in order to prove that they were ready to go home, led these girls during the remainder of this hour to engage in productive discussion about the source of their hostility.

This approach, very different from that employed with neurotics, is necessary since the delinquent does not, as a rule, develop ideas which do not reflect his preoccupation with aggression and sex. It becomes the therapist's responsibility in working with delinquents to stimulate consideration of important feelings which should be dealt with in all analytic psychotherapy—such as, feelings of affection, humility, fear, etc.

If *induced discussion* occurs in group psychotherapy, it implies that a member is sufficiently in empathy with another's expressed feelings to talk about similar personal feelings. The emotional orientation of the narcissistic, character-disordered delinquent is such that induced discussion is a rarity except in relation to aggressive discussion or statements about sexual accomplishments. In these two spheres, the induction does not lead to *new* associations but merely prods into exacerbation pervasive dissocial feelings, which, as noted previously, should be controlled in order to avoid deterioration of the therapeutic session.

Since *forced discussion* implies the use of an aggressive attitude by the therapist to obtain information from group members, it is inappropriate in the treatment of delinquents who tend to be oversensitive and overreactive to aggression. This approach by the therapist would give the antisocial adolescent license to retaliate.

The concept of *vicarious catharsis* refers to the ability of a group member to identify with another member's expressed feeling, and thereby gain an understanding of his own personal problems. The character-disordered delinquent has little capacity to empathize with, or to tolerate the emotional problems of others. It often develops that while one group member is discussing something personal, the others engage in distracting activity. Since identity and empathy are closely related to the process of superego development (Fenichel, 1945), it is understandable why

[14] The reader will detect a repetition of emphasis on the existence of "problems" in these adolescents. This is an important re-educative aspect of psychotherapy with character-disordered delinquents who usually do not recognize that their adjustment is inadequate.

vicarious catharsis in group psychotherapy is beyond the emotional realm of the antisocial adolescent.[15]

Insight. The neurotic patient in interview group psychotherapy can frequently gain an understanding of unconscious conflicts through well-timed interpretation by the therapist or other group members. The therapeutic atmosphere of the group, which grows with the development of transference feelings, encourages the expression of suppressed thoughts, and may even result in the undoing of repression.

The group psychotherapy situation is unique in that under certain circumstances it provides an opportunity to gain insight through empathy with the problems of other group members. However, it also has the disadvantage of limiting the depth of self-examination because of the dilution of transference (Slavson, 1950a). Insight gained in group psychotherapy is often purely intellectual.

The character-disordered delinquent poses unique problems in regard to gaining insight in group psychotherapy. Regrettably, his character attitudes are aimed at avoiding displeasurable thought with the result that he rarely, if ever, develops spontaneous insight. Since he lacks empathic qualities, he does not "learn" about himself through identification with other group members. If the antisocial adolescent does not develop an authority-dependency relationship with the therapist, as described earlier, he usually does not gain an understanding of his behavior since he lacks motivation to change due to his low level of psychic discomfort.

When he comes to realize that he is dependent upon the therapist to recommend his release from the institution, the delinquent frequently "forces" self-examination, feeling that he must prove his self-under-standing. It is obvious that "insight" gained in this way is superficial. However, if repeated in individual and group therapy over a period of time, this type of self-awareness tends to become cumulative and eventually may encourage a reasonable degree of instinct control.

The following demonstrates the type of insightful thinking characteristic of such a group at the stage when they have developed a desirable transference. The group is made up of four adolescent girls (5th interview).[16]

---

[15] It might be pointed out that if it were possible for the antisocial adolescent to identify with others, he would not encroach upon the moral and social values of the community. In fact, the very existence of law and order can be traced in part to the complicated factors that make it possible for an individual to empathize with others (Freud, 1922).

[16] Since all the girls had been in individual psychotherapy prior to the start of this group, this accounts for the development of "insight" so early in the group therapy sessions.

The girls were worried about when they would be going home, and complained of missing their families. The therapist reminded them that as soon as they acquired a better understanding of themselves, that is, why they got into trouble, they could go home. Helen, feeling "obligated" to prove her self-understanding, said that girls get into trouble when they can't get along with their parents and have no one to tell them what is right or wrong. She continued, saying that if parents really cared for their child, they would sit down and discuss the child's problems with her. Irene picked this up and stated that she felt her problem was half her fault and half her parents' fault. Since her father always accused her of getting into trouble when she didn't, she "showed him." She also pointed out that she *knows something is wrong with her* because she is now at the treatment home. Both Violet and Gladys accused their fathers of neglect and aggression toward them. Violet felt that the "average" girl probably had a family who loved her and was kind to her. Her own father was drunk most of the time and would frequently beat her. The girls continued to talk about their problems at home, and the discussion ended in a burst of laughter when Gladys told how things did not really get bad in her home until her father hit her mother in the eye on Mother's Day.

It may appear to the reader that this type of thinking is not particularly profound and that it should be expected in group psychotherapy with maladjusted adolescents. However, it has been found that with character-disordered delinquents, this level of thought is not very common and depends on the development of a desirable transference.

Reality Testing. In the section dealing with verbal catharsis in group therapy with antisocial adolescents, it was noted that they demonstrated a deficiency in productive thought and verbal communication. This deficiency is neither fortuitous nor the result alone of cultural and social factors. Rather, it tends to be found as a certain type of personality in which delay of response to instinct is impaired.

Reality testing, that is, the examination of the adequacy of one's feelings, ideas, and actions, is considered to be directly related to ego strength. Thought allows an individual to anticipate his actions; and speech makes it possible to engage in more precise communication with the environment and thereby improve one's capacity to deal with external stress (Fenichel, 1945). The inhibition of direct response to instinctive demands is made possible by the exercise of thought and its verbal derivatives (Rapaport, 1951). It is the effect of the triadic constellation of action-orientation, thought limitation, and communication deficiency that must be dealt with if one is to be successful in treating the antisocial adolescent. It is for this reason that reality testing procedure, as it shall be described in this section, takes on particular significance in group psychotherapy with delinquents.

The neurotic in interview group psychotherapy frequently tests the adequacy of his feelings in the protected group setting, and then transfers what he has "learned" to everyday situations. The fact that he profits from the reactions of the group implies respect for the opinions of others and a desire to conform to social values. The antithesis is true of the antisocial adolescent. To him, social values tend to be oppressive because they restrict his instinct satisfaction. However, it has been observed that a limited type of reality testing can take place in group therapy if an authority-dependency transference is developed between the therapist and the delinquent. Without this relationship the group setting merely provides a fertile field for him to indulge his aggressive needs.

The technique employed in developing a transference with the delinquent places him in a position that is somewhat analagous to a child's relationship to his parents. However, in the present situation the parental figure remains firm and consistent, but nevertheless a benign authority who serves as a model after whom the delinquent can pattern himself. If the delinquent has this type of emotional tie with the therapist, the latter's efforts have a greater impact on him. The therapist can then use the group setting productively by introducing meaningful situations, obtaining the reactions (reality testing) of the group, and discussing the appropriateness of these reactions. This is a particularly sensitive phase of treatment requiring that the therapist be devoid of a sharp, critical attitude and that explanations of proper behavior be reasonably concrete in order to conform to the conceptual level of the group.

The purpose of this procedure can be restated as follows: It is to stimulate the development of a rudimentary value system based on identification with the therapist and introjection of his values, a consequence of the delinquent accepting the therapist as a more powerful and authoritative person than himself.

To illustrate, the following is the type of situation that can be created by the therapist in order to test the appropriateness of the group's reaction. The group is composed of five delinquent girls (13th interview).

About midway through the interview, the therapist initiated a topic on stealing which seemed to stimulate the group to engage in competitive discussion. They each told how they had stolen things at home, in school, in department stores, etc. The therapist did not "interpret" the motivation behind this behavior but instead asked the girls how they would feel if someone took one of their prized possessions—for example, a new dress.

Janet commented that if a person were "smart" enough to get it from her, then she should have it. Irene said she would fight to keep her things, whereas Violet thought she would retaliate by stealing something from the person himself. None of the girls seemed to feel that stealing was undesirable, nor was there any expression of unhappiness at having someone take advantage of them in this way. The therapist, at this point, commented that he thought all the girls had "strange" reactions to this situation and went on to say, as he had said many times before, that they didn't respond like *average* girls their age. He discussed the *normal* reactions that people have when others take their possessions and pointed out that ordinarily a person respects the property of others. To make the situation more meaningful and concrete, he elaborated upon an unfortunate experience of his own in which his watch was stolen. The group thought it was terrible that this had happened to him. The therapist in turn used their identification with him to point out the probable reaction of people they had stolen from.

The concept of what is average, normal, proper, reasonable, etc., is stressed repetitiously in this approach, until it is found that the group responds spontaneously with comments that they are not "average," or that they have problems. When this occurs, the therapist usually agrees with them and then uses these statements to encourage self-evaluation. The following is from a session with a group of five girls (16th interview).

The girls were discussing how they had sneaked off to be with their boy friends when they were supposed to be attending a meeting. The therapist commented that he didn't think this was a very smart thing to do. Irene said that she felt terrible afterwards and blamed the episode on their being "crazy mixed-up kids." The therapist agreed, and then wondered whether she knew in what way she was "mixed up." She gave this some thought and then said that if the therapist had a father like hers, he wouldn't be "normal" either. The other girls joined in to discuss how they also were not like other kids because of their unhappy family experiences.

In a therapeutic program geared to encourage control of instinctive demands, it can be seen that reality testing as described above, provides an excellent opportunity to portray for the delinquent what a normal milieu regards as proper behavior. With individuals who have not been receptive to social demands this takes on importance since they are usually not aware of what is expected of them.

One of the important requisites of planned psychotherapy is the formulation of a determinate goal, that is, a goal that considers the patient's psychological needs, the values of the community, and whether the prescribed therapy can be carried out in practice. These factors require special consideration in therapeutic work with antisocial adolescents because of the nature of their maladjustment and its extreme refractoriness to change.

Ideally, the goal in therapy with the character-disordered delinquent would be to effect sufficient personality alteration so that his energies become channeled into constructive, mature functioning, commensurate with his inherent potential. However, due to the nature and severity of his maladjustment, such a drastic character change could only come about if he were willing and able to come to grips with the core of his destructive psychic motivations. An additional complicating factor in considering therapy for this type of dissocial individual is that he proves contumacious when given the opportunity to examine his motivation (Eissler, 1949b, 1950; Schulman, 1952, 1955). He often maintains that there is absolutely nothing wrong with his behavior and may even become antagonistic when it is suggested to him that he is emotionally disturbed and in need of guidance.

In view of the resistance encountered in treating this type of delinquent, the goal of group therapy, as it is outlined in this chapter, has been defined pragmatically; namely, that it be employed as part of a more comprehensive effort directed toward stimulating control of antisocial impulses in a group of adolescents who have little respect for social values. The structural nature of delinquent character formation makes a more far-reaching goal somewhat impractical.

Since the goal of this treatment is aimed at developing control of instincts, it has been found that the role of *sublimation* in group therapy with antisocial adolescents is not of major importance.[17] This is due to the fact that sublimation, which results from a transformation of instinctive drives into constructive or creative energy, is hindered when repression is employed to control these drives (Fenichel, 1945). It is actually the delinquent's use of repression of instincts that constitutes our treatment goal.

Evidences of treatment "success" in our program of therapy with delinquents is their developing symptoms or behavior which reflects the effect of repression. Many of them develop compulsions or somatic symptoms, both of which are signs of internalized conflict often associated with repressed aggression. The following examples illustrate the type of symptom formation referred to:

[17] For a discussion of the role of *sublimation* in group psychotherapy see Slavson (1950a).

Jane, toward the end of her stay at the treatment home, became preoccupied with shining shoes. Each morning, after she had finished her shoes, she would go around to the other girls to see if they would let her polish theirs. She would become resentful if turned down. Violet, just prior to her transfer from the treatment home to a foster home, developed fatigue and leg pains. Though she had many symptoms of rheumatic fever, all medical tests proved negative. Her physical "ailments" persisted until she entered her foster home, demonstrating that her anxiety about this new situation was dealt with through internalization rather than by her previous pattern of aggressive, antisocial behavior.

It has been suggested that the delinquent who develops internalized conflicts, in the form of anxiety or other symptom formation, becomes amenable to deeper analytic therapy (Pearson, 1949). However, our attempts to involve improved antisocial adolescents in deeper therapy after they left the treatment home have always met with strong resistance. Opposition to analytic therapy was also encountered when it was suggested that they might prefer a new therapist.[18]

In using the group psychotherapy techniques described in this chapter to treat character-disordered delinquents, certain important factors must be considered. Since the therapist assumes responsibility for recommending the delinquent's release from the institution, these adolescents should have the same therapist for both individual and group treatment. It has been found that this does not create unusual tension nor rivalry, inasmuch as the narcissistic emotional orientation of the antisocial adolescent limits the depth of his personal involvement with the therapist.

It has also been found desirable that members selected for group therapy be as nosologically homogeneous as possible; this is particularly important when treating character-disordered delinquents whose aggressiveness, lack of empathy with other group members, and need to exploit situations for personal gain make them therapeutically incompatible with neurotic delinquents and a serious threat to delinquents with early psychotic symptoms.

It should be emphasized, in concluding, that the depth of emotional distortion in the character-disordered delinquent precludes the effective use of group psychotherapy as the sole treatment method. However, if this type of therapy is integrated into a program of treatment that includes individual psychotherapy and planned environmental manipula-

---

[18] Eissler (1950) has expressed the view that psychoanalytic therapy with delinquents must be divided into two phases: an initial or preparatory phase, and a secondary or analytic phase, with a different therapist for each. Our experience has been limited to what is comparable to Eissler's preparatory phase.

tion, it rounds out a concerted effort to deal with a very serious character deformation. When removed from his pathogenic milieu and placed in a controlled environment, the delinquent is helped to develop an identification with the therapist who encourages the formation of an authority-dependency relationship. However, it is a relationship that does not exploit the delinquent who has hitherto come to expect this of such situations. It is the formation of this type of relationship analagous to a parent-child interaction, that makes it possible for the delinquent to develop a more constructive conception of authority and social values.

BIBLIOGRAPHY

Aichhorn, A. (1935), *Wayward Youth.* New York: Viking Press.
Breuer, J., and Freud, S. (1895), *Studies in Hysteria.* New York: Nervous and Mental Disease Publishing Co., 1936.
Bromberg, W., and Rodgers, T. C. (1946), Authority in the Treatment of Delinquents. *Am. J. Orthopsychiat., 16:*672-685.
Eissler, K. R. (1949a), Some Problems of Delinquency. *Searchlights on Delinquency.* New York: International Universities Press.
—— (ed), (1949b), *Searchlights on Delinquency.* New York: International Universities Press.
—— (1950), Ego-Psychological Implications of the Psychoanalytic Treatment of Delinquents. *The Psychoanalytic Study of the Child, 5:*97-121. New York: International Universities Press.
Fenichel, O. (1945), *The Psychoanalytic Theory of Neurosis.* New York: Norton.
Freud, S. (1922), *Group Psychology and the Analysis of the Ego.* New York: Liveright, 1949.
Friedlander, K. (1947), *The Psychoanalytical Approach to Juvenile Delinquency.* New York: International Universities Press.
Gersten, S. (1951), An Experimental Evaluation of Group Therapy with Juvenile Delinquents. *Int. J. Group Psychother., 1:*311-318.
Grinker, R. R. and Spiegel, J. P. (1945), *Men Under Stress.* Philadelphia: Blakiston.
Johnson, A. M. (1949), Sanctions for Superego Lacunae of Adolescents. *Searchlights on Delinquency.* New York: International Universities Press.
McCorkle, L. W. (1953), The Present Status of Group Therapy in United States Correctional Institutions. *Int. J. Group Psychother., 3:*79-87.
Pearson, G. H. J. (1949), *Emotional Disorders of Children.* New York: Norton.
Peck, H. and Bellsmith, V. (1954), *Treatment of the Delinquent Adolescent.* Family Service Association of America.
Rapaport, D. (1951), *Organization and Pathology of Thought.* New York: Columbia University Press.
Schulman, I. (1952), The Dynamics of Certain Reactions of Delinquents to Group Psychotherapy. *Int. J. Group Psychother., 2:*334-343.
—— (1955), Dynamics and Treatment of Anti-Social Psychopathology in Adolescents. *Nerv. Child* (in press).
Slavson, S. R. (1947a), Contra-Indications of Group Therapy for Patients with Psychopathic Personalities. *The Practice of Group Therapy,* ed. S. R. Slavson. New York: International Universities Press.
—— (1947b), An Elementaristic Approach to the Understanding and Treatment of Delinquency. *Nerv. Child, 6:*413-423.

—— (1948), Milieu and Group Treatment for Delinquents. In: *Bulwarks Against Crime,* Yearbook of the National Probation and Parole Association, New York; also in: *Proceeding of the National Conference of Social Work,* 1948.
—— (1950a), *Analytic Group Psychotherapy.* New York: Columbia University Press.
—— (1950b), Group Psychotherapy in Delinquency Prevention. *J. Educ. Sociol.,* September, 1950.
—— (1950c), Social Re-education in an Institutional Setting. In: *Advances in the Understanding of the Offender.* Yearbook of the National Probation and Parole Association, New York.
—— (1954a), A Contribution to a Systematic Theory of Group Psychotherapy. *Int. J. Group Psychother.,* 4:3-29.
—— (1954b), *Re-Educating the Delinquent,* New York: Harper & Bros.
—— and Shulman, H. M. (1936), Re-educative Activity for Delinquent Youth. *Jewish Soc. Serv. Quart.,* June.
Szurek, S. A. (1942), Notes on the Genesis of Psychopathic Personality, *Psychiatry,* 5:1-6.
Thorpe, J. J., and Smith, B. (1952), Operational Sequence in Group Therapy with Young Offenders. *Int. J. Group Psychother.,* 2:24-33.

Chapter XII

CHILD GUIDANCE

●

Child guidance clinics were initially established in 1922 as demonstrations by the National Committee for Mental Hygiene and the Commonwealth Fund. Notable precursors were the Juvenile Psychopathic Institute in Chicago which concerned itself with the study of juvenile delinquency, the Phipps Psychiatric Clinic in Baltimore and the Boston Psychopathic Hospital; these two latter institutions accepted children as outpatients.

Although variations exist in structure, in specific practices and in the use of the professional disciplines involved, child guidance clinics are distinguished by their primary concern with the emotionally disturbed child. The clinical team utilizes the integrated skills of psychiatrist, social caseworker and psychologist in diagnosis and treatment. Originally, only children were treated, and parents were used as sources of information and as executors of direct suggestions from the clinic for handling of the children. However, with increased awareness of parent-child interaction, work with parents evolved from information getting and advice giving to the present recognition that most often the emotional difficulties of children are so closely interwoven with the personalities and symptomatology of the parents that treatment of both is necessary.

While the individual face-to-face interview with the therapist remains the predominant vehicle of the child guidance clinic in its psychiatric, casework, guidance, and counseling services, group psychotherapy is progressively attaining increased use as a therapeutic tool. This significant development has emerged from the recognition that certain cases require a group setting for the achievement of any therapeutic gain, in addition to individual treatment, that certain others can be treated more effectively in groups, and still others would respond to group treatment only. The group meets man's age-old needs to be with his fellow beings; offers support to the fearful; activates the constricted; provides a diluted therapeutic arena for those children and parents who are psychically incapable of assimilating the intensity of the face-to-face treatment relation. The group gives the individual a concrete experience in sharing his difficulties with others in similar straits, leading to the discovery that they no longer are alone with their troubles (universalization), and thus diminishing painful feelings of shame and stigma. There is a number of different types of therapy groups that are employed in child guidance clinics which will be briefly outlined in subsequent pages.

Activity group therapy conceived and developed by S. R. Slavson, as were also play and activity interview groups to be described presently, addresses itself to children in the latency period on a selective basis. It utilizes a distinctly permissive atmosphere to provide a healing, corrective, and maturing experience for personally disturbed and socially maladjusted children. Small groups of five to eight members meet weekly for two-hour sessions in a simply furnished meeting room where a variety of arts and crafts materials, tools and group games are available.

In this setting the children are permitted to express their destructive and constructive impulses, their dammed-up hostilities and sibling hatreds; their wishes to act as infants or their cravings to be adult and powerful. A typical scene from an activity group therapy session might show two or three carefully working with tools; another hammering vigorously against the wall; one sitting at a corner table with his back to the others in an attitude of withdrawal; still another running hyperactively about the room; while a few may vociferously compete for the therapist's attention.

Refreshments are served at each session. Depending upon the level of maturity, contemporary regressive need and length of time in treatment, the food may be thrown about, sucked up in an infantile manner, or eaten neatly and calmly.

Expressions of antisocial behavior and hostile and destructive feelings encounter neither criticism nor punishment; neither are they condoned. Rather, this behavior is understood and accepted as being an expression of the child's contemporary emotional stresses, needs and conflicts. Through free acting out in the group, pent-up tensions accumulated through earlier traumata and frustrating familial relations are liberated, bringing about a progressive lessening of the need for antisocial media of expression. These released emotional energies can then be used by the child in the service of his current growth process and adjustment to family, school and peers.

In such an atmosphere, therapeutic regression to earlier levels of fixation is facilitated. Thus children in whom there exists considerable tension adhering to an anal period will quickly gravitate toward such materials as clay, water and paint. They will often spend many sessions handling these with intense interest and satisfaction and making "concoctions" of sticky materials with obvious pleasure. As no limitations are imposed, interest in this activity subsides until it gives way completely to a more mature and masculine activity such as woodwork.

For effective treatment to occur there must reside in the group an inherent potential for the establishment of a comfortable equilibrium among the diverse personalities composing it. Grouping is then of prime import. A group composed solely of, or overloaded with, highly aggressive children would only create a turbulent and tumultous, tension-ridden atmosphere which would severely impede treatment gains. Similarly, an overweighting of withdrawn and constricted members would produce a relatively arid emotional climate in which social interaction and mobility, both necessary for progress, would be minimal. Experience has demonstrated that a group of eight should contain no more than two very aggressive members and no more than three of the highly withdrawn category; the others should fall between the two extremes. The inclusion of one or two socially active children in each group has been found to be necessary, for they stimulate interpersonal reactions and bring members into emotional contact with each other.

As in all treatment methods, here, too, the therapist plays a crucial and pivotal role. *Neutrality* and *passivity* comprise the two major facets of his therapeutic attitude; these permit the children to interact freely and to reveal openly their inner conflicts and tensions. Also, members are free to utilize the therapist according to their individual need, whether this be to ignore him coldly, fear him or to seek him out as a warm and protecting parental figure. In keeping with his role, the therapist does not interpret, moralize, punish, assign tasks, intervene or mediate in disputes between members. The neutrality on the part of the "parent" in the group "family" produces a basically democratic atmosphere in which children are extended the fullest freedom to develop their strengths and capabilities.

The child, whose relationship pattern with adults is one of compliance and ingratiation, will offer to make things for the therapist or to help him in cleaning the room at the conclusion of sessions. The therapist's response to these offers with a casual "if you want to," eventually assures the child that the adult has no need for him to act self-effacingly. He is then enabled to act as he really wants to, discovering and establishing his own identity in the process.

The infantilized child who has previously only experienced acceptance when helpless, dependent and "cute" soon discovers that the therapist will not cater to these tendencies but will rather allow him to function on his own, to struggle and compete and develop his capacities for independent functioning. The child who, in response to his life history, has developed patterns of provocativeness toward adults which generally elicit rejection and punitiveness, encounters in the therapist a calm, unruffled acceptance. This unique relation with the therapist gradually changes the child's view of adults as being on the one hand weak and easily manipulated by him to react on his level and on the other hand as counterattackers.

It can thus be perceived that within his defined neutrality and passivity, the therapist must be acutely sensitive to the unique personality adjustments and basic problems of each child in the group in order to be prepared to act in the most telling therapeutic manner. He also functions catalytically in the process by which the child relates himself to and becomes a part of the group. It is his pervasive acceptance, helpfulness, readiness to praise and encourage, and his respect for the human dignity of the children that enables them to behave similarly toward each other.

Because of the presence of diverse personalities within the group, the nature of the setting and the great number of different interpersonal situations that arise, opportunities for countertransference are multiple. The constant demandingness of the orally deprived child, the seductiveness of the ingratiator, the open competitiveness of the child in oedipal rivalry with his father—all may activate the therapist's own feelings and propel him toward negation of his therapeutic role unless he is sensitively attuned to his reactions. In the execution of his responsibility he must be able to restrain his own needs actively to control, guide and direct children, to be liked and to be included in their games and activities.

Activity group therapy has been found to be generally unsuitable for the severely psychoneurotic child and those with severe libidinal distortions. Moreover, because of the characteristic permissiveness of this treatment approach, it cannot assimilate the unbridled aggression of the psychopath or psychotic. The physically stigmatized, i.e., the blind and crippled and those too short or too tall, cannot be treated in these groups. Children, like animals, display strong aversion to marked divergence from the norm. Placing such handicapped individuals in these groups would only serve to emphasize their difference.

Although each case must be evaluated as to suitability for this treatment milieu on its own merits, nuclear and peripheral problems and dynamics, some general categories of cases have been found to respond to this medium. These include the behavior disorders (with or without neurotic traits), mild psychoneurotic types such as found in those individuals who have acquired fears rooted in specific external situations, some schizoid and borderline cases where the degree of fearfulness and psychological atypicality is not too marked, and some character traits and disorders, i.e., infantile and submissive characters, effeminacy in boys and masculinity in girls. In dealing with this last category of character disorders, groups can be effective in changing misplaced and defective identifications and ego ideals in that the whole group environment exerts a corrective pressure upon the particular malformed personality trait.

Play Groups. In play groups, children of preschool age reveal their problems in play on a fantasy level with dolls, doll houses, clay, toy animals, water, and blocks. At opportune intervals the therapist helps the children to understand their jealousies and resentments in language geared to their level of comprehension. For a fuller discussion of this type of treatment see Slavson (1945a, 1948, 1950).

Activity Interview Groups. For children from six to ten years of age who present more serious neurotic problems than can be adequately affected by activity groups, activity interview groups are employed. Here activity is combined with group and individual discussion. Play materials, especially suitable for eliciting the expression of aggressive feelings and libidinal strivings, such as toy guns, doll houses, dolls, clay, paints, masks, and toy animals are supplied. In an extensive paper, Gabriel (1939) has given a graphic description of this work. See also Slavson (1952).

Transitional Groups. After a period of group therapy, children are frequently ready to adjust to a less sheltered social arena as "Y" or community center. In the period of accommodation to the new setting, the group therapist may accompany the children and serve as the leader of the transitional group until it is securely established within the community environment.

Interview Groups with Adolescents and Parents. In interview groups with adolescents and adults, the group discussion method is employed exclusively with the goal of basic personality change toward emotional health through verbal catharsis and insight. The supportive presence of others with similar problems and anxieties has been found to be a strategic factor in helping clients freely discuss their problems, air their guilts, and ventilate their long-buried, unconscious resentments and jealousies.[1]

Guidance Groups for Parents. The recent development of guidance groups for parents offers a promise of precious dividends in family emotional health and the prevention of psychic disability in oncoming generations. In these groups, the goal is not directed toward changing the basic personalities of the parents carefully selected for these groups, but rather is aimed at bettering the daily living relationship between parent and child. To accomplish this, parents are helped to cross the 30-year gulf in understanding between child and adult. Parents bring into the group specific problems and situations, other members give their own experiences with similar problems and the group leader guides them toward understanding of the child's behavior and motivations, and helps them evolve more adequate tools for fashioning a more harmonious family life. In a noncritical, helpful atmosphere with the emphasis maintained steadily on the child, misconceptions and erroneous attitudes concerning children are clarified and corrected by the parents themselves. Mothers and fathers who enter these groups holding beliefs that children are basically selfish, ungrateful, or even vicious, have left with a totally changed perception of, and sensitivity toward, their children.

One father, Mr. Jonas, in his third group guidance session, participated in a discussion of obedience and respect in which several members complained of the absence of these virtues in their sons. When the leader asked the group how these feelings were developed in a child, a silence ensued, broken after a long moment by Mr. Jonas, stating almost incredulously, "You mean you have to respect a child first!"

For Mr. Jonas, whose previous relationship to his son had been marked by a sarcastically domineering attitude, this sudden insight opened new paternal horizons. At subsequent sessions, he reported having sought and considered the boy's opinion in planning the family vacation, talking things over with him in general, and having a more shared, harmonious and mutually accepting life with him. One could say that through the group Mr. Jonas found his son. In this he was aided by the other members' comments, suggestions and illustrations; from his equals in the group he was able to accept ideas and even criticism about his handling of his son much more readily than he could have from the leader who might symbolize all the resented authorities in his life. The leader in his role was noncritical and accepting of Mr. Jonas, continually giving him a feeling of being a person worthy of respect for his own individuality.

---

[1] For a fuller discussion of this type of treatment, see Chapter IX.

After experiencing this, Mr. Jonas was then enabled to enact similar attitudes with his son.

Through these groups[2] parents find ways to eliminate whole areas of stress and conflict, resulting in that happier family living which is the first requisite for emotional health and maturity. One mother, prior to entering the group, had constantly nagged and fought bitterly with her son each morning to get him up on time for school. After discussion of her problem in the group and at the suggestion of her group mates she bought an alarm clock for the boy and and left the situation in his hands. Fred responded positively to his mother's changed attitude which catered to his innate trend toward growth and independent functioning. He proudly saw to it that he awakened on time. A whole battleground had been dissolved, shutting off a chain reaction of tension in which Fred's upset feelings each morning had carried over into his relationship with teachers, classmates, friends, and family.

Problems such as bed wetting, stealing, thumb sucking, masturbation, disobedience, and school failure have been eradicated completely or significantly lessened as a consequence of wiser parental handling based on greater sensitivity to children's needs. In an atmosphere blending therapy and education, vital concepts are imparted. Parents gain awareness of the great differences between children and adults in media of expression and in emotional perspective. They learn to recognize, accept, and constructively canalize the natural spontaneity of children and their organic needs for physical mobility.

Although varied structures may be encountered in different agency settings, group therapy is generally an integral segment of the services offered to patients. Group therapists are usually drawn from the permanent casework or psychiatric staff, though under certain conditions they may also be recruited from related fields as part-time workers.

Cases are referred to group therapy either directly from intake, after completion of the initial study of the family and problems presented, or from the individual therapists who have been treating the child or parent. Depending upon the needs of the individual, a child or parent may be treated exclusively in group therapy or cooperatively with concurrent individual therapy. Cases may also be divided with one member of a family in a group and another in individual treatment. In certain situa-

2 Slavson who has evolved and tested this technique for six years has named it "child-centered group guidance of parents." A book by him dealing with this method is to appear soon.

tions a child and both parents may become members of three different groups.[3]

At regular intervals group therapists prepare progress reports on members of their groups in which they describe the individual's adjustment: the nature and degree of his interaction with fellow members, his attitude toward the therapist, his status and role in the group and other data significant for assessing and evaluating treatment. Studies are also made of the patients' adjustment in school, in the family and in the community.

At four-month intervals, integration conferences are held on each case in group therapy for formal evaluation of the individual's therapeutic progress. These conferences bring together all of the personnel involved in treatment of the family; thus, in a *cooperative* case, both group therapist and caseworker, as well as their respective supervisors, would contribute to the integrating process.

Because group psychotherapy is a relatively new field, agencies utilize the services of a consultant, necessarily a person with wide experience in group psychotherapy. In addition to providing leadership and technical direction for the group therapy program, his services include the training and supervision of group therapists, participation in integration conferences, in treatment conferences and in decisions involving suitability of clients for group therapy.

The following case is an example of the application of activity group therapy to a disturbed boy in latency.

Donald was referred to the Child Guidance Institute at age 9½, with problems of nocturnal enuresis, continuous since birth, intense rivalry with his brother, 3 years younger than himself, difficulties in socialization, with Donald having no friends of his own but usually playing with his brother's friends or engaging in isolative pursuits. There were conduct difficulties at school, mainly in the nature of clowning, several incidents of stealing of money from his mother and brother. Donald also exhibited a generalized, sullen resentfulness. When seen at intake Donald was observed to be a rather small, sad-looking youngster who made a somewhat pathetic attempt to conceal his feelings of timidity and weakness beneath a clowning façade.

As a result of her own upbringing by a driving, dominating mother and a weak, distant father, Donald's mother did not establish adequate feminine identifications and subsequently felt trapped in her role as wife

---

[3] A detailed study of a family treated under this plan was presented at the 11th Annual Conference of the American Group Psychotherapy Association, January 1953, and will be included in Slavson's forthcoming book.

and mother. After marriage she continued to work and to take college courses in obvious attempts to evade her wifely and maternal responsibilities. Donald's father, a weak, unassertive person, allowed himself to take over much of the operation of the house and child care functions.

Donald's crucial developmental years were marked by inconsistent handling as his mother vacillated between overprotectiveness and pressing the boy toward rapid achievement. There were also indications that his progress toward adequate masculinity had been blocked by the mother's deeply ingrained hostility toward male figures and the father's inability to provide a suitable object with whom Donald could identify.

Referral to activity group therapy was made with the view of providing Donald with a consistently warm, accepting, maturing and noncompetitive situation which could counteract his negative and frustrating experiences within his family which had caused him to decide that it was not worth while to grow up. It was also anticipated that the group could exert a stimulating effect upon Donald socially, that acceptance by the therapist and the group would strengthen his debilitated self-esteem and reinforce his weak masculine identifications.

In the therapist's "first impression report" on Donald, written after his first five group therapy sessions, he was described as being generally aloof and separate from the group. In this initial period he completely avoided the therapist, to the extent of not greeting him in any way upon arrival at the sessions. Shortly after this when Donald was seen for an individual interview by the group therapy follow-up worker, he spontaneously expressed his liking the group, saying that he especially liked the refreshments and "the kidding around." With reference to friends he stated with unconvincing bravado: "I've got trillions, scads of them." However, he later implied that he was still dependent upon his brother and the latter's friends as playmates.

At the treatment conference held after Donald's first three months in group therapy, he was described as quiet and self-contained, with a certain elusiveness about his personality which kept him on the periphery of the emotional flux within the group. He worked by himself at pasting shells and making lanyards. A tense, puppet-like jerkiness of his movements was described, and a pattern of silent departures from sessions immediately after refreshments was noted.

For a period of some months Donald, at first cautiously and then with increasing openness, acted out hostile and aggressive feelings which reached their climax at one session when Donald threw hammers violently at the walls. The therapist did not react in any way, and this behavior soon tapered off. Following this, Donald entered a phase of sibling rivalry in which he competed with another member for the therapist's attention and company at the ping-pong table.

After thirty sessions the mother reported that Donald seemed happier and "more grown-up." He was able to travel to group sessions without her having to accompany him any longer. He also had made a friend of his own age on the block where he lived with whom he played ball, an activity he had previously avoided.

Emerging changes were noted in the second progress report after eight months of group treatment. Although Donald had not formed any friendships with other boys in the group, he seemed much more relaxed in their company. He had begun to relate positively to the therapist, greeting him by name and proudly showing him his constructed crafts work. A widening of the scope of his activity had occurred in that Donald had begun to work with more resistive materials such as wood and metal which necessitated such masculine activity as hammering and sawing.

After one and a half years of treatment, the group therapist wrote, "Donald has lost the jerky quality which he had previously exhibited in his movement; rather, he now seems to walk with a certain carefree bounce. The sombre facial expression has given way to a quick readiness to smile."

At a psychiatric conference, diagnosis of character disorder was established. Donald's enuresis, school difficulties and stealing were seen as reactive to the marked maladjustment between Donald and his mother and her repudiation of him which was implicit in her rejection of her maternal role. The clowning and bravado were understood as having been Donald's reaction formations to his deep-seated feelings of weakness and castration.

When Donald had been in treatment for one and a half years, an interview with the father was arranged to explore the boy's adjustment outside the group. It was found that the enuresis and sibling rivalry continued, the latter symptom having diminished in intensity. Donald's conduct had improved at school. Whereas he had previously clowned disruptively in class, he currently seemed to be turning his talents for humor into socially approved channels, having written a comedy for a class play which had been successfully received. In the area of socialization, Donald had two friends of his own peer group and had enrolled in a neighborhood play center which he attended several times weekly. The father summarized that in general Donald was happier, more relaxed and spontaneous.

The following excerpt from the recording of a group session illustrates the changes effected over that period in a boy who had been initially remote, self-contained and elusive to one who had become able to zestfully share his life with his fellows:

"Donald arrived at 3:55, gave me a hearty hello and immediately asked the others if he could play ball also. Roy gave him the ball and glove and Donald and Charles began throwing to each other. Donald played with a certain relaxed, athletic grace and easily discussed baseball with Charles during their play. Later, Donald and Larry got into a long discussion on a variety of topics which included cars, the history of World War II, and camp. As I have indicated in previous reports, whenever Larry and Donald converse, a real rapport exists between them. All the other members were attracted to the conversation and at intervals contributed to it. Donald announced happily that he was going to camp for the first time. Later, Ben challenged Donald to a 'chicken-fight'; Henry and Tom joined in and the four boys continued at this in friendly fashion until refreshments were served."

In reviewing Donald's progress, it would seem that the permissive aspects of the group situation were crucial in nurturing his maturation. Initially guarded and withdrawn, he discovered that no pressure was exerted to socialize, to be likeable, courteous or friendly. His abandonment of isolation and psychological advances toward the group were made on the basis of his own inner readiness to do so. In the process of being allowed to adapt himself at his own pace to the social reality of the group, Donald encountered a unique regard and respect for his autonomy. The acceptance of his needs to withdraw and to function in isolation, in the absence of concomitant demands that he satisfy the needs of others, had significant repercussions in strengthening his self-image. At the time of his referral Donald's clowning reflected his inner self-appraisal, proclaiming in effect: "Look, I make myself funny. Therefore I am really not adequate or a threat to anyone." As his estimation of his own worth was enhanced in the curative group atmosphere, Donald was enabled to drop his self-deprecatory clowning in favor of a considerably more mature and adequate presentation of himself to the world.

In the therapist, Donald found a *consistently* calm, accepting, yet strong figure who had no need to be liked by the boy, but who was ready to meet him psychologically when Donald, after considerable testing, was finally assured of the adult's trustworthiness. In this vital relationship Donald's previously established conceptions of adults as punitive, pressuring and authoritarian figures were modified. In this process emotional pathways were laid that led toward more harmonious relations with parents, teachers, and camp counselors.

Other therapeutic elements involved were the manifold opportunities afforded for masculine identification with the therapist and the other boys, and the diminution of inner tensions through release of hostility accrued over the years in unsatisfying and frustrating familial relations. In his interaction within the group (family) with fellow members (siblings) and therapist (parent), Donald was free to work out one of his major presenting problems—his feelings of resentment toward his brother by whom he felt displaced. His discovery that there were neither preferred nor rejected members in the group led to measurable amelioration of his prior feeling of resentment involving his brother.

It should be noted that gains were achieved in this case despite negative factors involved in the resistance of both parents to involving themselves in treatment.

The following case illustrates a situation in which treatment in activity group therapy is contraindicated. *Andrew* was referred at 10 years of age for severe conflict with mother and sister, aged 14, disruptive behavior at school, constant restlessness and hyperactivity at home and school and inability to concentrate. There were fears of the dark, nightmares and nocturnal enuresis. Andrew displayed strong sexual interests and made frequent comments, with obvious excitement, on the breasts and buttocks of his mother, sister and women on the street.

The intake study determined that Andrew had shared the parental bedroom until age 6 and thereafter had slept in a room with his sister. The father assumed a subordinate role in the home and was distant toward Andrew. The mother seemed to relate to Andrew on a sibling-like level, being easily provoked to screaming at and hitting him. At the same time there were seductive elements in her permitting him to see her unclothed.

The evidence from the symptomatology and the salient developmental details points clearly toward intense neurotic conflicts in this boy engendered by the dangerously close relationship with the mother. This oedipal situation has been exacerbated in the presence of a weak father who has not stood firmly between the boy and his impulses toward the mother. Sexual stimulation has been rife through the unhealthy sleeping arrangements and maternal seductiveness, and this leads to the assumption that the enuresis is probably sexual in nature. It may also be assumed that Andrew's constant restlessness is the outer manifestation of marked inner sexual anxieties.

Intensive individual psychotherapy is needed here. Through the transference relation and the therapist's interpretation, Andrew can be helped to express his drives toward the mother, to understand and eventually recanalize them. This core of sexual anxiety could not be reached in the nonverbal, noninterpretive setting of activity group therapy. If put in a group, his pervasive inner tensions would only result in increasing hyperactivity and destructiveness. Activity therapy groups are geared to the latency period with its accelerated ego-integrative processes and the relative quiescence of sexual and libidinal conflicts. Dynamically speaking, Andrew has unfortunately had no latency period.

Group psychotherapy, as a treatment method, cannot be universally applied either to children, adolescents, their parents or adults generally who come to child guidance settings, nor can it substitute for, or displace individual therapy for patients suffering from severe, deeply rooted psychoneuroses. However, in the case of children in whom there is a basic social hunger to be accepted by their peers, activity group psychotherapy can be instrumental in modifying and eliminating pathological self-involvement and emotional isolation. In the social laboratory of the group the individual is prepared for the harmonious merging of his life with others in meaningful and positive societal living.

The following illustrates the effectiveness of child-centered guidance groups in achieving changes in ingrained attitudes of parents and in developing sensitivity toward children's needs.

Roy F. was first referred for treatment at age 10 years for nocturnal enuresis since birth, temper tantrums, conflict with his parents and several incidents of stealing money from his mother's purse. Additional difficulties were restlessness and hyperactivity, nail biting, teeth grinding, and misconduct at school. Roy was unplanned and unwanted; his mother repeatedly attempted to abort him until the sixth month of pregnancy. Toilet training commenced at age 7 months and was rigidly enforced. A sister was born when Roy was 9 years old. He shared the parental bedroom for the first 10 years of his life.

The mother, a tense, rigid and compulsive woman, infantilized and overprotected Roy. She bathed and dressed him until he was quite grown; in her fear and anxiety for his safety, she stealthily followed him about on the streets to see that he did not get into accidents.

The father, a taxi driver, was the oldest of three children, having a younger brother and sister. The paternal grandfather had owned a tailor shop; at age 7 Roy's father had been pressed into delivering clothes to his father's customers. The family had been economically deprived and as a child he had visited a friend so that he could play with the latter's toys. Roy's father repeatedly stated that he wanted Roy to have the things of which he as a child had been deprived. In his dealings with Roy, Mr. F.

alternated between severe physical punishment and overindulgence. Though he would beat Roy severely with a strap after the stealing episodes, he would at the same time give the boy rather large sums of money, becoming quite anxious when Roy would spend it, and would offer the boy a partnership in stamp and coin collecting hobbies. Roy was allowed to handle all of the money involved in these ventures. The father continually discussed with Roy the latter's enuresis and moralized on the subject in the hope that the boy would cease the annoying "habit." The father was obviously attempting to compensate for his own deprived childhood through his treatment of Roy. When seen in an individual interview prior to his assignment to a group, Mr. F., in a slip of the tongue, referred to himself as "Roy."

Mr. F. attended 23 group guidance sessions. At the first session, after listening to other members describe some of the difficulties with their children, he commented that his son's "problem" was "anxiety," but did not expand on the subject. He complained that on Sundays, Roy was unwilling to accompany him on visits to the paternal grandparents and preferred to go to the playground. He ignored the statement by another and older member of the group who suggested that this seemed like a healthy reaction in the boy and reiterated that his son had "too much anxiety." At the close of this session, Mr. F. referred briefly to Roy's enuresis which he ascribed to "nerves" and expressed strong criticism of the boy for "drinking water before going to bed."

At the second session that Mr. F. attended, he reiterated his complaint that Roy preferred to play with friends rather than visit with him and added, "Kids are out for themselves." Later he was critical of a fellow group member who was unresponsive to his son's conversation about science, stating: "The trouble with you is that you're not interested in the things your boy does." In the next session, Mr. F. was less communicative and listened attentively to a discussion of physical punishment by the others, which led to the conclusion that it served only to alienate children from the parents rather than helping them to control themselves. His only comment was that Roy was "nervous" and seemed to resent anything he, the father did.

At the fourth session Mr. F. told of his difficulties in getting Roy to wash his hands before mealtimes and his resistance to being of any help to his father. However, instead of expressing resentment or criticism, he now wondered if this was due to "immaturity" in the boy. He described feeling hurt that Roy seemed to consider friends more important than him. The leader explained this as a normal developmental phase in which children, much less secure in the acceptance by their peers than by parents, naturally catered more to friends. Mr. F. seemed both impressed and appreciative, saying, "So that's why he's so nice to his friends? I'll have to take that idea home."

In the succeeding several sessions, Mr. F. continued to voice defensively superficial and rather meaningless statements to the effect that "nerves," "anxiety," "tension" were causing his son's difficulties. In echoing statements of other group members, he continued to make frequent use of platitudes such as "time is a great healer," or "that's human nature." On one occasion he was observed to wink broadly at another man in the group as he coyly asked the leader whether parents "made too much of a fuss over children." The leader remarked that it sounded like a loaded question, and Mr. F. laughingly admitted that it was.

At his seventh session, he indicated that he closely supervised Roy's homework every night and would criticize him for his "sloppy" handwriting. He did not respond when another member wondered why Mr. F. was so upset as long as the boy's writing was acceptable to his teacher. When one of the men noted that his son never told him what went on in his treatment at the clinic, and a second commented acceptingly, "That's his privilege," Mr. F. seemed highly surprised, averring that it was a totally new concept for him and adding, "I guess they need privacy, too." This marked the first time that Mr. F. had displayed any regard for the person of his child—a change obviously induced by the attitudes of other members in the group.

The eighth session marked a turning point for Mr. F. One of the members reported that his boy had confided to him his worries about school. Sadly Mr. F. remarked that Roy never told him anything, and "he doesn't want any part of me." From this point on Mr. F. presented a different and changed attitude in the group and began sincerely to grope for help in bettering his relationship with his son. In a serious manner he said that he now realized that his "old methods of nagging and hitting Roy" had not worked; he would have to try something new. At the close of that session, he sought out the leader and asked several questions about camp opportunities for his son. In this Mr. F. seemed to be testing the leader's acceptance of him.

At the next session Mr. F. again renewed his complaints about Roy's refusal to go visiting with him on week ends. He had modified his approach somewhat, he said, by offering first to play ball with the boy before going to visit his parents, but Roy still refused. Here, another of the group members told Mr. F. point blank: "Why don't you ask him what *he* wants to do and then do it." Apparently this direct thrust by a peer superimposed on Mr. F.'s growing awareness of his son as an individual with desires and rights of his own had its effect, because at his thirteenth session, Mr. F. announced with pride that he now had a "new system" for getting Roy to go to bed which eliminated the nightly conflict around retiring for the night. He now allows Roy to choose his own bedtime, he said, and after some experimentation, the boy had selected a reasonable hour.

At the succeeding session Mr. F. gave further evidence that he had made significant strides toward increased understanding of and sensitivity to the nuances of parent-child relationships. He said, among other things, that despite his own anxiety and misgivings, he had given Roy permission to go on a long bicycle trip, and it had worked out well. He then added significantly: "Sometimes we want to let them [children] grow up and go out on their own, but when they're ready to go, we get frightened."

At the sixteenth session one of the men described how he became upset when his son picked his teeth with a fork. The father's abrupt admonition to the boy to stop had touched off a lengthy conflict between them. In discussing this situation, Mr. F. said to the man, "I'm getting grey-haired but I'm finally getting smart. I've finally learned that the more you harp on a kid, the less good it does." Later, a new member expressed his frustration over his son's misconduct by exclaiming, "How do you teach a kid discipline?" Mr. F. replied gently: "With patience, my son."

At a later session, Mr. F. told of having awakened Roy during the preceding night to take him to the bathroom, explaining that it was a chilly night and that he did not want the boy to catch cold if he wet the bed. Other members questioned the advisability of this act, pointing out that he was being overprotective of a boy who was now almost 13 years old. Mr. F. in an abashed manner said, "I guess I'm going back to treating him like I did when he was 3 years old." At another session where a discussion of the parents' involvement with their children's school performance took place, Mr. F. declared that he had learned in the group that a parent "has to be more of a pal to a child and not a teacher." To another parent who had consistently visited the school in attempts to effect changes of class and teacher for his son, Mr. F. pointed out that a parent is not helping a child by fighting all his battles for him since this prevents him, the child, from learning to handle situations on his own.

For a long while, despite his progress in understanding of children's motivations and behavior in other areas, Mr. F. was unable to think objectively about Roy's enuresis. He would still frequently make resentful comments to the effect that the wetting was still a problem and "if he would only stop." On various occasions he expressed being tempted to use a mechanical device to control this symptom. Finally, at one of his last sessions, Mr. F. voiced awareness of the close relationship between Roy's enuresis and his infantilization by the parents and concluded by saying, "We did everything for him and that way kept him a baby. No wonder he wets today."

In his adjustment to the group, Mr. F. first presented strong resistances to involving himself in a meaningful way. He voiced his son's problems by superficialities, used platitudes, and sought to defeat the leader. The unwavering acceptance by the latter, the example set and support given by fellow members as they earnestly sought solutions for their difficulties with their children, enabled Mr. F. to drop his defenses and join in the common group effort toward better parenthood. The emotional gratification of being accepted and respected, and of being allowed to follow his own course and pace enabled him in turn to re-enact these attitudes toward his son.

Follow-up interviews with Mr. F. after termination of the group revealed significant improvements in Roy. The enuresis lessened in frequency, conduct disorders at school ceased and the boy showed growing ability to accept responsibility as reflected in his finding for himself a part-time job to cover his own expenses. He had also bought at his own initiative presents for the parents and his sister on their birthdays. He evidently now perceived his father as a more positive and generous person, one to whom he could now give in return. It should be noted in passing that the mother had also been in a child-centered guidance group from which she seemed to benefit as much as did her husband from his group.

BIBLIOGRAPHY

Allen, F. (1930), Evolution of Our Treatment Philosophy in Child Guidance. *Ment. Hyg.*, 14:1.
Amster, F. (1944), Collective Psychotherapy of Mothers of Emotionally Disturbed Children. *Am. J. Orthopsychiat.*, 14:1.
Gabriel, B. (1939), An Experiment in Group Treatment. *Am. J. Orthopsychiat.*, 9:1.
Goller, G. (1942), Criteria for Referral to Group Therapy in a Child Guidance Clinic. *Smith College Studies in Social Work, 13.*
Hamilton, G. (1947), *Psychotherapy in Child Guidance.* New York: Columbia University Press.
Lowrey, L. (1943), Group Therapy for Mothers at the Brooklyn Child Guidance Center, *News Letter of the American Association of Psychiatric Social Workers.*
Rosenthal, L. (1951), Group Psychotherapy in a Child Guidance Clinic. *J. Soc. Casework,* 22:8-337.
—— (1953), Group Therapy with Problem Children and Their Parents. *Fed. Probation,* 17:4-27.
Schiffer, M. (1952), Permissiveness Versus Sanction in Activity Group Therapy. *Int. J. Group Psychother.*, 2:255.

Slavson, S. R. (1943a), *An Introduction to Group Therapy*. New York: International Universities Press, 1951.

—— (1943b), Treatment of Aggression Through Group Therapy. *Am. J. Orthopsychiat., 13*:3.

—— (1945a), Differential Methods of Group Therapy in Relation to Age Levels. *Nerv. Child, 4*:96.

—— (1945b), Treatment of Withdrawal Through Activity Group Therapy. *Am. J. Orthopsychiat., 15*:4.

—— (ed.), (1947a), *The Practice of Group Therapy*. New York: International Universities Press.

—— (1947b), Qualifications and Training of Group Therapists. *Ment. Hyg., 31*:3.

—— (1948), Play Group Therapy for Young Children. *Nerv. Child, 7*:318.

—— (1950), *Analytic Group Psychotherapy*. New York: Columbia University Press.

—— (1952), *Child Psychotherapy*. New York: Columbia University Press.

Witmer, H. L. (1940), *Psychiatric Clinics for Children*. New York: Commonwealth Fund.

Chapter XIII

FAMILY SERVICES

●

Family service agencies are rather widely scattered throughout the United States, with the highest concentration in the cities east of the Mississippi. Some 256 of these agencies are affiliated in the Family Service Association of America—a national body primarily delegated to the setting up of standards in this field.

The core professional staff of a family agency is composed of social case workers with a minimum educational requirement of two years graduate training in a school of social work. Not infrequently other specialists are employed for specific services in relation to the total program of the organization, such as home economists, nurses, homemakers. There are also special staff consultants, usually psychiatrists and clinical psychologists.

The modern family service agency had its precursor in the Charity Organization Society of the last century. Following the example of similar movements in England around 1870, these organizations combined the broader attack against social evils of the day, with attempts to dispense charity to the destitute in a coordinated fashion. By the turn of the century a body of procedures had begun to emerge from the practice of the volunteer charity workers. There was a growing awareness that in identifying the needs of individuals in distress and in providing adequate resources for help, specific skills were called into play. This trend toward the specialization of social work as a professional entity received particular impetus with the founding in 1898 of the first training school of philanthropy (now known as the New York School of Social Work) and with the publication of Mary Richmond's *Social Diagnosis* in 1917.

During the early 1920's, as experience became crystallized further and as social work education began to be influenced by psychoanalytic psychiatry, a newer orientation emerged. Family caseworkers began to emphasize the importance of studying the broader forces affecting families in need of help, coupled with a better understanding of the individual applicants. Furthermore, in meeting needs for immediate financial support, the goal of utilizing all of the agency's services toward establishing the family as an independent operating unit in the community was kept in the foreground.

During the economic depression in the thirties, private family agencies were unable to maintain their earlier function of giving financial relief and many of them relinquished this completely. The emphasis shifted to what is termed "composite" casework directed toward helping with problems of personal and family adjustment. In a recent statement the central purpose of such agencies was described as contributing to ". . . harmonious family interrelationships, to strengthen the positive values in family life, and to promote healthy personality development of various family members."[1] These purposes in the program fall into the following two major categories: (a) providing casework services; (b) participating in community planning. Some of the agencies have also evolved selected secondary functions, such as group education, professional social work education, and research. Family casework services are applied to manifold problems ranging from help with marital or children's adjustment problems, through disturbances in vocational functioning, to planning for the care of the physically or mentally ill, the handicapped or the aged. In all of these, the emphasis on the family as a unit is paramount. The family is seen as playing a major role in the emotional and social adjustment of its members. The study of the interaction of psychological, social, economic and cultural forces in family life is basic to family casework.

The initial step in this casework approach is that of adequate exploration to obtain a full understanding of the problem at hand as well as of the capacities of the individual and the family. This exploration is achieved within a framework of the caseworker's acceptance, interest and respect for the client as a person with integrity, dignity and rights of self-determination.

On the basis of the information obtained, the caseworker formulates a psychosocial diagnosis which represents an evaluation of the pertinent physical, economic, personality and cultural factors involved in the client's and the whole family's functioning.[2] From this, he hypothesizes

[1] *Scope and Methods of the Family Service Agency.* New York: Family Service Association of America, 1953, p. 3.
[2] This is presented from the point of view of the so-called "diagnostic" orientation. For another theoretical approach see Kasius (1950).

what needs to be done about the factors which appear to be interfering with adequate adjustment with special reference to the capacities of the client or family for accepting or utilizing help. Carrying out the treatment plans is the final step in casework. These three phases—exploration, diagnosis, and treatment—are not seen as separate, formal entities, and at any one time they can be operating as a unit.

Generally speaking, two kinds of treatment goals have been delineated in family casework, depending on the diagnostic and prognostic elements in each case: (a) treatment aimed at maintaining adaptive patterns; (b) treatment aimed at modification of adaptive patterns.[3] In the first-named treatment aim, the emphasis is on supporting the client in such a way as to maintain or improve his level of functioning. This may involve temporary planning at a point of crisis for some specific resource, as for example, homemaker service.

In other instances, a long-term contact may be called for, especially with individuals whose ego is weak and who find it difficult to cope with the pressures of everyday living. A supportive relationship with a caseworker frequently can mitigate enough of the panic and emotional pressure of the client to allow him to regroup or develop his ego strengths so that he feels more able to face the problems before him. This kind of treatment planfully avoids attacking a client's defensive structure nor is there any conscious aim at promoting insight. Among the ego-supportive techniques utilized toward this end are: environmental manipulation, suggestion, persuasion and guidance (Bibring, 1947).

In the second treatment aim there is a primary intent of changing the individual's patterns of functioning through enhanced self-understanding. While not aiming at personality reorganization with its focus on eliciting unconscious material, as is the case in deeper psychotherapy, this approach utilizes preconscious material to help the client increase his awareness of his motivations. Besides the utilization of ego-supportive techniques, a primary method here is clarification of feelings, attitudes and adaptive patterns. It is envisioned that the individual's relationship with the caseworker sets the stage for a corrective emotional experience with opportunities for the internalization of new ideals and attitudes which ". . . have the effect of strengthening the ego's capacity for reality testing and of lessening or increasing the demands of the superego."[4]

In discussing the functions of the family service agency, we have referred earlier in this paper to group education. This activity has developed over the years as agencies were approached by community groups

---

3 *Scope and Methods of the Family Service Agency*, pp. 18-20.
4 *Ibid.*, p. 20.

to furnish them with speakers, discussion leaders and the like for the dissemination of knowledge in the broader field of mental hygiene. In 1946 and again in 1948 two separate committees of the Family Service Association of America surveyed the various kinds of educational group services in individual agencies. The recent trend has been that of encouraging discussion series instead of the earlier single sessions. This program, known as "family life education," is offered to interested *groups* in the community, such as civic or parent-teacher associations. The purposes are primarily educational and preventive in goal, involving the dissemination of concepts of mental hygiene, of child development and of family relationships.[5] Family life education is quite different from group psychotherapy and will, therefore, not be discussed in this chapter. In contrast to such group education programs which are made available to community groups, group psychotherapy is utilized as a resource for clients receiving direct treatment in the agency and is, therefore, generally viewed as a "complementary service" to the core casework program.

Group psychotherapy, while strongly entrenched in clinical settings, is a very new development in the family service field. Its adoption by a very selected number of agencies within the last few years appears to be due to a number of factors. First of all, there is the earlier discussed newer emphasis in these agencies on personality pathology which has increased the utilization of psychiatric consultants. In addition, the interest in the family as-a-whole, in the practice of group supervision and in family life education, served to impress the field with the motivational forces inherent in small face-to-face groups. There has also been a constant search on the part of agencies for new and more effective methods of helping, particularly for specialized categories of clients, such as adults who are inaccessible to casework contact, children or adolescents, unmarried mothers, and so on.

In the late thirties, the Jewish Social Service Bureau of Chicago, a family organization, together with the Jewish Children's Bureau and the Institute for Juvenile Research sponsored an "Experimental Project in the Integration of Casework and Group Work Services for Children" (Spiker, 1943). This project, modeled after Slavson's work, was directed by Spiker and Svendsen of the Institute for Juvenile Research and served children between the ages of 8 to 16 and occasionally those of preschool age. These were called "protected groups" and were utilized for children who had difficulties in socialization and could not get along in the usual community groups. Most often children were sent to such groups follow-

5 See articles on family life education, *Family Service Highlights, 19,* 1953.

ing a period of casework help in the various cooperating agencies. A similar program founded in 1942 by Redl in Detroit became known as the "Detroit Group Project." While originally organized by three casework agencies, among them the Jewish Social Service Bureau, its sponsorship shifted within a year to the Detroit Council of Social Agencies and the School of Social Work, Wayne University. Described by the founder of the project as "an agency to serve other agencies," the original focus was on the formation of "protected groups," not unlike those described above, which were attached to group work agencies in the community. The major aim was at first to obtain diagnostic material on children with problems (Redl, 1944). Subsequently, clinically oriented therapy groups were also organized. While the earlier-mentioned Chicago undertaking appears to have been discontinued, the "Detroit Group Project" is still in operation.

It should be noted that in both these efforts family service associations served as co-sponsors of groups operated in the community for a number of casework agencies. It was not until 1947 that a family agency, the Community Service Society of New York, adopted group treatment as an integral part of its own program of helping families. This work was directed by S. R. Slavson till 1952. In this setting group therapy is available only to individuals who are in active treatment in the agency. Consideration of a client for group therapy is based on the fundamental casework steps of arriving at a psychosocial diagnosis and appropriate treatment goals. Following such an evaluation, the most effective method of help, or a combination of methods, is considered. For example, in addition to group therapy, clients may receive the services of a public health nurse, of a homemaker, of a dentist and so on. The introduction of group treatment requires careful timing in relation to the individual's readiness and his use of other measures of help.

From among a multiplicity of types and levels of group psychotherapy, the agency initially adopted "activity group therapy" for children between the ages of 8 and 14 years. This method of group treatment, originated by Slavson, has been adequately covered in the literature (Slavson, 1943). In addition to activity therapy groups[6] with their emphasis on the children's *acting out* of behavior patterns and conflicts, there was also some experimentation with discussion groups for adolescent girls and for mothers of young children (Grunwald et al., 1951; Stauffer, 1951). In these, the major channel of communication were verbal interchanges among the group members and the group therapist. Subse-

[6] See Chapter XII.

quently, the possibilities of applying the concepts of family casework to discussion groups for adult clients have been studied in considerable detail. The level of work with such groups approximates the earlier-described casework treatment aims of changing the client's adaptive patterns. The discussions focus on the individual's conscious and preconscious attitudes toward himself and his environment, and on his interpersonal relationships. It is self-evident that this method differs from the deeper, analytic types of group therapy which are widely practiced under specifically clinical auspices.

The group therapy program at the Community Service Society is administratively a part of the Division of Family Services. The responsibility for its over-all delineation and development resides in the Division's administrative head with the assistance of the Chief Psychiatric Consultant and others. In the district units which are located in various areas of the city, it is the district administrator who has the responsibility for planning and implementing group therapy practice. The local districts carry responsibility for maintaining the group meeting rooms and group records; for the joint consultative processes between group therapists and caseworkers; and for recommending caseworkers as candidates for training in group therapy. The agency maintains no separate group therapy department. Instead, group treatment constitutes an integral part of other services offered to clients. All group therapists are practicing caseworkers, part of whose time is allocated to group therapy. As was pointed out elsewhere (Taggart and Scheidlinger, 1953), experience has confirmed the value of such a plan in furthering the integration of group therapy with the total services offered by the Society.

The agency employs a Group Therapy Consultant whose function it is to provide leadership in the development and evaluation of group therapy practice in the local districts; in the supervision of group therapists or of group therapy supervisors by means of individual supervisory conferences; in conducting an in-service training seminar in group therapy; in interpreting group therapy to the agency staff and to the community. The Group Therapy Consultant is a member of the consultation staff of the Division of Family Services. He is responsible both to the Director of District Administration as well as to the Chief Psychiatric Consultant. There is also close interchange with the Casework Associate who leads in the development of the quality of casework practice in the agency.

Prospective group therapists are recruited from among the more experienced caseworkers who have expressed interest in this form of treatment. Besides above average skill in casework, these people must possess a good sensitivity to interpersonal relationships, a high degree of self-awareness and an ability to command attention of a group. Following about a year's period of participation in the group therapy seminar, the workers are assigned to carry a group. Besides continued seminar attendance the group therapists have regular supervisory conferences. In these, the detailed recordings of the group sessions are analyzed, techniques are discussed, and theory is related to practice.

The actual formation of groups, their general composition, age range and sex are determined by factors of need and also by availability of physical facilities and trained therapists. Following a tentative decision to establish a particular group, the caseworkers in the district (or in adjoining districts) are asked to submit summaries on clients who fall into the particular category and who might benefit from group treatment. Some of these cases are suggested for group therapy by the district psychiatric consultants in the course of their conferences with workers. In the instance of groups for adults, a psychiatric consultation precedes the final acceptance of each client for group therapy. With activity groups for children where criteria for selection and methodology are by now firmly established, routine psychiatric consultations or psychological testing are not required. Such conferences may be held when the readiness of the child for such treatment is questioned because of the kind or degree of disturbance present. In all instances, the general suitability of individuals for group therapy or the advisability of placement in a particular group are evaluated with great care. Creating an optimum group balance—placing together clients who would tend to enhance the therapeutic interaction with a minimum of threat to the weakest individuals—becomes a paramount factor in determining the final group composition. As might be expected, the treatment plan in each case varies. With respect to children, some of them receive group therapy alone, because this method is considered best adapted to their problems; others may be included in a group with the objective of making them more accessible to casework treatment later; others receive both kinds of help simultaneously. Adults, on the other hand, have not been treated exclusively in groups. They have at all times some casework contact in addition to the group experience.

Besides their value as a resource for long-term treatment, our children's groups have been found extremely helpful for purposes of observation which facilitated arriving at an adequate psychosocial diagnosis and treatment planning. This is especially helpful in a family agency where in work with large families with serious pathology, it is often impossible to obtain pertinent individualized descriptive data on each child. Such observation in a group may subsequently lead to further use of group therapy or of other services.

Whenever a client is assigned to a group, the caseworker and the group therapist maintain a continuous contact with each other. The group therapist needs to know about happenings in the family and especially about significant incidents affecting the client. The caseworker is informed about the individual's behavior in the group. Besides such informal interchanges between caseworkers and group therapists, integration conferences on each group member are held twice a year. These represent the formal way of integrating the group treatment with the other services offered to each client and to the family as-a-whole. Such conferences are also held in the interim if needed. In addition to the caseworker's working with the family and the group therapist, the district psychiatric consultant participates in these conferences. The discussions are geared to the material in special summaries prepared by the caseworker and the group therapist for this occasion. Following the interchange of relevant data, the group member's general adjustment is evaluated within the framework of the broader family picture. Joint treatment plans are formulated.

As is true with any client seen at the agency, a psychiatric consultation may be sought at an appropriate time on the client in the group or on a member of his family. Such consultations may be initiated by the caseworkers or the group therapist. In either instance, they follow the usual pattern of consultations in the district. The group therapist participates in all psychiatric conferences held on members of his group or their families. The minutes of such consultations and of the integration conferences are filed in the group therapy record, as well as in the family case record.

Another family agency, the Brooklyn Bureau of Social Service and Children's Aid Society has utilized group treatment for several years (Greving and Grunwald, 1953). Termed "group counseling" this method was introduced in the hope that through it more clients could be reached, among them those who had failed to respond to casework. In the descriptions of this program stress is laid on the fact that it is "a method of choice, not merely an auxiliary or substitute service" (Grunwald, 1954). Most of this agency's experience has been with groups of mothers. It is not altogether clear from the literature what detailed criteria are used in the selection of these clients. They were described at one point as being homogeneous with respect to age, intelligence and social background with their psychological make-ups being of similar structure (Grunwald, 1954, p. 189). At another point, they were considered to be women with mildly compulsive or hysterical neurotic disorders. At the same time, however, the idea was expressed that selection of group members was based on a "similarity of situational conflicts and a similarity of functioning in areas of ego intactness" (Grunwald, 1954, p. 184). In addition to mothers' groups, the agency has also organized groups for young unattached adults, for adolescent boys who had been discharged from an institution for delinquents, and groups for children under foster care.

An interesting feature of such "group counseling" is its length. In contrast to the earlier described therapy groups at the Community Service Society where the treatment may proceed for as long as a year or even two, depending on each client's need, at the Brooklyn Bureau of Social Service the average group holds no more than 18 to 20 weekly sessions. Certain group members can have individual contact as well, preferably with the group leader.

In discussions of the dynamics of "group counseling" a number of factors are stressed. Ego strengthening is believed to occur through mutual support and identification and through the ventilation of feelings. In addition, belonging to a group serves to break the feelings of isolation and with loosened defenses, readjustment of adaptive patterns of behavior can occur. The role of the "group counselor" is a neutral one at first. He does not plan discussions or summarize them, but instead the group is encouraged to engage in "associative thinking" (Slavson, 1950). The worker uses universalization as a means of fostering a positive climate and "points out reality-adaptive patterns" to the clients. The "interpretation of feelings" or of transference reactions is avoided.

In the description of "group counseling" the authors take great pains to distinguish this method from group therapy. They say: "In psychotherapy, modification of basic adaptive patterns is attempted: It is a medically oriented method for the treatment of seriously disturbed individuals for whom resolution of problems is attempted through the achievement of major insight into the unconscious dynamics of behavior and personal interrelationships" (Greving and Grunwald, 1953, p. 1).

A still more recent group therapy program has been in operation at the Jewish Family Service of New York City.[7] There are about 12 groups, ranging from fairly homogeneous ones (with respect to social role—not personality type), such as a group of mothers of adolescents or mothers of children in their latency, to socially heterogeneous groups composed of adults of both sexes and of mixed marital status. Most of the groups are conducted by social caseworkers of advanced standing who, in addition to

[7] The following material is from a personal communication to the authors by Mr. S. N. Sherman, Assistant Executive Director.

this work, also do individual casework. Three of the group leaders, trained in group therapy, are not permanent members of the staff, and are employed only to conduct groups.

Following the example of the Brooklyn Bureau of Social Service, this agency has, for the time being at least, chosen to call their work "group counseling." They appear to have some misgivings about this term in view of its didactic connotations. Their stated aim is to develop a treatment process in working with groups that is an adaptation of and bears a close kinship with the treatment process in individual casework. There is no aim of promoting "character change" through these groups. The goals involve "strengthening of the ego towards reality adaptation of the personality." The group interaction and the individual relationship of clients to the counselor are viewed as the basic medium. The methods employed by the leader are "support, explanation and clarification."

Clients for groups are drawn from the active case load of the organization and from among pending applications for service. Clients are seen individually by the group counselor as part of the selection and preparation for the group experience. Where indicated, individual interviews are offered in the course of the group counseling.

In view of the agency's focus on the family as a whole, more than one member of the family is apt to be in individual casework or in group guidance, and sometimes in both. In one district office three parallel groups were described: a group of adolescent girls; a group composed primarily of mothers of these girls; and a third group comprising the fathers of the adolescent girls and the husbands of the women in the second group.

In so far as the group counselors are attached to specific districts, they were found to serve as integrating factors between individual casework and group guidance. They also form a cohesive, agency-wide group for seminar and workshop purposes. This training is under the leadership of a consulting psychiatrist who has been related to the agency's casework practice over the years. In view of the new and experimental nature of this program, further details about it could not be obtained at this point.

From the reports received by the Family Service Association of America only one family agency outside of the New York City area appears to have attempted group therapy. This agency, the Jewish Family and Children's Bureau of Baltimore, Maryland, has been conducting a mothers' group which has been organized this year.[8] Most of the nine mothers in the group had been in casework with the group leader. They were appar-

8 From a written communication to the Family Service Association of America.

ently chosen on the basis of their concern about the children, and this was set as the purpose of the group discussions. It was envisioned that through the medium of such discussions, the mothers would gain in self-awareness and consequently become more relaxed in the handling of the children.

After a brief period of mutual exploration, the mothers expressed their feelings of anger and frustration against the agency for having failed to give them specific advice regarding the handling of their children. This was followed by a discussion of how they felt when their children's behavior provoked them to anger. The therapist offered support throughout these interchanges and began to help the women in their attempt to understand the need for both freedom and discipline in the handling of young children. There was focus on the mothers' awareness of their own reactions as well as those of the children. They had also began to talk about how one could accept dependency feelings in oneself and in others. Since this single group has been formed very recently, further material about it is not available.

The introduction of group therapy to the family service field is in its very beginnings. Its advent was made possible by the newer orientation in many of the agencies toward a fuller understanding of personality problems in all the clients, no matter what the complaint at application, culminating in a psychosocial diagnosis. There was also a developing clarity regarding the differences among treatment goals, treatment methods and treatment levels. Some of these concepts continue to be the subject of controversy in the family casework field, between the so-called "diagnostic" and "functional" orientations.

The increased utilization of psychiatric consultants who had contact with group therapy in other settings, as well as the caseworkers' beginning awareness of the potentialities for personality growth inherent in small groups, served to give additional impetus to the interest in group therapy.

It is noteworthy that the questionable argument of saving time or money through the use of group treatment is rarely advanced. Instead, there is justified emphasis on seeking new and more effective approaches for helping clients, in addition to the basic casework method. It is also gratifying that there has so far been a minimum of confusion between other group programs traditionally operated by some of the agencies and between group psychotherapy. The latter, with its planful concentration on helping people with recognized problems in small, carefully balanced groups, stands in clear contrast to other group programs, usually with a mental hygiene orientation, such as camping, institutions for children and adults or "family life education." There is no reason why group therapy cannot operate simultaneously with the other approaches within a given agency.

There appears to be a justified concern that group therapy in family agencies should correspond to the goal of family casework—improvement in the functioning of individuals with social and personality impairment. Since group therapy has experienced its greatest development under directly clinical auspices, such as child guidance clinics or in hospitals, there is the problem of borrowing some of its techniques without at the same time imitating the goals and levels of practice of these settings. This is less of an obstacle in the instance of activity group therapy for children in view of its more or less standardized character and its admitted emphasis on patterns of ego adaptations. Actually, the adoption of even group treatment for adults to a family agency setting need not present any undue difficulties as long as the goals and levels of such treatment are clearly defined. For, it must be remembered that even in a strictly psychiatric set up, there can be a multiplicity of therapy groups with a variety of levels, ranging from "group analysis" to groups which planfully do not foster undue regression, focusing on the conscious and preconscious ego-adaptive patterns of the patients. Family casework has repeatedly assimilated concepts and techniques from psychiatric practice without necessarily increasing the "depth" of treatment. It must be stressed, however, that group therapy, no matter what its level, is in many ways a more delicate instrument than individual treatment, requiring therefore, the utmost care and discrimination.

In setting up a group therapy program it is essential to have specially trained and supervised practitioners with the availability of psychiatric consultation. The selection of clients for a group requires utmost caution. For, some individuals can use some form of group therapy only in conjunction with individual help. Other persons are never ready for any kind of group therapy either because of their inability to weather the emotional impact of the group process or because their behavior might exert unduly harmful effects on other group members or on the therapeutic group climate as a whole.

Group therapy would appear to be a particularly suitable service for a family agency to develop. It is well known that personality formation or malformation have their roots largely in the individual's experience in his first group—the family. A therapy group, in a sense, re-creates a family. Family conflicts are spontaneously re-enacted in such a setting; they can be corrected through the supportive elements inherent in the group experience. The reality of a group of people, each with his own needs and reaction patterns, offers an opportunity for testing and modifying one's own social behavior.

The data derived from observations of the client's responses and of his verbalizations of attitudes in a group setting are helpful to the caseworker who is involved with other members of the family. The continuous interchange between group therapists and caseworkers, and the inclusion of psychiatric consultants in the planning and evaluation, can serve to evolve a stimulating and effective team approach to the family as a unit.

BIBLIOGRAPHY

Bibring, G. L. (1947), Psychiatry and Social Work. *J. Soc. Casework, 28*:205.
Bruno, F. J. *Trends in Social Work—As Reflected in the Proceedings of the National Conference of Social Work—1874-1946.* New York: Columbia University Press.
Eliot, M. M. (1953), The Family Today, Its Needs and Opportunities. *Soc. Casework, 34.*
Family Service Association of America (1949), Current and Future Developments in Family Service Program. *Family Service Highlights, 10* (February).
—— (1953), Family Life Education. *Family Service Highlights, 14.*
Fraiberg, S. (1952), Some Aspects of Casework with Children. *Soc. Casework, 33.*
Garrett, A. (1942), *Interviewing: Its Principles and Methods.* New York: Family Welfare Association of America.
Greving, F. T. and Grunwald, H. (1953), Group Counseling—A New Family Service. *Better Times, 35*:1-7.
Grunwald, H. (1954), Group Counseling in a Casework Agency. *Int. J. Group Psychother., 4*:183-192.
—— et al. (1951), The Case of Jean Case. *Int. J. Group Psychother., 1*:64-77, 154-171.
Hamilton, G. (1951), *Theory and Practice of Social Casework.* New York: Columbia University Press.
Kasius, C. (ed.) (1950), *A Comparison of Diagnostic and Functional Casework Concepts.* New York: Family Service Association of America.
Redl, F. (1944), Diagnostic Group Work. *Am. J. Orthopsychiat., 14.*
Richmond, M. E. (1917), *Social Diagnosis.* New York: Russell Sage Foundation.
Scope and Methods of the Family Service Agency (1953), New York: Family Service Association of America.
Sherz, F. H. (1952), Intake: Concept and Process. *Soc. Casework, 32.*
Slavson, S. R. (1943), *An Introduction to Group Therapy.* New York: International Universities Press, 1952.
—— (1950), *Analytic Group Psychotherapy.* New York: Columbia University Press.
Social Casework, Generic and Specific: An Outline (1929), A Report of the Milford Conference, American Association of Social Workers, New York.
Spiker, D. (1943), Protected Groups in the Treatment of Young Children. *Am. J. Orthopsychiat., 13.*
Stauffer, M. (1951), Group Psychotherapy in a Family Agency. *Int. J. Group Psychother., 1*:348-355.
Swithun, B. (1949), The Nature and Definition of Social Casework. *J. Soc. Casework, 30.*
Taggart, A. D. and Scheidlinger, S. (1953), Group Therapy in a Family Service Program. *Soc. Casework, 34*:378-385.

Chapter XIV

SEX AND MARRIAGE PROBLEMS

•

When men and women are relieved of excessive preoccupation and anxiety involved in obtaining the means of sustenance, they become concerned with measures for maintaining and improving their own physical health and general welfare and those of their children. And when it is necessary they can limit their families and/or space their children to the best advantage for themselves and their offspring. Further, when they are not harassed by the daily care of excessive numbers of children for whom they cannot perforce adequately care physically and emotionally, and are as a result healthy and at ease with themselves and with their children, they seek the knowledge and the skills necessary to assure happiness in their roles as husbands, wives and parents.

As a first step, their major need is information in areas they themselves recognize as most important for human relationships, namely, sex and reproduction, areas about which there is more secrecy, misinformation, superstition and taboo than in any other aspect of contemporary human life. The facts are few and relatively simple to impart to adults. To transmit them to children is much more difficult, however, and the manner in which this is done by parents reflects their own state of development and points up the importance of attitudes as they are associated with and involved in such personal and intimate questions.

The Margaret Sanger Research Bureau has been organized to render service and education and to conduct research in the fields of contraception and infertility, preparation for marriage and parenthood, and marriage consultation to men and women who seek help in problems of their marital relationships, particularly in the areas of sex and reproduction.

The nature of the problems as seen in the Bureau is fraught with much conscious and unconscious anxiety and guilt because of the extant taboos and superstitions about sex and reproduction. The ease with which the therapist or counselor deals with these subjects, the directness of the approach and the good feeling resulting from sharing with others what is so intimate a problem, are among the factors that contribute greatly to whatever success is achieved.

A variety of potency disturbances, problems of infertility, and sterility are presented in contraceptive and infertility clinics. The physical examination, diagnoses, treatment, and recommendations for treatment of the emotional aspects which patients discover as causing or contributing to physical conditions, help greatly in their accepting psychotherapy.

At times the sex problems that occur early in marriage are the only ones the men and women are concerned with; but it is also possible to impart knowledge of, and then insight into, their immediate problems to the total emotional relationship, as well as to their own specific conflicts. Increasingly, as men and women seek greater happiness and contentment in their marriage, as all other aspects of their interpersonal relationship are brought to light, these are dealt with in marriage consultation service, and the approach to these problems is psycho-bio-social. It implies that a man is a total person, with a body, intellect and emotions. He has a genetic inheritance and acquired characteristics as a result of having been in a particular sequence and relation in the family constellation and in a particular environment. One is never isolated or alone; one is always involved in relationships and always in a social environment which influences one and which, in turn, one influences.

The existence of varied capacities of an individual, constitutional in nature, are stressed. This points up an important factor in indications for, and treatment of, emotional disturbances. Some of our patients are puzzled by the fact that though the same psychopathology with severe mental emotional disorders is present in some patients, it yet allows them to function in areas in which well-adjusted persons do not. It brings clearly to focus the uniqueness of the individual, and also that an identical pathology may be quantitatively different. They discover that stronger constitutional capacities in a disturbed person may make the difference between adequate and inadequate functioning.

Psychotherapy in our Service is used as a method of treatment of emotional disturbances as palliative, curative, and preventive. The psychotherapy is psychoanalytically oriented, eclectic in nature, emphasizing both Freudian and non-Freudian concepts, whatever applies in the particular case or group.

It was found that group treatment offers a more realistic approach to many problems of interpersonal relationships as we see them in our Service than does individual counseling and treatment. Emotional needs that can be satisfied by a person himself without involving others are relatively few. Most of these are satisfied through or in relation with some other person. Satisfactory adjustment to living when it involves another person is dependent upon the manner in which one acts and reacts in a relationship, on how feelings, thoughts and actions are expressed, modified or repressed out of consideration for the other individual involved. In a group one discovers not only why one behaves in a particular manner, but also how this behavior appears to others, how and why they accept or reject it, and how they think one should modify it.

All our group sessions begin with a 10 to 15 minute discussion by the therapist of the psychodynamic factors in the particular problem under consideration. General mental hygiene concepts, social values, and sociological changes as they affect the problem, are also discussed. Beyond this the sessions are unstructured.

When dynamic concepts are presented or behavior interpreted, the language used is simple and easy to understand, and since they may be wholly new to the group members and at variance with their beliefs and knowledge, statements are often made in the following manner: "It may seem strange, but—," or, "what we think or feel may be exactly opposite —." Concepts and interpretations are usually general in short-term group therapy. In the long-term groups they are individualized.

The number of treatment sessions in a particular group depends, as does the content and technique, on the goals. Additional factors that may influence the number of sessions for a group are the number of people we desire to reach and the time available to the personnel and their availability for evening sessions, which is the only time feasible for most patients. The number of groups is limited by the availability of patients necessary to form a group. We usually list double the number of patients needed for a group since we expect that about one half of them will withdraw after accepting group treatment. The number of sessions for different groups ranged between four and fifty. Sessions are held once a week for two to two and a half hours, usually in the evening, although some groups met during the day. All members of groups are seen six months after discharge for follow-up interviews.

After experimenting with varied numbers in groups we determined that the optimum is between six and eight. In the short-term groups no new members are added after sessions begin. In the longer series new patients are admitted through the third session. The types of patients treated at the Bureau are socioeconomically of the low, middle, and occasionally of the upper classes. The groups, therefore, usually consist of a mixture of these. The ages of the members are usually in the late 20's and early 30's. Fees are nominal, but if excessive for a patient, they are adjusted to his or her capability to pay. It may be of interest to note that the therapist is a part-time unpaid worker.

We have experimented with groups consisting of

1. Women with sexual difficulties
2. Premarital groups (preventive)
3. Group of couples with varied marital problems
4. Group of men with potency problems
5. Group of men with azospermia
6. Infertility groups
   a. Mixed
   b. Those with repeated miscarriage
   c. Those with no physical defects.

Group therapy at the Bureau was introduced for women who came to the "contraceptive clinic." These women had also sexual problems, consisting primarily of lack of sexual response or orgasm. At the present time most women we see experience some sexual gratification, and the problems they present are primarily the lack of "vaginal" orgasm or orgasm with penetration, or impotency problems of their husbands. This means that our original goal is no longer valid and treatment of the groups at present must be long range with a fair number of the patients prepared for referral for psychoanalytic help.

All of the groups were at first exploratory in nature to determine what personality factors or specific emotional conflicts existed in the particular problem; groups could facilitate this. It has consistently been shown that there is no specific, uniform basic personality structure in the various problem areas, nor specific, uniform conflicts. The experimental groups have revealed that they can also be, and some already have been, used as desirable therapeutic techniques for particular problems.

The general results of group treatment need not be narrated here. They are well known to all who are working in the field of group therapy, and we shall instead give some details of the following types of groups: (1) women with sexual problems; (2) premarital guidance; (3) problems of married couples; (4) problems of infertility.

Group Therapy in Sexual Maladjustment. All women in these groups are referred from the Contraceptive Service. Several questions in the history form taken at the initial interview which are related to the sexual adjustment reveal potential sources of difficulty. Some women come for contraceptive advice, specifically in the expectation that the use of another form of contraception than the one they are using will improve their sexual adjustment. There is, therefore, an ample source of patients for these therapy groups.

Since a physical examination is part of the routine of the Contraceptive Clinic, data are available to exclude women with physical abnormalities and local inflammatory conditions that may interfere with adequate response. Many women and, for that matter, many men believe that their sexual difficulties are the result of some organic disturbance or physical abnormality. The reassurance patients derive from negative findings after a thorough physical examination is in itself of great psychotherapeutic value.

The idea that a disturbance is psychological rather than organic in origin may, on the other hand, be a source of considerable distress to some, for to their way of thinking it is a reflection on their mental health. An attempt is therefore made at the initial interview to allay such anxiety. Psychological causes underlying cases of sexual maladjustments are explained to the woman, or to the couple if the husband is present, and the need for a more thorough exploration pointed out. Usually the opportunity for further help is readily accepted. The initial interview is also used to uncover in detail the nature of the particular problem, and whether the couple is suitable for group therapy and whether the group is acceptable to them. Those who do not fit into a group or for whom the group idea is unacceptable are referred either for individual treatment or to another treatment facility when this is indicated.

In all groups the therapist opens the discussion with some of the basic factors involved in the sexual relation. Brief mention is made at this time of the frequent lack of preparation on the part of women for the sexual side of marriage, of the differences in the attitudes of men and women, of the degree and frequency of spontaneous desire in women, the importance of adequate arousal, and the nature of the orgasm whether achieved through stimulation of the clitoris or of the vagina. It is pointed out that sexual difficulties may result from either physical or psychological causes, but that adequate coital techniques may help to overcome some of the psychological barriers to complete the response.

By the end of this preliminary talk which lasts about 15 minutes, the members of the group are usually quite at ease and ready to participate in the discussion. Often the character and the content of the preliminary talk provides immediate clarification and yields understanding. Examples of some of the remarks made by group members as recorded in our notes follow:

Mrs. A.: "I have already learned something I did not know. Now I understand why I am here. I have been married 15 months and have not gotten my satisfaction yet. I am aroused when my husband plays with me, but as soon as he enters I lose all feeling. I lose it, and I don't get it back again, and I get disgusted. Often I start crying. Now I see some of the reasons for our trouble."

Mrs. B.: "I think that my problem is tied up with the fact that I was brought up in complete ignorance. I was married, and all of a sudden I was supposed to know everything, and I knew nothing. I blamed myself all the time. The whole atmosphere was so bad that I could not talk to anyone about it. For the first time now it is becoming clear to me what the relationship is."

Facts in the patient's sex history are often brought to the surface spontaneously and at times with a great deal of emotion. At one point, for example, one of the women suddenly stated, with much anxiety: "This has nothing to do with what you are talking about, but when I was a young girl I used to masturbate," and she burst into sobs. The reaction of the others was extremely reassuring, as they, in turn, told of their own sex experiences in childhood.

As for specific results: some usually achieve orgasm by penetration, others by clitoral stimulation or by acceptance of a clitoral response, and some require referral for long-term therapy.

Group Discussions with Engaged Couples. In a democratic family system young men and women are granted freedom in their own choice of a mate. As a rule they are not hampered in their choice, and even when parents object, they frequently yield to the inevitable. But freedom to choose does not mean that young men and women are emotionally ready for the responsibilities of marriage and parenthood. Young men and women are now marrying earlier and are not always economically ready for marriage. In some groups, parents are expected to support them during the schooling or the training for business or careers which they continue. The young people desire privacy, they want to set up their own family units and are reluctant to live with their parents or have the parents live with them. Where it is absolutely necessary for a father and mother to live with the couple, the children consider it a burden.

Expectations of parents, society and that of the young men and women themselves are greater than ever before. Those entering marriage expect to derive through each other the utmost mutual satisfaction of their own basic needs for love and emotional security, sex and parenthood. They are expected to maintain their relationship through their own efforts. They are expected to grow and develop together in this relationship, plan for children and equip themselves to be good parents so that their children can be given the love and security they need for their own emotional development to maturity.

There is nothing, however, in the emotional development of an individual that specifically prepares him for the marital relationship. Such a relationship is neither instinctive nor intuitive. A good marriage is learned by precept and example.

To the young men and women who have had the experience of living in a happy home and received appropriate sex education from their parents and schools, premarital education highlights and reinforces the knowledge they have and gives the additional information they need for their own marriage. But to the many who have not had this favorable background, more is needed and there is much that needs to be undone. These young men and women are not well prepared, or even adequately prepared, to give to the marriage so as to receive what they expect from it. Only the awareness of their own particular capacities to contribute to the desired goal, knowledge of what to do with these capacities, and their willingness to do so, can secure their objective. Premarital guidance was instituted as a positive contribution to marital adjustment and stability by the prevention of maladjustment. The results obtained in sexual disorders gave rise to preventive group treatment. It was thought that young couples about to marry would greatly benefit by such help. Experience in these groups had shown that a fair number of sexual problems are due to lack of information, and the presence of misinformation and incorrect attitudes. Only engaged couples are accepted for these groups. The question can be raised here as to whether it is feasible to have groups that include both the men and the women. Would the young women feel too shy to raise questions particularly related to problems of women if men were present? It has consistently been found that there is an advantage in having couples present together because of the fact that they both receive information at the same time and in the same way, and have an opportunity to learn about another.

The content of the series of sessions is planned on the dynamic concept that people marry to satisfy certain basic needs such as love, sex and parenthood, and that these needs are influenced by early childhood experiences, by social and cultural forces which either reinforce positive attitudes and values or produce negative ones. The lack of information, the misinformation, the fears and anxieties from the prohibition of normal release of sexual needs, the difficulties resulting from inadequate child-parent relationships—all adversely affect the capacity to love and prevent the development of a mature personality, culminating in difficulties in marital adjustment. It is anticipated that the presentation of these concepts inculcate more positive attitudes and help to develop insight into what the young people, as individuals, are bringing to their marriage and what the marital relationship involves.

A series of three sessions is held to deal respectively with love, sex and parenthood. This number has been found adequate to present the material and to insure full discussions. Each session usually lasts from three to three and a half hours. Most of the young people are interested primarily in contraceptive advice, but some in more information about sexuality. The approach is to treat sexual adjustment in marriage as part of a total emotional relationship.

The first session is devoted to a discussion of sexual anatomy and physiology, the nature of the sex act, differences in responses between men and women, and the question of family planning and contraception. The next session involves a discussion of psychosexual development, of sexual curiosity in the young child, the usual prohibitions he encounters, attitudes toward masturbation, and the changes in development that come about during puberty.

As an example of the freedom of discussion of early sexual experiences the following is taken from our notes:

Mary said that she never heard the word masturbation until she had read it recently. The other three girls said that they had no sexual feelings or desires that they remembered until they were engaged. Ellen said that she had overheard boys talking about masturbating in order to arouse themselves. She had been frankly shocked. Arnold said that he had masturbated by himself, and with a group of boys, but he felt guilty about it as he was sure that his family would disapprove. Robert said that if you were told it was wrong, then you would feel that what you were doing was wrong. Ellen had watched a man masturbate until he had ejaculated, and said that his wife was in the room with him but not near him. She couldn't understand why anyone should do that. This was discussed. Then Robert said that many men would masturbate for the first orgasm, and then they could take a long time to stimulate the woman and not have trouble holding themselves back. Arnold said that in the Army boys would get into trouble if they were caught masturbating, but Robert felt sure that there were always ways of not being found out.

The aim is to help the group understand the prohibitions that society has placed upon them all their lives, and the fact that the inhibitions that they have developed are not automatically shed when a religious or legal ceremony had been performed. This makes it possible for the group to consider their role in marriage as something that will take a period of time for them to work out to their greatest satisfaction, and is of help to young people, many of whom have read books on sex, have high expectations for themselves, and are full of anxiety that they will not be able to perform adequately.

In the third session the discussion is centered on what is involved when two people begin a life together. This includes a discussion of personality development and the influences of early experiences in the life of the individual. Such considerations are necessary to help a couple recognize that marriage alone does not bring about basic personality changes. A discussion on the development of a mature love relationship and its important role in marriage follows from this. The entire question as to how much one changes in making a good marital adjustment, and on what level these changes occur is of great interest to most of our groups. We accept the fact that the group participants are to be married soon, and, therefore, do not focus on the question of choosing a mate. Rather, emphasis is placed on helping the partners in the approaching marriage see the ways in which they would be adjusting to each other.

Whenever possible a follow-up session is held after six months. There is, as a rule, very free discussion of all aspects of their marital adjustment. Most achieve satisfactory sex relationship and take their other adjustments in stride. When some express difficulty, they know they can ask for help. They all feel that the premarital sessions have helped them, not only in the factual information they had received, but also because they had come to realize what is necessary for a successful marriage and how a marriage relation develops.

Group Treatment of Married Couples. From the very beginning of our work with women with marital problems, we recognized the value of interviewing their husbands, whenever possible, to learn their points of view as to their wives' problems and for additional information, as well as to enlist their cooperation in solving the problems should this be necessary. The men were interviewed separately. With the passing of time, however, the more constructive attitudes which evolve so rapidly between husbands and wives, especially when they are interested in helping one another, made it seem more advantageous to interview them together. In the Marriage Consultation Service of the Bureau we encounter all types of marital problems. These are dealt with individually and in couples: men and women are seen together first, then separately, and together again whenever indicated.

Our own impression and the frequent request from the men and women themselves that they meet together substantiated our conclusion that husbands and wives involved in intimate interpersonal problems need to be treated as a unit. We later discovered that group treatment could be administered to a number of couples just as it was with one couple.

The results of treating married couples together can best be expressed in the words of the participants. One said: "It's nice to know that other people reach a compromise. It's not a brick wall you are up against." Another, "It's good to be together. One partner may not be aware of the real problem if we come independently." And still another, "If someone breaks the ice, it's easier. So many people having the same type of problem makes you feel less peculiar and different."

Group Treatment of Infertile Women. The basis for the psychological approach to the problem of sterility is that emotional conflicts can be a factor contributing to infertility; on the other hand, childlessness can itself cause emotional disturbances. Many theories have been suggested to show the mechanism of psychogenic sterility, but as yet there is not enough evidence regarding the mechanisms involved.

Two major theories have been advanced in this connection. One is that through the hypothalamus, now considered the seat of emotions, there is a direct communication with the anterior pituitary which, in turn, causes changes in the hormonal system thus affecting the physiology of reproduction. The second is that the smooth muscle fibers of the fallopian tubes and uterus are affected through the autonomic nervous system causing local spasms. There is no doubt that the spasm of smooth muscle fibers is one of the most common visceral responses to emotional tension.

It has also been suggested that sterility may result from long-standing hypermia and congestion of the fallopian tubes and ovaries due to emotional conflicts. One of the earliest explanations was given by Sellheim who said that there may be a premature maturation of an ovarian follicle that is not ready for fertilization. Emotional conflicts, furthermore, may alter the specific chemical and physical properties of secretions in contact with the sperm and ovum.

Attention to the psychological aspects of infertility was first called by couples who, after many years of infertility, adopted a baby and then the wife conceived. This motivated some psychiatrists to investigate the role of psychic factors in infertility. For conception to take place it is postulated that a woman must have not only the physical structures and hormones of a female, but that she must *feel* that she is a woman and *accept* her sex. A girl child becomes, and feels herself developing into a woman if she has made proper identification with her own mother, and thus accepts her femininity. She must also accept masculinity in men as represented by her father, and later by her husband. Being a woman means acceptance of her primary role, that of conceiving and bearing children; being a woman means readiness and capability to rear children and to foster their physical, emotional and mental development.

For conception to take place, the male must deliver a sufficient number of sperms of proper structure and viability. He must be willing and able to have normal sexual relations so that the sperms may be deposited inside the vagina where they readily enter the uterus. He, too, must have made proper identification with his own father, and accept femininity in women as represented by his mother, and later by his wife.

And yet, we know that there are women who have the proper psycho-organic dispositions as described above, and still do not conceive readily and frequently. This fact should give pause to those who are now espousing psychological concepts exclusively without recognizing other factors, as for example inheritance and the fact that there may be a quantitative factor present as well. Women with genetically low fertility and massive psychopathology have lesser chance of becoming pregnant than the woman of low fertility with a milder form of psychopathology, and a woman of high fertility may be able to overcome marked psycho-pathology.

Group treatment of infertility cases has as its goal to explore whatever emotional conflicts exist, to release tension, produce relaxation and give ego support. Helping a patient to accept her infertility without conflict, especially in cases of secondary sterility, or to consent to adopt a baby or, when it is indicated, artificial insemination, is a part of the therapeutic aim with infertile women.

All couples accepted by the Infertility Service attend an orientation lecture. The Director, Dr. Abraham Stone, gives a lecture-discussion which involves anatomy, physiology and psychology of infertility, and begins the ego support which the infertility couples receive throughout their investigation at the Bureau. These discussions conteract the feelings of inadequacy, of being different, which are characteristic of most of the couples. In a few instances these sessions were sufficient to facilitate pregnancy and no further investigation and treatment was necessary.

The Psychiatric Service of the Infertility Clinic introduced group treatment early in its existence. The original plan was to treat cases with obstructed fallopian tubes with no demonstrable structural pathology, and in cases where no organic cause for infertility was found either in the husband or the wife. Since at that time there was an insufficient number of these, a "mixed" group was formed. The first group consisted of one case each of closed tubes, anxiety state, and amenorrhea, and two cases with husbands who had premature ejaculation.

Discussion of general dynamics usually brings forth material from these patients around one or more factors which a number of the members of the group have in common. As the sessions proceed there emerges an increasing recognition of the impact of emotional processes on their thinking and feeling and on the conduct of their everyday life. Most become more relaxed as a result and develop healthier attitudes toward their husbands, and, strikingly enough, they begin to accept their infertility without anxiety and feelings of inadequacy they originally had had.

The specific results of this particular group were that two of the patients whose husbands had premature ejaculations conceived, but miscarried. The patient with amenorrhea had a few menstrual cycles without hormonal therapy. The woman with anxiety state became greatly improved, and one with closed tubes became pregnant and delivered a normal full-term infant.

Mr. and Mrs. S. had been married for five years. They had used contraceptives for the first two years and had since been trying to conceive without success. It had been a devastating fact for Mrs. S. to find that she could not become pregnant. She had always done everything she was supposed to do. According to her, life had always been good and easy; everything was fine, she had no complaints, and nobody had complained about her. "Everything was always lovely," she emphasized.

Mrs. S. is an attractive woman of 28, meticulous in appearance and manners: no hair out of place; not a wrinkle in her clothes. She came from a middle-class family, the youngest of two children. The maternal grandmother always lived with them, and the home was a place where all the family congregated. Her aunts and uncles and their children were always visiting and it was all very lovely. Her father and mother got along very well, and she was very happy with her elder brother who was good to her. She got along well with teachers and students; after graduating from high school, she obtained a job as secretary in which she was very happy with her boss and fellow workers. She had boy friends and had no problem with them, they never "bothered her." It was not until she met her husband that she permitted any physical contact. Her husband and she got along beautifully. He was a salesman. She kept on working for a few years, they saved money and now had a beautiful house in a suburb with an extra room ready for a child.

She was disappointed when after extensive efforts she could not conceive. Her brother, a psychologist, suggested that she consult the present author to determine whether a psychological factor contributed to her infertility. It was obvious at the first interview that the girl was a functioning compulsive personality. In a discussion with the brother, the therapist suggested that intensive psychotherapy for his sister's infertility was indicated, since, in her way, she functioned adequately in other areas. It was, however, thought advisable as an exploratory measure to include her in a group with women with no physical defects in which she could participate and receive whatever benefits she could without too much probing of her defenses.

She participated very little in the group discussions and was not urged to do so. On a superficial level and because of her character, she made good contact with the other women who participated more freely. Finally, and with the group support, she was able to express resentments against all the members of her family whom she had seen as so "lovely" and to whom she had been so "lovely." Despite this new recognition Mrs. S. retained a good relationship with them which did not vary much from her previous pattern. The release of some of her hostility and the support the group provided to the release of tension made possible a pregnancy within a few months after the group sessions were completed. Mrs. S. had a normal delivery and her baby was healthy in every respect.

Conclusion. Psychotherapy, particularly group psychotherapy, as an integral part of medical services in various problems of marriage proved a valuable contribution to the solution of these problems as presented by patients which they had considered as exclusively physical in nature. It aids in the treatment palliatively, curatively and in prevention. Group techniques emphasize the universality of basic needs, the uniqueness of the individual and the inevitably resulting differences in behavior and attitudes. In the area of interpersonal relationship in marriage, especially in sex and reproduction, it is a realistic approach to the problems of men and women. Group psychotherapy furnishes an excellent exploratory medium for research as well as a method of teaching students in this field of endeavor.

BIBLIOGRAPHY

Anshen, R. N., ed. (1949), *The Family: Its Function and Destiny*. New York: Harpers.
Dunbar, F. (1947), *Mind and Body: Psychosomatic Medicine*. New York: Random House.
Duvall, E. M. and Hill, R. (1945), *When You Marry*. New York: Association Press.
Ford, C. S. and Beach, F. A. (1951) , *Patterns of Sexual Behavior*. New York: Harpers.
Kinsey, A. C., Pomeroy, W. B., and Martin, C. E. (1948), *Sexual Behavior in the Human Male*. Philadelphia: W. B. Saunders.
—— (1953), *Sexual Behavior in the Human Female*. Philadelphia: W. B. Saunders.
Landis, J. T. and Landis, M. G. (1948), *Building a Successful Marriage*. New York: Prentice Hall.

Levine, L. and Brodsky, J., *Group Premarital Counseling*. Pamphlet.
—— and Gilman, M., *Frigidity*. Pamphlet.
—— and Stone, A., *Group Treatment of Sexual Maladjustment*. Pamphlet.
Portnoy, L. and Saltman, J., *Fertility in Marriage*. Pamphlet.
Stone, A. and Levine, L., *The Dynamics of the Marital Relationship*. Pamphlet.
Stone, H. and Stone, A. (1935), *A Marriage Manual*. New York: Simon and Schuster.

Chapter XV

PRIVATE PRACTICE

●

Group psychotherapy had its beginnings in outpatient clinics of general hospitals, in mental hospitals, social agencies, and child guidance clinics. For some years an increasing number of psychiatrists have employed group psychotherapy in private practice. They have been adapting techniques and modifying goals to suit the type of patient who is being treated in the privacy of the doctor's office. The adoption of group psychotherapy for the treatment of adult patients in private practice has been greatly stimulated by its extensive use in the armed services, where many physicians had an opportunity to come in close contact with this new method and where they have learned much about its advantages and limitations. However, the opinion was prevalent that private patients would be unwilling to expose their inner problems, preoccupations, and feelings to other patients. Practice has shown that these misgivings were not justified (Hulse, 1954).

The well-known fact that the type of patient whom we find in the private office differs widely from the psychiatric patients in clinics and institutions has its impact on group psychotherapy in private practice. The existing reports on this type of group psychotherapy are predominantly concerned with adults suffering from psychoneurotic and psychosomatic illnesses (Baruch, 1945; Baruch and Miller, 1947; Foulkes, 1948; Loeser, et al., 1949; Bronner, 1954).

A number of reasons account for the difference in patients in private practice and in patients who are treated in clinics, hospitals and agencies. In the first place, the psychoneurotic represents a large majority among private patients. Many physicians, however, carry also a good number of ambulatory psychotics. In contrast to many agency settings where children and adolescents are predominant, in private practice

fewer children are treated than adults. The majority of children brought
for treatment are boys who act out. Individually, and still more so in
groups, they need special facilities because they are frequently over-
aggressive and destructive. It is therefore understandable that very few
psychiatrists can provide play and work rooms to accommodate therapy
groups for emotionally disturbed children. This type of treatment is,
therefore, still primarily carried out by agencies and institutions.

This chapter is based on the author's experience with group psychotherapy in private practice over a period of nine years, on a study of the
literature, and on personal contacts and correspondences with group
psychotherapists in and outside of the United States. A detailed questionnaire (Hulse, 1954) was circulated among a selected group of psychiatrists and the answers received have been of great help in carrying out
this study.[1] Modified questionnaires aiming at similar goals are circulated by Professor Don D. Prosser, Karolyn B. Prosser and Solon D.
Samuels, M.D., of the Research Commission of the Group Therapy
Association of Southern California at Los Angeles and by Dr. Simone
Blajan-Marcus of Paris representing a group of French psychoanalysts
interested in group psychotherapy (both studies unpublished). Experiences with group psychotherapy in private practice in England have been
reported by Foulkes (1948) and others.

Concerning the question of all-male, all-female, or mixed groups, opinion seems to weigh in favor of mixed groups but in many instances the
number of female outnumbers by far the number of male patients, a
factor that may cause imbalance in the groups. About one half of our
respondents prefer mixed groups. For the rest, all-female groups out-
number all-male groups.

The preference for clinically homogeneous or heterogeneous groups
is subject to the limitation of a private office practice. As a rule, private
practice does not provide the psychiatrist with a large enough number of
patients with the same pathology, as can be found in a hospital clinic or
social agency. Some psychotherapists hold that it is unnecessary and even
not conducive to successful treatment to put patients with the same or
similar symptoms in the same group. In psychoanalytically oriented
therapy (78 per cent of the group psychotherapists answering our questionnaires designate their procedure as "analytic" or "psychoanalytically
oriented") the focus is not so much on the symptom as on the deeper
mechanisms which produce symptoms. We try to create in our patients

---

[1] This study was undertaken by the Commission on Group Psychotherapy in Private
Practice of the American Group Psychotherapy Association, Inc., of which the present
writer was chairman.

the awareness that common symptoms very often only give the appearance of homogeneity, and that patients with great variations in symptomatology often have very much in common when the unconscious roots of psychoneurotic behavior are reached. In the group process the common symptom is, therefore, often used as a defense: instead of going deeper, patients exchange information about their physical symptoms (headaches, duodenal ulcers, compulsions, etc.). The good results reported with heterogeneous groups as used widely in private practice might therefore be a useful stimulus for those who until now have been working by preference with homogeneous groups.

The specific goals of a given therapeutic group are, of course, an important determining factor for heterogeneous as well as for homogeneous groups.

The terms "homogeneity" and "heterogeneity" have to be understood. There are a number of definite considerations to be observed in the process of selecting and grouping of patients who can serve as therapeutic agents for each other. Patients of very low and very high intelligence are often incompatible, the former resenting what they consider oversophistication or "show-offness" in the more intelligent members. The latter, on the other hand, protest against the retardation of interchange that the mentally slow need in order to be comfortable and cooperative. Differences in educational backgrounds are less important and should be worked out in the group, i.e., a basically intelligent person can, through the therapeutic process, overcome awe, resentment or inferiority feelings toward another patient with higher academic achievements. Differences in color, religion or national backgrounds should not be deterrents, but may provide fertile material for the working through of attitudes and values.

Some private practitioners believe that resistant and diffident patients should be accommodated first and should have a say as to the selection of their co-members in a group. Such problems seem to be of greater importance in private practice than in hospitals or agencies where candidates for therapy often feel more as "charity patients" and therefore in the begining submit more easily to (but revolt later against) the authority represented by the hospital or agency. The self-paying private patient might act (and act out) differently. We feel that the composition of the group has to remain the prerogative of the therapist and that negative attitudes of a patient, being resistance phenomena, should be handled as such. A greater number of individual sessions may have to be devoted to the development of rapport before the therapist can place such patients in a group.

Differences in age cannot be completely overlooked, especially in the early stages of a newly composed group. In the beginning stages patients become uncomfortable and drop out if they have too little in common with each other and if specialized problems of certain age groups or social situations are permitted to take up most of a group's time. If a new group is organized, it is advisable to limit the age range for adult patients to about 15 years, i.e., 20 to 35, 25 to 40, 45 to 60, etc. It is not advisable to mix adolescents below 20 with adults over 25.

One of the most important factors in the future development of group psychotherapy (as well as in most other branches of medicine) is a definite understanding of therapeutic indications and contraindications. In group psychotherapy we still have a long way to go before the treatment results from patients of various nosological categories will be predicted with reasonable certainty. Many are still puzzled by the fact that a given method helps some patients while it fails with others. While the results of research to date do not yield definite solutions for this problem, our present knowledge can offer some valuable leads and suggestions that can be put to good use.

Most psychiatrists using group psychotherapy in private practice agree that anxiety states, anxiety neuroses and anxiety hysterias, i.e., patients who manifest a great amount of free-floating anxiety are good prospects for group psychotherapy. Anxious patients are often less disturbed in groups than in individual sessions where they have to face the therapist alone and where they often project their fear of the punishing parent into the therapeutic situation. They derive support from the group where some patients have already "learned" to manage their free-floating anxiety. This often results in rapid symptom improvement and in a greater ability to work through basic problems in the ensuing, sometimes prolonged psychotherapeutic process. Their anxiety is useful to the group in providing the fuel which is needed for group movement (Hulse, 1950). Similar phenomena diagnosed in children as behavior disorders are of such a nature that it is easily understood why behavior disorders respond well to group psychotherapy (Slavson, 1952).

Private practice deals frequently with patients who are acutely anxious, and who therefore do not fit into the psychotherapeutic arrangements of one or two sessions a week as provided by outpatient clinics or agencies. Such patients can profit from the specific therapeutic elements provided by group psychotherapy, but they often need additional support. The questions of group sessions two or three times a week or concomitant individual and group psychotherapy will be discussed later in this chapter.

Severe hysterias of the "grande hystérie" or the conversion types are not very frequent in private practice in our culture. They are treated by preference with classical psychoanalysis. Only in later stages when weaning them from psychotherapy becomes an important task, may group psychotherapy be considered. The same is true for reactive depressions who at first need and should receive intensive individual therapy and who later, during the convalescent stage, may be considered for group psychotherapy.

While most acute psychoneurotic illnesses in adults can be treated to greater or lesser advantages by group psychotherapy—often in combination with individual psychotherapy—the widest field for the use of group therapy in private psychiatric practice seems to lie in the area of character neuroses. The treatability of patients in this category through group therapy has been well established by our correspondents as well as by our own experiences.

The literature gives ample proof of successful group psychotherapy with mothers of children with behavior disorders (see Chapter IX). It is characteristic for many of these mothers that they had never tried to get treatment for their extensive chronic neurotic disturbances, usually of hysteric, phobic, compulsive and obsessive nature, and that it was only increasing difficulties in the management of their children that forced them to seek help. The achievement of ego syntonicity which is typical for character neuroses is a severe handicap in individual psychotherapy, as the patients frequently deny their own anxiety and discomfort and continue to accuse environmental factors, especially children, mates, in-laws, employers, etc., as the cause of their unhappiness. This type of patient is frequently found in private practice, especially in connection with marital and other intrafamily conflicts. The patients' fear of change, their lack of motivation toward individual psychotherapy or psychoanalysis, their rigidity and combativeness are the main causes of their refusal to submit to therapy or their early failure in treatment. Group psychotherapy offers great advantages for these patients to accept therapy in the beginning, and to endure it for an adequate length of time (often several years), in order to permit character changes.

The group provides patients with character neuroses with a more social setting and a lesser degree of threat as compared with the individual face-to-face situation. Group psychotherapy permits denial and "passing over" attitudes in the beginning phases and gives hostile and righteous individuals a wide range for argument and verbal acting out. While the patient permits himself such release, he does not have to attack the parental figure (the therapist) directly but can live through less threatening battles with sibling figures. It is, of course, inadvisable to compose a group exclusively of compulsive and hostile members. It may be necessary to give a high degree of support to anxious and phobic members who are frequently attacked during the early stages and who identify the compulsive member with their own parent. After a short initial period, the need to act as therapists to each other and the ability to recognize one's own character traits in others appear as therapeutic elements characteristic of group psychotherapy.

In later stages of group psychotherapy the impact of group action increases when patients join in the effort to remind a fellow patient over and over again that he had "understood" before the meaning of a neurotic symptom or of an anxiety-provoking life experience and therefore cannot withdraw from the insight obtained previously into vagueness and denial (Hulse, 1953). The generally observable phenomenon of superego relaxation in groups adds further to the progress of patients with character neuroses.

When discussing the selection of patients for group psychotherapy in private psychiatric practice we prefer to use the classification "schizophrenias" to "psychoses" for practical as well as theoretical reasons. The psychotic and prepsychotic patients in ambulatory therapy are mainly schizophrenics; other psychotic categories (organic, general paresis, toxic, manic, depressive, etc.) exclude themselves frequently from ambulatory group therapy by their general behavior and their lack of contact with reality. All patients with seriously disturbed reality contact (free hallucinatory or delusional states) or with severe depressed or suicidal traits should be excluded from private group psychotherapy because of the disturbing effect they have on other patients. These patients also need a much closer contact with the therapist than group psychotherapy by its very nature can provide.

For ambulatory schizophrenic patients, the dangers are usually remote. The experience of many group psychotherapists shows clearly that such patients can be successfully treated in heterogeneous groups without dangers to themselves or to others. Their treatment in ambulatory homogeneous groups does not apply to private practice.

Ambulatory schizophrenic patients in private practice can be divided into two major categories: psychotic or postpsychotic patients on one hand, and potentially psychotic on the other. The latter category is frequently referred to as "borderline state," a term which appears semantically indefinite and nosologically undetermined. It seems that these patients can very definitely be diagnosed as schizophrenic, even while not removed from reality. For our discussion, they are considered basically different from "schizoid personalities," i.e., normal persons with schizoid inclinations and character coloring.

A large number of ambulatory "borderline" schizophrenic patients are, in the opinion of more than half of our respondents, suitable for group psychotherapy in heterogeneous groups, i.e., in groups that have a majority of psychoneurotics and patients with character neuroses. These schizophrenic patients have to be carefully selected and due to their tendencies toward aloofness, moodiness and self-isolation, there should not be more than two of them in a group of eight. On the other hand, they contribute to the group by their ability to understand and to verbalize preconscious processes, and to interpret lucidly material produced by other patients. Despite occasional outbreaks of hostility, they are often well liked by the other group members, and their contributions are well accepted. They derive and use support from the group and show ego growth and maturation if exposed to a prolonged therapeutic process.

We have observed several patients of this category over a number of years and have been gratified by the results obtained. One of these patients, Miss X, who had had previous psychoanalysis of a modified kind for a two-year period with another psychiatrist but had remained socially withdrawn and unemployed, has had a continuous successful employment adjustment during three years of group psychotherapy. Her social relations as well as her sexual adjustment had greatly improved. Her basic difficulty in deep relationships was not resolved, but it seems to be undergoing slow changes toward improvement. She has been able to verbalize basic conflicts in the group; for instance, she described in definite terms the ego-threatening anxiety of approaching orgasm and her fears that she may never be able "to come back" from the disintegrating feeling of "getting lost" in orgastic relations to a mate. She improved greatly, without ever threatening the safety of other members. Neurotic fellow members have definitely profited from her ability to verbalize feelings about primary processes. Similar experiences have been related to me personally by other group therapists.

The majority of group psychotherapists seem to admit only rarely antisocial character deviates or severe psychosomatic disorders to clinically heterogeneous groups.

Patients with character disturbances such as alcoholics are often disturbing elements in heterogeneous groups. Some of our correspondents also feel that stutterers and epileptics do not improve in heterogeneous groups, but our own experiences have shown that the special problems of stutterers and epileptics can be worked through in intensive psychotherapy in mixed groups.

Minor psychosomatic ailments like skin eruptions, occasional asthmatic attacks or hay fever are frequent concomitants of neuroses and do not present specialized problems in the private practice of group psychotherapy. Severe psychosomatic illnesses are usually treated in specialized groups, but in private practice it is rarely possible to establish groups composed exclusively of obese patients or of persons suffering from multiple sclerosis, poliomyelitis, colitis, colostomy or other type of psychosomatic symptomatology. Such groups are usually organized in hospitals or outpatient departments. An exception has been group psychotherapy in the private office of an allergist (Baruch and Miller, 1947).[2]

The private psychiatrist working with a new form of psychotherapy develops empirically over a number of years certain preferences in his methods and techniques. It is a gratifying experience when he finds later that others, confronted with similar problems, have come to the same conclusions and are using the same techniques. It seems that in several areas of private practice group psychotherapy, the empirical process has created well-defined new therapeutic standards[3] (Slavson, 1952).

A brief survey of specific mechanics of private practice group therapy might be of help to those who are newcomers to this branch of psychotherapy.

Size of Groups. The number of patients in a therapeutic group is usually six to eight. A number of group psychotherapists carry as many as nine to ten patients and report good results. Most therapists feel that the increased number dilutes the therapeutic intensity; few are able to observe and record adequately the reactions and the interchange in a very large group. We have found that a large number of participants interferes with sufficient verbal release of the individual patient during a given time (Hulse and Goldfeld, 1953).

The Time Element. A high degree of consensus in regard to the time element has emerged from empirical findings. Short group sessions do not permit an adequate "warming up" period, prolonged sessions create general tiredness and increased irritability, and also impair the therapist's ability to observe and to treat if he has to work with many patients and without pause. Most therapists questioned by us prefer group sessions of 90 minutes' duration, the rest are about equally divided between those who treat for one hour and those who treat for two hours.

---

[2] These types of specialized groups in private practice may be made possible in the future by establishment of central clearing offices and exchange by means of which psychiatrists could refer patients with specific problems to private group therapists specializing in the treatment of such psychosomatic categories.

[3] Panel Discussion at the Ninth Annual Conference of the American Group Psychotherapy Association, New York, 1952.

Only very few therapists use less than one hour, or more than two, and this occurs only in highly specialized settings.

Frequency of Sessions. The number of sessions per week is well settled by what is practically unanimity. With very few exceptions one or two sessions per week are the general rule in private practice group therapy, with a definite preferential leaning toward once a week.

Placing and Discharging Patients in Groups. While a number of authors, who have described the use of groups for diagnostic and general mental hygiene purposes, have placed new and unprepared patients in such groups, the private practitioners in a large majority prefer to prepare patients carefully for the new experience of group psychotherapy. There is of course no general standard procedure for the preparation of patients. Many therapists do not place patients in a group until they are assured that they have developed definite rapport with the therapist, a process which may take several weeks or months. Beginners who want to proceed safely until they themselves have acquired adequate experience in the new field should at first use patients of long standing in individual therapy for a process of "weaning" (Foulkes, 1948; Slavson, 1952). This "tapering off process" may be at first a combination of group and individual therapy ending with group treatment alone. Other practitioners accept patients for group psychotherapy after a short and rather perfunctory individual contact. Bronner (1954) and Mullan (1953) have dealt in great length with the pitfalls of premature introduction of patients and with the unconscious countertransference phenomena that play a role in the therapist's procedure before the patient actually reaches the first group session. The patient will of course be faced with a basically different situation depending on the fact whether he joins an open or a closed group.

When all members start group psychotherapy at the same time, the beginning is easier for all, but the process in therapy and therefore the time of ending cannot be equalized. If the private practitioner wants to end the group-therapeutic process for all his group members at the same time, he has to restrict the "working through" to selected and very limited areas of his patients' maladjustment. He also will find himself in difficulties, searching for patients who will be able to start and to end together within a prearranged limited time schedule.

These specific problems of private practice find their expression in the preference for "open groups without time limitations." Patients are discharged individually from groups as they improve, or, if found unsuitable for further group psychotherapy. As long as a nucleus of several well-integrated patients remains, the group continues, and new patients are admitted to maintain the group at optimum size. Some therapists permit the members to decide about new admissions, others manage admissions and discharges as their prerogative. If the patients remaining in a depleted group are not suitable for the formation of a nucleus, they are transferred to another group or into individual psychotherapy. Patients can remain in a group over extended periods of time, if they have been able to go through the inevitable initial adjustment period of the first few weeks.

It is easily understood that the admission of a new patient into an open group that has been in progress for an extended period of time has its special and intricate problems. Not only the patient has to be prepared but also the group. Many group members go through all the emotional difficulties of facing the birth of a younger sibling whenever a new group member joins. This is very often a welcome opportunity for the repeated analysis and working through process of basic conflict material (Wolf, 1949/1950; Bronner, 1954). Hostile manifestations against the newcomer are frequently conscious, but their unconscious roots have to be analyzed. The newcomer, of course, needs often protection and support when the "older siblings" attack him, sometimes with the admitted intent to make him leave. Prados (1952) permits new patients to sit next to him; others (Hulse, 1953; Hulse and Goldfeld, 1953) have described various analytic methods and observations concerning the inner forces of the group that can be mobilized in order to prevent early traumatization of a new patient.

While the admission of new patients creates special situations that can become therapeutic if well handled or are traumatic if not adequately recognized, so does the discharge of group members if and when they have improved or have been found unsuitable for a specific group. Transfer of a patient from one group to another is occasionally an advisable procedure if a patient has become involved in problems with one or several patients, problems that are not sufficiently analyzable in a given group setting. This happens occasionally in the case of hostile and compulsive character neuroses. Better progress might be achieved in a new group. Very disturbed patients who have to be transferred to individual therapy or to institutions are often upsetting elements before and after their removal, but they afford a realistic confrontation with the fact that group therapy is not a "cure all" and that failure in therapy for one patient does not endanger the prognosis for others.

Patients who have made good progress and are able to discontinue therapy are threatening for many group members who become anxious over the question: why is he cured and not I? The group process provides ample opportunities for the working through of such anxieties and for the establishment of the truth that no two patients ever have the same therapeutic goals.

We have observed groups as very effective therapeutic agents in preventing patients from leaving prematurely. Much better than an individual therapist is a group able to impress upon a patient the extent of remaining symptoms or disturbing character traits. If the patient accepts the group's attitude, the other group members will often pay special attention to these remaining maladjustments and become highly effective therapeutic agents.

Concomitant Psychotherapy. Of the many technical variations that different group therapists are using in their special settings, a few deserve special attention here. There is, for instance, the wide use of concomitant individual and group psychotherapy in private practice.

About 80 per cent of our respondents used individual and group psychotherapy concomitantly. Some apply combined treatment to all patients, others use it as indicated. Only a few did not use it at all. Good results have been obtained with psychoneurotics when combined treatment was used in "the tapering off" process, i.e., as a device to wean patients toward the planned ending of individual treatment. We have observed continuous stimulation of the individual treatment situation through the group experiences which the patient lived through in the presence and with the participation of the therapist. The advantages which the patient derives from concomitant use of group and individual therapy have been described in detail by Fried (1954), Hulse (1953), and others.

Specialized Projects. A number of specialized group projects have been reported that are concerned with new fields and with different aspects of group psychotherapy. Groups consisting solely of alcoholics or psychosomatic patients are employed. Mothers' groups are frequent. Some of the latter start as guiding or counseling ventures but soon lead to the recognition of personality problems and from this point on to group or individual psychotherapy. Several therapists carry psychotherapeutic groups of pregnant mothers, others are experimenting with parent and marital groups, i.e., they include husbands and wives in the same group or treat children together with their parents.

Some concern themselves with group therapy for children, a technically difficult problem in private practice. Schiffer (1947) conducts a unique venture in New York, an "Activity Group Therapy Center for the Maladjusted Child," the first private clinic for the practice of activity group therapy. Wm. Moore of Akron, Ohio, has treated children in groups together with their parents, using techniques developed by Dreikurs (1951).

The treatment of marital problems has been tried for husband and wife in parallel as well as in the same group. A psychoanalytic group setting was started by Samuel Rosen in New York, in which each group consisted of only three persons: the husband, the wife and the therapist. More than 30 couples had been treated by this method when the untimely death of Dr. Rosen prevented its continuation.

The use of hypnotic and suggestive methods in private practice group therapy has been described by Schmidhofer (1946), while McCartney (1951) has organized didactic groups of 30 to 40 patients who attended sessions once a week for six weeks.

Fees in Private Practice. The literature on group psychotherapy in private practice does not provide us with information about the fees charged. Our own experiences and inquiries furnish us with a limited amount of information.

The wide range of fees charged is in striking contrast to the degree of agreement that private group therapists have reached in the matter of treatment methods.

One third of our correspondents charge uniform fees, that is, all patients pay the same fee per session (or per month). But the range of these uniform fees is very wide, namely from $2.00 to $20.00 per session and from $15.00 to $45.00 per month. Only a small number of psychiatrists charge a monthly fee, however. If the fee for group therapy sessions is expressed in percentages of the fee for individual sessions, it ranges from one seventh (with six to eight members present), to the full fee for individual sessions. The average fee seems to lie betwen $2.50 and $10.00 per session. The maximal charge is $20.00 per session, the minimum is 50 cents. Some therapists contract with the group as a body (for instance, $20.00 per session) and leave it to the group to appoint a member to be responsible for the collection of fees. This method is not widely used.

BIBLIOGRAPHY

Baruch, D. W. (1945), Description of a Project in Group Therapy. *J. Consult. Psychol.*
—— and Miller, H. (1947), Interview Group Psychotherapy with Allergic Patients. *The Practice of Group Therapy,* ed. S. R. Slavson. New York: International Universities Press.
Bronner, A. (1954), Observations on Group Therapy in Private Practice. *Am. J. Psychother.,* 8:55-62.
Dreikurs, R. (1951), Family Group Therapy in the Chicago Community Child Guidance Centers. *Ment. Hyg., 35.*

272   FIELDS OF GROUP PSYCHOTHERAPY

Durkin, H. (1954), *Group Psychotherapy for Mothers of Disturbed Children.* Springfield, Ill.: Chas. Thomas.
Foulkes, S. H. (1948), *Introduction to Group-Analytic Psychotherapy.* London: Heinemann.
Fried, E. (1954a), The Effect of Combined Therapy on the Productivity of Patients. *Int. J. Group Psychother., 4:*42-55.
—— (1954b), Benefits of "Combined" Therapy for the Hostile-Withdrawn and the Hostile-Dependent Personality. *Am. J. Orthopsychiat., 24.*
Friesen, A. R. (1952), Practical Aspects of Group Procedures in Private Practice. Panel Discussion at the Ninth Annual Meeting, American Group Psychotherapy Association, New York.
Hulse, W. C. (1950), The Therapeutic Management of Group Tension. *Am. J. Orthopsychiat., 20.*
—— (1954), Dynamics and Techniques of Group Psychotherapy in Private Practice. *Int. J. Group Psychother., 4:*65-73.
—— (1955), Transference, Catharsis, Insight and Reality Testing during Concomitant Individual and Group Psychotherapy. *Int. J. Group Psychother., 5:*45-53.
—— and Goldfeld, R. (1953), Self-Reporting in Group Psychotherapy. *Psa. Rev., 40.*
Klapman, J. W. (1949), *Social Adjustment and Resurgo Magazine.* Chicago: Resurgo Associates, Inc., 1949.
Loeser, L. H., et al. (1949), Group Psychotherapy in Private Practice. *Am. J. Psychother., 3.*
Low, A. A. (1943), *Technique and Self-Help in Psychiatric After Care: 3 Volumes and Recovery Journal.* Chicago: Recovery Publications, 1943.
McCartney, J. L. M. (1951), *N. Y. State Med. J.*
Mullan, H. (1953), Counter-Transference in Groups. *Am. J. Psychother., 7:*680-688.
Panel Discussion at the Ninth Annual Conference of the American Group Psychotherapy Association, New York, 1952.
Papanek, H. (1954), Combined Group and Individual Therapy in Private Practice. Eleventh Annual Conference, Am. Group Psychotherapy Assn., New York.
Peck, H. B. (1952), Some Unique Contributions and Possible Limitations of Group Psychotherapy in Private Practice. Panel Discussion at the Ninth Annual Meeting, American Group Psychotherapy Association, New York.
Prados, M. (1952), Group Analysis Technique in Private Practice. Annual Meeting, American Psychiatric Association, Atlantic City.
Schiffer, M. (1947), *The Practice of Group Therapy,* ed. S. R. Slavson. New York: International Universities Press.
Schmidhofer, E. (1946), Therapeutic Relaxation. *J. Nerv. & Ment. Dis.*
Slavson, S. R. (1943), *An Introduction to Group Therapy.* New York: International Universities Press, 1952.
—— (1952), Some Problems in Group Psychotherapy as Seen by Private Practitioners. *Int. J. Group Psychother., 2:*54-66.
Wolf, A. (1949/1950), The Psychoanalysis of Groups. *Am. J. Psychother., 3:*4.
—— et al. (1952), The Psychoanalysis of Groups—The Analyst's Objections. *Int. J. Group Psychother., 2:*221-231.

Chapter XVI

COMMUNITY MENTAL HEALTH[1]

•

It is idle to talk about mental health for the individual without taking cognizance of the setting in which he lives and functions. Total health can be attained only when life and relations favor it. Man does not live in a vacuum, nor can he insulate himself from the impingement of his environment; whatever effort he invests in attaining personal well-being is fully or partially defeated, directly or indirectly, by too adverse circumstances and oversevere stress. One cannot view the mental health of the individual, therefore, as unrelated to conditions, environment and relations. The individual is inexorably entwined in his climatic, physical and emotional environment in which he strives to survive as a biological entity and a social atom. Whether he is aware of it or not, he constantly makes organic and social adaptations to tacit and active demands of his world. As a moral being he absorbs the values and codes of that world and internalizes them to form the inner authority that guides his life; they are also the root of his fears and anxieties. Whether he wills it or not, he must submit to the authority of his group and that of his society and modify himself in accord with their demands and codifications.

In order to survive as a social unit and preserve his self-esteem, the individual is impelled to fit into his immediate group as well as into the larger community. While usually yielding much gratification, this process of adaptation is also the source of frustration, deprivation, and self-denial. His instinctive trends for self-indulgence and satisfaction and his crass cravings and urges are not acceptable to his culture and evoke stigma and punishment. Thus the individual is torn between his anarchic urges and the social controls which he has to resolve according to his lights and

[1] A portion of the content of this chapter has appeared in the *Int. J. Group Psychother.*, 4:210-217, 1954.

psychic strengths. He may yield to his instinctive propulsions at the cost of social castigation or repress and inhibit them. Either choice results in conflict and unhappiness. To bring himself in harmony with social impositions the individual has to exercise a great deal of self-control and self-denial. He must learn the arts of repression and sublimation. The tragedy is that the channels for sublimation are not always at hand, however. Instead, society exerts direct inhibition and suppression. Schools, church, and various government agencies regulate conduct, prohibit or condone attitudes; they seldom *guide* toward better ways of living and finding self-fulfillment. Particularly are schools derelict in this respect. Instead of helping children find constructive outlets for their raw instincts, they rather build up fear and guilt and the inevitably resulting resentments that finally find release in antisocial attitudes, misology or neurotic self-blame. They breed antagonism both to the world of men and the world of ideas. Instead of conditioning children to identify with their fellow men and to draw delight from the world of thought and knowledge, schools turn most against both.

The low level of material security cannot but enhance instinctive fear, aggression or retreat that follow in its wake. The anxieties and insecurity that result from lack of permanent assurance of material survival add further to the unhealth of the average individual. To them are also denied the essential feelings of success and self-esteem because of social and economic inequalities. These further strengthen feelings of inadequacy, weakness and failure. Of equal deleterious effect are the over-rigid cultural, ethical and moral codes. Though necessary in and of themselves within limits they suppress the individual's spontaneity and instinctual gratifications because of their gratuitous rigidities and guilt-evoking effects.

The cumulative result from socially generated unfavorable contingencies and demands is frustration, guilt and anxiety. These, in turn, give rise to misanthropy and hostility that is reflected in every arena of man's political, social, economic and professional efforts. The disharmony between these feelings and the need to fit into the social mold create insurmountable difficulties for the psyche and uncontrollable tensions in interpersonal relations, thus vitiating the total social climate. However, social life is not all a debit situation. All the humane attributes as anthropologists have clearly shown, result from accommodations to and stimuli from fellow men. The ancient Greeks have rightly said that "Man without the work of man is nothing," and our own formulation, "That which is human in us is given us by other humans," is justified in fact. These truisms need no proof. Man's fulfillment and his redemption lie in his society and in his relation to it, for the group is the milieu from which man's health and unhealth are derived. Our concern is *the ways* in which this occurs, not *the fact* of it.

Psychotherapy in its final results helps man to carry his burdens with less stress and greater spiritual equanimity. It cannot by and of itself change the conditions of society. At best, it can help the individual mobilize powers to improve his lot. It cannot by and of itself change the community beyond the indirect effects that healthier people create a healthier society. Even if it were to leave the clinical frontiers and enter the stream and vortex of community life in its multiphasic manifestations, it is doubtful whether psychotherapy as such could solve or mediate its wider problems. Rather the accumulated knowledge emanating from psychotherapy distilled and adapted as a form of social psychology and social psychiatry and applied to relations in the home, school and industry may be applicable to the large canvas of social living. This would require understanding man not only as a disparate organism, but more so as an interacting and socially integrative mechanism. The function of the ego and the sources of the superego, as well as the shaping of the id and libidinal expression will then be viewed from a different perspective and with new understandings. A new nonrepressive and truly democratic society will then emerge.

The relation of psychotherapy, social psychology and social psychiatry to the social scene can best be established through group psychotherapy by applying the knowledge about man's behavior in groups derived from the unrestricted interactions in therapy groups. Beginnings in this direction are evident in a number of settings and different localities. This development is reflected in a recently published symposium on the "Applications of Group Psychotherapy Techniques in Nonclinical Settings."[2] The following were among the areas and social instrumentalities that have been described as employing group therapy techniques in modified form: with executives of departments in the United States Government (Laughlin, 1954); with personnel in industry (Blum, 1954); with teachers and other school personnel (Herrold, 1954); in counseling mothers in ways of dealing healthfully with their children (Grunwald, 1954); in training of staff in a correctional school (Kotkov, 1954); in work with social offenders (McCorkle, 1954), and in its use on radio as a means for mental health education (Steiner, 1954).

In the present volume as well, some of the chapters reflect this trend. Among these are Chapter X, describing spontaneous nondirective dis-

[2] *Int. J. Group Psychother.*, 4:163-217, 1954. For contributors, see Bibliography *sub* individual authors.

cussions among prenatal unmarried mothers; in Chapters IX and XII the work with mothers and fathers in a clinical setting is described and its importance and implications for preventing personality problems and social maladjustments in children as a prophylactic measure and the preparation and guidance of parents is pointed up. The application of group therapy in a family service agency is of a similar significance (Chapter XIII). The study of the uses of group psychotherapy in industry is described from the point of view of a psychiatrist in Chapter XVI; finally, its values in training psychiatric and other personnel is delineated in Chapter XVII.

Reference has been made by a few of the contributors to this volume to my "Child-Centered Group Guidance of Parents."[3]

In this method conversations with carefully selected fathers and mothers at the group sessions are focused exclusively upon the parents' understanding of their children's behavior and motivations and upon responding to them in an appropriate and understanding manner so as to foster mental health in their offspring. Each parent evolves his own techniques for dealing with his children and managing the home in the light of his new insights derived from these free discussions. Emphasis is laid upon *sensitization* of the parent to the child and placing himself in empathy with the child's mind, needs and cravings. Out of this enhancement more empathic responses result. The child is seen in a new and more helpful light.

This technique grew out of my work with mixed groups of mothers and fathers in the community, not at a clinic, in 1948. They were the parents of babies under 18 months of age, and the discussions were a step toward *preventing* difficulties with them. This work, when sufficiently widespread, holds great promise for mental health in the community, for there is not gainsaying the fact that the foundations of mental health are laid in the home.

Though only in their beginnings, these efforts of reevaluating human relations in the light of new understandings of what mental health is gives it an altered dynamic meaning. "Mental hygiene" was treated in the past as though it were a special and separate subject and was presented to the public and in classrooms in an academic manner as a special topic unrelated to the conduct of everyday living. But mental hygiene is not a subject to be taught; it is a way of life. Having the facts does not guarantee their use. Mental health has to be incorporated in every aspect of

[3] See Chapters XI and XII. A volume dealing with this type of group guidance is now ready for press.

living, in discharging responsibilities and in daily relationships. It can be attained only when living itself is carried on healthfully.

The papers referred to in the preceding pages describe how persons in places of power and authority, whether as parents, teachers, government officials or foremen, evolve new awarenesses of their effect upon other humans by virtue of their positions. Through actual demonstration by the leader, who is a psychotherapist, of his acceptance, his tolerance, secure self-control and freedom of expression of ideas and feelings, the participants assume new, more healthful and more effective leadership and followership roles.

The application of such techniques is only one of many attributes of a democracy that reaches beyond the political field. In fact, the formulations concerning the group in psychotherapy reflect fully the awareness of the inherent nature of democracy, for only in a democratic culture can group psychotherapy, group work and group guidance emerge. Only a culture in which the sanctity of the individual is the rule of life could give birth to a humanistic psychiatry; and only where the recognition exists of the interdependence of each with his fellow men can free group associations become pre-eminent and group psychotherapy flourish. The striking rapidity with which this form of treatment has spread in some countries is a barometer of the social climate of their civilization.

Just as dynamic psychiatry, group psychotherapy, too, has wider applications to life and culture beyond clinical frontiers, and for obvious reasons probably even more so. Roberts (1954) states in this connection: "If one inquires as to the unique contribution of the group psychotherapist to the general study of the group process, the answer would probably be that the group psychotherapist has had an easy and ready access to the accumulated knowledge along the dimension of internal reaction of the individuals participating in the group. The group psychotherapist generally has had his basic professional training in the psychological theory contained in psychiatry, psychoanalysis, psychology and social casework."

The principles of the interpersonal processes and reactions and of emergent group patterns in a democracy lead to understanding of social processes generally. However, in any discussion of the peripheral uses of group psychotherapy or its adaptations to areas other than psychiatry and clinical practice, the basic differences must be kept in mind between it, group psychotherapy, and release, guidance, counseling, group learning and reorientation of attitudes.

A basic characteristic of group psychotherapy lies in the fact that patients considered for groups are first studied as to their etiological, nosological and dynamic factors, and clinical diagnoses are established or hypothesized in advance. The patients are then grouped in a manner that would prove therapeutically effective for each of the participants. In other settings such as schools, social centers, industry, guided discussions, and in like situations where groups are used for education and re-education, this rigid choice and grouping is neither possible nor desirable. In such settings individuals have to be accepted by and large, as they come.

In the papers and chapters to which reference was made, the outstanding characteristic is the humanistic approach to people derived from the understandings of psychology and psychiatry. One is impressed with the attitudes of the authors, their awareness of the social forces in operation, and their empathy and feeling for the people with whom they are working. No longer are we cradled in the belief that people must conform, that they must function "properly," as we understand it, at the peril of punishment, getting poor school marks or of losing the job. The new attitude is one of understanding and helpfulness. Psychology and psychiatry are greatly responsible for these changes.

The literature also points up a new type of effort in altering relations in the family with a view to creating a climate in which children can grow into wholesome members of the community. Perhaps of all the areas in which we attempt to work, that of family relations is of the greatest importance and holds the greatest promise. Influencing attitudes of parents toward one another and toward children on a widespread scale in the community through parents' societies, through high schools and colleges, through voluntary church and other groups, women's clubs, rotary and other such organizations, is the most sound way of integrating mental health practice into the day-by-day living process, rather than treating it as an isolated discipline or academic subject matter for lectures or classroom teaching.

It is becoming increasingly evident that in important matters people cannot be dealt with *en masse*. Largely because children force this upon them by their unregulated behavior, teachers are beginning to recognize this fact. Fewer and fewer pupils are as easily manageable as they had been in the past; they are no longer as afraid nor as submissive. They discharge their justified hostility, act it out, are defiant and create tensions and difficulties in the classrooms, on the campuses and in the community. Teachers are, therefore, forced to attempt to understand what it is that is causing these difficulties. They are only now beginning to recognize that immobilization of children is well-nigh impossible; that children must be considered and treated as dynamic, reactive human beings with feelings, needs, cravings, desires, urges, aggressions, hostilities, friendships, love, and needs for love, for security and, above all, for respect. While schools are leaning toward these new directions we cannot be too sanguine about the changes either in their quality or frequency. However, the movement is in the right direction.

Similarly workers in shops, factories, offices and in private and government agencies are not treated as authoritatively and tyrannically as was the case in the past. Greater consideration is given them as persons, as individuals requiring status, freedom, participation and individual and group autonomy.

This attitude has been conditioned by many social and economic forces which fall outside the scope of this perusal, but the *modus operandi,* the techniques for expressing and managing these new needs have undoubtedly been influenced by group psychotherapy, as the literature unmistakably reveals. Group psychotherapy has shown that even if they cannot be directly transplanted, basic psychiatric understandings and group psychotherapy techniques can be redistilled for dealing with and management of groups and in the approaches to human behavior and needs. These changes constitute a true revolutionary step in human relations.

Not quite two decades ago few, if any, would have suspected that Freudian psychology could be applied to group management. Group psychotherapy has demonstrated that this is not only possible but essential. Dealing with groups on a more sensitive, more enlightened and humanistic basis has been stimulated and made possible as group therapists demonstrated the importance in human relations of the individual's unburdening himself of resentments, hostilities and dissatisfactions. This is now being absorbed in the most difficult of all settings—industry. No longer are workers viewed as automatons, but rather as individuals whose unconscious and irrational motivations must be understood and dealt with. Industry is beginning to recognize that group techniques are effective in the reconditioning of attitudes and in attaining cooperation beneficial both to labor and to employers. This discovery is of first magnitude, and as it spreads as a doctrine and as a practice in ever wider areas, a healthier community will emerge. No claim is made that psychology, psychiatry, or group psychotherapy can create a healthy community by themselves. Basically, man lives by how he earns his living and that, of course, has to be changed and made more favorable, more remunerative and more secure for the workers.

What can group psychotherapy offer to the schooling[4] of children? An example of this may be more clarifying than a purely theoretic disquisition. A boy of sixteen was described by his father, a professional man, as nervous, a poor sleeper with difficulties in social relations and poor achievement in studies. At home he was aggressive and unmanageable, requiring strict disciplining from his father, though with little effect. Because of his failures in high school, his general maladjustment and obvious emotional disturbances, the boy was placed in a school with which I was associated some thirty years ago. The school was psychoanalytically oriented and conducted on "progressive" lines with group participation as its base. Most of the teachers at the school had had a personal analysis and by tradition individualization of pupils and the educational program was the rule. The emphasis was upon each pupil's interests as the center.

About six months later the father told me: "You know, I can't believe my eyes. What's happened to James? Not only does he look better and is better in every respect, but the other day he told me to wake him up at six o'clock because he had to study. Now, we fought with him day and night that he do his lessons and he always refused. So I asked him, why the change? 'You see, Dad, we don't get individual marks,' said the boy. 'The class as a unit is marked and if I fail in my work, I reduce the the mark of each member of the class. I've got to keep up so that I will not hurt the boys and girls with whom I work on the project.'" An individualized group process not only motivated James to study, but also changed his personality and social function.

We cannot go into the details or the dynamics of these changes at this point. Certainly the most important factor operating was that James wanted to be a part of the group but only after he had been fully accepted by it as he was when he came to that particular school. I have designated this craving as "social hunger." In the new school he was not treated unfeelingly as he was at home and in the public high school.

It would seem that on the basis of our new knowledge changes in the schooling of children should occur in six distinct areas. These can be described briefly as follows:

(1) Education must be reorganized along lines so that awareness of the needs of pupils and respect for the individual's potential and creative powers find full expression and not only intellectual learnings and acquisition of information emphasized.

---

[4] I have always differentiated between "training," "schooling" and "education." Particularly is it important not to confuse schooling and education. Most often schools are anti-educational.

(2) The basis of all education should be acceptance of the child as a unique individual, rather than a member of a mass with no specific assets and limitations, needs and strivings. Blanket criteria as to abilities and standards of achievement are entirely unsuitable. Even on a postgraduate college level one must accept the students' ignorance in order to educate them.

(3) We must recognize the importance of a permissive, though conditioned, environment suitable for children at different ages and of different talents on the basis of the principle of *graded reality* (Slavson, 1943).

(4) The role of the teacher must be changed from that of a taskmaster to be feared and placated to one of a friendly guide and helper.

(5) We must recognize the importance of suitable occupations not only for groups, but also for individual children which should be the basis of their education. This is not intended to minimize group participation, exclude group learning and group activity nor the elimination of formal subjects, but the core of all education must be the recognition of individual needs and talents in a group setting and in an atmosphere of free interaction and participation (Slavson, 1939b, 1940).

(6) Classrooms must be reorganized, physically and in every other way, so that pupils could find abiding and sustaining interest and, what is even more important, would be accessible to one another rather than being regimentally seated face to back. People cannot learn the facilities of face-to-face relations in a back-to-face position. In order that people may develop social attitudes, learn how to interact constructively and to respect and appreciate each other, they must be accessible to one another. Classrooms make them physically as well as emotionally inaccessible so that pupils cannot acquire social patterns in a guided and conditioned environment which the classroom should be.

Our film "Activity Group Therapy"[5] unmistakenly demonstrates how children improve in a free, constructive atmosphere not only as individuals, but also in their social development. Since it is still restricted to clinical personnel, the film was once shown to a group of teachers, experimentally, with an experienced group therapist present for the purpose of obtaining their reactions to it. The viewers were asked to state their opinion as to the value of the film in their work with children. Parts of several of the responses will be reproduced here.

[5] Distributed by the Center for Mass Communications, Columbia University Press, New York, to clinical personnel and other workers and students in the fields of Mental Health. It is hoped to make it available in the near future to teachers after some suitable additions to the film are made.

Naturally [wrote one teacher] my reaction to the film was channeled toward modification for use in the school. As a matter of fact
I have been so influenced that on two or three occasions it has acted
as a deterrent to me where I might formerly have taken action. For
example, yesterday during the seventh period, E. N. had violated the
school regulation by leaving the (school) yard to buy potato chips.
When he returned he very defiantly munched them in my presence.
At the same time he tried to claim his turn in the basketball game,
attempting to take the ball from B. C., who told him that he had
forfeited his turn because he had violated the rules. After some
resistance, E. N. walked away and skipped his turn. He took his turn
when it came around again. All this time I was impelled to interfere,
but restrained myself. I had the pleasure of seeing this conflict and
violation resolved by the dynamics of group activity.

I have been very much influenced by the film. This influence has
led me to interfere much less frequently in problem situations and
to wait much more patiently for the boys to resolve their differences.
However, I must be honest. I find that I have a tendency to interfere
in some cases and not to do so in others. When I analyze this I find the
toleration being extended to those who are markedly aggressive and
fractious. I am now in the process of *thinking through* [italics mine]
this situation with the purpose of determining whether this development is helping my work with the boys.

That is very hopeful. Another reaction was:

The film was a revelation to me. It was exciting and vastly impressive.
I realized more than ever the good effects of permissiveness. The first
step in reaching a boy is to accept him and make him feel that you
like him. The film showed me that (1) it is possible to make boys feel
better about their lives; (2) it is possible to help them resolve their
inner difficulties; (3) my attitude is of great importance; (4) I must be
patient—results come slowly. I think group therapy can do a great
deal for education if we can affect the thinking of teachers.

Now, what can we do for adults in working with groups as a result of
our group-psychotherapeutic knowledge? I should like to suggest four
ideas in this regard.

(1) Treatment of adults must be such that they feel accepted and respected. This gives the participants in some instances for the first time in
their lives, and certainly for the first time in a group situation and on
their jobs, a feeling of status. Their opinions, whether agreed to or not,
should be listened to and respected by the psychologist, by the industrial
consultant, the plant official, the executive, the principal or superintendent, as the case may be.

(2) The members of groups must be accessible to one another. Interference with free communication is inconsistent with a free, democratic

culture and mental health. Individuals must work through their feelings toward each other and reveal themselves in a way that others could accept and understand them.

(3) Expression of feelings needs to be encouraged and the participants permitted to voice discontent and irritation and even their hostilities so that the quantum of repression by the ego in holding down these feelings is at a minimum. When the ego is not overloaded, the result is emotional and physical development.

(4) Because of discharge of emotion and resulting release, the participants are enabled intellectually to understand the problems and solutions involved, as well as to accept their part in the situation. They are able to objectify it and accept what other people and they themselves are doing.

Some of the values of group counseling for parents who do not present serious personality disturbances consist of the facts that (1) the parents identify with a wholesome parental figure in the person of the leader; (2) the group emphasizes the positive values in the parental role; (3) parents are helped through "mirror reaction" from the other participants in the group to see their own behavior more objectively; (4) empathy with children is increased through the discussions; (5) factual information and knowledge concerning child nature and child behavior is acquired; (6) universalization of problems and difficulties in the group discussions result in reduced guilt feelings and a strengthened ego for dealing with the day-to-day situations in the family setting. Of note is the work with mothers that has been done in St. Louis, Mo., and described in several reports (Buchmueller et al., 1949; Kahn et al., 1951; and the prophylactic work with women in pregnancy described by Caplan, 1951).

These techniques and processes stem from group psychotherapy, specifically, and from dynamic psychiatry generally. The dynamics in therapy groups have their counterpart in the work described. The warm, accepting relations and mutual regard in the guidance and re-education of groups correspond to the transference syndrome in group psychotherapy; expression and release of feeling correspond to catharsis, and understanding is the counterpart of insight. Though it is on a less intensive basis and less emotionally charged, we see the parallel between this work and group psychotherapy.

Of special value is the use of various types of free group interaction in training of personnel whose work involves emotional strain and unconscious attitudes. Some of these groups consist of nurses, especially those who work with mental patients, psychiatrists in training and interns in general medicine, all of whom unconsciously resist acquiring and applying psychologic insights in their work. This situation is described in Chapter XVII in this volume; also a number of papers dealing with this aspect of the problem have been published (Kotkov, 1954). Teachers, as well, should be provided with these emotion-releasing group experiences so that they can pass on their relaxed state to the children in their care.

The application of modified group therapy and group interaction is comparatively widespread in colleges and universities. A notable example of this is the University of Minnesota (Hinckley and Hermann, 1951), but reports reach us that the method is applied in a number of other universities as well. It must be noted that most of these groups are not designed for direct treatment. They are rather aimed at the emotional reorientation of students with a view toward better scholastic achievements and social adaptation.

Another important and more recent development in the use of modified group psychotherapy is the "unstructured group" described by Amster (1954). These are "spontaneous and self-motivated" groups of persons in the community, not in a clinical setting, who have become aware of the interferences in their function and adjustment of their attitudes and reactions. None of the participants in the four groups of men and women presented serious enough problems that would require intensive psychotherapy, but all felt that they could function more effectively and live more happily if they could eliminate some of the affective reactions that caused them stress or inconvenience. One group consisted of housewives; another was made up of members of parent-teacher associations, and two of university students. In all of the groups the "here and now" problems and situations formed the content of the conversations. However, Mrs. Amster reports that despite the preoccupation with practical and immediate problems "many of the principles of group psychotherapy, manifest almost immediately, were utilized in group sessions," and that though "the original purpose formulated by them [the participants] was retained as a general theme, . . . was altered somewhat by the participants' emotional investments in the original purpose and by their academic interests." All participants in all the groups seemed to gain greater clarity of the conflictual situations in which they were involved and reasons for their inability to mobilize power for learning and concentration and, above all, their own part in creating and perpetuating their difficulties. All felt a great sense of relief and evolved a more hopeful outlook for the future.

Another type of nonstructured group has been described by Lulow (1951) who has met with mixed groups of fathers, mothers and teachers of children in a nursery. These groups, also meeting outside of a clinical setting, aimed at engendering a better parent-child relation and an under-standing of small children and their needs. Other situations in which groups are employed in correcting personal adjustment are those of unorgasmic and infertile women, marriage and family counseling, and premarital counseling.

The motivating impulse in the work set forth here is the growing recognition that hostility is an integral and unavoidable characteristic of the human personality, and that a culture favors mental health when it prevents generating overintense hostility on the one hand, and permits and tolerates its expression on the other. A major burden of man is that he must bear up under feelings of hostility, some of which are projective while others are justifiable and realistic. Culture can be defined as the mode in which guilt, aggression and anxiety are tolerated and dealt with. In repressive cultures, guilt is kept at a high level and aggression is pro-hibited. The more humanistic and democratic a culture is, the lower is the level of guilt and the greater is its tolerance of the discharge of aggres-sions in direct and especially in sublimated forms. Freedom of speech, for example, is a guaranteed channel for the discharge of aggressive feelings toward authority and peers. Frequent political elections is another way of getting rid of older brother and father figures. Relaxed and flexible social codes hold down the quantum of guilt, and protection under law is a preventive of anxiety.

As persons in authority and power over others in school and home, factory and office deal with their subordinates with flexibility and con-sideration, self-esteem rises, security is felt and hostility, and therefore guilt and anxiety are reduced. However, the most important single factor in this social complex is that hostile feelings are allowed expression—verbal expression—and acceptable sublimations are provided for them. Harboring such feelings, and the guilt and frustration they generate, create a heavy load on the psychic energies of the individual, and are frequently the cause of many gastrointestinal, cardiac, vascular, neural and many other somatic disturbances. In view of the fact that repressive atti-tudes and measures are practically universal, the social climate created is one of tension, aggression and uncertainty that permeates every area of society—home, school, shop, factory, church, voluntary and demanded relations.

The employment of modified and adapted group psychotherapy for persons in power—parents, teachers, landlords, employers, policemen, judges, legislators, managers and executives—in the process of which they, in their own turn, can discharge their resentments and hostilities without fear of losing face or retaliation, relaxes them. They grow more secure, less tense and therefore less rigid and less punitive toward their dependents and subordinates. The superiors are then able without fear and hesitation to provide similar release and outlets to their subordinates through group discussions, gripe sessions, planning meetings and other means for increased participation that yield feelings of belonging and status.[6] This new attitude toward authority and self, if sufficiently wide-spread, begets a mentally healthy community.

The techniques already employed in personnel management and training derived from analytic group psychotherapy can be extended to deal with all social tensions, e.g., interracial relations. Because these atti-tudes are intensely emotionalized and strongly tinged with feelings toward self, with discomfort in the face of difference, and with strong sexual and homosexual feelings (Slavson, 1939), group discussions can be helpful, but they cannot be expected to solve the entire problem. The schism between races and nationalities will eventually be eliminated through free inter-action and relationships that will arise from direct, intimate contact. However, there are always a number of persons whose prejudices are not accessible to the ego and whose attitudes can be reoriented by cathartic and insightful group discussions.

In an ideal society no one would be entrusted with social power and authority who does not understand his own motivations and is not free of narcissistic, megalomaniacal and exhibitionistic strivings that plague the average politician and legislator. The members of government in a democratic society should rightly be chosen from the socially motivated and reasonably altruistic persons who place the welfare of the community above their personal advantage and aggrandizement. Such communities and such leadership cannot be envisaged before some remote future, but a degree of improvement in the present political, legislative and executive chaos could be achieved if the participants had some awareness of the personal drives and "blind spots" that interfere with their open-minded judgment and social interests. Personal or clique interest and the charac-teristic stubbornness of the weak and the fearful more often than not determine loyalties and decisions to the detriment of the community and frequently to the world as a whole.

Awareness of unconscious determinants and irrational elements in the thinking of persons in social authority would greatly diminish the poten-

---

[6] This is not to be understood to mean that *all* controls have to be removed. Char-acter is strengthened and health is assured where controls are so exercised that they are willingly accepted and incorporated by the child and adult. Unfortunately, few have the skill to exercise them in such a manner.

tial evil that results from them; and, as in the case of industrial and government executives, group interaction guided by professionally trained leaders in which emotional undercurrents are revealed would immeasurably benefit the community and society as a whole. This may seem at the present time a fantastic plan, but as human intelligence and especially good-will will be increasingly put in the service of mankind, this suggestion is not as bizarre as it first seems. Society should be governed by wisdom not by aggression, by the idealistic not the mundane, which is to a disturbing extent at present the case.

The effectiveness of the use of intelligence in social affairs is demonstrated in the phenomenon of the formerly "inevitable" economic depressions. In a conversation between the present writer and a vulcanologist, the latter related the benefits accrued to a number of South American communities as a result of his predictions months in advance of impending eruptions of volcanoes. The conversation took place in the 1930's, at the peak of the disastrous depression in the United States. I suggested that some day we shall reach a stage in our social development when similar predictions will be made in relation to economic depressions, which supposedly have to occur approximately every seven years, and perhaps some regulations instituted that would prevent them.

"But this is impossible!" exclaimed the highly trained scientist. "Economic depressions cannot be avoided!"

"If human intelligence can penetrate the subterranean blind forces of volcanoes as effectively as it does, I think the same intelligence, if applied to social problems, can solve them as well," was our retort.

Events of a quarter century since that statement was made have shown this to be the case.

All who worked with groups in the different settings outlined report that they encounter individuals who are unsuited for group participation. Some are too disturbed, others are so hostile or rebellious that they create tensions beyond the groups' ability to assimilate them. These situations exist also in psychotherapy groups. There are always individuals who cannot tolerate group relations, particularly when they are encouraged freely to discharge their feelings and where the usual restraints and controls are relaxed. Free group discussions and interactions can prove too threatening to persons whose ego organization is weak and who feel too guilty or inadequate to deal with strong emotions. They require individual treatment, though some of them resist that experience as well.

As we observe the behavior and reactions of most people in group situations, we cannot but be impressed with their inappropriateness to the realities of those situations. There are constantly in evidence in the attitudes of all of us feelings that militate against group cohesion and constructive group action. The adult who was an only child, for example, still behaves in groups as though he were such. One who experienced prolonged conflict and threat in his family setting will tend to create conflictual situations in other groups as well, and he who was rivalrous with siblings or parents will act it out later in group and interpersonal relations.

There are also in evidence irrational antagonisms and affinities in groups flowing from memories and unconscious sexual predilections. Defenses against homosexuality, for example, create much conflict among members of all groups, and the masochistic, activated as they are by a need for punishment, disturb the group climate. The fearful and withdrawn are social neuters, as it were, contributing little, while the defensively or sadistically aggressive block the free flow of group action.

It is with this awareness that we must deal in all, even the nontherapeutic, groups if we wish to render them creative, purposeful, and constructive. Neither devices, nor artifices, nor ignoring these phenomena, can take the place of this knowledge and awareness, though many makeshifts are currently being evolved. Those social scientists and psychologists who are laboring toward developing a science of "group dynamics" are tilling barren soil. There cannot be such a blanket instrumental science beyond abstract generalities. Each group acts differently and the difference arises from inevitable differences in constituency and in leadership. What we rather need is sensitivity to and understanding of human needs and strivings and their deviative and self-defeating as well as wholesome and constructive expressions that groups can bring forth in all of us.

BIBLIOGRAPHY

Amster, F. F. (1954), Application of Group Psychotherapy Principles to Nonstructured Groups. *Int. J. Group Psychother.* 4:285.

Blum, M. L. (1954), Group Dynamics in Industry. *Int. J. Group Psychother.*, 4:172.

Buchmueller, A. D. and Gildea, M. C. L. (1949), A Group Therapy Project with Parents of Behavior Problem Children in Public Schools. *Am. J. Psychiat.*, 106:46.

Caplan, G. (1951), Mental Hygiene Work with Expectant Mothers: A Group Psychotherapeutic Technique. *Ment. Hyg.*, 35:41.

Grunwald, H. (1954), Group Counseling in a Casework Agency. *Int. J. Group Psychother.*, 4:183.

Herrold, K. F. (1954), Applications of Group Principles to Education. *Int. J. Group Psychother.*, 4:177.

Hinckley, R. G., and Hermann, L. M. (1951), *Group Treatment in Psychotherapy*. Minneapolis: University of Minnesota Press.

Kahn, J.; Buchmueller, A. D., and Gildea, M. C. L. (1951), Group Therapy for Parents of Behavior Problem Children in Public Schools. *Am. J. Psychiat.*, 108:351.

Kotkov, B. (1954), The Group as a Training Device for a Girls' Training School Staff. *Int. J. Group Psychother., 4*:193.

Laughlin, H. P. (1954), Seminars with Executives on Human Relations in the United States Government. *Int. J. Group Psychother., 4*:165.

Lulow, W. V. (1951), An Experimental Approach Toward the Prevention of Behavior Disorders in a Group of Nursery School Children. *Int. J. Group Psychother., 1*:144.

McCorkle, L. W. (1954), Guided Group Interaction in a Correctional Setting. *Int. J. Group Psychother., 4*:199.

Roberts, B. H. (1954), Introduction to Symposium: Application of Group Psychotherapy Techniques in Nonclinical Settings. *Int. J. Group Psychother., 4*:163.

Slavson, S. R. (1939a), *Character Education in a Democracy.* New York: Association Press, pp. 204-218.

—— (1939b), Group Education for a Democracy. *J. Ed. Sociol.,* December.

—— (1940), A Plan for Group Education in the Elementary School. *J. Ed. Sociol.,* May.

—— (1943), *An Introduction to Group Therapy.* New York: International Universities Press, 1952, pp. 19-20.

—— (1954), Remarks on Group Psychotherapy and Community Mental Health. *Int. J. Group Psychother., 4*:210.

Steiner, Lee R. (1954), The Use of Radio as a Medium for Mental Health Education. *Int. J. Group Psychother., 4*:204.

Chapter XVII

INDUSTRY

●

In the field of business and industry, management is becoming increasingly concerned with the mental health of its employees. This reflects a growing recognition that productivity in the broadest sense is intimately related to such factors as the degree of cooperative effort, the level of morale and job satisfaction, the problem-solving skills of key personnel, the effectiveness of supervision and the uninterrupted two-way flow of communications. All of these variables are indices of the emotional well-being of plant personnel.

While for some people work is a source of great pleasure and deep satisfaction, it is for many frequently the arena for friction, strife, discontent and frustration as mirrored in statistics of turnover, absenteeism, accidents, illness and alcoholism. Too often one's vocation is solely a means to an end and is intensely disliked per se. It is not surprising, then, that in such a milieu many basic needs cannot be met, frustrations from other areas are intensified and additional stress is constantly being placed on an individual's capacity for maintaining emotional homeostasis and expending creative effort.

In every organization there are individuals whose primary responsibility is to facilitate the work of others. Thus, supervisors[1] are concerned with the mobilization and utilization of the productive energies of their subordinates. In addition to possessing technical and administrative know-how, it is imperative that the supervisor be able to work effectively with and through others. His effectiveness is closely related to the extent to which he is free from intrapersonal and interpersonal conflicts. He must have sufficient sensitivity to his own needs and those of others (Ar-

[1] This will be the term we shall use in this chapter to designate the individual responsible for a group's activities, whether high or low in the industrial hierarchy.

gyris, 1953) and to the dynamics of group activity so that he is able to deal effectively with human relations problems and to assist in developing a cohesive work unit. To the extent that he lacks these abilities, the difficulties referred to earlier occur, and enlightened management is including more and more into its traditional consultative and training programs services that utilize knowledge and skills derived from clinical experience to train supervisors to meet their responsibilities more effectively.

It has become apparent that group psychotherapy is not merely an expedient substitute for individual treatment but has unique advantages in its own right (Powdermaker and Frank, 1953; Slavson, 1950). Advantages are not confined solely to the therapeutic group, but can be obtained in other group situations as well. Valuable learning experiences can accrue to members of nontherapeutic groups when they are concerned with the emotional as well as the intellectual development of their membership. The increasing sophistication of the general population has placed heavier demands on clinically trained specialists to extend their services beyond treating the emotionally disturbed. There is a shift in focus of interest from the therapeutic to the preventive, and a concomitant change in role from psychotherapist to consultant. Organized segments of the community are making more frequent use of these services to improve the emotional well-being of personnel and to improve over-all organizational efficiency (Slavson, 1954).

Thus, in group settings supervisors can be trained to be more effective leaders by increasing their sensitivities to the needs of subordinates; staff personnel are helped to deal better with human relations problems; the skills of those who have training responsibilities in industry can be sharpened; and key personnel in top management are helped to work more effectively together, as well as with and through subordinates.

The line of demarcation between psychotherapy and training is not always a sharp one (Kelman and Lerner, 1952). Our main interest in training is in helping the trainees gain insight into *how* they act and react rather than *why*. Interpretations are rarely on the deep, dynamic level utilized in the more intensive forms of analytic group psychotherapy. A group, for example, is encouraged to inquire into how individuals react to its aggressive or critical members and to explore the resultant effects upon its activity rather than to be concerned with the environmental and emotional causes of behavior.

In an industrial training group, the trainee is primarily concerned with problems relating to his organization. He may find it difficult to deal with certain people; he may fail to perceive how his own actions frequently militate against the very objectives he is aiming at; his preoccupation with such questions as "how to change people's attitudes," and "how to get people to do things" prevents a realistic understanding of the interaction process. He frequently seeks manipulative devices which, when applied, deceive very few people beside himself. Preoccupation with personal needs often precludes any genuine interest in, concern for, or awareness of, the needs of others. Trainees may seek a systematic, realistic and integrated philosophy and system of values which will enable them to integrate their own needs and the needs of their subordinates and the organizational goals into a working system. They may be concerned with such problems as how to conduct meetings more efficiently, take account of the personal needs of subordinates, establish better working relationships, build better team relations, and reduce intergroup conflict between competing professional and technical subgroups.

To be sure, many of these problems have their roots deeply imbedded in the individual's personality structure and reflect unconscious needs. For many, an attempt to bring about better understanding and integration outside of a formal psychotherapy situation would meet with defeat or be unwise. There are, however, substantial numbers of people who are strongly motivated to improve their effectiveness and participate in less intense self-evaluative experiences. These persons profit considerably from "training."

As in group psychotherapy, the depth or superficiality of the procedure depends upon the frequency of sessions, the size of the group, the degree of motivation and sophistication of the individuals involved, and similar factors. In an industrial setting, some additional variables must be considered. Consultants should be aware of the "philosophy," reactions and degree of support of other individuals in the administrative hierarchy in addition to the group with which they are dealing.[2] The atmosphere and productivity of a group will vary in accordance with whether the meetings are on "company time" or on the individual's time; whether they are within the plant or away from it; whether attendance is voluntary or compulsory, no matter how they may be labeled.

A review of the clinical literature reveals that very little has been published regarding the application of group-psychotherapeutic principles to industrial training. The first and only book on industrial psychiatry was written by Anderson in 1929, but it makes no reference to any form of group procedure, although there are hints that the industrial psychiatrist may well extend his influence beyond traditional functions. In his chapter on "Industrial Psychiatry," Levy (1947) mentions the possibility of involv-

[2] See "Improving The Processes of Leadership Training." *Adult Leadership,* June, 1953.

ing the application of psychodynamic principles to problems of management, labor relations, public policy, internal organization, and again extending the psychiatrist's function beyond the traditional roles. Menninger (1948), in his chapter on "Mental Hygiene in Industry and Business," indicates that the psychiatrist in industry should have direction of training courses in the structure, function, and disorders of the personality, which would be given to all those in leadership positions from top management to the lowest supervisors.

Rees (1950), in discussing various aspects of preventive psychiatry, also touches on the use of "case conferences and discussion groups with trade union leaders, with workers, with management . . ." He does not, however, specify any of the procedures he discusses. Similarly, McAttee (1951) mentions that the industrial psychiatrist's activities should include supervisory training in human relations. Here too the specific program is not detailed. In 1951, Laughlin and Hall discussed for the first time the use of a modified form of group psychotherapy in an industrial setting. It was their belief that "what represents treatment to emotionally sick patients might become an educational process of considerable depth to 'normal,' 'successful' people." In 1954, Laughlin again described similar work, and indicated that the therapeutic process was designed to reach a "deep and significant level"; no lecturing or presentation of principles was involved. He pointed out that this method can be in fact an important adjunct to existing training methods in industry.

In contrast to the clinical literature, the current writings in the fields of psychology, industrial relations, adult education, and group dynamics are replete with references to various group programs in industry. Reviews of recent developments in leadership training can be found in Dooher and Marquis (1952), Gordon (1951), Maier (1952), Planty and Efferson (1952), and Hoslett (1951).

McMurry (1953) points out that many management problems could be approached more efficiently if managers would develop "empathy." In another paper, McMurry (1952) describes status and power conflicts in the administrative hierarchy and the ways in which destructive competition interferes with organizational efficiency. Roethlisberger (1953) sees many failures in personal relations due to lack of simple communicative skills and concludes by saying that he finds it reasonable to believe that there are simple skills of communication which can be taught, learned, and practiced. Three recent articles deal with various aspects of organizing and conducting group training programs. Buchanan and Ferguson (1953) give an excellent description of the first two years of a supervisory development program. In a second article (1954) they consider some of the unresolved problems in this type of training program. Tannenbaum, Kallejian and Weschler (1954) point out some of the limitations of conventional training programs, and say that training which is "vertically oriented"[3] has greater chances of bringing about permanent changes in behavior. They point out the difficulties a trainee experiences in altering his behavior when he receives training apart from the individuals with whom he works.

The rapid development of this area of application and the moderate success which has been achieved have engendered the feeling in some that training in human relations is a "cure-all" for organizational problems. Unquestionably many factors operate to disrupt the equilibrium of an organization. However, when supervisors possess adequate leadership skill, they can help provide an atmosphere in which individuals can solve problems more effectively, and many of the other disrupting forces (e.g., social, economic, etc.) can be minimized.

As already stated, the primary objective of the programs to be described is to increase the personal effectiveness of individuals in dealing with problems in human relations. This objective is attained by helping trainees gain greater awareness of themselves and others, develop a sensitivity to the dynamics of group behavior, become aware of the defenses they employ, learn more effective ways of dealing with conflict and tensions, and implement their emotional understandings with useful skills.

The formats of programs that can be instituted to meet these goals vary considerably and can be organized in various settings. They can be conducted under the aegis of a university and bring together personnel from different plants or they can be conducted within a given plant. In an in-plant training program, groups can be organized with individuals at the same level of administrative hierarchy, or with individuals from various levels of the hierarchy. Training procedures can be added to the usual activities of a functioning group, e.g., a departmental staff, committees, work teams, and similar groupings.

The most frequently utilized program involves the formation of a new group organized specifically for purposes of training. Trainees are drawn from different areas in a plant and have no on-the-job relationships with one another. In such a group formal status differences are minimized, and frequently they are essentially strangers to each other at the initial meeting. In a large plant, such a training group is organized as part of the regular in-service program of the organization and attendance is frequently voluntary.

[3] The term "vertically oriented" designates the plan in which all of the members of a given organizational unit are in one group regardless of status differences.

The initial objective of the consultant in such a group is to establish a permissive atmosphere, and stimulate the free flow of communication between all members of the group. The amount of structure introduced into the meetings, especially at the beginning, depends upon the sophistication of the participants and the previous information they have been given regarding the purpose and nature of the program. The consultant makes a constant effort to increase the group's interest in, and attention to, its own processes, including the interpersonal feelings which exist, the barriers to communication that arise, and the forces that determine the group's operation. These awarenesses enable the group to determine its own needs and to act appropriately upon them. In such a setting, valuable emotional as well as intellectual learning takes place. Trainees learn to narrow the gap between theory and practice.

As problems are discussed, interest may develop in such topics as interviewing, counseling, dealing with "difficult" individuals, and group leadership. When appropriate, discussion is supplemented by the use of films, didactic material, and "role playing"; such a group can develop remarkable cohesion and become very productive. A group of this type might consist of fifteen to thirty members and meet weekly for two to three hours, for ten to twenty sessions; or it may continue indefinitely with new members being added as others drop out. As the group develops, and depending on the skill of the consultant, more complex and more difficult and comprehensive problems can be included in the group's activities.

In this type of group, no unusual demands are placed upon the consultant. However, since trainees are less highly motivated and less likely to be preoccupied with personal problems than in a therapeutic situation, the consultant has considerably less initial prestige and must utilize great skill if he is to promote the development of a productive situation.

Working with a *natural work group* (i.e., a group which is already in existence with a work orientation) involves somewhat different considerations (Tannenbaum et al., 1954). A natural group may involve top level staff, a group of line employees and their supervisor, or a group of supervisors of unequal rank from a given division. In such "vertically oriented" natural groups supervisors and subordinates are together and existing status differences are likely to increase resistance to training, especially as the trainees experience greater anxiety when exposing their feelings to those with whom they work rather than to strangers.

Usually, the services of a consultant are requested for such a group when the responsible member becomes aware that increasing interpersonal tensions are resulting in impaired performance. Frequently, the consultant is requested to help the group think through organizational or inter-personal problems between its members and other segments of the organization.

Although basically the procedures employed with such a group are similar to those previously described, in this situation the consultant is constrained by additional factors. Here, formal status relationships already exist among the members, and patterns of interpersonal relations have already been established. In this setting, the consultant is primarily concerned with reducing the group's tensions to the point where mean-ingful problems that interfere with day-to-day work performance can be identified. If the consultant has established effective relationships with the members of the group, he can slowly introduce techniques that would assist in the solution of these problems. Although the natural training group moves more slowly than the artificial group, it has the advantage that any changes brought about in working relationships are likely to carry over to on-the-job situations. Also, since the group continues to function after training, procedures that help the group maintain and improve its efficiency can become a permanent part of the organizational activity (Fleishman, 1953).

Prior to the actual meeting of the natural work group, the consultant may wish to familiarize himself with the plant setting and the organiza-tional structure (Menninger, 1948). He may find it helpful to have indi-vidual interviews with the prospective participants in order to establish some degree of rapport, evaluate motivation for training, and familiarize himself with the "jargon," problems, existing relationships, and the gen-eral work atmosphere. Since the success of the program is crucially de-pendent upon the support of the person with the highest status in the group, it is advisable when appropriate to counsel with him prior to and during the administration of the program.

When working with higher echelons of management, perplexing and persistent problems often arise which do not appear on the surface to be "human relations" problems. Generally, these are approached from the viewpoint of administrative or technical concepts. New perspectives on such problems may be gained, however, through a consideration of the impact of the human factors that generate and maintain them. Obviously, the consultant can never duplicate the accumulated experience of the leaders with whom he works. He can, however, help them apply *their* knowledge more effectively. For example, the perennial problems of com-munication in a large plant are more easily solved when managers acquire awareness of their *own* contributions to communication failure and better understand the emotional factors involved. Blockings to communication may occur (a) when individuals attempt to raise their status at the expense of others; (b) when they are apprehensive about the ways in which information may be utilized; (c) when they become antagonistic because of real or fancied misuse of power; and (d) when they fear that activities will be interpreted as inadequate or incompetent. When supervisors understand these problems in themselves and others, they are in a much better position to deal with them effectively.

At the present stage of development, adequate data are not available from which to specify the optimum conditions for training. If meetings are too widely spaced, the training may have little effect since forces cannot be generated to break through resistance. If the intervals between meetings are too short, individuals do not have the opportunity to integrate new learnings. The larger the group, or the greater the number of supervisory levels which the group encompasses, the more difficult it is to create the desired atmosphere. The difficulties of evaluating training programs are even greater than those encountered in clinical settings where records of diagnostic tests and treatment are available.

Since each participant influences in turn many other people, changes resulting from training sessions easily filter through an organization. What may appear as superficial understanding or insight may often have profound effects on an organization. Records of two incidents that follow illustrate the types of insights that can be derived from training.

Incident No. 1. During the third meeting of a training group, the discussion centered on staff conferences. The suggestion was made that such a conference be "role-played." Fred took the role of the superintendent of a large manufacturing concern meeting with his key department heads. Although his aim in calling the meeting was to "sound out" their views regarding a particular problem, Fred gave them little opportunity to do so. He dominated the meeting with his own ideas, and seemed not to hear what others were saying. The role playing was interrupted, and the group commented on Fred's actions and pointed out what he was doing. They indicated that he really did not delegate any responsibility to his subordinates, but shouldered it all himself. He accepted the group's comments and proceeded again with the role playing. For a few minutes he seemed to be making an effort to act differently, but shortly slipped back into character. The ensuing discussion of the group made it clear to Fred that his urge to assume responsibility was very strong and a definite part of his personality (the dynamics, or genetic origin of this need was not explored).

The revelation of this facet of Fred's personality came as a surprise to him. Even though he held a position of considerable responsibility, he had never been aware before of this aspect in his dealings with people; more importantly, he gained greater insight into how these actions affected those with whom he worked. The ensuing discussion regarding the relationship between delegation of responsibility, initiative and personal growth helped many members of the group clarify their thinking with respect to this aspect of administrative practice.

Incident No. 2. This incident dramatically illustrates one effect of the permissive atmosphere of a training session. A training group in a university setting had met for nine sessions and had reached a point where members communicated freely. The topic of leadership had been discussed for several meetings. The group finally reached an impasse and turned to the consultant for "expert" comment. When none was forthcoming, there was a good deal of hostile, negative feeling expressed about the lack of leadership being demonstrated. This discussion was culminated by Jack's remark that he should not only get his money back for the course, but should instead be paid by the consultant for coming, since he, Jack, had at least contributed to the discussion. At this point, the consultant explained to the group what was happening; namely, that while they were frustrated and unhappy they were also able to express their feelings openly, and as a result, the consultant could understand how they felt. The analogy to their on-the-job situations was quickly recognized. Of course, their subordinates are frustrated at times and unhappy, but are they, the participants, the last ones in the plant to know how their workers really feel unless they have established a relationship allowing free expression? Jack was convinced. He now claimed he had gotten his money's worth for the whole series in this one discussion. The interchange that ensued from this incident not only clarified the concept of "leadership," but helped each person understand his own role in raising barriers in his relationships with the people with whom he works.

As in group psychotherapy, the experience of communicating with a wide variety of individuals in a permissive atmosphere produces a greater appreciation of individual differences, more insight into oneself and one's impact upon others, and yields a clearer understanding of the bases of success or failure in human relations. The sensitivity and skills acquired help individuals to become more effective in group activities, both as leaders and as group members. Reports from participants in the training groups as well as from individuals with whom they work confirms the fact that these groups succeed in accomplishing the specified objectives. Reports indicate that following training, participants feel more comfortable, their tensions are diminished, and their efficiency in the management of manpower is enhanced.

It is to be stressed that a socially motivated group psychotherapist is not primarily interested in those individuals in the community who present gross signs of emotional disturbances only. He is also interested in the average, so-called "normal" person who is subject to the many stresses inherent in our society. The procedures described here are not to be confused with psychotherapy, nor are they in any way to be substituted for therapeutic methods, when the latter are indicated. The industrial consultant has to be aware of all the implications of a therapeutic situation, but at the same time meet the needs of his group members, other than in psychotherapy. The therapist is concerned with support, insight, interpretation. The consultant's functions are that of discussion leader, giver of information, teacher, stimulator and clarifier, as well as interpreter.

The impact which the consultant exerts, the extent to which he can be nondirective in his approach, the degree of insight trainees can achieve, are in direct proportion to the motivations, the psychological sophistication of the trainees, and to the degree of support they receive from their superiors. Some participants expect the training groups to follow the pattern of the classroom, which had set the pattern for learning for them as children and adolescents, and in some cases also as adults. They expect to have case material presented to them and to hear lectures. At first they resent the fact that they themselves are to provide the material for study and to participate actively in the discussions. Frequently participants expect training in human relations to consist of a system of rules and "tricks." They, therefore, find great difficulty in adjusting to an unstructured setting devoid of easily memorized generalizations. However, they gradually learn to close the gap between theory and practice. Because there is a certain threatening aspect attached to the use of this method with persons who do not regard themselves as patients, we would go astray indeed if we aroused more anxiety than we allayed. The industrial consultant must exercise careful judgment, and considerable demands are placed upon his clinical skill in dealing with the resistances he inevitably encounters. As groups become active, the consultant needs to evaluate carefully the quantum of anxiety individuals can absorb and deal with constructively. His clinical training and skills give him the understanding of underlying and deeper individual and group reactions which are not interpreted to the group, but do serve as guides to the consultant in his work.

The importance of effective training activities cannot be overestimated for all too often individuals rise in administrative hierarchies because of technical competence, but lack the human understanding and skills in establishing constructive relations necessary for adequate job performance (Himler, 1949).[4] The atmosphere of our industrial society, with its emphasis upon technical knowledge, logic and facts, and the social stereotype of how people ought to or do behave leaves little room for training in human relations. The lack of such understanding is the basis for countless frustrations and anxiety which have repercussions on many other people. Supervisors who have failed to acquire such understandings in the process of development have little opportunity to do so except through programs of the type discussed here. It might be noted in passing that the type of training described here in the field of industry is equally applicable to many other segments of the community. Programs of this kind are currently under way in hospitals, government agencies and service organizations. Teachers, school administrators, and leaders of labor organizations are likewise making use of such programs.

Perhaps the greatest impact in the training experience is achieved through the behavior of the consultant as a member of the group. Through the nature of the relationships that he establishes and his conduct in the group and toward individual members in it, he provides a behavioral model for new values and modes of behavior. It is this system of values coupled with the conceptual knowledge generated by the group experience and discussions that provide the basic framework for sound procedures in management of manpower.

BIBLIOGRAPHY

Anderson, V. V. (1929), *Psychiatry in Industry*. New York: Harper.
Argyris, C. (1953), *Personality Fundamentals for Administrators*. New Haven: Labor and Management Center, Yale University.
Buchanan, P. C. and Ferguson, C. K. (1953), Changing Supervisory Practices through Training. *Personnel, 30*:218-230.
—— (1954), Some Controversial Issues Concerning Supervisory Development. *Personnel, 30*:473-481.
Dooher, M. J. and Marquis, V. (eds.) (1952), The Development of Executive Talent. *A Handbook of Management Development Techniques and Case Studies*. New York: American Management Association.
Fleishman, E. A. (1953), Leadership Climate, Human Relations Training, and Supervisory Behavior. *Personnel Psychol., 6*:205-222.
Gordon, T. (1951), Group-Centered Leadership and Administration. In: *Client-Centered Therapy*, ed. C. Rogers. Boston: Houghton-Miffin.

4 See also "The Application of Psychiatry to Industry," Report No. 20, Group for the Advancement of Psychiatry, July 1951.

Himler, L. E. (1949), The Place of Psychiatry in Industry. Paper presented to Annual Meeting, Michigan State Medical Society, September 23, 1949.

Hoslett, S. D. (1951), *Human Factors in Management.* New York: Harper.

Kelman, H. C. and Lerner, H. H. (1952), Group Therapy, Group Work, and Adult Education: The Need for Clarification. *J. Soc. Issues, 8*:3-10.

Laughlin, H. P. (1954), Seminars with Executives on Human Relations in the U. S. Government. *Int. J. Group Psychother., 4*:165-171.

—— and Hall, M. (1951), Psychiatry for Executives. *Am. J. Psychiat., 107*:493-497.

Levy, D. M. (1947), *New Fields of Psychiatry.* New York: Norton.

Maier, N. R. F. (1952), *Principles of Human Relations: Applications to Management.* New York: John Wiley.

McAttee, O. B. (1951), The Establishment and Function of an Industrial Mental Hygiene Service. *Am. J. Psychiat., 107*:623-627.

McMurry, R. N. (1952), Executive Neurosis. *Harvard Business Review.*

—— (1953), Empathy: Management's Greatest Need. *Advanced Management.* New York: Society for Advancement of Management, Inc.

Menninger, W. C. (1948), *Psychiatry in a Troubled World.* New York: Macmillan.

Planty, E. G. and Efferson, C. A. (1952), Developing Leadership for Tomorrow's Tasks. *Dun's Review.*

Powdermaker, F. B. and Frank, J. D. (1953), *Group Psychotherapy.* Cambridge: Harvard University Press.

Rees, J. R. (1950), Diagnosis and Prophylaxis in Psychiatry at Home and Abroad. *Am. J. Psychiat., 107*:81-86.

Roethlisberger, F. J. (1953), The Administrator's Skill: Communication. *Harvard Business Review.*

Slavson, S. R. (1950), *Analytic Group Psychotherapy.* New York: Columbia University Press.

—— (1954), Remarks on Group Psychotherapy and Community Mental Health. *Int. J. Group Psychother., 4*:210-217.

Tannenbaum, R.; Kallejian, V.; Weschler, I. R. (1954), Training Managers for Leadership. *Personnel, 31.*

Chapter XVIII

TRAINING

●

In medical schools psychiatry is being taught by the time-honored techniques of didactic lectures, assigned reading, demonstration clinics, seminars, conferences, and work with patients. As a result, the average student at the time of graduation has nowadays a better understanding of mental illness than had graduates in the past. His knowledge of psychotherapy, however, is seldom adequate, because the same methods for teaching this branch of psychiatry are not wholly satisfactory. The psychotherapeutic relationship is such a delicate and dynamic one that attempts at demonstrating it to students are not sufficient. In most training programs cases are assigned to the students for treatment and a senior psychiatrist is appointed to discuss the case with him, offer suggestions and direct the treatment program. It is difficult to demonstrate techniques under these circumstances even though they may be described and discussed freely and fully. More effective teaching methods are necessary in the case of psychotherapy.

In addition to psychiatric training and a personal analysis, the student in a psychoanalytic school is required to treat a specified number of cases under supervision of an experienced analyst in order to qualify as an independent practitioner. It is recognized that in this directive role the instructor cannot enter into the relationship with his trainee's patient. Instead, his supervision is confined to reviewing with the student the patient's productions. He then offers whatever suggestions and interpretations are indicated. He cannot be present to observe the conduct of the trainee. He has to depend upon the student for his interpretation or report on the development of the treatment and the emerging situations. Despite the experience with techniques that the student gains from his own analysis and the supervisory experience, more effective training methods are desirable.

The Commonwealth Fund Conference (1947) on teaching psychotherapy testifies to the recognized need to improve teaching techniques. Although this Conference was designed primarily to evolve better methods of teaching psychotherapy to students and general practitioners, there is also evident the need to improve methods of teaching the techniques of psychotherapy to psychiatrists in training so that they may acquire proficiency during residency and training periods.

The extended uses of group psychotherapy in many fields caused some practitioners to recognize its possibilities for teaching psychiatry and for training in psychotherapy, and some favorable reactions to its use have already been reported in this connection. The utilization of group therapy in teaching and training has varied somewhat with different practitioners, and can be roughly divided into two techniques. In one, students at the undergraduate or graduate level attend group sessions of patients under treatment as members, as observers and reporters, or as ancillary therapists. The students meet after the sessions to discuss with the therapist significant incidents of the session. Important psychological phenomena that occurred during the sessions are pointed up and the material brought forth by the patients is evaluated. The manner in which the therapist dealt with various reactions of patients is critically examined. Students thus get the "feel" of participation. In the other method, the students themselves constitute the therapy group, and eventually their own patterns of behavior and reactions are examined.

An early report on the first type of group teaching was made by Hadden (1947), who had volunteer medical students attend group sessions of patients for a full teaching year. In this group most of the patients were veterans discharged from the service because of various types of psychoneurotic disabilities. A large percentage of them came with visceral complaints. The medical students became familiar with the problems of the patients in advance by taking their histories and later by obtaining progress reports during brief interviews preceding group sessions. Although these senior undergraduate students were initially regarded as observers, they were also encouraged to ask any questions they felt would contribute to the clarification of a point in the discussion. In the early sessions there were efforts through discussions to help the patients recognize their physical disorders as induced by emotional tensions.

The patients as well as the students became thoroughly familiar with the fact that a state of emotional disturbance can cause dysfunction of almost any organ and produce any symptom. Much to the surprise of the somatically oriented students, patients soon began to evidence varying degrees of relief of their symptoms. Before there was "mass flight" into cure, discussions were initiated into the role of the unconscious in the production of illness and inappropriate behavior. Few patients dropped out after they experienced relief from physical distress. The therapeutic process could then proceed to deeper levels.

The students freely participated in the group discussions and often contributed a great deal to them. Following each group session the students and the therapist spent about an hour reviewing what had transpired in the group session. At first they were prone to accept the fact that cardiac irregularity, nausea, and other visceral symptoms could be produced by emotion, since most of them had experienced some such disturbances, but rejected every attempt to attribute headaches and various other pains to psychogenic causes. The role of tension in the causation of these symptoms seemed foreign to most of the students. While they were impressed with the effect group therapy had upon the visceral symptoms, the opportunity for observing the working of the ego-defensive mechanisms such as repression, projection, rationalization, etc., was even more gratifying to them. Their awareness of transference and countertransference manifestations was an experience that was impressive and helpful.

The hours following the patients' groups sessions soon grew into therapeutic sessions for the students. Their resistances, transferences and countertransferences were examined so that not only the patients benefited from it, but many of the students admitted to personal improvement as they acquired insight into their own neurotic defense mechanisms and underwent psychologic changes as a result. On termination of this group the students were asked for comments, and their statements were very helpful in evaluating this technique. One of the first students who participated in this teaching effort wrote as follows, while in the army two years after graduation:

> Observing a group of patients over a period of several sessions impressed upon me much more of the psychodynamics than I had been able to grasp anywhere else, despite the fact that my interest had always been in psychiatry. . . Some of my most vivid recollections of group psychotherapy have to do with the hate, fear, explosive antagonisms, guilt and sorrow that would unfold like a dream during an evening's session. Having witnessed the handling of these reactions has helped me infinitely in coping with similar situations that I am now facing.
> [Another wrote:] Sitting in on group therapy sessions is comparable to assisting at a surgical operation. In a group session you actually

participate intellectually and emotionally and get the feel of something you cannot otherwise appreciate, no matter how much you read
about it or discuss it. No one would be allowed to practice surgery or
medicine without supervised training, and this [participation in a
therapy group] seems to be the ideal way of getting supervised training
in the art of psychotherapy.

One of the most gratifying results in this experience was the breaking
down of students' resistance to psychiatry. Votos and Glenn (1953) report
a similar experience when medical student groups were formed in which
they discussed with an instructor the interviews they had with patients.
As this material was examined and turned to the patients' benefit through
psychotherapeutic measures, the students came to regard psychotherapy
as a valid, helpful measure. Their previous resistance was largely displaced by an increased interest in psychiatry. Subsequent use of a similar
technique with graduate students has further demonstrated that the presence of trained observers and therapists will help the presiding therapist
become more aware of his own countertransferences, as recorded by
Hadden (1953).

Almost everyone who has had the opportunity to be present at a group
in action has been impressed with its potentialities as a way of teaching
psychotherapy. Slavson's (1950) sound film, which made it possible to
observe portions of a number of sessions of an activity therapy group,
has made this technique more palpable to the viewers than could have
been done by other devices. The utilization of a group in which patients
are actually treated is an ideal way for demonstrating psychotherapeutic
techniques. It affords the student the possibility of seeing how various
mental mechanisms are utilized in the therapeutic effort and causes him
to participate emotionally as well.

The therapist must feel secure in his role before he can permit observers to be present and the group must have full confidence in him and
assurance that they are not exploited as guinea pigs. In a demonstration
group the therapist must have established by his behavior a firm relationship with his patients so that they feel their treatment is the principal
activity of the group and the observers only incidental. In the shooting of
Slavson's film the cameras had been concealed and for a long time before
the actual filmings were done the children were accustomed to working
and behaving naturally under the lights and in the setting. All action in
activity therapy groups is "nonverbal," but they afford a rare opportunity
for studying the meaning of children's behavior and observing the role of
the therapist.

I have never in my prolonged practice of including students found patients disturbed by their presence provided the groups had been properly prepared. They are always informed that the students are there to learn, and that their presence is part of regular medical training. It is desirable that students be constant in their attendance, and I have found it helpful if they are seated behind the patients. This, I feel, advisable because often students cannot conceal their surprise, disapproval or other feelings, and patients may become disturbed by such reactions. I have discovered that it is much easier for patients to discuss their problems before students in a group than it is when an instructor attempts to conduct a therapeutic interview with a single patient with one or more students present. The presence of other patients minimizes anxiety, and many verbalize their preference for group treatment.

Some patients have commented that they were glad to see students receiving this type of instruction, since they were aware of the fact that many physicians had little or no knowledge of the problems of the neurotic. Other patients who had been initially hostile toward psychiatric treatment have revealed that before they realized the fact that students were being trained through the group, they were not receptive to any psychiatric treatment. The presence of students lent validity to the psychiatric approach and their resistances lessened.

In a recent paper, Miller, Kwalwasser and Stein (1954) reported on an experience with group psychotherapy in a voluntary mental hospital. For over a year their residents employed group psychotherapy in the management of their patients under close staff supervision. As each conducted the session with his patients the other trainee sat in as recorder and observer. Once a week the residents met with the supervising psychiatrists and discussed the records of the group sessions. Significant changes in the attitude of the residents were soon observed. Rather than viewing the patients as a peculiar collection of abnormal complexes, drives and conflicts, and their illnesses as a series of abnormal symptoms resulting from these, they began to see patients as human beings whose illnesses represented a failure of adjustment to life situations, whose symptoms were defenses against suffering and attempts at restitution. They were able to recognize the rationality of the patient's behavior in the groups. The reality of the patients' problems and their insight into their "failures" and need for change impressed them, and the residents' ability to gauge the patients' ego strength caused them to alter prognostic views. It is obvious from this report that enthusiasm for their work was greatly stimulated. Both patients and residents benefited from the experience and the authors were encouraged by the possibilities of the group as a teaching device.

Wender and Stein (1953) point out that group psychotherapy not only makes it possible to demonstrate therapeutic attitudes and techniques but permits residents to acquire experience under supervision. They too, regard it as a real "clinical method of teaching psychotherapy."

A description of the application of a group-psychotherapeutic technique for training is contained in Berman's (1953) paper on a project designed to help workers achieve an optimal level of professional proficiency in such fields as clinical psychology, social psychology, social anthropology, and to aid social workers and others who offer services to individuals and groups. Ten to fifteen students or professional workers met weekly for twelve to fifteen two-hour sessions with a group leader who had had psychoanalytic training. The participants were called upon to describe situations from their daily work which they had found upsetting or which caused them undue or prolonged emotional stress. The group and the therapist explored the whys of such irrational reactions. This led to a limited and selective exploration of pertinent childhood and adolescent situations. Eventually examination of the emotional responses of group members to each other was encouraged, and from the discussion the therapist was able to demonstrate various psychological phenomena that are otherwise difficult to grasp meaningfully in conceptual and didactic teaching. Berman feels that the increase in self-understanding brought about as a result was based on the fact that preconscious material was brought to the conscious, rather than the bringing of deeply repressed memories from the unconscious into the conscious. He regards the goals and benefits of his work with these groups as similar to those of brief psychoanalytic psychotherapy rather than akin to formal psychoanalysis.

In a follow-up study most of the participants considered the group experience to have been of value in increasing their understanding of themselves and of others. A few felt that the course was a disappointment because it did not go far enough in intensive, frank self-examination and examination of each other. Although Berman does not comment on this, it may be interpreted as the result of anxiety evoked in some members as well as a desire and possibly also a need for more extended treatment. The author does point out that as a rule the psychologically vulnerable members dropped out early in the group's existence. Out of seventy participants, three discontinued almost at once and one who was traumatized dropped out in the middle of the course. In the case of one member of the group who had developed acute anxiety after one session the symptom subsided after a single individual interview with the group leader. The author rightly points out that in unskilled hands the procedure is fraught with danger. In his project every safeguard was provided against negative effects upon the participants.

At the eleventh annual meeting of the American Group Psychotherapy Association in New York in January, 1954, Patton (1954) reported on a group experience of staff members at the Sheppard and Enoch Pratt Hospital which he considers very helpful in training of hospital staff. The initial group therapy sessions in the residential units where active treatment of patients was carried on were begun with some trepidation since group psychotherapy was new to most of the doctors involved. Because of this the prospective leaders arranged group sessions among themselves before they had begun the sessions with their groups of patients. When the sessions with the patients started the nursing personnel was required to attend. As the sessions progressed, the patients began to complain about rules, hospital policy, and the like. The doctors tended to interpret these complaints as directed primarily toward the nurses. Since the nurses were present, great anxiety was induced among them and a physician-nurse seminar became necessary. The nurse-physician sessions were "therapeutic," since the discussions revolved around the group therapy sessions of the patients and the complaints that were registered there. Through these discussions a greater awareness of the nurses' problems was induced in the doctors. They then recognized transference phenomena entering into the physician-nurse relationship, and the nurses in turn became more aware of their own unwarranted anxiety. Patton regards these groups as very valuable aids in training of hospital personnel and in integrating them into a therapeutic team. It is significant that similar groups are planned for personnel at the attendant level, for persons in this echelon can wreck a program in a hospital very easily.

Glenn (1951) has reported upon the benefits of discussion groups with psychiatric aides, including nurses, in a 900-bed mental hospital. Weekly sessions were held over an eight-month period with very gratifying improvements in the interpersonal relations between patients and personnel. The free discussion of incidents that occurred on their wards, and especially exploration of feelings in regard to the situations as they arose, was a helpful experience for all. The acceptance of feelings reduced anxiety, hostility, guilt and acting out on the part of the aides; they became less upset by the patients' regressive behavior and were, therefore, more permissive and helpful to them. As the aides came to understand their own role in the care of patients, they felt more significantly a part of a therapeutic team and became more valuable on the job. A significant decrease in personnel turnover was observed.

Boganz (1951) and Weitz and Boganz (1952) appropriately point out that psychiatric techniques are seldom used, as they should be, in dealing with personnel problems in psychiatric hospitals. They introduced a conference system with staff supervisors in which the basic tenets of group psychotherapy were employed. They report marked improvement in the smoothness of the hospital's operation.

In any institution where group psychotherapy is to be employed, especially where patients are in residence, I feel that the personnel at all levels should be fully informed and constantly acquainted with the procedures, or they will soon sabotage the program. Because of the permissive attitude necessary in an effective group, the personnel who supervise the patients feel threatened by the complaints that invariably are voiced about them in group sessions. In one restraining institution no progress could be made by dealing with the patients until sessions with the personnel at all levels were introduced by the present author. Like those of Patton and Glenn, the group sessions became essentially therapeutic, since the anxieties, hostilities and rivalries that became apparent had to be dealt with, interpreted and resolved before all participants could become enthusiastic about the project. As the members of the personnel came to realize that their authoritarian roles released in patients pent-up feelings of hostility which had initially been produced by unreasonable parents, they began to understand why their harshness, sarcasm and scorn did not help their charges. Soon they began to behave more like the parents the "poor kids" should have had, and beneficial changes followed.

For a long time there has been considerable concern about the number of medical students and physicians who are unstable or even psychotic. From Cornell Medical College, Kohl (1951) reports that in a fourteen-year period during which psychiatric services were available to medical students, 25 per cent have on their own requested psychiatric help, many of them for serious disturbances. Strecker, Appel, Palmer, and Braceland (1937), as a result of a study of senior medical students by means of a comprehensive questionnaire, concluded that:

31.6 per cent could be classified as normal
21.8 "   "   "   "   "   " mildly neurotic
19.4 "   "   "   "   "   " definitely neurotic
24.6 "   "   "   "   "   " markedly neurotic
2.6 "   "   "   "   "   " markedly unstable with a
                                               precarious prognosis

They also concluded that there was little possibility of any student with neurotic predisposition benefiting from the stress of four years in medical school.

With such disturbing revelations it is desirable that at some time during the four years at medical school an attempt be made to help students resolve emotional problems, as well as to make them better therapeutic agents for their patients. It is comforting to note that efforts are being made in this direction. The best-known work in this regard is that of Whitaker (1953) of Emory University where, for the first two years, students in the medical school take part in group experiences of a self-exploratory nature. Improved personality integration as well as a better understanding of the maladjusted person is the reward. It may be pointed out that Whitaker's use of multiple therapists in the handling of a single patient affords an excellent method of training at the graduate and undergraduate levels to a limited number of students, as does the work of Dreikurs (1950), Dreikurs, Shalman and Mosak (1952), and Hayward, Peters and Taylor (1952).

Peltz, Steele, Hadden, Schwab and Nichols (1955) present a modification of Whitaker's technique in that groups of about ten students met for eighteen weeks to discuss their emotional reactions to patients under treatment by them. Although this experiment was rather brief, it holds promise in that students not only acquired insight into their responses to patients but recognized transference phenomena entering into their own relationships with each other and other people. It is particularly significant that negative countertransferences were commonly met with in these students when they had to deal with patients who did not have a readily recognizable organic disease. From the discussions of this feeling of annoyance with patients, the students soon realized that the absence of physical symptoms produced anxiety in them because patients without them made a demand upon them as persons, not only as doctors. They frequently reported a feeling of inadequacy to deal with emotional problems of many of their patients and were surprised to discover that patients would talk to them so freely. They soon realized that such patients are often benefited by "sympathetic listening."

One of the unexpected observations of this experience was that so many students were disturbed because the training staff was not didactic. Throughout the years in college and medical school they had become conditioned to didactic teaching so that the nondirective, permissive atmosphere produced considerable anxiety in them. They were also upset when differences of opinion among the supervising staff came to the fore. The resemblance of these disagreements to family strife was the obvious interpretation. Many of the students reported, and observers confirmed the fact, that following the group experience they dealt with all types of patients much more confidently than in the past and some, for the first time, recognized that the physician, as a person, is an important therapeutic agent.

The students in the groups had known each other and had been together for more than a year. Initially there was considerable resistance to self-revelation. Resistances were acted out by dropping out of the group, absences, tardiness, manifest distractiveness, digression, intellectualization, and all other common methods. Progress was slow as the students "tested" the therapist and the situation. Interpretation by the leader was minimal throughout the group experience because of the obvious danger, but in a few sessions toward the end of the group's existence some of the content of earlier sessions, not regarded as potentially traumatic, was interpreted. The students were surprised to discover the real significance of some of the material they presented, and there was general agreement on their part that the exposure to the group discussions was helpful to them in acquiring a better understanding of themselves and their relations to their patients.

Semrad and Arsenian (1951) have used the group process in teaching group dynamics to groups of diverse composition. These were variously composed of psychiatrists, psychologists, and social workers, along with other hospital personnel at different stages of training. Their groups varied in size from ten to thirty, and met from six to eighty times. In each instance a group emerged because the central figure exercised some structural influence. Their report deals primarily with observations during the sessions and they draw only a few conclusions. Of the participants 70 per cent liked the experience, 14 per cent did not; and the others were ambivalent. The authors feel that "the bridge between theory and practice is readily crossed by the method of teaching and many people come away with new insights into how to observe or conduct both themselves and group meetings more effectively."

Rhoads and Dlin (1954) who were entrusted with the counseling and psychiatric care of student nurses reported on the use of group therapy in dealing with the emotional problems of these students. There is little doubt that direct and modified group psychotherapy will be used more widely in educational institutions to protect and improve the mental health of students. It is hoped that qualified psychiatrists will take a more active part in this development.

In his psychodramatic setup Moreno (1940) affords an excellent rehearsal situation in which social workers, physicians, psychologists and others can re-enact specified situations. In this area, and as a means of inducting catharsis in therapy groups, psychodrama finds its most profitable application. In reticent adolescent groups the play acting of a specific situation can frequently accelerate catharsis and initiate progress, but in adult groups, except as a rehearsal technique, there seems little need for psychodrama. The average group is so spontaneously dramatic as to obviate the need for planned psychodramatic productions. Hagan and Kenworthy (1951) found the psychodramatic approach in the training of Red Cross workers an invaluable aid at St. Elizabeth's Hospital.

Although he has not reported fully on his experience, Wolf et al. (1952) and Wolf (1954) has had psychoanalysts in training participate in analytic group-psychotherapeutic sessions, and he regards this as a very valuable aid in such training. In a preliminary report dealing primarily with psychoanalysts' objections to the psychoanalysis of groups, he indicates that a group analysis of previously analyzed professional people is progressing satisfactorily and that he will report on this later. The results of his work lead him to feel that such groups will be increasingly useful in the training of analysts and psychiatrists.

In a paper that he presented at the Annual Conference of the American Group Psychotherapy Association in 1946, Slavson (1947) suggested that as a preliminary to becoming group psychotherapists, psychiatrists and other qualified psychotherapists should have a prolonged and intensive seminar in dynamic psychiatry, and another in group therapy. He also suggested sessions for the trainees in groups as well as intensive individual supervision. He also required that prospective group therapists have supervised field work or internships in hospitals and child guidance clinics and should become acquainted with current and historic developments and the literature in the field. Administration, recording of sessions and the integration of group psychotherapy into the total treatment program was another of Slavson's requirements and, significantly enough, he recommended "a psychiatric consultation service for students."

The successful use of the Gesell (1941) room (one-way screen observation room) for observation of children and their behavior has been effectively employed in the training of psychiatrists. These rooms have afforded psychiatrists and students in training the opportunity to observe sessions of therapy groups as well as individual therapeutic interviews. When such a room as this was offered to me I initially welcomed it with enthusiasm, but as the arrangements were being completed my anxiety mounted. I could not, comfortably, visualize myself betraying patients' confidences and allowing others to observe them without their knowledge and consent. While I do not feel that I can function satisfactorily under these circumstances, others may be able to use the Gesell room as an effective method of teaching. I have not employed it myself, and prefer to bring students and physicians into a group after an adequate preparation.

For demonstration purposes I have conducted group psychotherapy sessions for six to eight patients with as many as eighty observers present. Though the observers sat in the back or to one side, the patients were fully aware of their presence. It was made clear to them that all observers were professional people interested in a treatment technique with which they were unfamiliar. The patients did not seem to be disturbed even by the large group of observers and the sessions were successful. When many observers are present, therapy groups soon appear to be unaware of them, but only when the therapist concentrates on the patients' discussions and does not appear to be giving a performance at their expense. While it is difficult to incorporate a large number of observers into a group of patients, two to four can be allowed to take part provided they are properly identified and the group is assured that it does not exist for the benefit of the visitors. Teaching must be kept incidental to teaching; the tail must not wag the dog.

Free discussion with the students can be held after the patients leave, and they can critically examine what had transpired. During the group sessions, however, observers must not interrupt or overtly respond to what occurs in the group. However, in the after-session meetings with the students or physician observers, their vicarious participation readily becomes apparent. Eventually these conferences become therapeutic for the observers themselves, and are recognized as such by them.

In the teaching of psychotherapy, group-psychotherapeutic sessions provide a clinical method that is being more widely applied. It is of great aid in presenting psychiatric and psychotherapeutic procedures in a more effective fashion to medical students and psychiatrists in training. Because many students need psychiatric assistance, group psychotherapy should be provided for them wherever it is possible, so that they can be helped toward a better self-integration. The use of group discussion in the training and management of personnel in mental hospitals has been very helpful and is finding increasingly wider use in equipping persons to carry on their duties more effectively and with deeper understanding that results in greater satisfaction. Group psychotherapy should not be used by unskilled therapists, for much harm as well as good can be wrought through this potent technique.

BIBLIOGRAPHY

Berman, L. L. (1953), A Group Psychotherapeutic Technique in Training in Clinical Psychology. *Am. J. Orthopsychiat., 23*:322-327.

Boganz, C. N. (1951), Psychiatric Aspects of Hospital Administration. *Am. J. Psychiat., 108*:277.

Commonwealth Fund Conference (1947), *Teaching Psychotherapeutic Medicine. An Experimental Course for General Physicians.* New York: Commonwealth Fund.

Dreikurs, R. (1950), Techniques and Dynamics of Multiple Psychotherapy. *Psychiat. Quart., 24*:788-799.

——; Shalman, B.; Mosak, H. (1952), Patient-Therapist Relationship in Multiple Psychotherapy. *Psychiat. Quart., 26*:219.

Gesell, A. L. (1941), *Developmental Diagnosis.* New York: Paul B. Hoeber.

Glenn, J. (1951), Values of Group Discussions with Psychiatric Aides in a Mental Hospital. *Int. J. Group Psychother., 1*:254-263.

Hadden, S. B. (1947), Utilization of a Therapy Group in Teaching Psychotherapy. *Am. J. Psychiat., 103*:644-648.

—— (1953), Countertransferences in Group Psychotherapy. *Int. J. Group Psychother., 4*:417-423.

Hagan, M. and Kenworthy, M. (1951), The Use of Psychodrama as a Training Device for Professional Groups Working in the Field of Human Relations. *Group Psychother., 4*:1-2.

Hayward, M. L.; Peters, J. J.; Taylor, J. E. (1952), Some Values of the Use of Multiple Therapists in the Treatment of the Psychoses. *Psychiat. Quart., 26*:244.

Kohl, R. N. (1951), The Psychiatrist as an Advisor and Therapist for Medical Students. *Am. J. Psychiat., 108*:198.

Miller, J. S. A.; Kwalwasser, S.; Stein, A. (1954), Observations Concerning the Use of Group Psychotherapy in a Voluntary Mental Hospital. *Int. J. Group Psychother., 4*:86-94.

Moreno, J. L. (1940), A Frame of Reference for Testing the Social Investigator. *Sociometry, 3*:4.

Patton, J. D. (1954), Group Psychotherapy: A Training and Teaching Method in a Private Psychiatric Hospital. *Int. J. Group Psychother., 4*:419-428.

Peltz, W. L.; Steel, E. H.; Hadden, S. B.; Schwab, M. L.; Nichols, F. (1955), Group Therapeutic Experience as a Method of Teaching Psychiatry to Medical Students. *Int. J. Group Psychother., 5*:270-279.

Rhoads, J. M. and Dlin, B. M. (1954), Problems of Group Psychotherapy with Nurses. Read at the Tenth Annual Meeting, American Group Psychotherapy Association.

Semrad, E. V. and Arsenian, J. (1951), The Use of Group Processes in Teaching Group Dynamics. *Am. J. Psychiat., 108*:358-363.

Slavson, S. R. (1947), Qualifications and Training of Group Therapists. *Ment. Hyg., 31*:386-396.

—— (1950), Activity Group Therapy: Sound Film. Distributed by Center of Mass Communication, Columbia University, New York, 53 minutes.

Strecker, E. A.; Appel, K. E.; Palmer, H. D.; Braceland, F. J. (1937), Psychiatric Studies in Medical Education, II. Manifestations of Emotional Immaturity in Senior Medical Students. *Am. J. Psychiat., 93*:1197.

Votos, A. S. and Glenn, J. (1953), Group Techniques in Overcoming Medical Students' Resistance to Learning Psychiatry. *Int. J. Group Psychother., 3*:293-301.

Wender, L. and Stein, A. (1953), The Utilization of Group Psychotherapy in Teaching Psychotherapy. *Int. J. Group Psychother., 3*:326-329.

Weitz, P. and Boganz, C. N. (1952), Application of Group Therapy Principles to Hospital Administration. *Int. J. Group Psychother., 2*:245-249.

Whitaker, C. A. (1953), An Experiment in the Use of a Limited Objective in Psychiatric Teaching, Paper #28 presented at Meeting of American Psychiatric Assn., May, 1953; not published. Not indexed in Index Medicus.

Wolf, A. (1954), Personal Communication.

——; Locke, N.; Rosenbaum, M.; Hillpern, E.; Goldfarb, W.; Kadis, A. L.; Obers, S.; Milberg, I.; Abel, R. (1952), Workshop for Group Psychoanalysts. The Psychoanalysis of Groups: The Analysts Objections. *Int. J. Group Psychother.*, 2:221-231.

Chapter XIX

RESEARCH

•

The quickening of group psychotherapy to its present phenomenal development inevitably leads to careful stocktaking. A longitudinal account of the general literature will not be attempted here. Published reviews of the literature on group psychotherapy can be found in a number of sources.[1] This survey will confine itself to selected experimental contributions that have appeared in the field since 1950.

The Character of Research. The apparition of the age-old split between clinical research and experimental research looms as large in group psychotherapy as it does in individual psychotherapy. The clinician has cautiously avoided the application of quantitative methods to information based upon hasty, limited, or oversimplified observations. Perhaps no expert has expressed this concern more vigorously than Powdermaker and Frank (1953): ". . . preoccupation with controls and experimental design is premature and is based on the misapprehension that these methods in themselves lead to the discovery of significant relationships" (p. xi).

Earlier, Eysenck (1952) decried the lack of experimental methodology in individual psychotherapy. In a review of publications, he discovered an inverse relationship between the depth and extent of psychotherapy

[1] A pioneer review of the literature on group psychotherapy was made by Thomas (1943). This initial effort covered the sparse literature that was then extant. He organized the material with a surprising appreciation of basic problems. Meiers (1945) contributed to the origin and development of the field. Burchard, Michaels, and Kotkov (1948) stressed the lack of uniform reporting and offered a schema of variables for improved communication. Dreikurs and Corsini (1954) presented a supplementary digest of the literature. Certain publications are cited in the *Annual Review of Psychology* and *Progress in Neuropsychiatry*. Generous abstracts of current articles are reported in the *International Journal of Group Psychotherapy*. See also Report to the World Federation for Mental Health (1952).

and the percentage rate of persons who recovered. Seventy-two per cent of the patients improved under custodial care, 64 per cent by eclectic treatment, while only 44 per cent improved by means of psychoanalysis. Yet Eysenck observed that these figures "appear to be remarkably stable from one investigation to another, regardless of type of patient treated, standard of recovery employed, or method of therapy used . . . In view of the many difficulties attending such actuarial comparisons, no further conclusions could be derived from the data whose shortcomings highlight the necessity of properly planned and executed experimental studies into this important field" (p. 320).

The merger of intuition and controlled experimentation is for the good of the species. Only blighted products can result from weak contacts. The clinician needs the manipulative character of variability procedures. The experimental investigator cannot plan without the clinician's hunches, hypotheses, generalizations. Experimental solutions rest on clinical assumptions. The solutions are true to the extent that the assumptions are valid.

Current experimental research in group psychotherapy has been limited to the use of small samples. The methodologist has argued that it is better to obtain an approximation than not to make the attempt at all. Subjects are usually rare. Circumstances for undertaking research are usually extremely difficult. The cost in time and manpower is usually prohibitive. Occasionally, research accomplished with a small sample is just as valid as that carried out with a larger sample. A sip of whisky is just as adequate for testing purposes as the conventional shot. The drawback is that we are not sure of small samples. If subjects are limited, more could be added later and the project continued.

The mechanics of clinical research permit a combination of many observations. It leaves unanswered, however, the precise manner in which the logical steps have been calculated. Cattell (1952) felt there should be no sharp boundary between clinical and statistical research:

> One of the fondest illusions of the clinician, for which he has paid heavily in loss of research time and effort, is the belief that there is a "clinical method" of research. Although there is a clinical method of *treatment,* in the realm of applied psychology, the method of *research* in the clinical realm are either the methods of experiment or the methods of statistics—or nothing! . . . the clinical reader . . . will point out, that . . . acute powers of observation combined with a good memory have succeeded, for example, in establishing certain invariable sequences, i.e. in pointing to causality, and have also resulted in the recognition of certain syndromes which repeatedly occur and which have only much later had their patterns established by statistical

analysis. This is quite true, but it actually supports the argument for the non-existence of an independent clinical method. When the clinician behaves in this way he is being a statistician . . . he has succeeded in extracting correlations, in recognizing invariable sequences and in appreciating factor loading patterns by exactly the same quantitative *principles* as are used by the statistician, though at an unconscious level of inference [pp. 5, 6].

How close has the Cattel ideal been approximated in psychotherapy? Statistical research in psychotherapy is a complicated enterprise. Can biopsies be performed and reported without violence to the total situation?

Miller (1951) published an enthusiastic article on the application of rating devices, methods of control, and Q techniques to nondirective psychotherapy. Cartwright and Zander (1953) edited a series of papers on group dynamics. Some of the problems that face the group psychotherapist in experimental research were presented by Frank (1950, 1951). Locke (1952) outlined basic statistical considerations and safeguards as applied to group psychotherapy.

What is the current status of research in group psychotherapy? Although textbooks on research outline various approaches, clinical research has come to be regarded more and more as synonymous with experimental control.

The most fertile hypotheses for current research in group psychotherapy come from the scouting expeditions of the clinician. Problems in group psychotherapy are numerous, intricate and difficult. The clinician has the most comprehensive grasp of anyone in the field. Deprecating innuendoes, although justified as a prophylaxis against rigidity and stagnation, do not cancel out existing experience, theory and normative surveys but subject them to the rigor of more refined quantitative standards. Sound experimental design stands independent of theory, but its conclusions are merely the result of a preparatory exercise without an initially sound clinical hypothesis.

The older clinical approach to research requires little or no change in the customary psychotherapy plan. The natural elasticity of the situation remains untampered. The volume and complexity of the data lends itself easily to skilled interpretations. It is the only technique available for organizing a running account of the underlying unconscious meaning of seemingly bewildering, irrelevant, peripheral intermember exchanges.

The danger of a "pure" clinical assessment lies in possible misinterpretations of behavior-verbal compounds where no control is available on intuitive inferences. The use of judges with comparable training, who would arrive at their own interpretations *independently,* would

greatly increase subsequent reliability calculations of the original readings and yield a basis for more objective and quantifiable connections.

Group psychotherapy is defined in this chapter to mean: the development of verbal and emotional interactions and part-identifications in an
initial collection of unrelated malfunctioning individuals, led by a qualified psychotherapist, purposely motivated toward the common goal of the
alleviation of reality problems on a conscious level.

Experimental Investigations. Those studies will be included under
experimental research which have employed some form of a quantitative
measure of variability and/or sufficient control. The use of an objective
measure per se does not meet the former criterion. The introduction of
an observer alone, for example, without some test of the reliability of his
observations does not meet the latter criterion.

About 2 per cent of published papers in group psychotherapy can be
designated as experimental research. Of the latter, 60 per cent reported
on effects, 20 per cent on process, 10 per cent on selection, and 10 per cent
on the therapist. A survey of unpublished doctoral dissertations in group
psychotherapy disclosed that 41.7 per cent were studies of process, 33.3 per
cent of effects, 12.6 per cent in the comparison of therapies, 8.3 per cent
of the therapist, and 4.1 per cent of goals.

This crude actuarial survey discloses the paucity of studies that have
applied experimental principles of research to group psychotherapy
material. Experimental research in group psychotherapy has centered
upon studies of process and the effects of group psychotherapy. Published
studies have investigated effects primarily, while unpublished doctoral
dissertations[2] have assayed the group process. Although the quantification
of group process has been ingenious and trailblazing, it has been confined
to behavioristic manifestations. Despite this, there is still room for much
experimental spadework on peripheral considerations before treading
upon more refined and more perplexing methodological problems that
are shared in common with all clinical studies.

Only a trickle of experimental research has been applied to such
gross problems as selection, the role of the therapist, comparison of
therapies, and the goals of group psychotherapy. Workers, with an experimental bent, should snatch every opportunity to investigate the
tremendous variety of clinical hypotheses that, hitherto, have had but
little or only coarse quantitative confirmation.

Effects. Interesting methods have been applied to equally diverse
patient populations. Mehlman (1953) reported on a project involving

---

[2] For a report of unpublished doctoral dissertations not included in this section, see
Hobbs (1951) and Borgatta (1953).

thirty-two white, institutionalized endogenous mentally retarded children with an age range of 5 to 12 years. He divided his total population into three matched groups consisting of a nondirective play therapy group, a movie group, and an inactive group. A battery of pre and post tests were administered within a six-week period: Form L of the Revised Stanford Binet, Revised Form II of the Grace Arthur Point Scale of Performance tests, the Rorschach test, the Haggerty-Olsen-Wickman Behavior Rating Scale, and the California Test of Personality. A statistically significant increase in adjustment occurred in the play therapy group only, as measured by the Haggerty-Olsen-Wickman Rating Scale. A significant increase in the Rorschach F% baffled the author, since supplementary evidence did not support intensified "intellectual constriction" or "anxiety." He felt that this change could not be explained "other than chance basis." The investigator concluded: "Here the group that was more aggressive, less cohesive as a group, and more involved in contact with the therapist made the greater gains in adjustment" (p. 60).

Also employing nondirective play therapy, Bills (1950) had subjects comprising eight third-graders who were classified as slow learners. Bills tested the hypothesis that substantial change would occur when the variable of nondirective play therapy was introduced. The design called for three block periods of thirty school days each. The first block period was used as a control, the second for nondirective therapy, and third as a follow-up. The experimenter proceeded on the basis that personality variables could be more sharply controlled by using the same subjects than if they were matched with another group of subjects. The Gates test of Paragraph Meaning and the Gray Oral Reading Paragraphs were administered. A substantial improvement was found in reading ability during the block period of play therapy only.

Gersten (1951) applied an experimental approach to a group of juvenile delinquents using a conglomeration of therapeutic techniques: interview group therapy, directive and nondirective therapy, and such adjunct methods as handicraft, films, psychodrama, etc. Handicraft was introduced at the beginning of the sixth session because his subjects did not verbalize readily, were tense and self-conscious. Forty-four boys from a State Training School were divided equally into an experimental group who had twenty sessions of group therapy and a control group who had no therapy. They had an average age of 15 years and 7 months and a mean I.Q. of 85.6. Several tests were administered: the Wechsler-Bellevue Intelligence Scale, the Stanford Achievement Test, the Haggerty-Olsen-Wickman Rating Schedules, and the Rorschach test. The results showed a rise in I.Q. and a significant difference in school achievement. Better adjustment was also reflected in the Rorschach scores M, FC and CF, H and P. A study of case histories disclosed no differentiating criteria. However, phonographic recordings evaluated by four judges consisting of a psychiatrist, a director of social service, a case supervisor at one training school and a group psychotherapist at another training school, agreed to the following changes as having occurred as the result of group experience: emotional release, initial insights, and more emotional security and social maturity for the experimental group (Haggerty-Olsen-Wickman ratings).

Sheldon and Landsman (1950) investigated the effects of group psychotherapy with students in academic difficulty. A group of twenty-eight potentially capable college freshman students, who were below expectation in academic performance, were invited to join the Academic Method Course. The total sample was divided into a control group (which pursued the usual lecture and discussion method) and an experimental group (led by a qualified nondirective therapist). Both control and experimental group met five times a week. The experimental group, however, substituted two of its periods a week with group therapy. Pre and post evaluations were made with an array of tests which included the Iowa Silent Reading test, the California Test of Personality, the Ohio State Psychological test, and grade point averages. The experimental group obtained significantly higher grade point averages.

A study by Chenven (1953) was geared to test a hypothesis that communication could be inhibited by emotional concomitants of brain injury as well as impairment due to the injury itself. Sixteen patients, ages 31 through 60, were selected from several hospitals and institutions by means of the Wechsler-Bellevue Performance Scale, the Eisenson Test of Aphasia, and the Head-Chesher Aphasia Test. The patients were then randomly assigned in groups of eight either to speech therapy alone or to speech therapy and group therapy. The Metropolitan Achievement Battery Forms R and S of the Elementary Series (tests of reading, vocabulary, arithmetic, language usage and spelling), and a Picture Story Test devised by the investigator were administered pre and post to measure language achievement and oral expression. The results indicated that the improvement of those who had combined speech and group therapy was significantly greater than those who had speech re-education alone.

Some experimental approaches have been attempted with psychotics. Harrow (1951) measured the effects of twenty-five psychodramatic treatment sessions on twenty male schizophrenic veterans of World War II, with particular reference to defined scales of realism, interaction and spontaneity. The Rorschach test, the MAPS test, and a specially devised

Role test were administered to the patients pre and post therapy. A control group of ten subjects received no therapy. A significant difference was found in favor of the psychodramatic group on the Realism scale by means of the Role (action) test and the Rorschach test.

The Porteus Mazes and Mirror-tracing test, tools said to be sensitive to social adjustment were given by Peters and Jones (1951) to Negro male schizophrenic veterans within a week following admission to a Veterans Hospital. Patients were assigned alternately to a control and an experimental group. The senior author treated the latter group in weekly psychodrama sessions over a four-months period. Significant differences were present in favor of the treated group. The problem-solving tasks were interpreted as showing increased understanding, performance facility, and motor reactions.

Therapies contrasted. Closely allied to the study of effects were investigations which attempt to compare the results of different therapeutic formulations. Imber (1953) conducted a study to determine the efficacy of short-term group therapy for thirty-six male psychotic patients through the use of directive and nondirective psychotherapy. This study also aspired to clarify the relationship of psychotherapeutic success to technique and the therapist's personality. Patients were assigned at random to one of four experimental groups or to one of two control groups until a total of six subjects were allocated to each group. The control groups participated in reading and literary discussions. All groups met for two one-hour periods a week for five consecutive weeks. Since exposure to therapy was brief, the author selected tests purporting to measure changes in attitude rather than personality. Only the experimental groups showed changes significantly different from zero by means of Hildreth's scales and Berger's questionnaire. No special benefits were recorded in favor of either directive or nondirective psychotherapy, nor could the two therapists be distinguished in terms of psychotherapeutic success.

Another comparative study was conducted by Page (1953). He proposed to measure the effects of three different group emphases: Mowrer's sign and solution learning (1950, 1953), Coffey's social role, and Rogers' reflection of feelings as modified by Glad (1951). Three groups, of five individuals to a group, were selected from a freshman psychology class based upon a sociometric technique consisting of members who mutually rejected each other. Three group therapists were rotated among the three groups so that each therapist was never twice in succession with the same group. Pre and post applications of three tools were used in an interval of fifteen sessions, as follows: (1) a modification, following Hartley (1950), of the Q technique developed by Stephenson (1953); (2) notations of overt verbal behavior detailed by Sanford (1952); and (3) Jeffers' (1953) quantification of the Stein Sentence Completion test. The results, in terms of "a more adequate social functioning," indicated that the learning theory technique brought about the greatest number and degree of changes, social role techniques was next, while reflection of feelings was found least effective. The author does not discuss the possible influence that mutually rejecting members and rotating therapists may have in favoring the most intellectual approach.

Process. More and more studies have attempted to adapt Bales' (1950) interaction system to psychotherapeutic groups or used some sociometric device. A project by Evans (1950) reported difficulty in obtaining adequate reliability in the recorded observations of two observers. A 49 category list had to be reduced to 32 and then to 12, resulting, however, in a summation of error. By excluding categories with less than 5 per cent scored interaction, correcting for difference in rate of scoring, and conversion to a 12 category list, agreement between observers improved.

Croley (1951) scored behavioral interrelationships on the basis of characteristics subsumed under the categories of feelings, role, and content. Fine (1953) constructed a participation index for measuring changes in group behavior. De Haan (1951) developed a method for graphically depicting group life in growth, participation, and leadership behavior. Roberts and Strodtbeck (1953) used the Bales technique with paranoid schizophrenic and depressed patients. The authors attempted to measure the nature of the environmental contacts and the ways in which hostility was expressed. Four observers conducted the scoring. The expectations of the investigators were met with "the depressed patients being higher than the paranoid schizophrenics on (a) ratio of positive acts, (b) per cent of acts to participants other than the leader; and lower than the paranoid schizophrenic group on (c) rate of acts per minute."

Lewis (1952) found a relationship of group therapy focus to group cohesiveness and the therapeutic goal of increased socialization. The goal of socialization is a worthy one for a psychotic population, but one may wonder how ambitious or psychotherapeutically effective a goal it is for a college freshman class in psychology. Could not socialization be achieved, in time, through class associations alone, by joining a club or a church social?

Role of the therapist. Grob (1950) proposed the hypothesis that the leader selects the patients who ultimately stay in group. His approach, however, was aimed more at a contrast between the individuals of one group that failed to consolidate with individuals of another group that had relative success. Chance (1952) requested patients to rate their relationship to the therapist and their most important parent. A modified form of the Q technique was employed and ratings were obtained. The author acknowledged the exploratory character and shortcomings of her research, but concluded there is some evidence of a correspondence between attitudes and feelings toward the therapist and an important familial figure.

Selection. Kotkov and Meadow (1952, 1953) conducted Rorschach studies of continuing and noncontinuing patients in group psychotherapy. The subjects consisted of a heterogeneous group of twenty-eight veterans at a V.A. Mental Hygiene Clinic and fifty-eight obese patients of a Public Health Service weight maintenance project. A discriminant function was applied to three Rorschach variables, FC-CF, D% and R. The coefficients of the discriminant function disclosed that the FC-CF variable contributed most, the R variable helped a little more, while the D% variable was negligible. The following prediction formula was obtained: $Z = .00241397x_1$ plus $.00006969x_2$ plus $.00038326x_3$ in which x_1 = FC minus CF, x_2 = D%, and x_3 = R. In its application to new groups one may substitute the empirically determined FC minus CF, D% and R values for each individual and calculate his Z value. Selecting the best cutting point among the Z scores, the authors made 68 correct placements and 30 incorrect ones.

Kotkov and Meadow (1953) attempted to validate their prediction formula with patients in individual psychotherapy. Although they met with corresponding accuracy, others have had varying success. Auld and Eron (1953) tried the formula on a smaller sample (21 continuing and 12 noncontinuing) with results little better than chance. Utilizing a larger patient population, Gibby et al. (1954) applied the prediction formula with 61 per cent success. The strongest value of the Kotkov-Meadow formula is that it is more successful in locating patients who do not continue (88%) than those who continue psychotherapy. Gibby et al. found that by using the Rorschach R (number of responses) alone, 69 per cent of the patients could be located correctly. The cutting point may differ from clinic to clinic: with Auld and Eron, continuing patients had more than 18 responses per Rorschach protocol; with Gibby et al., continuing patients had more than 35 responses.

Recent research in group psychotherapy discloses some modest attempts to control and quantify an initial conjecture, a theory, a generalization. For justifiable reasons, most of these efforts have been crude. Investigators are usually snarled with many obstacles in the crucial steps of problem solving required in the testing of a hypothesis. Some of these difficulties accrue in the planning stage involving petty details such as administrative clearance, scientific comradeship, "altruistic surrender," financial arrangements, and so on. Other difficulties are more technical in nature. They involve localizing a problem that will include the least number of contaminating variables. They involve the use of observers who will introduce the least number of emotionally toned interfering factors, inadequate training or premature and inadequate masking of the results through a clumsy prosecution of the investigation. They involve careful sampling, trustworthy measuring scales, and a sufficiently large number of people and observations in order to eliminate the sources of error by an averaging process.

Progress in group psychotherapy was manifested in the march of new experience, the acquisition of new knowledge, and the formulation of new generalizations. Most reports on group psychotherapy have dealt with people who were not sick enough or who were too sick for individual psychotherapy.

From the few controlled studies that are available on group psychotherapy, the following implications appear warranted: (1) groups receiving psychotherapy benefit substantially more than groups receiving no psychotherapy; (2) the crystallization of group-psychotherapeutic effects cannot ensue without a psychotherapeutically oriented catalyst; (3) a collection of illnesses per se does not constitute a therapeutic group; (4) the content should be specifically directed toward the alleviation of illness or malfunctioning to be of more than ephemeral value to the patient; (5) patients who make contacts easier and who associate more freely are the most likely to remain in psychotherapy.

Unpublished doctoral dissertations in group psychotherapy have been more daring but also more vulnerable, for the most part, in their presentations: (a) by introducing clinical distortions in experimental design; (b) drawing too extensive generalizations from shaky experimental controls; (c) accepting lower standards of significance on variables where measurements are as yet too inexact.

In the past several years the experimentalist has crashed the barriers of clinical research, although he is still struggling and his future is as yet uncertain. Out of the vast store of clinically recorded material, there is a fertile field for this stranger, when he comes of age; not merely for the creation and modification of designs for research but also for an intimate, powerful respect for traditional reticence toward quantitative procedures.

The experimentalist is a toddler in the group psychotherapy scene. His cry is lusty. His demands exceed available resources. As yet his re-

326　　　　　FIELDS OF GROUP PSYCHOTHERAPY

search is naive and elementary. He is on surest terrain when dealing with broad generalized hypotheses and controls.

BIBLIOGRAPHY

Auld, F. and Eron, L. D. (1953), The Use of Rorschach Scores to Predict Whether Patients Will Continue Psychotherapy. *J. Consult. Psychol., 17*:104-109.

Bales, R. F. (1950), *Interaction Process Analysis.* Cambridge, Mass.: Addison-Wesley.

Bills, R. E. (1950), Nondirective Play Therapy with Retarded Readers. *J. Consult. Psychol., 14*:140-149.

Borgatta, E. F. (1953), Some Research Findings on the Validity of Group Psychotherapy as a Diagnostic and Therapeutic Approach. *Am. J. Psychiat., 110*:362-365.

Burchard, E. M. L.; Michaels, J. J.; Kotkov, B. (1948), Criteria for the Evaluation of Group Therapy. *Psychosom. Med., 10*:257-274.

Cartwright, D. and Zandor, A., eds. (1953), *Group Dynamics, Research and Theory.* New York: Row Peterson & Company.

Cattell, R. B. (1950), *Personality: A Systematic, Theoretical and Factual Study.* Boston: McGraw-Hill.

—— (1952), P-Technique Factorization and the Determination of Individual Dynamic Structure. *J. Clin. Psychol., 8*:5-10.

Chance, E. (1952), A Study of Transference in Group Psychotherapy. *Int. J. Group Psychother., 2*:40-53.

Chenven, H. (1953), Effects of Group Therapy Upon Language Recovery in Predominately Expressive Aphasic Patients. Unpublished Doctor's Dissertation, New York University.

Croley, H. T. (1951), A Method of Analyzing the Process of Group Therapy. Unpublished Doctor's Dissertation, University of Denver.

De Haan, R. F. (1951), Graphic Analysis of Group Process. Unpublished Doctor's Dissertation, University of Chicago.

Dreikurs, R. and Corsini, R. (1954), Twenty Years of Group Psychotherapy. *Am. J. Psychiat., 111*:576-574.

Evans, J. T. (1950), Objective Measurement of the Therapeutic Group Process. Unpublished Doctor's Dissertation, Harvard University.

Eysenck, H. J. (1952), The Effects of Psychotherapy: An Evaluation. *J. Consult. Psychol., 16*:319-323.

Fine, H. J. (1953), Interaction Process: The Analysis of a Group Therapeutic Experience in a Human Relations Seminar. Unpublished Doctor's Dissertation, University of Syracuse.

Frank, J. D. (1950), Group Psychotherapy in Relation to Research. *Group Psychother., 3*:197-203.

—— (1951), Some Problems of Research in Group Psychotherapy. *Int. J. Group Psychother., 1*:78-81.

Gersten, C. (1951), An Experimental Evaluation of Group Therapy with Juvenile Delinquents. *Int. J. Group Psychother., 1*:311-318.

Gibby, R. G.; Stotsky, B. A.; Hiler, E. W.; Miller, D. R. (1954), Validation of Rorschach Criteria for Predicting Duration of Therapy. *J. Consult. Psychol., 18*:185-191.

Glad, D. D. (1951), A Manual of Basic Maneuvers in Psychotherapy. Unpublished Manuscript, Psychopathic Hospital, Denver, Colorado.

Grob, S. (1950), A Clinical Investigation of the Role of the Therapist in Group Psychotherapy. Unpublished Doctor's Dissertation, Harvard University.

Harrow, S. (1951), The Effects of Psychodrama Group Therapy on Role Behavior of Schizophrenic Patients. Unpublished Doctor's Dissertation, University of Chicago.

Hartley, M. (1950), Q Technique—Its Methodology and Application. Unpublished Doctor's Dissertation, University of Chicago.

Hobbs, N. (1951), Group-Centered Psychotherapy. In: *Client Centered Therapy*, ed. C. R. Rogers. Boston: Mifflin.

Imber, S. D. (1953), Short-Term Group Therapy: An Experimental Investigation of Effectiveness for Psychotics and a Comparison of Different Therapeutic Methods and Different Therapists. Unpublished Doctor's Dissertation, University of Rochester.

Jeffers, J. (1953), An Exploratory Study of Individual Changes Occurring During Group Therapy. Unpublished Master's Thesis, University of Denver.

Kotkov, B. and Meadow, A. (1952), Rorschach Criteria for Continuing Group Psychotherapy. *Int. J. Group Psychother.*, 2:324-333.

—— —— (1953), Rorschach Criteria for Predicting Continuation in Individual Psychotherapy. *J. Consult. Psychol.*, 17:16-20.

Lewis, R. T. (1952), An Analysis of Group Cohesiveness as a Function of Different Types of Group Therapy Focus. Unpublished Doctor's Dissertation, University of Denver.

Locke, N. (1952), The Psychologist in Group Therapy. *Int. J. Group Psychother.*, 2:34-39.

Mehlman, B. (1953), Group Play Therapy with Mentally Retarded Children. *J. Abn. & Soc. Psychol.*, 48:53-60.

Meiers, J. I. (1945), Origins and Development of Group Psychotherapy. In: *Group Psychotherapy*, ed. J. L. Moreno. New York: Beacon House.

Miller, J. G. (1951), Objective Methods of Evaluating Process and Outcome in Psychotherapy. *J. Psychiat.*, 108:258-263.

Mowrer, L. H. (1950), *Learning Theory and Personality Dynamics*. New York: Ronald Press.

—— (1953), *Psychotherapy—Theory and Research*. New York: Ronald Press.

Page, C. W. (1953), A Comparative Study of Three Types of Group Psychotherapy Formulations. Unpublished Doctor's Dissertation, University of Denver.

Peters, H. N. and Jones, F. D. (1951), Evaluation of Group Therapy by Means of Performance Tests. *J. Consult. Psychol.*, 15:363-367.

Powdermaker, F. B. and Frank, J. D. (1953), *Group Psychotherapy*, Cambridge, Mass.: Harvard University Press.

Report to the World Federation For Mental Health (1952), *Int. J. Group Psychother.*, 2:72-82; 173-184; 274-283.

Roberts, B. H. and Strodtbeck, F. L. (1953), Interaction Process Differences Between Groups of Paranoid Schizophrenic and Depressed Patients. *Int. J. Group Psychother.*, 3:29-41.

Sanford, E. (1952), An Analysis and Systematization of Goals of Therapy. Unpublished Doctor's Dissertation, University of Denver.

Sheldon, W. D. and Landsman, T. (1950), An Investigation of Nondirective Group Psychotherapy with Students in Academic Difficulty. *J. Consult. Psychol.*, 14:210-215.

Stephenson, W. (1953), *The Study of Behavior Q-Technique and its Methodology*, Chicago: University of Chicago Press.

Thomas, G. W. (1943), Group Psychotherapy: a Review of the Literature. *Psychosom. Med.*, 5:166-180.

INDEX

Abel, R., 312, 315
Abraham, K., 81, 93, 105, 106
Absenteeism, 290-300
Acceptance operations, 197
Acting out, 134, 171, 190, 237, 261
Activity group therapy, 3, 15, 28, 216-220, 222-227, 237, 270, 281, 305
Addiction, *see* Drug addicts
Adolescents, 46, 99, 196-213, 219, 235, 237, 241, 260
Adoption, 171, 188, 192-193
Affect hunger, 111-112, 119, 182-183
Affects, 42, 105, 141
Aged, 6, 7, 11, 129-151
Aggression
  and addiction, 64, 69-70
  and allergies, 109-127
  and delinquents, 198-212
  and psychosomatic disorders, 42-56
  and society, 274, 285-288
  and stutterers, 101-102
  see also Hostility
Aichhorn, A., 198, 213
Aid to Dependent Children, 185
Alcoholics, 6-7, 11, 23, 26-27, 45, 76-93, 266, 270, 290
  treatment of in hospital, 26, 30-31, 35, 84
Alcoholics Anonymous (A.A.), 16, 26, 30-31, 78, 83, 86-87
Alexander, F., 42, 56, 104, 106, 108, 127
Allen, F., 231
Allergies, 6, 47, 108-127
Allison, S. G., 84, 93
Allport, G. W., 85, 93
Alonzo, A. M., 32
Alopecia areata, 42
Altruistic surrender, 325
Ambivalence, 66, 131, 165-166
Ambulatory schizophrenia, 265-266, *see also* Borderline cases
American Group Psychotherapy Association, 85, 222, 261, 267, 272
American Medical Association, 98, 106
Amster, F. F., 154-155, 168, 231, 284, 288
Anaclitic therapy, 44, 109
Anal stage, 105
Anderson, V. V., 292, 300
Anemia, 41
Anorexia, 81, 119-120
Anshen, R. N., 258
Antabuse, 85, 86
Anthropology, 274, 307
Antisocial character, 266, *see also* Delinquency
Anxiety
  and addiction, 67-68

and alcohol, 79-80, 82
and allergic patient, 115-116, 123
and society, 274
internalized, 199
neurosis, 263
of parents, 158-168
of pregnant women, 186-188
states, 53, 83, 263
Aphasia, 46
Appel, K. E., 309, 314
Argyris, C., 290-291, 300
Aristotle, 96
Arsenian, J., 311, 314
Art, 23, 26
Arteriosclerosis, 130, 149
Associative thinking, 203-206, 241
Asthma, 42, 47, 48, 108-109, 119-120, 122-123, 126-127, 159
Asylum, 17-19
Auld, F., 324, 326
"Autogenes training," 91
Auxiliary leader, 143
Azospermia, 249

Backus, O. L., 98, 106
Bacon, S. D., 77, 93
Bales, R. F., 78, 80, 93, 323, 326
Barber, V., 98, 106
Barnes, M., 157, 168
Baruch, D. W., vii, 47, 56, *108-128*, 260, 267, 271
Bauer, I., 156, 168
Beach, F. A., 258
Bed wetting, *see* Enuresis
Behavior disorders, 263-264, *see also* Activity group therapy, Character, Children
Bellsmith, E. B., 21, 38
Bellsmith, V., 197, 213
Berger, 322
Berliner, B., 62, 63
Berman, L. L., 307-308, 314
Bernard, V. W., 184, 194
Berne, E., 113, 127
Bernstein, L., 21, 32
Bibring, G. L., 235, 245
Bierer, J., 21, 32, 85, 93
Bills, R. E., 320, 326
Binger, C., 105, 106
Bion, R. W., 21, 32
Blackman, N., 46, 56
Blajan-Marcus, S., 261
Blepharitis, 42
Blethen, E. C., 185, 194
Blum, M. L., 275, 288
Boganz, C. N., 309, 314
Borderline cases, 4, 11, 219, 265-266